THIS FESTSCHRIFT

IS DEDICATED TO

DAVID BIDNEY

BY HIS FORMER STUDENTS ON THE
OCCASION OF HIS SEVENTIETH BIRTHDAY

III

DAVID BIDNEY

(On the Occasion of his Retirement from Indiana University)

James H. Keller
Indiana University

David Bidney came to Indiana University in 1950, appointed jointly by the Departments of Anthropology and Philosophy. This was not the customary division of disciplinary talents at that time, nor is it now for that matter, but it was quite consistent with the unique educational and experential background of this most uncommon man. And though he transferred fully into Anthropology in 1964, and later, in 1970, was one-quarter time in the Philosophy of Education, his research and teaching continued to reflect his original preferences.

A Canadian by birth, he studied at the University of Toronto where he received a Bachelor of Arts with Honors in Philosophy and Psychology in 1928, and in 1929 earned the M.A. as a George Paxton Young Fellow in Philosophy. Yale University, where he was a University Fellow in Philosophy, conferred the Ph.D. degree on him in 1932. He then returned to the University of Toronto as a member of the faculty (1932-34), held a postdoctoral fellowship at Yale (1934-35), served as an instructor at Yeshiva University (1936-38), was a Sterling Fellow at Yale (1938-39) and subsequently taught there (1939-40).

The emphasis during these years was formally within philosophy, and his revised dissertation, *The Psychology and Ethics of Spinoza*, now a standard reference, was published in 1940. However, David Bidney's association with anthropologists at Yale University and an opportunity to participate in a seminar concerning the philosophy of the social sciences served to re-focus some of his specific philosophical inquiries. Also, research leading to a major monograph concerning the "philosophical anthropology" of Ernst Cassirer led quite logically to the study and incorporation of ethnological data, particularly culture theory and its implications for understanding the human condition. From 1942 until assuming his position at Indiana University, David Bidney had the unparalleled opportunity to further this marriage of anthropology and philosophy while serving as a Research Associate and Assistant to the Director of the Wenner-Gren Foundation for Anthropological Research.

Anthropologists, after decades of study of human cultures in a multitude of places and times, had arrived at the prevailing conclusion that each culture stream was historically unique and, therefore, the search for "universals" in the human experience could not but fail. However, David Bidney held a contrary view. With an indepth awareness of the anthropologist's "science" and employing the critical perception of the humanistic philosopher, he dared to ask not only "what is Man?" but pursued the further question, "what ought he be or become?" The questing led into folklore and myth, ethics and religion, and the ideational province of human morality, and particularly how these were represented and conceived of in non-Western cultures. Along with these interests, his concern with human freedom was a continuing commitment. His numerous writings necessarily brought him into direct conflict with the prevailing anthropological orthodoxy, but that the questions were exactly the right ones and the answers challenging can best be demonstrated by reference to a review of his *Theoretical Anthropology*, a comprehensive historical critique of the discipline:

> ...if we do not accept his prescription for a mature science of anthropology, one comprehending nature and will, science and the humanities, the question does remain--just where do we go from here?

The critical probings which characterized David Bidney's writings and which contributed to making him a Guggenheim and a Ford International Fellow, were similarly apparent in the classroom. He was a master teacher with the master teacher's sense of mission. Systematic, thorough, and demanding--Socrates had a peer--I can speak from experience that a student attended his class unprepared only once. Yet if high standards were applied in the evaluation of student performance, it was soon apparent that the teacher did not exempt himself from an even higher expectancy. A

VI

class under David Bidney was an intense and memorable intellectual experience, and although he has now retired from the formal teaching portion of the academic role, the content of that experience will continue through his students to generations of others.

The ideal university has been described as a "city of the mind." David Bidney represents the kind of dedicated and inspired citizenry necessary for the creation of that community. Let me, as a former student and now a colleague, and on behalf of those who know him best, say how grateful we are for the opportunity we have had of knowing David Bidney; we eagerly anticipate seeing the fruits of his retirement years soon published.

SELECTED PUBLICATIONS OF DAVID BIDNEY

Theoretical Anthropology: Second Augmented edition, Schocken Books, First Paperback edition, 1967. Copyright 1953 by Columbia University Press; Introduction Copyright 1967 by Schocken Books, Inc.

David Bidney, editor. The Concept of Freedom in Anthropology. The Hague, 1963.

"Phenomenological Method and the Anthropological Science of the Cultural Life-World" in Phenomenology and the Social Sciences, Maurice Natanson editor, 2 vols,; Northwestern University Press, Evanston, Illinois, 1973, (vol. 1, pp. 109-140).

"The Philosophical Anthropology of Ernst Cassirer and Its Significance in Relation to the History of Anthropological Thought" in P.A. Schilpp, ed., The Philosophy of Ernst Cassirer (Evanston, Illinois, 1949) pp. 465-544.

"Vico's New Science of Myth" in Giambattista Vico: An International Symposium, Giorgio Tagliacozzo, editor, The Johns Hopkins Press, Baltimore, 1969, pp. 259-277.

"Paul Radin and the Problem of Primitive Monotheism" in Culture in History: Essays in Honor of Paul Radin, edited by Stanley Diamond, Columbia University Press, New York, 1960, pp. 363-79.

"The Concept of Value in Modern Anthropology: in A.L. Kroeber editor, Anthropology Today: An Encyclopedic Inventory. Chicago, 1953, pp. 682-699.

"Cultural Relativism" in Internation Encyclopedia of the Social Sciences, David L. Sills, editor, vol. 3 pp. 543-47, The MacMillan Company and the Free Press, 1968.

"The Philosophical Presuppositions of Cultural Relativism and Cultural Absolutism" in Ethics and the Social Sciences, edited by Leo R. Ward, University of Notre Dame Press, 1959, pp. 51-76.

"The Varieties of Human Freedom" in Anthropology, ed. by David Bidney, Mouton & Co., The Hague, 1963, pp. 11-34.

"So-Called Primitive Medicine and Religion" in <u>Man's Image in Medicine and Anthropology</u>, Monograph IV, Institute of Social and Historic Medicine, The New York Academy of Medicine, Iago Galdston, M.D., editor. Internation Universities Press, Inc., New York, 1963, pp. 4-56.

<u>The Psychology and Ethics of Spinoza</u>, Yale University Press, New Haven, Connecticut, 1949.

X

INTRODUCTION: THE LEGACY OF DAVID BIDNEY:

Bruce Grindal
Florida State University

The essays in this volume are the gifts to our teacher. They are offered as the separate statements of mature scholars who owe in common the experience of having been taught by David Bidney, whose humanistic influence has left its mark upon their intellectual lives. Each of the essays reflects this tradition. Thus, to begin, we must first speak in tribute to the man, David Bidney, as scholar, teacher and friend.

David Bidney's major contribution to the scholarly world has been his collection of essays, Theoretical Anthropology. Within its covers is outlined the prescription for a renewed discipline of anthropology in which human beings are the rational creators of their cultural life. This humanistically oriented, if not enlightened, view of culture has had to contend with the more positivist strains of social thought characterizing much of anthropology today. David Bidney's defense of enlightened tradition and his critique of modern thought has presented the anthropological profession with its first serious philosophical challenge.

David Bidney taught us to question our basic assumptions about the nature of human existence. What in fact is the nature of man? What has been the manner of our psycho-cultural evolution? Is anthropology merely a positivist critique of human behavior or is it possible to view humans as creatures of their own making? For David Bidney, only human beings have the ability to reflect upon self and the larger experience. Only man, the imaginative creature, is able to formulate his world in symbols which extend into the uniquely human realms of myth, poetry, and art. And finally, only man is in possession of reason and is involved in the quest for intelligibility, meaning and value.

Central to David Bidney's concept of a humanistic anthropology is the idea of freedom. For Bidney,

the issue of freedom is tied to our understanding of
the moral bases upon which human life is predicated.
At the most basic levels, we may choose to understand
freedom as the natural and culturally relative constraints imposed by human life. Yet, it is also necessary to see human actions as dictated in accordance
with rational ideals which ultimately posit the human
good. While each culture creates both the possibilities
and constraints for human life, the scope of value must
not be seen merely as relative in time and space. As
anthropologists, we must be able to transcend the boundaries of our contemporary situation and view freedom as
emergent in history, as an inherent quality of psycho-
cultural evolution. It is this moral basis of freedom
which David Bidney has chosen to emphasize, and with it
our necessary commitment to reason and progress and to
the human quest for liberation.

In turning toward the crucial questions facing
the modern world, David Bidney has stressed this need
to acknowledge common values. Today it is often difficult to separate the struggle of ideologies from the
quest for power. As heirs to the thought of Nietzche
and Marx, we have been taught that ideals always serve
the interests of some group or class in society, that
out consciousness is determined by the conditions of our
our social and political life. To this David Bidney
responds by posing the possibility of an objective good
which, instead of committing us to a philosophy of perpetual crisis, would provide a common frame of values
through which human beings could live in harmony. To
this end, David Bidney has charged anthropology to assume its role as a "reformer's science" and to undertake the task of understanding the human condition in a
universal ideological framework.

As a teacher and scholar, David Bidney introduced a generation of students to a tradition of scholarship not usually included in the standard world of
anthropology. Here one learned the philosophical foundations of John Locke and Immanuel Kant; the new science of Giambattista Vico, Authur Lovejoy's great chain
of being, the symbolic philosophies of Ernst Cassirer
and Susanne Langer, the pragmatic and existential
statements of John Dewey and William James. David Bidney's ideas thus are a tribute to the whole tradition
of Western scholarship, laying open the philosophical
and humanistic roots of anthropological thought. Students who learned from Dr. Bidney received an education
of the most profound kind.

In the courses taught by David Bidney there reigned the decorum of the highest traditions of scholarship and thought. It was this rigour which gave to his classes their most memorable qualities. There was discipline for high standards, but there was also understanding and sensivity. What you learned from David Bidney stayed with you, influencing the subsequent directions of your ideas and career.

In his courses, students were expected to demonstrate serious participation. This included not only writing substantially researched papers but also getting up before the entire class and giving formal presentations. As was his custom in both undergraduate and graduate classes, one student was always assigned the task of preparing a summary critique of the previous class. Each student was given a particular class period in which to prepare an address. This meant not only listening attentively, but also researching further the ideas and thinkers that Dr. Bidney presented to us.

Memorable also were the occasions when one had personal conferences in his office. Students who did research papers were expected to come prepared not only to present their topics but also to defend them in discussion and often in mild debate. These meetings were both formal and highly pleasurable. They demanded one's rigorous attention, yet they were also touched by Dr. Bidney's particular sensitivity to the deeper professional and personal concerns of each student.

In sum, I reserve the highest tribute for David Bidney as gentleman and scholar. In the conduct of his relationships with students, decorum and good manners were always maintained. There was demand for high standards, but this was accompanied by understanding and a strong feeling for the well being of each student.

* * * * *

The separate contributions to this volume must in the end speak for themselves. Nonetheless, each is a statement concerning the method of anthropology which at its root is the human experience. In the experience of anthropological fieldwork, the individual anthropologist crosses the boundaries of his or her understanding and enters a different cultural world whose usages, meanings, and values create a challenge to further understanding. In this process of interaction,

XIII

the anthropologist must forego the tendency toward judgement so as to place himself within the vital framework of another's understanding. Such self-placement involves the anthropologist in the creative acts of others who in their day to day encounter with reality fashion meaning and value for human life. To witness this process, to respect it in others, and above all to be influenced by it is a goal of an anthropological humanism.

Beginning with the possible theoretical orientations of a humanistic anthropology, Jon Wagner's essay opens an important discussion on human creativity and normative value. Starting with an examination of Enlightenment thought, Wagner presents a critique of positivist thought from the conservative social theories of St. Simon and Comte to the present day interpretations of anthropological science. As a counter critique, Wagner urges anthropologists to consider the measure of culture as the genuine response to human needs and creative potentials, and proposes study aimed at these questions. As anthropologists, Wagner concludes, we must redefine and reassert our role as a "reformer science," one in which we are experientially and morally involved in the human conditions we study.

Bruce Grindal's essay on synergy begins with an appraisal of Edward Sapir and Ruth Benedict in order to evaluate different cultural realities as fulfilling human needs. Do cultures provide individuals with a set of meanings which allow them to grow with a relative absence of frustration and with a sense of creative and participatory belonging, or do they foster antagonistic relationships and aggressive and insecure personalities? From an interdisciplinary perspective, Grindal examines the quality of interpersonal encounter from the standpoint of synergetic relationships, and, in so doing, suggests a possible orientation for a humanistic anthropology.

Frank Cunningham's essay advocates a modified version of the rationalist tradition in assessing our understanding of tribal societies. Are people in these societies less intelligent or mature than those in modern ones? Or is any consideration of this question impossible due to the relative circumstances in which any society finds itself? In response to these questions, Cunningham presents a critical analysis of some philosophical currents in present-day social theory and argues that each offers only a partically adequate way of conceptualizing tribal thought.

Referring to her anthropological field research in various areas of the world, Lola Romanucci-Ross considers the effects of our own conceptual systems upon the recognition and solution of problems in other cultures. By comprehending our own culture as an open system, our contact with other cultures provides for the constant renewal of consciousness in a world which is dynamically moving toward a consensual validation of its different phenomenological realities.

Arthur Newman examines the implications of humanistic psychology and its affinity to humanistic anthropology. In agreement in Bidney's position, Newman argues that human history is replete with examples of man's transcending--through the exercise of deliberate, creative decision making--his sociocultural milieu. In pointing up the close theoretical and empirical affinity between Bidney's ethnological position propounded by the humanistic psychologists, Newman demonstrates that, in spirit and in letter, an interdisciplinary society of humanistic scholars is very much in evidence.

In approaching the questions of intercultural understanding and social change, Dell Hymes opens the second section of the Festschrift with a discussion of language and religion in order to gain understanding of native American humanities. Hymes begins by asking himself -- and by extension the white American -- how one, as a non-Indian, can understand the Indian. How is it possible to cross the cultural distance which separates our communication with one another so that there may be a common basis of understanding? Exploring the roots of humanistic inquiry, Hymes examines the nature of language and religion with the purpose of creating bridges for intercultural understanding. Concluding with respect to native American humanities, Hymes argues that language is the vital element in maintaining the integrity, value and religious definition of any culture, since it is through language that a people conceptualize and express their collective way of life. In the case of the American Indian, whose cultural existence is threatened by destruction, these questions are ever more relevant.

Dennis Warren and Ronald Duncan apply the humanistic perspective to the entangled dilemmas of socioeconomic change in traditional societies. So often in

the encounter between modern society and its traditional counterpart, there is a strong element of paternal
ethnocentrism and condescension, which, instead of
serving the ends of positive social change, function to
widen the gap between rich and poor and to impair mutually constructive forms of communication. Warren
argues that dialogical approaches in applied anthropology can greatly facilitate communications between indigenous societies and directed change agents, enhancing the possibility for viable development. Employing
the methodology of ethno-science, Warren emphasizes our
understanding of indigenous knowledge systems and the
viable involvement of local populations in the design
and implementation of development projects. In a similar vein Duncan argues that social change should be
directed toward removing the barriers that prevent
people from producing autochthonous change that is
self-generated and culturally relevant. Emphasizing
the radical principle of cultural freedom, Duncan outlines a practical method for the self-generation of
behavioral modification and social change.

Edwin Segal's essay likewise takes up the problem of intercultural communication with respect to
planned social change and urban development in an East
African city. As Segal argues, all behavior requires
an appropriate setting, and the existence of proper
social relations is often crucial for defining the
propriety of particular behavior and thus the expression of a culture's norms and values. Too often, however, professionals involved in development planning
disregard these arrangements and thus unwittingly impose a dichotomy between the new cultural order and the
past. The problems of anomie and dissonance result,
and the people faced with changing conditions are
forced to make a polar choice of becoming modern or remaining traditional. As his essay illustrates, the
vital role of the anthropologist is to ensure that such
transitions are made with a minimum of cultural disruption and distortion.

Jon Wagner's contribution discusses social
change from the standpoint of "cultural crises" from
which arise the visionary experiences of charismatic
leaders and the formation of utopian alternatives to
cultural life. Wagner focuses on a utopian group in
the midwestern United States as an example of a communal society which has arisen in a cultural milieu
which has failed to satisfy the basic needs of its members. As the author points out, this group, as many

similar groups, is a microcosm for our understanding of modern society and the problems it manifests when the social routine no longer serves human needs and aspirations.

The article by Malvina Rosatt McNeill involves field research in the elementary schools within the state of Rio Grande do Sul in Brazil. Here, she takes up the perennial problems of human and economic wastefulness in the school system as particularly reflected in the high rate of failure and dropping out of school. Utilizing documents and statistics, as well as numerous interviews with principals, teachers, and supervisors, McNeill presents a clear picture of the problems involved in age-grouping and promoting students within the educational system. As she points out, such an approach often ignores the cultural background of the students and serves more to organize rather than to educate students.

Finally, Marea Teski presents an engaging and highly relevant discussion of the role of the old in society. Beginning with an examination of traditional societies, Teski demonstrates the links between the improvement of subsistence conditions and life expectancy. In modern society, she further demonstrates that the welfare of the old is tied to the extent of their economic participation. Then, in the best traditions of a "reformer science," Teski concludes by advocating the general improvement of the economic conditions of the old, and a further widening of the constellation of meanings through which the old may meaningfully participate in communal life.

The final group of essays concerns the ethnography of human experience and its symbolic representations. Here emphasis is given to the differing methods of ethnographic inquiry. Life history, folklore data and analysis, ethnographic science, and historical linguistics--each is employed as a practical vehicle for understanding the encounter between the ethnographer and the stranger.

The essay by Alan Dundes looks at the popular culture of America and presents a most engaging psychoanalysis of American football. As he argues, football is a virtual national festival in the United States which, like folk rituals in other societies, strikes a responsive chord in a people's collective psyche. In order to account for its extraordinary popularity,

Dundes surveys the popular or folk terminology associated with the game and associates football in the United States with ritual contests involving the expression of adolescent masculinity, which belongs to the general range of male rituals around the world in which masculinity is defined and affirmed.

Nahoma Sachs offers a textual analysis of the symbolic meanings and metaphorical expressions of the annual Koleda ritual of a Yugoslav Macedonian village. The chanting of Koleda has its roots in pre-Christian times, and represents a classic inversion ritual in which serious insult is transformed into symbolic jest. The themes of sexuality are given symbolic meaning in terms of the Macedonian complexes of honor and shame, and the metaphors of the Koleda provide a vehicle to transform the feelings and intuitions derived from personal experience.

Glynn Custred ponders one of the most basic and enduring conceptualizations of the human psyche - that of the soul. Specifically, the paper deals with the idea of the soul as it existed in the southern Andes just prior to and shortly after Spanish conquest. Employing evidence from historical documents and contemporary ethnographic and linguistic data, Custred reconstructs the semantic domains and cultural significance of the Quechua concept which accounts for the essence, life, and character of individual human beings.

The essay by Oswald Werner and Allen Manning emphasizes the use of ethnoscientific methodology in coming to comprehend the subtle boundaries of meaning which unite and separate human communication. As Werner and Manning state, "We must concentrate on a better understanding of the nature of cultural units from the level of the individual all the way to the level of terrestrial human culture." Focusing on the dialect boundaries of the Navajo language, they present a thorough treatment of the semantic components of important concepts in Navajo culture. The methods employed here are indeed instructive to a further investigation of the problems of thought and communication.

The essay by Charles Adams seeks to forward an understanding of intercultural communication with a critical analysis of aurality and consciousness in the symbolic culture of the Bosotho. In discussing the relationships between aesthetic perception and logical thought, Adams endeavors to unravel the complexities of meaning and value which taken together point us toward the fuller dimensions of human consciousness.

Vernon Howard concludes with a philosophical discussion of semiotics relative to culturally acquired forms of cognition. Howard's thesis is the same for anthropology as for psychology: to avoid self-fulfilling prophecy, one's taxonomy of symbols must be logically independent of any anthropological or psychological theories of their acquisition and uses. In developing a theory of "representations," Howard seeks to address a broad range of interdisciplinary questions such as the symbolic preferences of individuals and cultures and the various contexts in which symbolic activity occurs.

TABLE OF CONTENTS

I. ORIENTATIONS FOR A HUMANISTIC ANTHROPOLOGY

By the concept of a normative science of
culture I mean a science of culture concerned with the formulation of cultural
ideals as possible means and ends of socio-
cultural life.

(From Theoretical Anthropology, 1953, p. 416)

THE HUMANISTIC PERSPECTIVE IN ANTHROPOLOGY:
A BRIEF OVERVIEW

Jon Wagner
Knox College

The set of essays before us centers on the theme
of encounter--encounter between the human being as a
seeker of knowledge and the human being as an object
of understanding. It is an encounter that the anthropologist may pursue halfway around the world, but
one which ultimately takes place inside his own skin.
This sort of anthropology, which emphasizes the common humanness of both observer and observed, can be
termed "humanistic anthropology"; indeed each of the
authors who have contributed to this volume identify
their work in some way with this rubric. But what
really is meant by "humanistic anthropology"? At
worst it could be merely a vague term of self-con-
gratulation, meaning little more than "sensitive" or
"broad-minded." At its best, it refers to something
less smug and more specific.

Anthropology, the comparative study of humankind, might be seen as a dialogue based on the dual
nature of human existence. Human beings are, like
their fellow creatures, subject to forces and influ-
ences that they do not will into existence and which
often escape their understanding. The individual,
for example, is the recipient of both a biological
and a cultural heritage, and these are in turn the
products of long-term processes of change and development that can operate independently of our acknow-
ledgement or approval. At the same time, and somewhat paradoxically, the human species alone has the
capacity to foresee (however dimly) its possibilities
and to strive (however haltingly) for the realization
of some over others, based on normative conceptions
of truth, goodness, and beauty. Perhaps it is the
task of humanistic anthropology to focus upon this
second facet of human existence, not in order to dis-
credit the nonconscious, determinative aspects of

3

human life or the methods used to study them, but to contribute to the richest and most balanced approach of which anthropology is capable.

There is nothing new about what we are calling humanistic anthropology. Even putting aside the Greek, Muslim, and other traditions of anthropology, we can see in the anthropology or "universal history" of many Enlightenment philosophers a fundamental commitment to humanistic precepts. The central motivation for Enlightenment anthropology was normative; it was predicated on the idea that cultural understanding is linked directly to cultural improvement. The Philosophes held to the assumption that the human being is the creator and the measure of culture, and that human beings are endowed with needs and potentials that may transcend the limitations of particular cultures (assumptions which, as we shall argue, are essential to humanistic anthropology). Their doctrine of human perfectibility was not a sanguine illusion that everything was about to be "okay." It was, rather, a faith that although culture "makes" humans, humans ultimately have the capability of redesigning it so that it makes them better. According to this view of culture and society, it is possible that the critic of the existing order may be more "right" than the norms he criticizes; the criterion is not the "needs" of the social system but the potential for human development.

The Enlightenment preoccupation with transcending the existing social order does not mean that no attempt was made to apply scientific analysis to detect and explain the patterns and regularities of cultural development. In fact, there is little indication that the Philosophes saw any tension between the normative-humanistic and the scientific aspects of their anthropology; such tension is the child of another age.

St. Simon, Comte, and other conservative social theorists of the early nineteenth century, horrified by the chaos that followed the French Revolution, were quick to blame the Enlightenment belief that reasonable people stood above the social order and were qualified to judge it. For this humanist creed they substituted the proposition that all human good stems from the social order -- imperfect though it may be -- and that those who presume to judge society and advocate its disruption are their own worst enemies. Society was often depicted as an organism and the

individual as a cell therein, a mere abstraction except when considered in relation to the whole. From
such a viewpoint it becomes absurd to think of the
part as the measure of the whole, or the human being
as the measure of society. The individual who pretends to see beyond the current order is only a cancerous cell which threatens to disrupt the welfare of
the organism. The maintenance of the social system is
seen as the ultimate end and human beings are but the
means, and it is presumed that all social behavior and
cultural ideology -- of which individual behavior and
thought are only reflections -- is justified to the
extent that it contributes to social ends. Thus ele-
vated almost to the status of a deity, the sociocultural entity becomes the creator and the measure of
individual human consciousness, and the idea of supra-
cultural standards of judgment is discarded. Along
with this "positivist" outlook comes a specific methodology, which rejects the "metaphysical" approach
of Enlightenment humanism and purports to restrict itself to an objective understanding of the workings of
the social order, an understanding arrived at by means
of a strict empiricism and a supposed rejection of
metaphysical and subjective perspectives.

It is important to emphasize that, notwithstanding the ultra-scientific self image of its advocates,
positivism in anthropology is not coterminous with the
scientific approach. Positivism, unlike science, is a
doctrine that specifically rejects the dialectic nature of anthropology, advocates a narrowly empirical
approach, and categorically rejects the validity of
all problems, strategies, and concepts not manageable
within the framework of its self-styled scientism.
The term "science," on the other hand, refers to a
variety of paradigms and strategies which share certain methodological standards including a commitment
to replicable observation, self-correction of findings
through continued empirical tests, and a tendency to
focus on describing processes and relationships while
temporarily bracketing ethical and aesthetic considerations. While there is a clear contradiction between
humanism and positivism, as the two are defined here,
no such conflict need exist between humanistic and
scientific approaches in anthropology.

The currents of humanism, science, and positivism
all run strong in anthropology, and few anthropologists or schools of thought could legitimately be placed within one of these traditions exclusively. The

5

"classical" 19th century evolutionary anthropology of
E. B. Tylor and others, while searching for a "scientific" understanding of cultural evolution, shared
with the Enlightenment a central emphasis on progress,
reason, and the normative aspects of cultural change.
Franz Boas, who advocated a more rigorous empiricism
than the evolutionists had practiced, nonetheless devoted much energy to the promotion of sympathetic understanding of cultures, showed great concern for
problems of meaning and the role of the individual,
and trained many of the central figures in twentieth
century humanistic anthropology. Even Alfred Kroeber,
who frequently argued for culture's determination
over human consciousness, nevertheless occupied himself with the question of normative evaluations of
culture (1944).

It would be misleading to suggest, however, that
humanistic concerns have enjoyed unflagging popularity in anthropology; on the contrary, some strong intellectual currents in anthropology contradict humanism, and the strongest among these are cultural determinism and cultural relativism. Although the advocates of determinism and relativism differ significantly among themselves, they share certain propositions in common. One might argue for specific determinative relationships between culture and the individual without being a doctrinaire determinist, but
determinism as a doctrine states that the perceptions,
values, and motivations by which an individual guides
his or her actions are entirely determined by cultural heritage. This doctrine is consistent with, and
typically accompanied by, the doctrine of relativism
which states that all modes of thought, including
concepts of value, are the products of specific cultures and can therefore be judged only from the particular viewpoints of those respective cultures.
Sumner's Folkways, initially published in 1907, held
as a main thesis that "the goodness or badness of
mores consists entirely in their adjustment to the
life conditions and the interests of the time and
place" (1940:79). Forty years later, Herskovits expressed the viewpoint of many of his fellow anthropologists when he stated that "Evaluations are relative to the cultural background out of which they
arise," and that "The primary mechanism that directs
the evaluation of cultures is ethnocentrism" (1947:
350,356 original italics).

6

.Again, it is possible to recognize specific instances of relativity or to use relativism as a methodology without becoming a doctrinaire relativist (cf. Bidney 1968), but to accept relativism as a philosophy is to deny the possibility of any values except those imposed by specific cultures. Ironically, the orthodoxy of cultural relativism seems to have grown out of the humanist tradition of liberal tolerance and empathetic understanding (e.g. Benedict 1934). As such it may well be the beginning of wisdom, but as an uncompromising doctrine relativism denies the possibility that cultures themselves are subject to legitimate evaluation. Cultural determinism and cultural relativism deny what humanism affirms: that individual human thought can to some degree be liberated and liberating; and that there exist, in addition to cultural differences, some fundamental realities of human existence which we are capable of sharing and which can allow some standard for judging cultural forms.

The humanistic approach in anthropology has never been without able supporters. Edward Sapir's milestone article "Culture, Genuine and Spurious" (1924) outlined in bold strokes some possible criteria for reckoning the human value of cultural forms. Although Ruth Benedict was in certain respects a thoroughgoing relativist, her ideas on "synergy" and "human waste" reflected a similar desire to evaluate cultural differences (1934). Robert Redfield attacked relativism not only for its inhumanity but also for its logical inconsistency, noting that the relativist doctrine as set forth by Herskovits and others contained its own value judgments which were gratuitously placed beyond the relativistic cul de sac (1953; cf. Bidney 1952).

One of the most consistent and capable supporters of humanistic anthropology has been David Bidney. Bidney's doctorate in philosophy, combined with a career of teaching and research in anthropological theory, placed him in a uniquely advantageous position for the criticism of anthropology's philosophical underpinnings. It was this critique, especially as applied to cultural evolution, relativism, and determinism, that constitutes the theme of most of his writing and teaching. Each of the contributors to this book was, in his or her own way, influenced directly by Bidney's scholarship.

7

One of Bidney's central assertions has been that anthropological theorists too seldom confront honestly the philosophical roots and implications of their statements. This theme is particularly developed in Bidney's critique of cultural relativism, which is likely to stand as one of his most lasting contributions to anthropology. It is characteristic of his meticulous scholarship and his fairness that he never launched a dogmatic, all-out attack on cultural relativism, but chose instead to recognize its methodological and humane potentials while opposing it in its extreme and dogmatic forms, wherein it attempts to assume the status of a comprehensive moral philosophy (e.g. 1952;1968). Bidney's position on determinism was also a synthetic one: rather than shrilling about the unbounded freedom of humankind, he advocated an approach which recognizes an element of indeterminacy and creativity in culture, within the limits imposed by nature and history:

> The issue, then, is not whether man's "will" is free, in the sense of being undetermined or causeless, but whether man as a whole is or is not to a limited extent the active agent and efficient cause of the cultural process and whether culture, if its historical conditions are understood, is subject to human control in the interests of human well-being. I maintain that human freedom and causal determinism are quite compatible and that no irreconcilable conflict is involved (1967:123-24).

Despite Bidney's reputation in some quarters as an "indeterminist" (Harris 1968:300), it should be apparent from the above quote that his position converges with that taken by such prominant "determinists" as Frederick Engels (1972:58) and Marvin Harris (1977:xii,195), both of whom have argued that the ultimate value of knowledge about deterministic forces lies in its potential to enhance human control.

Concerning the question of relativism, anthropology shows signs of retreating from the uncompromising position taken by Herskovits and others. Marvin Harris, for example, is a hard-nosed advocate of an anthropology styled on the natural sciences; yet he is not abashed to say that science ought to aid in the selection of "better" forms of cultural life, and is more than willing to criticize exploi-

tation, injustice, and dishonesty in human societies
(1975;1977). Redfield was probably not wrong in his
1953 (145) prediction that relativism was "in for
some hard times." This can be attributed not only to
such intellectual critiques as Bidney's, but also to
the inherent inadequacy of relativism in a world characterized by violent change and intersocietal conflict. The complexities of the modern world have
made it clear that no culture enjoys the privilege of
moral or practical isolation. Many of the younger
anthropologists have themselves taken part in the social criticism of the late 1960's which attacked academia's apparent moral detachment. Still, there has
as yet been no coherent movement to construct an anthropology based on humanist commitments. Perhaps
the positivism in our intellectual background has
given us a more-than-healthy skepticism of anything
smacking of philosophy. Certainly concepts like "human nature" and "individual creativity" are easier to
debunk than to verify, and anthropologists are de-
bunkers by inclination and training. Furthermore,
the credibility of such concepts has sometimes been
damaged by the naivete and even ethnocentrism with
which they were put forth. Our foot-dragging is understandable, for the development of humanistic anthropology will require new commitments and will bring
troublesome issues that can be resolved only partially
and with difficulty. It is encouraging to note, however, that some other social science disciplines are
grappling with similar issues and show signs of growing interest in humanist perspectives (e.g. Flynn
1977).

Leslie White (1959) once made the claim that
man's control over culture is "an anthropocentric illusion." The assertion implies an Olympian perspective from which such specifically human notions as
freedom are revealed as the mere imaginings of limited beings. Even supposing that such a perspective
were attainable and in some sense true, its value is
subject to challenge. We are, after all, human
beings whether we like it or not. It is realistic to
accept the fact that our objectivity, valuable as it
is, exists always in the context of our peculiarly
human limitations and purposes. We must ackowledge
the importance of categories of experience and modes
of perception that are rooted in a specifically human
nature rather than "pure" objective intelligence or
absolute reality; that is, we must set aside the desire to be gods. In our dual role as actors and ob-

9

servers we are experientially involved with, and morally accountable for, the conditions we study. We are engaged in the perception and selection of human possibilities as well as the description of cultural reality. This means appreciating our species quest for meaning and all the elusive ghosts--responsibility, empathy, justice, awe, creativity, beauty, the numinous--that go with it, and identifying ourselves with that quest.

Of course, all this assumes the existence of some attributes, needs and potentials that go deeper than specific cultures; in other words, human nature. It assumes also that we can sufficiently liberate ourselves from culture-bound modes of thinking to gain some sight into these human qualities, and that such insights will turn out to be useful. Only if we accept these propositions of human unity and freedom can we adopt the view that human beings, both in the individual dimension of critical, creative thought and in the collective dimension of human nature, are the measures of culture.

To argue that there is a need for humanism in anthropology is not to claim for this approach an exclusive window on the truth. The importance of such things as creativity and normative meaning does not exclude other phenomena from consideration. It is only prudent to recognize that freedom operates within a multitude of constraints and that the more we know about them the better off we are. Opposition to genetic, ecological, or other specific causal explanations simply on the grounds that they insult our dignity is not humanism but hubris. One might hope for an anthropology that treats human behavior as the product of multiple levels and kinds of processes which can best be comprehended through an open-ended dialectical approach. Knowledge of the culturally specific informs our conception of human nature, and understanding of determinative forces clarifies our perception of freedom. The establishment of theoretical orthodoxy, be it idealistic or deterministic, is the end of dialogue. In the final analysis it is encounter--encounter with the alien, the familiar, and most of all, the inconvenient--that nourishes understanding.

REFERENCES CITED

Benedict, Ruth

 1934 Patterns of Culture. Boston: Hough-
      ton Mifflin.

Bidney, David

 1952 The concept of value in Modern Anthro-
      pology. In Anthropology Today: Selec-
      tions, Sol Tax (ed.), pp. 436-453. Chi-
      cago: University of Chicago Press.

 1967 Theoretical Anthropology. New York:
      Shocken Books.

 1968 Culture: Cultural Relativism.
      International Encyclopedia of the
      Social Sciences. New York: Mac-
      millan.

Engels, Frederick

 1972 Socialism, Utopian and Scientific.
      New York: Pathfinder Press.

Flynn, Charles

 1977 Orientations of Humanistic Sociology.
      Anthropology and Humanism Quarterly
      Vol. 2, No. 4:9-11.

Harris, Marvin

 1968 The Rise of Anthropological Theory.
      New York: Crowell.

 1975 Cows, Pigs, Wars and Witches: The
      Riddles of Culture. New York:
      Vintage Books.

1977   Cannibals and Kings: The Origin of Cultures. New York: Random House.

Herskovits, Melville

1947   Man and His Works. New York: Knopf.

Kroeber, Alfred L.

1944   Configurations of Culture Growth. Berkeley: University of California Press.

Redfield, Robert

1953   The Primitive World and its Transformations. Ithica: Cornell University Press.

Sapir, Edward

1924   Culture, Genuine and Spurious. American Journal of Scoiology. 29:401-429.

Sumner, William Graham

1940   Folkways (3rd ed). Boston: Ginn & Co.

White, Leslie

1959   Man's Control over Culture: An Anthropocentric Illusion. In Morton H. Fried, ed., Readings in Anthropology, Vol. II. New York: Thomas Y. Crowell Company. Pp. 548-566.

SYNERGY: A THEORY AND PRAXIS FOR HUMAN LIFE

Bruce T. Grindal
Florida State University

The Views of Sapir and Benedict.

In his seminal essay, Culture, Genuine and Spurious, Edward Sapir (1924) spoke of the possibility of studying and evaluating cultures with respect to how well they provide suitable environments for human existence. Along a general continuum, he saw the genuine culture as one which begins from the needs of the individual while at the same time functions as an integrated and meaningful whole. It is able to strike a harmonious relationship between the vital strivings of human beings and the cultural soil in which they are nurtured. According to Sapir, a genuine culture expresses "a richly varied and yet somehow unified and consistent attitude toward life in which nothing is spiritually meaningless in which no part of the general functioning brings with it a sense of frustration, or misdirected or unsympathic effort (p. 410)." The spurious culture, on the other hand, is external to the individual producing a feeling of subservice to arbitary demands and fostering an attitude of nonparticipation and alienation. While the genuine culture serves to nurture the creative potential of human beings, the spurious culture is inherently frustrating, fragmentary and wasting of human endeavor and sentiment.

Reflecting upon Sapir, the author strongly believes that he was on to something that the subsequent course of scholastic anthropology has largely neglected. For at issue is the whole question of human value and the possible emergence of an anthropology capable of addressing this question both scientifically and ethically, with an emphasis on the measure of cultural satisfaction. In other words, cannot anthropology blend its scientific perspective with some general definition of human value, and begin pursuing research and thought which would be in service to this value? The response of this paper is affirmative, and the following ideas are in large part a response to the challenge of Sapir's thinking.

The standpoint which is proposed involves the idea of synergy. Stated simply, synergy pertains to the cooperative or harmonious relationship of parts within a system. Most notable in anthropology, this idea is contained in the posthumously published writings of Ruth Benedict (Maslow and Honigmann 1970). According to Benedict, synergy exists when the acts of individuals in society are in mutually reinforcing relationships so that the valued ends of individuals complement those of the social body. From the comparative material, she finds that highly synergetic societies are characterized by a low incidence of aggression, meaning here behavior the aim of which is injury, expulsion or humiliation of another person. As Benedict contends, a society is like a joint stock company in which its members share the profits and pool the risk. While differences in wealth and status may exist, the individual nonetheless experiences his or her position in society as just, inculcating a faith in the rewards of cooperative social living. The course of life convinces one that one's own goods are the goods of society. In such a society,

> Will to power over people has not been called
> into being by his experience: fear of desertion,
> fear of humiliation, are only deterrents to im-
> proper behavior; and desertion and humiliation
> will not fall to his lot unless he defaults; he
> does not live in a threatening universe, and he
> does not have to snatch and grab to maintain
> himself. (Maslow and Honigmann 1970:327)

Conversely societies of low synergy are characterized by opposing and antagonistic relationships and foster personalities which are variably aggressive, acquisitive, and insecure.

For Sapir the problem of human cultural existence is one of creative participation. Do cultures provide members with a consistent set of meanings which allow the individual to grow with a relative absence of frustration, and in a sense of creative and participatory belonging. Sapir's answer is yes; some cultures are more genuine than others. For Benedict the problem of human being resides in the quality of human

14

relationships which in turn is related to the institutional structures of society. That human relations are cooperative or antagonistic is expressed in the varied forms of aggression and social injustice.

As a concept, synergy assumes the existence - or at least potential existence - of orderly systems, and may be applied not only to discussions of socio-cultural phenomena but also to the areas of biology, medicine and psychology. In this paper, therefore, I should like to explore the idea of synergy from an interdisciplinary perspective and in so doing suggest a possible orientation for a more humanistic anthropology.

Human Well-Being and the "Wisdom of the Body".

If by radical we mean getting to the root of the matter, what better place to begin an analysis of synergy than with the most fundamental processes of biological functioning. As Paul Weiss (1970) notes in his discussion on metabiology, the biological organism may be likened may be likened to a set of Chinese boxes in which living matter is represented in a hierarchy of concentric subsystems. At its root lies the gene and at its furthest extension the limiting membrane of skin which separates the interior milieu from the external environment. Thus, "...the genes are embedded in chromosomes, chromosomes lie in the nucleus, the nucleus is surrounded by cytoplasm, the cells are incorporated in the tissue matrix bathed by the internal milieu of blood and lymph, and the whole body faces the outer environment (Weiss 1970:97)." Each of these systems or shells constitutes the environment for its inner neighbor and in turn is contained within the more inclusive environment of its outer neighbor.

In approaching the idea of synergy, it is well to bear in mind the kind of thinking set forth in Weiss' discussion. Synergy pertains to the property of systems, and specifically to systems where the relationship of parts are harmonious and where the integrity or well being of both the part and the whole is maintained. From Weiss' perspective, the biological organism - or more precisely, the healthy biological organism - is synergetic. The processes of respiration, digestion, circulation, neural and endocrine function exist in the final analysis to maintain the conditions of cellular life. The welfare and integrative functioning of the organism is therefore not at odds with the life of the cell. Were this relationship to

15

become unsynergetic, were the organism to create an aggressive or cancerous partnership within its cellular milieu, the conditions of life would cease.

In his early discussion on the subject of homeostasis, Walter Cannon (1932) stated that the human body possesses an "instinctive" wisdom by which it seeks to maintain the necessary conditions for existence. This process is a highly complex set of bodily interactions, which regulates the uniform functioning of the organism as it encounters different environmental situations. Thus when the body performs muscular activity, reactions are triggered which balance bodily temperature, the appropriate levels of blood sugar, and the elimination of bodily wastes. For the most part this process operates unconsciously and is governed by the neural activity of the limbic brain and autonomic nervous system, and the regulation of the secretion of bodily hormones. Homeostasis adapts the body to states of activity and returns it to a state of rest and reintegration. As Cannon (1932:267) states, "every change in the outer world, every move in relation to the outer world, is attended by a rectifying process in the inner world of the organism." The concept of homeostasis thus posits an inner dynamic through which the body seeks to create an optimal balance between the individual's creative encounter with environment and the maintenance of his or her own inner integrity. Major disruptions of this process, the individual's inability to synergetically relate to its existential situation, create illness which may permanently strain the individual's capacity to adapt, and ultimately to survive.

In recent years, Cannon's ideas have gained renewed interest in the area of stress research. According to Hans Selye's (1956) original treatment of the subject, stress pertains to the nonspecific reactions by which the organism responds to demanding circumstance and through which it restores bodily and mental equilibrium. Stress may be caused either by the pressure of a foreign body or pathogen in the organism or by the frustrations and problems of everyday life. By its nature stress is adaptive, triggering certain neural and endocrine reactions, causing the body to resist the source of stress (stressor) and to restore bodily function. If the body is unable to restore equilibrum, stress becomes a chronic condition which in time gradually destroys physical and emotional well being.

In a more recent treatment of this general problem,

Howard and Scott (1965) view human behavior--or for that matter, the behavior of any living organism--as a problem solving phenomena which responds to situations demanding solution. Such responses may range from the largely unconscious regulation of physiological process as in the disruption of homeostatic balance, to the sociocultural and symbolic problems which stem from group living. Considering these processes, they point out that it is necessary to distinguish between the efforts at problem solving, the mobilization of the organism's energy resources, and the actual resolution of the problem. Thus the organism may act by diverting its energies away from confronting problems or else by failing to mobilize its resources altogether as in the case of paralysis. The "tension that results from the organism's inability to master presenting problems and its consequent need to devote excess energy and resources to maintenance activities is termed stress (Howard & Scott 1965:141)."

This process thus possesses a normative dimension, which is at first approximation we may define as health or well being. Specifically a healthy organism is one in which instinctual capacities and environmental requirements are mutually regulated so as to create a maximum condition of adaptibility and a minimum condition of negative feedback or stress. If an organism is able to adapt to the insult of a bacterial pathogen or injury, its very adaptiveness is the condition of its health (Selye 1956). In the same vein, from a psychological perspective, the human organism must deploy its resources to integrate the internal symbolic stimuli of self consciousness and the resultant behavioral effects upon others in the social environment. In other words, the individual is able to synergetically perform his social role while continuing to satisfy or realize his basic needs.

In turning to a discussion of human growth and development, two important dimensions emerge: one, the inner dynamic which represents the potential being of any life form, and secondly, the interaction of this potential within temporally successive environments. Beginning then with conception, the organism comes into existence as a bundle of inherited and yet-to-be-realized genetic potentials. In the nurturant environment of the mother's womb, these potentials unfold and are modified by the stimuli of this outer world. The phenomenon of birth is essentially the trading of one environment for another, and the encounter with the new

17

environment further develops these new potentials. As Gardiner Murphy has stated, the organism, human or otherwise, "is a tissue system undergoing changes partly because of interaction with the outer world. [It] is 'acquiring' new characteristics all the time, never by accretion but always by modification of what is (1947: 51)." Thus as long as life continues, the individual is engaged in a dialectic project of its own development, both acting upon and reacting to the total field of its existence.

In a very real sense, the healthy growth of the human being may be likened to that of all organisms. Thus the gardener knows that a particular seed requires certain conditions for its proper nurturance. In the same way, we can begin to explore the "cultural soil" in which human beings develop; indeed, Maslow suggests this when he speaks of "growth-fostering" and "growth-inhibiting" cultures. The question of culture, of course, adds a new dimension or as Gerald Weiss (1975) has stated, a new realm to the order of existence in which human behavior is governed by not only genetic but also symbolic principles. This greater complexification (Huxley 1956) of the human experience renders any biological explanation at best partial. Yet our basic being rests upon a biological substratum, and as Malinowski has so well perceived, our culture is a product of these "basic needs." To divorce culture from biology, is to reject the most fundamental dimension of the human problem, and that is the dialectic interplay between our genetically endowed nature as life forms and the conditions which we have socially and historically created for ourselves. That this relationship is synergetic, that it fosters healthy growth as well as a rational basis for social living, is the problem at issue.

Synergy and The "Lessons" of Evolution

From an internal biological perspective, the primary purpose of existence is the maintenance of orderly functioning within the living system. If, however, we move beyond the protective membrane of the skin, the external reality which the organism encounters is not necessarily integrated with the same determinancy as within its successive environments. In other words, a hiatus exists between the inner instinctual potential of the biological/psychic world and the natural world of "unyielding facts" which does not automatically respond to the "wishes, hopes, and fears" of the

18

organism (Maslow 1968). This hiatus involves adaptation or the organism's ability to maintain a relationship to the vicissitudes of its external situation while at the same time preserving the survival and basic integrity of its biologically constituted self.

In response to this hiatus, the generally agreed "biological lesson" is survival or the successful struggle in the competition for life. As Paul Weiss states, "biological nature condones the resolution of conflict by victory rather than conciliation. Outfighting, outbreeding or outsmarting a competitor are the approved means of evolutionary progress (1970:10)." Yet the question of survival is not altogether a simple matter. Few, if any, species exist as solitary creatures; even at the simplest taxonomic levels (e.g. cell colonies), species survive in aggregations. It is logical then to theorize, as does Wilson (1975), that natural selection favors not only genetic traits conducive to individual survival but also "altruistic" potentials which socially band co-specific organisms and favor group survival. As phylogenetic adaptations, these traits extend the range of ambiance beyond the protective membrane of the skin to the social group and progressively favor the overall adaptability of the organism (Sahlins 1960).

Viewing this in the context of biological evolution, it may be argued that synergy is an emergent phenomenon. Historically, lesser forms of organization progressively transform or "self-transcend" (Huxley 1956) into more complex forms of organization. Beginning with the evolutionary emergence of multicellularity, separate cells come together in such a way that the metabolic activities of one do not interfere with the metabolic activities of the others. This cooperative metabolism is a form of altruism which from the "cell's point of view" becomes a form of collective egotism. "The choice between egotism and altruism does not arise between the cells of a single multicellular body; within its confines, there is no motive for competitive fight (Selye 1965: 283)." Likewise, homeostasis represents an evolutionary trend toward more precise regulatory mechanisms and toward greater overall adaptability to the situational changes of the environment (Curtis 1965). This involves greater awareness and responsiveness to external stimuli and a greater need to interrelate such stimuli to internal biological functioning. Finally, the evolution of the cerebral cortex, as it pertains to mammals, primates

19

and especially man, even further increases the organism's capacity to perceive and come to generalized
associations about its environmental condition, and in
turn, fosters an even greater imperative to integrate
awareness or consciousness with biological well being.
The course of general evolution then involves a reciprocal interaction between the organism's sensory awareness of and overall adaptability to environment and the
hierarchical complexification of its biological functioning (Huxley 1956) (Sahlins 1960).

In viewing human evolution, the problem of synergy
increasingly entails the question of consciousness, and
particularly symbolic consciousness. Unlike other animals, humans relate to the conditions of their existence through historically acquired symbolic forms.
The biosphere of the human organism is thus contained
not only within a physical environment governed by natural law but also within a cultural environment where
the measure of meaning and order are governed by symbolic represenations and their extensions into artifacts and interpersonal relations. Culture is a self-
maintaining system organized about intercommunicating
human beings and transmitted interpersonally through
the organs of symbolic awareness. As such it exists as
a systematically meaningful "outer membrane" or noosphere (Huxley 1956) (Teilhard de Chardin 1956) which
is as necessary for human survival as the bio-organism
is for the life of the cell.

The evolution of this noosphere represents a progressive mediation between the genetically coded organism and the material requirements of life. On the
one hand, humans are the only animals who are conscious
of themselves in terms of publicly coded symbols. As
Hallowell (1959) argues, it is this capacity for symbolic self consciousness that lies at the basis of
human moral systems which are the collective representations of symbolic values. Further, this very ability
to symbolically code experience is part of man's phy-
logentic heritage and is thus imprinted upon his biological nature, the very coding of his DNA. On the
other side of the equation, the evolution of the noosphere has also meant the progressive modification of
the natural environment. "Progress" or evolutionary
advance as Sahlins (1960) states, entails the ever increasing capacity to utilize the energy potential in
the environment and adapt it in the service of collective human needs. As human beings have fabricated
their environments through technology, they have

progressively removed themselves from the purely natural conditions of life. Thus, the lesson of human evolution has been one of the mergence of organism and environment through the "self-developing framework of thought" (Teilhard de Chardin 1961).

Convergence is thus a distinguishing characteristic of human evolution. Unlike other animal species, whose evolutionary directions have been those of adaptive radiation and differential speciation, humans emerge from the course of hominid evolution as a single species. Further, the direction of human cultural development has imposed centripetal forces upon the potentials for differentiation and fragmentation. Less complex forms of social organization have given way to more complex and inclusive forms; less efficient technologies have been replaced by more efficient ones; and in the process humankind has moved, albeit not without suffering and moral irony, from the simpler ambiance of nomadic bands to the more intense and organically interrelated conditions of modern life.

However, merely because human evolution is characteristically convergent does not necessarily mean that the relationship of the enculturated human being with his or her cultural environment is necessarily synergetic. There still remains the hiatus between organism and environment, and while human cultures strive to mediate this gap, the success of their adaptations and symbolic meanings cannot merely be assumed. Thus unlike the genetic ally coded interrelationships of biological functioning, the existence of synergy at the level of culture is not an accomplished fact and always represents indeterminant potential or, as the author contends, an ideal of moral attainment.

Order and Aggression in Nature and Human Nature

From the discussion so far, we can detect the emergence of two kinds of values, which the author will call unitary and opposing. In nature we find these values reflected, on the one hand, in the interaction of intraorganism processes and in the cooperative or "altruistic" (Wilson 1976) relations among populations of co-specific organisms. On the other hand, the opposing tendency is reflected in the aggressive rule of individual natural selection--the natural law involving competition for scarce resources and the struggle for survival and dominance. Commenting upon these unitary and opposing values in a human dimension, Paul

Weiss (1970:10) states: "Being the animal he is, man has inherited a flair for polarizing issues. Instinctively, he fans their conflict breeding potential by laying stress on divergence and disparity; doing so he amplifies the centrifugal separative forces which threaten to disrupt the crucial cohesiveness without which no living system, including the human race, can survive." In contrast to this "Darwinistic" view of what Weiss calls biological man, he posits the idea of civilized man who seeks to counteract, through the power of reason, this fatal trend to excessive polarization by making "the most of his rational faculties by adopting the broad perspective which would let moderation defuse the explosive charge of fanatical antagonisms (1970:11)." Thus, there emerges a kind of oscillation between the selfish or "biologically" impelled side of our nature and those values which lay stress on altruism, cooperation and reason.

In his examination of the condition of contemporary America, Jules Henry (1963) approaches this question in a similar vein when he distinguishes between values and drives. Commenting upon modern America, he states that we are a "driven culture," driven on by the impulse toward achievement and competition, and by the drives for security and higher material standards. The basis for this driveness arises from the narrowly egotistic nature of our psycho-biology. Unlike hunger and thirst, the social drives are generated by our culture; still human beings yield to them in the same as hunger and thirst. Since their sphere of influence is limited to the individual's own ends, such drives are predatory and create conflict and antagonism both within self and in one's interpersonal relations. As Henry (1963:15) states, "In the American conception, drives can become almost like cannibals hidden in a man's head or viscera devouring him from the inside [and consuming] others by compelling them to yield to [this] drivenness." The consequences of such drives breed problems ranging from heart attacks and ulcers to alienation, cruelty and ethnocentrism. By contrast, values are the sentiments which work in the opposite direction; instead of polarizing and aggressively opposing groups within the social body, they seek to unify human diversity through "gentleness, kindliness, and generosity."

In searching for the causes of aggression and altruism, it is necessary both to interrelate and to distinguish between biological and cultural bases. Beginning then from a comparative or ethnological standpoint,

22

it is significant to note that, with the notable exception of man, co-specific organisms tend to avoid
situations which are mutually injurious. This is
usually facilitated by "ritual" forms commonly associated with mating, hierarchical behavior, and territorial defense (Curtis 1975) (Eibl-Eibesfeldt 1970). Such
forms not only defuse or buffer situations of potential
violence but also promote cooperation and preserve order in co-specific populations. If, however, changes
occur in the environment which place pressures upon a
population's capacity to survive, as in the case of
overpopulation, centrifugal tendencies develop which
promote intra-species aggression and "a breakdown of
the supporting and order-preserving social structures
(Autrum 1966)." Such situations of scarcity engender
stress symptoms causing the hyper-activation of the
sympathetic nervous system, and promoting not only
intraspecific aggression but also such abnormal functioning as impotence, inability to lactate, and cannibalism (Eibl-Eibesfeldt 1970).

From a general standpoint aggression is a response
to threat. All of existence presents the organism with
conflict; and as the organism develops through life, it
must continually adapt to new circumstances through the
appropriate modification of awareness and behavior.
Aggression arises when the channeling of the organism's
energy is sufficiently frustrated so as to interfere
with its striving toward need directed goals (Dollard
et al 1939). This inability to create a satisfactory
cathexis between states of need and the requirements
of the environment results in acts of violence against
co-specifics or acts of self-destruction as evidenced
in pathological stress reactions. To argue that aggression is innate (Ardrey 1966) or reactive (Dollard
et al 1939) is to impose a false dichotomy. In essence
it is an instinctual potential which is activated by
conditions which threaten survival. In the animal
world, this is evidenced by disturbances of the "homeostatic" balance between organism and environment, or
in the case of social species, by circumstances which
disorder the mutually adaptive mechanisms of group survival.

In formulating his theory of natural selection,
Darwin drew strongly upon the thinking of Malthus when
he spoke of selection in terms of the competition for
resources. Those organisms which "adapt to their own
advantage in the struggle for life" are those which are
most capable of utilizing the environment in a superior

23

manner. Those which don't "lose," so to speak, since
the measure of success is not only individual survival
but also reproductive or phylogenetic continuity. As
Hockett (1973) so well illustrates, the "power of
death" is the norm; almost all organisms die without
reproducing. The rule of natural selection is thus
order-opposing, and is based upon a dynamic disequili-
brium between the biosphere and the material resources
which sustain it. Thus the success of any one adaptation is measured aggressively against the failure of
other adaptations. Yet out of this process, there
emerges in general evolution more complex forms of
intra-species cooperation which progressively minimize
the "power of death" by creating greater overall adaptability to the material conditions of survival.

The situation of humankind is a good case in point,
noting here the ever-increasing impress of culture and
the development of technologies which prolong human
mortality. However, there is an irony to human existence. On the one hand, human evolution represents a
pinnacle in terms of altruistic forms of co-specific
bonding and interthinking frameworks of communications.
Yet, as Freud (1961) has so profoundly queried, it is
"so hard for men to be happy." Indeed, the greater
part of the Western Christian tradition, which so en-
obles the value of love and universal humanity, has
placed a rather low estimation upon human life and the
possibility of happiness. This tradition's history of
predatory conquest and warfare, race and class oppression, and downright cruel acts in the name of God give
one cause to share Freud's pessimissism. Further, any
survey of the cross-cultural material would illustrate
that the forms of human aggression are legion, incom-
parable in variety and intensity to those of any other
animal species. One need only think in our own society
of the sado-masochistic "games people play" in interpersonal relations to know how aggressive behavior is
hidden beneath the sham and pretension of everyday symbolic usage.

In the first analysis, the unique causes of human
aggression would seem to reside in the learned symbolic
forms and thus cortical control over behavior. Holloway (1974), in his general discussion of primate aggres-
ion, notes the significance of cortical enlargement and
the rise of self consciousness in primate evolution.
This self-consciousness is capable of assigning value
to both self and the group, and thus accounts for both
the relatively stable bonding of primate groups and the

24

stronger reactions of xenophobia and group-related aggressive behavior. Like Hallowell (1969), Holloway argues that the evolution of self-consciousness is a foundation upon which the distinctly human forms of symbolic consciousness built, and that man must be seen in terms of his primate phylogenetic development. Thus ideas and symbols, mediated through the cerebral cortex "can drive aggressive behavior far beyond that known in any other primate (Holloway 1974:7)." The relationship between self-consciousness and new forms of aggression suggests then that the price of increased cortical control is a loss of control with respect to the fixed motor patterns which inhibit dangerous behavior in most species.

This idea of "cortical super control" and its relationship to aggression closely approximates Freud's theory of the personality. For Freud, the human ego or self-consciousness if formed in the interaction of two disparate poles: the id and the super-ego. The former represents man's animal nature, which like that of any creature is driven by the needs for gratification and is governed by the principle of pleasure. The super-ego is the symbolic consciousness which is derived through cultural learning and serves to render the world as morally ordered. This super-ego is the individual's micro-cosm of the larger culture, and facilitates adaptation to the cognitive, aesthetic and ethical frameworks of fellow human beings (Sprio 1951). That these cognitive forms adequately serve to regulate and adjust the mutual relationships of human beings cannot be assumed. For Freud, human existence involves the cost of repression, the denial of instinctual needs, and the problem of human life essentially reduces to that of the "economics of happiness" in which the healthy ego is capable of directing its instinctual energies along culturally prescribed forms of gratification.

Nonetheless, the process of becoming human invariably involves a measure of frustration. Toward the conclusion of his Civilization and Its Discontents, Freud argues that the cost of repression and neurotic compromise is a powerful share of aggressiveness, and he notes ironically that the very blessing of modern civilization have at the same time accelerated the level of human violence. Thus, for civilized humankind,
"...their neighbor is for them not only a potential helper or sexual object, but also

25

someone who tempts them to satisfy their
aggressiveness on him, to exploit his
capacity for work without compensation,
to use him sexually without his consent,
to seize his possessions, to humiliate him,
to cause him pain, to torture and to kill
him. Homo homini lupus." (1961:82)

Thus, Freud saw aggressive drives as responses to
the inherent frustrations of adapting to social values.
The culturally resolved solution to aggression, as
Freud saw it, is neurosis in which the individual
learns to repress sexual and aggressive strivings in
order to conform to codes of social morality. Such
forms of an aggression are usually self-directed often
leading to somatic disorders and distorted psychological adaptations.

This notwithstanding, Freud also saw aggression as
innate. The sham imperialism of World War I and the
rising spectre of fascism convinced Freud in his later
years that the human race possessed a strong instinct
toward destructiveness and disorder. Further, his life
encounters with the irrationality of anti-Semitism and
the hypocritical standards of Victorian morality laid
open to Freud a vast underground of human discontent
and convinced him of the intractable conflict between
biological man and his cultural ideals. Freud saw aggression as innate, not so much because he did not
understand the underlying psycho-dynamics creating it,
but because he lacked the sensibility of critical
social thought. Indeed, the absence of any thoroughgoing examination of Marxist thought and his steadfast
embrace of bourgeois values attest to this. Thus the
times in which he lived were taken as the standard by
which to assess the totality of humankind. To Freud
then, man is inherently a wolf, clothed in but a thin
veneer of civility.

As stated above, aggression is innate insofar as
it represents a potential response of frustration and
danger, and while it may be argued that a certain
amount of aggressive behavior is inevitable, the cultural conditions which create it are variable. Agreeing with Marcuse (1962), any form of human living contains a certain amount of "basic repression"--if we
mean by this the unavoidable frustrations involved in
human growth and adaptation. At its root, basic repression stems from scarcity or inherent disparity
between human desires and their material fulfillment.

26

However, some forms of social existence engender a surplus of repression, an added deprivation, so that the requirements of the economic and social life are more strenuous or frustrating. To Marcuse, surplus repression is a result of human inequality which he defines as the unequal distribution of scarcity in civilized society. Surplus repression emerges in human history with the evolution of urban society with its aristocratic culture and values, its institutions of servitude and public violence, and the increase of human suffering and alienation. The institutionalization of human inequality in modern society gives its cultural expression in the "logic of domination" which morally justifies the restraints and material deprivation which the ruling classes impose upon the greater part of the population. This logic of domination further creates in society an aggressive and predatory posture; crime and other forms of deviance become institutional realities as well as wars of conquest and imperial rule.

In way of conclusion, there emerges from this discussion the sensibility of a dialectic interaction between processes which are order-creating or altruistic and those which are order-opposing or aggressive. The on-going and creative endeavor of any culture is toward building systems of order and meaning which facilitate man's adjustment to reality and which give life a sense of moral and aesthetic value. Yet not all cultures are able to master the historical and environmental circumstances in which they find themselves nor are they necessarily able to create harmonious relations between inter-thinking human beings. The measure of aggression is thus a measure of a society's failure, an index of its stupidity. The forms of aggression include not only outright acts of violence but also any thought or behavior which threatens to disorder human relations, to alienate individuals from one another, and to imbalance the reciprocal relationship between man and nature. Aggression is a response to threat whether in the form of rational danger or neurotic anxiety, and as a response only serves to intensify the conditions which create it.

Synergy as a Theory of Communication

From the foregoing, the idea synergy may be seen as pertaining to order-creating processes, processes which serve to mediate the potentials of aggressive behavior, so to affect more harmonious systems of order.

To begin a theoretical examination of synergy,

27

it may be best to consider it as an aspect of communication, we mean the flow of information among organs of awareness. This idea further implies the notion of transaction, in which any particular event has mutual effect upon organs of awareness. The latter term, organ of awareness, is used so to distinguish between communicative processes within a living organism and those which occur among organisms and between organism and the environment. Thus within a biological organism there develop out of the individual's bio-chemical heredity certain patterns of action and response, or in cybernetic terminology, patterns of feedback and redundancy (Bateson 1972). Within an organism, physiological events occur in complex webs of relationship; cortical stimuli affect limbic functioning; limbic functioning affects the secretion of enzymes, this in turn modifying the homeostatic regulation of the living system. Since these relations are mutual in nature, the ontogenetic nature of growth is one in which patterns of mutual adjustment develop. By the same process the growth of self consciousness is a communication between intra-psychic impulses and the culturally construed world. The self, fashioned by the symbolic representations of others, is carried in the informational content of events, persons, and objects. Humans thus assume the masks, roles and meanings which society gives; yet this is done only by adjusting them to the restraints and potentials upon which human life is structured.

Beginning with the genetic template, information is transmitted which reacts to its outer environment and in turn helps construct it. Thus, we can form chains of intercommunication and causation. As Weiss notes there exists within the organism the sequence of gene, chromosome, cytoplasm, cell, tissue, organism, and environment. In this we can recognize a continuum of complexes of phenomena which retain their identity or "persistence of pattern" and also influence the lesser and greater environments in which they are contextually situated.

A similar continuum may also be extended beyond the individual into successively larger environments. As Francis Hsu (1971) has stated, we must view the human being not so much as an individual atom, but as a personage whose conscious reality and identity are tied to both the individual's expressable consciousness and his or her intimate society and culture. The processes of early growth and identity formation occur at

28

this level which is, in terms of the individual's enculturation, his or her primary social space. Here
affective ties are formed and the cultural heritage inculcated (Spiro 1951). Beyond this level, which Hsu
terms the jen, his "psychosociogram of man" includes
three further levels: the operative society and culture, the wider society and culture, and the outer
world. These levels are distinguished primarily by
lessening degrees of affective and direct participation.
In the wider society and culture human relationships
are characterized by usefulness rather than by attachments of feeling. Such spaces characterize the latter
stages of enculturation, and particularly the areas of
growth and development in Western industrial society.
The institutional settings of the school, the market
economy, and often the community itself would be included. Beyond this Hsu distinguishes between those
role relations in which we enter into some personal
sense of transaction such as student, employee, custom-
er and the like, and those where our attachments are at
best indirect or vicarious. This wider society and
culture would include "human beings, cultural rules,
knowledge and artifacts which are present in the larger
society but which may or may not have any connections
with the individual (1971:27)." To use Hsu's example--
until recently most black Americans were in this layer
for the majority of white Americans. The average person's knowledge of theoretical physics would be another
example, in which knowledgeable involvement would be
minimal. The final layer which Hsu postulates consists
of those "...peoples, customs and artifacts belonging
to societies with which most members of any society
have no contact and of which they have no ideas or only
erroneous ideas (1971:28)." This final layer sets the
furthest boundaries of human knowledge and ethnocentrism.

While one could debate on the exact number of
levels, we nonetheless can draw a continuum of interactions beginning with the gene and extending to the
furthest horizons of the knowable world. At each level
there occur transactions in which communication events
transform themselves from one level or sequence to the
next. The bio-chemical configuration of the gene communicates information to the chromosome which in the
process is transformed into new sets of information.
Likewise the development of the self begins with the
bio-psychic structure of the human being which receives
and transmits information with respect to the social
and material environment. Through this interaction

there develop systematic transformations or patterns which define as a culturally endowed human beings.

From this perspective culture may be seen as derived through the inter-thinking transactions of human beings fashioning adaptive relationships to the social and material conditions of life. In this sense, culture is a form of adaptation in which the self modifies its ideas and behavior to conform to the material requirements of life. Yet culture also is a vehicle through which individuals perceive existential needs, and as such, exists ideally to foster the actualization of these needs. The human purpose of culture then would be to provide an ambiance in which the individual is able to secure the satisfaction of basic needs, to develop in a healthy direction, and to gain creative mastery over the conditions of life. From a humanistic standpoint culture is a form of human expression and creation. It provides human beings with a vehicle through which inner potentials are communicated into the outer world of people and things. The process is one of interaction and mutual transformation; culture is at one and the same time both a "model for" creative action and "model of" the material world to which it must adapt (Geertz 1966).

Synergy and Its Implications for Human Life

What then are the implications of this approach? Initially, it would seem that the idea of synergy is relevant to the empirical examination and evaluation of order-creating processes of communication. The problem of human well being is essentially one of maintaining the homeostatic order of creatively adapting to life. This involves effective communication; thus if the individual is to be physically and mentally healthy, the body must be able to communicate both within its internal milieu and in the environmental context of other people and material things.

In its cultural form, synergy is best expressed in the idea of consenses. As Benedict stated, a synergetic culture is one which harmoniously relates individual needs and collective needs. It establishes a working consensus, in which the labors of human beings are equitably distributed and in which the individual has an opportunity to express personal aspirations and gain a just part of society's rewards. The synergetic culture, then, fosters a sense of value which effectively links the communication of human beings in a common

30

pursuit of individual and collective ends.

For Freud, however, the possibility of the human race ever attaining such a relationship was highly improbable. For the biological requirements of man, his inherent sexual and aggressive drives, are necessarily at odds with the moral requirements of the social life. From these conflicts are derived the periennial problems of neurosis and aggression. In the modern world, as Marx and Marcuse argue, these conflicts are compounded by the requirements and consequences of the techno-economic sphere of culture and the consequent problems of human inequality and injustice. For Marx, of course, the solution lies in a communist revolution; yet if one is to look at Marxism in practice, the "logic of domination" continues to persist and so also the problems of aggression, alienation, and suffering.

Thus synergy represents not so much an accomplished fact, but an ideal of moral attainment. It communicates the idea that the achievement of personal happiness and self-fulfillment is concurrent with the happiness and fulfillment of others. In the words of Immanuel Kant, "to treat humanity whether in thine own person or in that of another, in every case as an end, never only as a means (1909:47)." The "golden rule" of Jesus Christ immediately comes to mind as well as the utopian ideas of Plato and Spinoza. What is essentially being addressed is the universal value of love which speaks to the union of the individual with somebody or something outside oneself. Through such unions, individuals create the conditions of personal happiness, freedom and power, and peace of mind. As Erik Fromm (1956) has stated, "Love is the only satisfactory answer to the problem of human existence."

In turning to the "lessons" of biology, Hans Selye closely parallels this orientation in his discussion of altruism. Beginning with the human body, the manner of its healthy functioning is a question of the altruistic cooperation of its tissue systems. In the realm of interpersonal relations, this value is expressed in the cooperative and adaptive relationships of individuals to fellow human beings. The stress of life is the process by which human beings deal with the problems of cooperation and adaptation, and the solution to the problem of stress lies in altruism, or as Selye would state, in human acts which secure the well being and gratitude of other human beings.

31

It seems to me that, among all the emotions,
there is one which, more than any other, accounts for the absence or presence of stress
in human relations: that is the feeling of
gratitude--with its negative counterpart, the
need for revenge. It is curious how closely
the mechanism which deals with stress within
the body of one man resembles that which meets
the stress of social relations between men
(Selye 1956:284).

Thus those individuals who create environments in
which conduct is rewarded by the gratitude of others
act in the interests of their own happiness, health and
well being. Conversely those who act in aggressive
ways sow the seeds of anger, fear, and revenge. For
revenge is the awakening in another person of the wish
that the aggressor should not prosper because of what
he or she has done. Revenge then threatens the security of the aggressor and creates an environment which
further promotes stress and suffering. Thus the condition of human well-being clearly emerges as that of
love and affection.

As Erik Erikson (1963) has stated, the development
of the healthy ego depends upon a "recognition that
there is an inner population of remembered and anticipated sensations and images which are firmly correlated
with the outer population of familiar and predictable
things and people. In order for this to be effected,
there must exist some nurturant ambiance, which Erikson
calls, "basic trust," in which the experience of mutual
regulation occurs without an inordinant amount of pain
or frustration. Insofar as this is accomplished, the
parent must be capable of inculcating in the child some
somatic conviction that the relation between the inner
and outer worlds is meaningful. Thus even though a
certain amount of frustration is inherent in socialization, the fact that such frustrations possess societal
meaning gives the child possession of means to cope
with frustration.

Maslow (1968) speaks in a similar vein when he
states that the process of growth takes place in steps
in which each encounter with the environment is made
possible by the feeling of safety. Viewing the mother-
child relationship as a case in point, he states (1968:
46-47)

....growth forward....takes place in little
steps, and each step forward is made possible
by the feeling of being safe... We may use
as a paradigm the toddler venturing away from
his mother's knee into strange surroundings.
Characteristically he first clings to his
mother as he explores the room with his eyes.
Then he dares a little excursion, continuously assuring himself that the mother's
security is intact. These excursions get
more and more extensive. In this way, the
child can explore a dangerous and unknown
world. If suddenly the mother were to disappear, he would be thrown into anxiety, would
cease to be interested in exploring the world,
would wish only the return to safety, and
might even lose his abilities, e.g., instead
of daring to walk, he might creep. (1968:
46-47).

Through such an interactive process, gratification
breeds increased motivation, and the lesser or more
basic needs, as they are sufficiently gratified, give
rise to new and higher needs. The healthy or "fully
realized" individual, therefore, is one who has developed in the nurture of basic trust, love and acceptance.
This milieu, promoting healthy growth, allows for the
development of the autonomous individual capable of
creativity, spontaneity and self-sufficiency. Such a
person in Maslow's view possesses the strength of character to deal with life's stresses and to grow by these
experiences, widening the horizons of his or her knowledge and relatedness to others. In sum, the healthy
or self actualizing person is synergetic, capable of
communicating inner emotional demands or needs with the
outer realities of his roles in society.

The alternative to synergetic growth is born in an
environment of frustration and mistrust. Instead of
the smooth flow or cathexis of energy between inner and
outer worlds, this energy is frustrated resulting in
repression or "intrinsic counter cathexis" (Maslow 1968).
Instead of promoting a feeling of well being, the individual comes to distrust self and to project upon the
outer world similar fear and hostility. To survive,
such a person erects defensive barriers to understanding, denying those parts of self which he or she fears
or does not wish to surface to consciousness, and at
the same time stereotyping or rigidifying the world
of outer awareness. This person is diminished or

stunted, and much of his or her behavior is self-defeating and a waste of energy, energy which otherwise may have been utilized toward more rational and charitable ends.

The cultural implications of these ideas is well illustrated by James Prescott (1975) in his study of the relationship of body pleasure and the origins of violence. As a neuropsychologist Prescott points out that conditions of somatosensory deprivation and pain create behaviorial reactions which underlie aggression and interpersonal violence; whereas conditions promoting bodily pleasure favor reactions relating to love, trust and cooperation. Illustrating his argument his information draws upon cross-cultural data to measure the relationship between the level of physical affection during infancy and the presence of adult physical violence. His findings show that, "in 36 of the 44 cultures studied, a high degree of infant affection was associated with a low degree of physical violence-- vice versa (1975:13)." Additional comparisons also point out correlations of violence with strong prohibitions upon pre-marital sex (a form of somatosensory deprivation), and the use of drugs and alcohol (an intoxicating substitute for real pleasure). Thus concluding upon the theoretical implications of his study, Prescott states:

"I believe that the deprivation of body touch, contact and movement are the basic causes of a number of emotional disturbances which include depressive and autistic behaviors, hyperactivity, sexual aberration drug abuse, violence and aggression (1975:11)."

Thus, a basic precondition for human synergy is an environment in which one experiences physical pleasure and in which one is allowed to grow to his or her full potential in relationships of cooperation, trust and love. Further, this assumes that the organization of the social life is such that it renders to the material needs of human beings in a manner creating mutual adaptation among people and between the society and its material environment. In viewing society, then, it is important, as Hsu (1971) has pointed out, to see human life as existing upon mutually interpenetrating levels. The level of the gemeinschaft or jen is the first significant level, in which the individual comes to experience the culturally meaningful world of people and things. In this environment or "social space," the individual's identity is formed through interpersonal transactions, a formative process which in turn affects the individual's transactions with the wider, more impersonal and more utilitarian society. Conversely, the institutional arrangements of the wider society feed back upon the quality of affective relations within the gemeinschaft. Thus if conditions of poverty and social oppression prevail in society, these wider social relations operate to increase the frustration of intimacy and the incidence of aggression in primary social relationships.

At the level of human psycho-biology health is a general state of homeostatic regulation in which the body's active encounter is counter-balanced by passive processes of rest and restoration (Cannon 1932) (Selye 1956). As this process is maintained and nurtured by the outer environment, the individual is allowed to grow, reaching out toward the full potential of his or her higher needs (Maslow 1968). If, however, this process is frustrated, if rigid boundaries and barriers are placed in the path of communication, the result is repression or the inhibition of cathexis. This inhibition causes individuals to compartmentalize life and foster antagonistic relations both within themselves and their social interactions.

This schism between self and outer existence is well illustrated by the idea of neurosis. As Maslow (1968) views it, neurosis consists of the defenses which the individual erects so to deny, distort or evade experience. Its motive force is fear (angst), causing the individual to impose barriers between self and outer experience, impeding the flow of communication. Repression, projective distortion, rationalization, and regression are all forms of counter-communication which prevent the adequate translation of experience and human meaning. Neurosis is thus a disease of human interaction; for the barriers imposed upon self are largely derived from others.

In the context of society, these schisms and barriers are the myriad forms of human alienation and their pathological consequences. With alienation the individual is divided from himself and other people. The sense of active participation and creative involvement with the outer world is stifled and the components of self and other are polarized. Thus in any society conditions which impose barriers between the sexes, generations, races and socio-economic classes create

35

unsynergetic conditions for human life. For by opposing groups they not only erect barriers of mutual ignorance but also quicken the potential for antagonism and
aggression. The sado-masochism of everyday life is but
a microcosm of the institutions of warfare and socio-
economic oppression. In both cases the mutual transactions of love and cooperation have failed; and in
response, individuals create rigid boundaries between
themselves and others. The institutional expressions
of egotism, sexism, racism and the other varied forms
of ethnocentrism polarize the "we--they" distinction
and create human relations which are both fearful and
angry.

This attitude of love and consensus not only bears
upon relationships among human beings, but also to the
reciprocal and equilibrated balance between human material needs and the potentials and limitations of the
natural world. Thus if a human population exhausts an
environment's capacity through overpopulation or technological exploitation, the negative conditions of
scarcity will feed back upon human beings and future
generations of human beings as deprivation and suffering. A truly "affluent" society, to use Marshall Sahlins' (1968) formulation, is one which defines its material values as a realistic appraisal of a people's
technological capacity and the environment's ability to
sustain this capacity. Ironically, as Sahlins demonstrates, this quality of affluence is most characteristic of "simple societies," particularly hunting and
gathering bands. Thus the advance of "civilization"
and particularly its predatory and exploitative values
have rendered a serious schism in environmental relations. The capacity of human survival is indeed the
major issue of our times, one demanding creative solution.

In conclusion, synergy is offered as a rational
theory and praxis for human life. Its central value
lies in the moral imperative of love and the interpretations of this value in the conduct of human affairs.
To the ends of preserving harmonious relationships,
the practical application of synergy lies in what may
be called the "politics of consensus." Thus, on the
one hand, we should seek to preserve human diversity
and autonomy, realizing that each individual and individual cultural tradition is an end in its own right
and that each has something to contribute to the collective problem of human existence. Thus we realize
the necessity of human beings living in morally ordered
cultures. As Plato conceived it, a just society is one

36

in which the individual can have and do what is one's own. It is one which can both contain and integrate the diverse needs and potentials of its people through the creation of orderly relationships. Marx, of course, saw this in his formulation of a communist society as did the enlightenment philosophers in their conception of a democratic state. Yet in practice we find that both have had many moral failures; one because of its rigid adherence to collective values and the other because of its exaggerated emphasis upon individual. True justice then is established on the basis of reciprocal needs, and far from being a rigid guideline for thought and action, it is a dialectic process which recognizes the historical indeterminacy of nature and culture.

REFERENCES

Allport, Gordon W.
    1955   Becoming. New Haven: Yale University Press.

Ardrey, Robert
    1962   African Genesis. London: Collins.

Autrum, H.
    1966   Tier und Mensch in der Masse. Munich.

Bateson, Gregory
    1972   Steps to an Ecology of the Mind. New York:
           Chandler Publishing Company.

Bidney, David
    1967   Theoretical Anthropology. New York:
           Schocken Books.

Cannon, Walter
    1932   The Wisdom of the Body. New York: Norton.

Curtis, Helena
    1975   Biology. New York: Worth Publishers.

Dollard, J., Doob, L., Miller, N., and Sears, R.
    1939   Frustration and Aggression. New Haven:
           Yale University Press.

Douglas, Mary
    1966   Purity and Danger. London: Routledge and
           Kegan

Eibl-Eibesfeldt, Irenaus
    1970   Ethology: The Biology of Behavior. New
           York: Holt, Rinehart and Winston.

Erikson, Erik H.
    1963   Childhood and Society. New York: W. W.
           Norton and Company.

Freud, Sigmund
    1961   Civilization and Its Discontents. New York:
           W. W. Norton.

Fromm, Eric
    1955 The Sane Society. New York: Holt, Rinehart
          and Winston.

Fromm, Eric
    1956 The Art of Loving. New York: Harper and Row.

Geertz, Clifford
    1966 Religion as a Cultural System: in Michael
          Banton (Ed.) Anthropological Approaches to
          the Study of Religion. New York: Frederick
          A. Praeger, pp. 1-46.

Hallowell, A. Erving
    1969 Behavioral Evolution and the Emergence of
          the Self, in Evolution and Anthropology by
          Betty Meggers (Ed.) Anthropological Society
          of Washington.

Henry, Jules
    1955 Homeostasis, Society and Evolution: A
          Critique, The Scientific Monthly, December,
          pp. 300-309.

Henry, Jules
    1963 Culture Against Man. New York.

Hockett, C. G.
    1973 Man's Place in Nature. New York: McGraw-
          Hill.

Holloway, R. L.
    1974 Primate Aggression, Territoriality, and
          Xenophobia. New York, Academic Press.

Howard, Alan and Robert A. Scott
    1965 A Proposed Framework for the Analysis of
          Stress in the Human Organism, Behavioral
          Science. vol. 10, pp. 141-160.

Hsu, Francis L. K.
    1971 Psychosocial Homeostasis and Jen: The Con-
          ceptual Tools for Advancing Psychological
          Anthropology, American Anthropologist.
          vol. 73, no. 1, pp. 23-44.

Huxley, Julian S.
    1956 Evolution, Cultural and Biological, Current
          Anthropology, pp. 1-25.

Kant, Immanuel
    1909 Critique of Practical Reason. London.

Kantt, Immanuel
    1909 Metaphysics of Morals. London.

Koestler, Arthur
    1967 The Ghost in the Machine. New York:
          Macmillan.

Marcuse, Herbert
    1962 Eros and Civilization. New York: Vintage
          Books.

Maslow, Abraham H.
    1968 Toward a Psychology of Being. New York:
          D. Van Nastrad Co.

Maslow, Abraham and John J. Honigmann
    1970 Synergy: Some Notes of Ruth Benedict,
          American Anthropologist. vol. 72, pp. 320-
          333.

Murphy, Gardiner
    1947 Personality: A Biosocial Approach to Origins
          and Structure. New York: Harper and Row.

Paz, Octabio
    1961 The Labyrinth of Solitude. New York: Grove
          Press.

Prescott, James W.
    1975 Body Pleasure and the Origins of Violence,
          Bulletin of the Atomic Scientists.

Redfield, Robert
    1953 The Primitive World and Its Transformations.
          Ithaca, New York: Cornell University Press.

Sapir, Edward
    1924 Culture, Genuine and Spurious, American
          Journal of Sociology, vol. 29, pp. 401-29.

Sahlins, Marshall D.
    1960 Evolution: Specific and General, in Evolu-
          tion and Culture by Marshall Sahlins and
          Elman Service (Eds.). Ann Arbor: University
          of Michigan Press.

Sahlins, Marshall D.
1968   Notes on the Original Affuent Society. In
        Man the Hunter, Edited by Richard Lee and
        Irven De Vore, pp. 85-89. Chicago: Aldine
        Publishing Company.

Sartre, Jean-Paul
1948   Portrait of an Anti-Semite. London.

Sartre, Jean Paul
1963   Search for a Method. New York: Alfred A.
        Knopf, Inc.

Selye, Hans
1956   The Stress of Life. New York: McGraw-Hill

Spiro, Melford
1951   Culture and Personality: The Natural History
        of a False Dichotomy, Psychiatry, vol. 14,
        pp. 19-46.

Stent, Gunther S.
1975   Limits to the Scientific Understanding of
        Man, Science. vol. 187, pp. 1052-1057.

Tart, C. T. (Ed.)
1969   Altered States of Consciousness. New York:
        John Wiley and Sons, Inc.

Teilhard De Chardin, Pierre
1961   The Phenomenon of Man. New York: Harper
        and Row.

Weiss, Gerald
1975   Culture and the Theory of Levels, Paper
        given at 74th annual meeting of the American
        Anthropological Association, San Francisco.

RATIONALISM, HUMANISM AND TRIBAL THOUGHT

Frank Cunningham
University of Toronto

Rationalism made its appearance in the 17th and 18th centuries as a champion of humanism. The rationalists vigorously combatted philosophical approaches which led to blind obedience to secular or divine authority, and they resisted the moral scepticism already apparent in the works of early empiricists. For two centuries rationalists campaigned for human progress and mutual understanding based on universal scientific rationality.

By the 20th century, however, the rise of the social sciences and especially of anthropology seemed to put rationalism on the side of the bad guys. Increased study of beliefs associated with tribal magic and religion revealed that tribal peoples held views quite foreign to anything entertained by even relatively uneducated people in the industrialized parts of the world. One effect of these studies — unfortunately quite widespread on the part of academics and others — was to adopt the view that the peoples of these societies had something wrong with them and were simply inferior to "civilized" humans.

This ethnocentric viewpoint, with its overtone of racism, persists to this very day in some quarters, and it has been unwittingly reinforced by rationalism. On rationalistic standards, beliefs of tribal peoples were grossly out of accord with science or reason, and therefore these peoples appeared more like lunatics or imbeciles than anything else for holding them. (This ethnocentric attitude is often reflected in the use of "primitive" to describe peoples whom I shall refer to as "tribal" for want of a better term.)

Those in the anthropological and other academic communities who shunned such a condescending attitude often reacted by rejecting rationalism. Some took

the view that tribal peoples have _superior_ insight into the truth of things, which, it is said, is hidden
by science and reason. A more common response was
(and is) to maintain that tribal beliefs are neither
superior nor inferior to those of people raised in
industrialized society as far as being closer to the
truth about things goes, but that they are simply _diff-_
erent. That is, in reaction to rationalism, many
adopted relativism.

I should like to make a few comments in defense
of the rationalist tradition, that is, the tradition
which shares with classic rationalists the optimistic
view that objectively discernable progress exists
in both knowledge and morality because of the
employment of science and reason. Quite apart from
other problems, anti-rationalist reactions to tribal
thought do not seem to me to promote a genuinely
supportive attitude toward tribal peoples. At the
same time, I believe that it is the case _both_ that
tribal peoples are intelligent, mature, sane people
and that they hold many beliefs which are just wrong
and which are arrived at by methods which have been
justifiably abandoned by other peoples in the course
of their histories.

The Superiority of Tribal Thought

The view that tribal peoples have superior insight into things seems to me almost always hypocriti-
cally advanced. If someone really, sincerely believed
that tribal thinking was superior to his own way of
thinking, then why would such a person not do everything in his power to _adopt_ this way of thinking? It
will not do to say that the mind formed by industrial
society is forever blocked from fathoming the tribal
mind. If this were true, then how could it be discovered that tribal thought is superior at revealing the
truth in the first place? To find this out, one would
have to know what that truth is, and if, as it is
claimed, it is tribal thought which reveals this truth,
then it must have been possible somehow to partake of
this thought. In the second place, _some_ actually
superior insights of tribal peoples have come to be
recognized and taken over (for instance regarding
preservation of the environment and some medical treatments). Why could not _other_ putative insights be
appropriated as well?

If the superiority of tribal thought theory is

44

not sincerely held, then it involves a far more condescending attitude than a rationalistically based perspective. It is the kind of condescension sometimes exhibited in discussions where one person disagrees with another, but pretends not to disagree thinking the other person incapable of either changing or accepting the fact that there is disagreement.

Sometimes the view that tribal thought is superior is associated with an attitutde which romanticizes tribal peoples. It is felt that tribal peoples have some exotic qualities denied to others. No matter how jealous one may be of these supposed qualities, this attitude is also condescending. It shares the ethnocentric view that tribal peoples are abnormal, with the difference that their abnormalities are to be envied. That ethnic chauvinist and racist attitudes carry with them both deprecating and idealizing dimensions is well known, at least by those subjected to ethnic and racist discrimination. The romanticization of tribal peoples' thought seems to me on a par with these attitudes.

Relativism

Relativists argue that contradictory beliefs can both be true depending on who holds them. (Or they hold some variant of this view, such as that it is not possible to judge from one standpoint whether beliefs of another standpoint contradict ones own.) Aside from philosophical problems with relativism which I do not intend to raise here, this perspective is also condescending in the end. In effect the relativist is saying to the tribal person: "You may think that your views about things are objectively correct while other views are wrong, but we, who are more philosophically sophisticated, know better." It does not make it any the less condescending toward tribal peoples that this attitude is also directed against anybody else who thinks their views are objective.

Some relativists will object that they are not at all denying objectivity to tribal thought, but are just making it relative to tribal peoples. They claim that tribal beliefs are objective for tribal peoples, just as any other beliefs are objective for those who hold them. There are well-known philosophical problems with this view, for example in determining just what force there is to saying that something is "objective for" someone who shares the general viewpoint of a community of believers, when it is denied that there is any way objectively to evaluate the viewpoint. In addition, this response approaches the attitude of those who think tribal thought superior. Tribal peoples have views which we cannot share or evaluate, but which are "true" in a realm of their own.

The theoretical stance of relativism was motivated by such things as a liberal rejection of elitism and dogmatism. Its sociological effects, however, can be quite illiberal. From the premise that one can never know what point of view is objectively right or wrong, a person can draw the liberal conclusion that therefore people ought to be tolerant of different points of view and not stand in judgment of them. But a person can just as well draw the conclusion that since nobody can know who is right and wrong objectively, then it is best to hold to the views of your own community of believers dogmatically -- that is, without consideration of whether they are justified -- to avoid being drowned in a sea of conflicting opinions.

One can even draw the further conclusion that beliefs are not the sorts of things to be objectively adopted and urged on others, but the sorts of things to be imposed on others by brute force if necessary. Relativism can thus lead to the view that might makes right. Mussolini was one epistemological relativist who apparently found no problem reconciling his relativism with illiberal modes of behaviour. Relativism is no guarantee that a liberal attitude will be taken toward others, and in particular it is no guarantee that tribal thought will not be depreciated in an ethnocentric way, or even obliterated (as in colonial or neo-colonial ventures).

Functionalism, Structuralism, Ideology

Suppose that somebody rejects both relativism and rationalism, how should such a person think of tribal thought? Let me list three approaches which might be taken, and which I believe have been taken, partly in response to what is perceived as the need to escape a relativist-rationalist dilemma.

It might be thought that functionalism offers a solution. From a philosophical point of view functionalism is pragmatic. It shifts from talking about the truth of ideas and the correctness of different ways of thinking to talking about usefulness in

46

maintaining a social equilibrium. Tribal thought is not superior or inferior to non-tribal thought, it is just more or less useful for promoting social coherence in tribal society.

This approach seems to me to fail in offering a non-condescending approach to tribal thought. While the pragmatic-functionalist might consider the ideas of those studied to be useful or not useful rather than being true or false, those people themselves surely consider their ideas true. If they did not, then it is doubtful that they would act on them, and hence the ideas would not be useful for maintaining the social equilibria functionalists see them as maintaining. Therefore, the functionalist perspective shares one condescending attitude of relativism: "You may think your ideas are true, but we more sophisticated social scientists know that they are just more or less useful parts of a social system."

A sufficiently radical structuralist might attempt to avoid a relativist-rationalist dilemma by maintaining that some views of tribal peoples are not really different from apparently contradictory views of non-tribal peoples, but that the two are just alternate ways of expressing the same underlying structural conceptualizations. Quite aside from the problem all structuralists have of explaining just what a "structure" is, this approach is not very different from the functionalist one.

Tribal peoples may think that they have certain ideas about things, but in fact they are mistaken, since they do not perceive the real, structural content of their views. This goes quite beyond rationalism. The rationalist may question tribal peoples' opinions regarding the truth of some of their ideas, but this structuralist approach claims that they are mistaken even about the content of their own ideas.

Closely related to a radical structuralist view is one which attempts to see ideas such as those associated with tribal religion and magic as merely "ideological", where this means that these ideas are nothing but window dressing. The tendency I am describing is to deny that tribal peoples really hold beliefs considered radically wrong. The suggestion is instead that they just pretend to hold such beliefs, perhaps to futher ulterior motives or maybe just ritualistically.

If such pretence is thought to be unconscious,

then this view would be similar to the structuralist one which doubts that people are aware of the content of their own beliefs. If it is a conscious pretence which is imagined, then it does not say much for tribal peoples that they engage in such systematic hypocrisy and self-deception.

Intelligence

In my view there is a grain of truth in all three of the approaches just referred to. But to make use of these grains, I believe that a rationalist viewpoint must be adopted. However, it must be a rationalism somewhat tempered by a more empirical attitude than classic rationalists favoured, especially toward the concept of human intelligence.

A widespread way of thinking about intelligence is as a common quality existing in different degrees in every human or as a faculty with different degrees of efficiency. Among other things, this view has led to the belief that I.Q. tests can be devised to ascertain "how much" of this intelligence different individuals possess. For a variety of reasons, I believe that this viewpoint should be abandoned. It is better to think of "intelligence" as standing for a variety of skills which humans have, and to think of these skills as continuous with the historically changing natural, technological, and interpersonal environments of those who exercise them. By this I mean that different historically given problems require different skills for their solutions and that the development and exercise of those skills depends on the existing natural and human environment, which is also historically given.

Take a tribal keeper of a herd who is good at keeping track of cattle using a simple number system, a schoolchild from an industrialized country who can do long division problems, and an engineer who can make accurate calculations with a slide rule. Who is smarter? It seems to me a mistake to ask the question. Each could be compared in the exercise of his or her skill with others facing the same problems and equipped with the same natural or artificial aids and with the existing knowledge at the time, but how could they be compared with one another? (It might be thought that the three could be compared by appealing to their relative ranking among their peers who face similar problems. Though it does not matter for the purpose of this essay, I think this would also be a

mistake, since it supposes the at least debatable view
that the same sorts of mental skills are required by
people facing different tasks and equipped with different aids.)

If human intelligence is thought of as comprising
several historically conditioned and task relative
skills, then degrees of intelligence can be distinguished from amount of knowledge. Of course the
schoolchild knows more about mathematics than the herd
keeper, and the engineer knows more than the schoolchild. But this does not make the schoolchild more
intelligent than the herd keeper any more than it makes
·the engineer more intelligent than the schoolchild.
Similarly, the method of using calculating devices to
arrive at the solution to a mathematical problem is
better from the standpoint of discovering mathematical
truth than the methods of the schoolchild or the herd
keeper, which are (let us assume) limited in application and more prone to error. But·what has this to
do with the intelligence of those who either have or
lack those devices?

Rationalists insist history has proven that the
various methods associated with scientific inquiry are
more reliable than the methods of following traditional
prescriptions embodied, for instance, in religious
practices for the purposes of arriving at true beliefs
and controlling the environment. These are facts
about the effectiveness of methods for reaching conclusions, not about the intelligence of people who use the
methods. Depending on the circumstances, there might
be legitimate questions about the intelligence of a
person who is fully aware of a method known to be
reliable for achieving some purpose and who knows how
to employ the method, but employs an inferior method
anyway. However, this does not at all mean that in
general using more or less reliable methods for arriving at conclusions about something is an index of
comparative intelligence.

Solving most problems for humans requires that
they acquire true beliefs about certain things, but
what things they must have true beliefs about differ
from problem to problem, and whether they are able to
acquire true beliefs depends on many factors outside
of the individual believer's control. I do not mean
to rule out as important such qualities as being "quick
witted" or having a good memory, though the extent to
which these qualities are acquired rather than

49

inherited is a matter of continuing debate. However, the most important factors which determine whether someone will have the ability to solve a problem seem to me the availability of what I shall call "tools of thought": the content and accessability of education in required problem solving techniques, the availability of historically accumulated information, and the existence and nature of technological aids. A person may lack true beliefs about something because in the circumstances it is not important to have true beliefs about it or necessary tools of thought are unavailable. One may have false beliefs due to having partially or wholly unreliable tools of thought.

Tribal Thought

It is well known that people in tribal hunting or farming societies are better at solving some problems than people in industrial societies — namely problems associated with hunting and farming without the aid of sophisticated implements. (Regarding some problems it has been discovered that they are better than those equipped with such implements.) This fact does not lead most people to think that therefore tribal peoples are more intelligent than people in industrial society. Why, then, should tribal peoples as a whole be thought less intelligent than non-tribal ones?

The issue usually revolves around tribal religion and magic rather than around tribal beliefs about hunting and farming techniques. I do not think that tribal religion and magic should pose any problems about tribal intelligence, no matter what theory of speculative cultural anthropology is adopted to explain the nature and origin of these things. Either tribal religion and magic are merely ritualistic, playing no cognitive role at all in tribal peoples' lives, or else, whatever other functions they may perform, they play a role in tribal peoples' attempts to understand their environment. If they play no cognitive role, then the issue of intelligence does not arise (unless one wants to question the intelligence of engaging in merely ritualistic behaviour, in which case there are   many more places to look for examples than tribal societies.

The issue of tribal intelligence is pertinent if tribal religion and magic are seen as attempts to gain and organize knowledge. In this case, they are what I have referred to as tools of thought. On the view to which questioners of tribal intelligence are most likely to appeal, magic and religion are tools for

50

attempting to solve the proto-scientific problems of explaining why there are the natural regularities and irregularities that there are. Debates can be carried on over whether desires of tribal peoples for such explanation are among the origins of magic or religion, but even if this is granted, there is no problem regarding tribal intelligence. A tribal person could not be faulted for coming up with false explanations of natural events due to lacking the inherited tools of thought it has taken centuries to develop, any more than he or she could be faulted for lacking sophisticated mechanical tools, which are dependent on prior technological history for their existence.

Rationalism

On a rationalistic view, progress in human knowledge is the history of acquiring better and better tools of thought. This means discovering new aids to thought and sharpening old ones. It also means discarding tools which lead to false beliefs, including those false beliefs incorporated in tribal thought. Epistemological debates between sceptics and anti-sceptics can be carried out over whether and how this progress is possible. Here I am assuming that the rationalist can withstand the sceptic's attack. I am arguing that it is not necessary to choose between reason and science on the one hand or respect for tribal thought on the other. Let me conclude my comments by returning to the grains of truth in the positions mentioned earlier.

The grain of truth in functionalism is that sometimes _false_ beliefs can serve useful purposes. Anthropologists have surely succeeded in demonstrating that tribal religious and magic beliefs often serve socially useful functions, even though those who hold them may not intend them to serve these functions or even be aware of the fact that they do. This does not mean that therefore performing these functions are their "real" or primary purposes, or that it does not matter whether the beliefs are true or false. It just means that beliefs, including false ones, can and do have a variety of effects in human societies.

Sometimes people become aware of useful, though initially unintended, purposes served by beliefs of theirs, and hence are reinforced in acting on and expressing those beliefs. This illustrates the grain of truth in the view that tribal ideas are ideological window dressing. In those cases where such beliefs

51

continue to be expressed even when they are known to be false, they are nothing but window dressing. But I suspect that it is more often the case that independent motivation reinforces actual, sincere belief. Imitations of the hunt, for instance, can be repeated both for the conscious purposes of practice, instruction, and morale-building and as a rite sincerely believed to have magical significance.

The grain of truth in the structuralist approach seems to me that we can empathize with tribal peoples' attempts to grapple with problems of theirs even though we cannot agree with some of the beliefs that they draw on in attempting to solve the problems. Despite the falsity of some tribal views they nonetheless "make sense" to us. In my opinion, the explanation for this is not that beneath tribal views lie hidden concepts which we share, but that we can understand why some false beliefs are held by tribal peoples in their circumstances. We realize that in their place we ourselves would most likely have the very same views.

For the rationalist it is this realization also that makes for a humanistic respect for tribal thought. Indeed, if our species lasts long enough, I suppose that our distant descendants will marvel at some of our own false beliefs and unreliable tools of thought. One would like to think that they could justifiably respect our intelligence all the same.

ON ANALYSES OF EVENT STRUCTURES AS PHILOSOPHICAL DERIVATES OF THE INVESTIGATING CULTURE

Lola Romanucci-Ross
University of California at San Diego

Through references to anthropological field research conducted in various cultures of the world by
the writer as well as those of predecessors in cul-
ture-personality studies, this paper will consider the
effects of conceptual systems of our own investigating
culture in intellectual problem-recognition, and prob-
lem-solving in psychological anthropology and struc-
ture-function anthropology.

David Bidney in his seminal work Theoretical
Anthropology (1953) was an early and influential pio-
neer of the idea that personality and culture cannot
be reified as separate categories. They are not only
complementary in process, but indeed the locus of
culture is the person. He pointed out that scientific
objectivity does not imply socio-cultural indifference; the Olympian attitude so often assumed by scientists is hardly appropriate to the socially conditioned animal which is man. (Bidney 1953:449)

The field researcher is a representative of the
investigating culture, a complex of information systems which may be bounded but are not closed. In his
training, the researcher should have learned that constant renewal of consciousness is a necessity; it is
the process which provides the only cognition and recognition of explanation. He may have learned in the
practice and re-visitations of his research that very
often explanation is the intellectual expression of
the investigative cultures of the world homogenizing
the varied experiences of others into sets that can be
logically looked at for cause and effect relationships.
Anthropological fieldwork itself is a culture contact
situation and those cultures we investigate may lose
or gain in translation. It is the investigative process itself as a derivative of the premises of what is

53

a worthy subject of inquiry at any given time that will
be considered here. How are the models of the researcher selected and what are the logical systematics
that produce these models? We will refer to the study
of a Mexican Village to initiate the discussion.

Ethnography as paradigm: mapping of mind on mind.

The ethnographic model in my study of a Mexican
village in Morelos can be characterized as a set of
internal analyses of structure and function (Romanucci-
Ross 1973). Not only was I, at the time, of the
structural-functional persuasion, but the exercise was
also the assertion of an effort against the larger
study of which I was a part. It can be seen as a personal attempt to escape from the major paradigm. The
larger study was headed by Erich Fromm whose basic instrument for this study was a long questionnaire as
well as a battery of psychological tests and psycho-
analytic interviews. He wanted to look at patterns of
maternal and paternal authority as well as patterns of
work and creativity. He hoped to introduce new forms
of economic activity that would raise the standard of
living of the village as our studies progressed.

Erich Fromm is well-known for his works that
elucidate the fit between character types and economic
structure of societies, and for translating Freudian
character types (anal, oral, sadistic, masochistic,
and combinations of these) into Marxist understandings
of exploiter-exploited (Fromm 1941, 1942). In this
study, he wanted to learn what constitutes the source
of social character: was it historical process, nuclear family interactions, or was it an intricate combination of both?

Open-ended questionnaires were given to 230
adults, as those given to German workers in 1930
(Adorno et al 1950). They were based on the premise
of latent and manifest content analysis characteristic
of the psycho-analytic interview or dream interpretation. Replies were then clustered into syndromes:
authoritarian/non-authoritarian, creative/non-creative,
mother-attached/father-attached. These were then
destined for multivariate analyses, with methods designed to correspond to clinical theory, e.g. a reply
had meaning in its syndromal context. These methods,
in contrast to factor analysis, allow a response to
have different meanings depending on the pattern in
which it occurs. These results have been published

(Maccoby and Fromm 1972). In our anthropological jargon, it allows for a little emicity in a tight-mashed, etic framework, which is to say that some insider views are sometimes visible by the reader. But such fragments are constrained, however, by the descriptive frames of the analyzers.

In the Maccoby and Fromm study summary, 700 persons are sorted through one-dimensional or several-dimensional sieves of graded receptivity or exploitativeness, so that the biophilia/necrophilia mode of human relatedness can be noted as a socio-cultural fact.

Our three years of direct field observations as anthropologists were to have been complementary to this study. Ted Schwartz and I helped re-shape the questionnaire; I was undoubtedly affected by the larger study, as we worked closely with Mexican psychoanalysts, psychiatrists, physicians, social workers, health and agricultural officials, politicians, lawyers and economists. We helped in the economic development projects; these included establishing clubs by sex and age groups for the purpose of introducing new skills in agriculture and animal husbandry or for the improvement of nutrition and public hygiene practices. For the most part, our attempts created a series of failures, featuring the leading fiasco, the indigenous pottery movement coupled with an attempt to establish a silk-screen processing plant. Our projects did not transform the village, but they did transform my understanding of it.

My anthropological colleague and I lived in the village. We designed a socio-economic survey instrument which included land tenure patterns which were later correlated with social character syndromes. We noted that the choice of crops planted by an individual was not random nor dictated by exogenous considerations of market and ease of negotiations. The more adjusted and mature persons (i.e. those more in control of all facets of their lives) planted the high risk, speculative crops such as tomatoes and rice rather than cane. The latter crop maximized dependency and was planted by the same persons who were on our debtor or heavy drinker lists (Romanucci-Ross 1973).

My own anthropological inquiries focused around events not covered by questionnaires and surveys.

These observations, often shared by my colleague, sensitized us to distortions in the formal instruments and helped us distinguish group-specific from family-specific from idiosyncratic responses.

Working in a team one learns how the same event elicits a multiplicity of views, or at least different emphases. One learns the true meaning of inter-scorer reliability, and can predict it well as the scorers become exhausted in argument. But the surveys and questionnaires will not help you understand how violence and conflict are defined in moral and legal contexts in the minds of the villagers. To learn how these concepts are interwoven in the village structure and reflect problems and process, the individual investigator must escape the major paradigm of the team approach, and, for a beginning, research the Agrarian Revolution of 1910, peruse historical documents and visit the courts for expanded data bases in which are to be found styles of murder and mechanisms of conflict avoidance. The rest of this non-directed research led this investigator to perceive the existence of moral codes and how they are used or constructed in calculating the outcomes of acts and events, and how social images of long duration affect village behavior and social roles. Then, how machismo and its symmetries, complementarities, and opposites sustain the emotional tone of the culture and shape future social change. Quite importantly too, how multiple bonds of kinship, friendship, god-parenthood (compadrazgo), and patronage in double-bonding or triple-bonding are used to meet various needs in a situation of limited resources. One could note what might be termed the contractual bond (an act on another logical level) which had the latent value of activating or de-activating the other four bonds.

What has been briefly described as ethnography or as paradigm, then, is that the fieldworker in this instance, was motivated in researching the subjects and events found of importance by the principal investigator as well as those that interested her personally. The latter can be referred to as distillates of what the anthropological discipline in America found important at the time, twined and clustered around some idiosyncratic notions of aesthetic latticing.

Other phenomenologies in the profession.

Looking at Mexican and peasant studies one notes

56

they can be categorized as follows: first there are
those concerned with definitions such as; what is
feudal?, what is capitalism? (Wolf 1959); what is
peasant? (Potter 1967); what is Mexican? (Foster 1967;
Romano 1968; Gonzalez-Pineda 1961). Definitions of
peasant seem reminiscent of the Georgics of Virgil or
ancient Roman treatises on agriculture. Secondly,
there are the re-visitation studies which are really
not re-visitations (Redfield 1930, 1956; Lewis 1951),
since someone else is looking at a modification of the
former field. There are symbolic structure studies,
dialectical materialism studies seeking economic determinants of which earlier investigators were usually
not aware (Tax 1953), and folk-urban studies culmi-
nating in the judgment that little communities are
better than big communities and that simplicity is
better than complexity (Redfield 1956). This micro-
cosmic ethic is recast cyclically in other knowledge
configurations. Recasting epistemes is not an un-
healthy exercise, but it is not a substitute for developing an awareness of our cultural collective intellectual processes.

There are studies of the sociological type telling us that we confront peasant everyday thinking with
our systematic thought and that everyone is a case in
point (Garfinkel 1967). This is indisputable, but the
intellectual problem has always been and continues to
be: how do you arrange, interpret and structure the
cases and the points? Or are we just to record behavior endlessly? Do these students of behavior maintain that everyday thought doesn't have a systematic
anchoring, whether the person every-daying-it is aware
of it or not? Or is the everyday person truly ran-
domizing, inventing constantly out of a constantly
changing everyday matrix?

Investigators suggesting that peasants are
plagued and transformed into Liliputian game theorists
by the limited good (Foster 1967) are reminiscent of
the wage-fund theorists and classical rent economists
such as Ricardo (1817). (It is not uninteresting to
note that the Spanish economists during the hacienda
period noted that land was limited, wealth was limited
and the Mexican poor were to take this under ad-
visement!)

Mapping experience and mind.

In our Mexican study neither the larger model nor

the minority paradigm concerned itself with such
topics as dissociational states, altered states of
consciousness nor modalities of thought, to name a few
areas of investigation that were not licit at the time.
This anthropologist did fill field notebooks with such
material, but it was indented and identified as marginal and of questionable value. Notes on modalities
of thinking were summarized with a Galilean (eppur si
muove) hesitation. To give a few examples of what I
mean by modalities of thinking: experience is the
answer to questions a person asks: to what questions
were the behaviors (structured as events) of these
villagers replying? Did certain details, such as
miniaturization of objects and persons as a linguistic
style, summarize a theory? Why was continuous data
preferred to discrete data in describing experience?
What of set learning? An analysis of the patronage
system will show that it was legislated away by agrarian reformers but only to usher in a half dozen
patroncitos where there had been one patron. What had
been learned was how one relates to the powerful person who exacts labor from you and gives you a small
part of his profits. This embedded learned relationship was not readily re-arranged.

Even as the anthropological study was prepared
for publication, a chapter on illness, disease, curing
and healing seemed to require an apology and was finally deleted by editors; yet illness was the lynchpin of
much that occurred in the village. As an opener to
many a conversation or as dramatic climax to many con-
flictful situations, body image and the uses of illness emphasized the complementarity of the sick and
well. This means its analysis is crucial in terms of
understanding the total configuration of the culture.

Social fantasy was found to have not only a creative role but also an immunizing or buffering effect
of what might be called institutionalized depression,
a mode of reacting that depends on reference levels of
positive or negative expectations. In this Mexican
village reference levels were set so low that real experience never fell below these reference levels. It
was counter-depressive. One found what these levels
were by looking at the songs and proverbs and the
levity of tone with which they were given or sung.
(Life is nothing! I would exchange it for tequila!;
We are all in the house of the soap maker, he who does
not fall is slipping!) In real life one puts his
faith in nothing and no one; if you helped anyone you

could be sure they would avoid you. When fantasy life and real life coincide, reality constructs not only expose what exists but are counter-depressive; they stop one short of a debilitating depression that would prevent the achievement of productivity. Strategies and interpersonal behavior are re-inforced by experience. Expecting betrayal, one betrays. One anticipates abandonment by abandoning. In fear of isolation, one isolates oneself. Fearing depression from within, and punishment from without, one lives on the surface. Denial becomes an important mechanism of defense.

Return and reflections.

Recently I returned to the village. I was interested to learn of the outcome of a land tenure case which involved a sulfur pool used for swimming, about to be commercialized by either one man or the village co-operative. The single protagonist lost. He and the village women had long ago correctly predicted the outcome to me (Romanucci-Ross 1973. Chapter 8). As they had prophesied, those who fought for the village invoking Agrarian Revolutionary heroes such as Zapata, after winning over the single protagonist and having him exiled, fought among themselve.. The winners were men from Mexico City with significant sums of capital for investment in the enterprise. On my re-visit, one of the women said to me, The old con-men have been conned by the young just as they conned the village years ago when you were writing about it. Now we have to pay ten pesos to enter this famous bathing pool, which is merely that old spring of sulphur water where we used to bathe for nothing. Catalino is gone down south, having seizures, that poor old intemperate hardhead, and the village got nothing out of it all.

The outcome was interesting because in this village information from women was considered gossip; some of the members of the study team thought the same, and yet I found the information from women to be the most reliable. Men, I had noted in my field notebook, do much fancy footwork with facts, since these facts seem to be needed to re-inforce the various male images. Women here were inconsequential and hence free to be truthful.

The village dream of the co-operative for the Bathing Pool Enterprise will join the other myths: the ghost of Zapata riding the hills on a white horse,

and the buried gold in the hacienda that will be found
by the village one day. The villagers were capable of
managing the fantasies and the real events except for
Tirzo, described in the earlier work as the macho. On
my return I learned he had been found dead in a canyon
for insisting that the village co-operative had to remain in control of the co-operative.

The village had changed with its Bathing Pool and
Recreation Center, and its Sunday afternoon rock band
concerts. There were now cars, buses and tourists as
well as the many new residents of middle-class folk
who wanted a home in the country. The researcher had
not really come home, and the opportunity to consider
the subjects that were not subjects then, was gone.

The field is real, not the model.

What informs ethnographic models and what is
learned from models has just begun to be considered in
anthropology. What informs a model is the experiental
history of the investigator and the trajectory of his
intellectual history of ideation with its emphases and
lacunae nurtured or starved within the broad historical arc of determinism of the investigating culture.
This does not mean our modelic activities are futile.
It does mean that non-recognition condemns us to repeat the same experiments again and again. What does
it mean to be flogged by a critic for having been
Weberian rather than Marxist, or Keynesian rather than
Milton-Freidmanesque? Such labelings are inflections
of insights in a dialectic of historical moments long
gone. Weber is Marx in causal inversion: perhaps a
difference that does not make a diⅎⅎⅇⅎence.

In the Mexican study I was part of a rather large
cast of intellectual migrants in what was probably the
longest study since the beginning of team research.
Perhaps it established the useful concept of diminish-
ing returns in such studies. Seeking a simultaneous
view of all the elements: cultural, social, political, economic, and looking for linkages to achieve a
synthesis as well as a periphery for end-linkages, I
did standard anthropological research in addition to
fulfilling my teamwork assignments. It was within
this frame I wrote about kinship, friendship, patronage, and godparenthood with its symmetrical and asym-
metrical aspects and the activating or de-activating
contractual bond for these linkages.

60

I would now address myself to the question we did not ask: just what are the mechanisms and processes that create the social character that functions well in a transformed society? I would look at it as a problem of continuity, discontinuity, and emergent evolution, of processes of information-flow. I would look very closely, as I did, at child-rearing practices, but as I did not nearly enough, as how these relate to the consciousness of women in their own sex role. I would note how change occurs not when everyone is sharing the same information system, but when there is noise in the channel, i.e., distortion of signals in information exchange (Bateson 1973). Most importantly, I would now use a model of identity developed in my fieldwork in Italy with personhood as the focus, and culture as the complexity of information systems. Culturally informed imagery not only includes but possibly begins with, and is derivative of, proprioception of body image in space and time, affected by group processes. Conceding this, we can then look at illness or social change as error introduced into a system.

An undisturbed population has the knowledge of its own cultural stochastic processes, i.e., an ability to predict the sequentiality of events and event probability in alternative hypothetical states (Romanucci-Ross 1975). Must we not at least, match this level of sophistication of our informants?

Ethnoscience, or learning to view the world through the categories of others encourages a consciousness of method in cultural inquiry. But, like cultural relativism, it provides insights that create serious problems. If, as in relativism, the good is defined only in its cultural context, is there then no absolute good? If, as in ethnoscience, knowledge is only relative to cultural categories, is there then no ultimate, testable reality? After many years of anthropological fieldwork and reflections upon its nature (Romanucci-Ross 1976), I was led once more to the concept of a normative science of culture that I had encountered as David Bidney's graduate student.

Whether we should invent new categorical grids for other cultures is and should remain problematic. Was it not totemic of a wine bottling aristocrat in France to say to me, Moi, je suis Barsac, mon beau-pere il est Beaujolais? We have overlooked many trans-cultural grids in our ad hoc inventions.

Achieving personhood in your own culture gives
you an identity; you are a center of cognition and affect as investigator and as a self. But a center
implies circumferential boundaries and the broad spectrum of all the other ways of being human demands more
of your training and another go at a new anthropology
based on past scholarly insights such as those provided by David Bidney. His insights have not been exhausted; in fact some of them have as yet to be applied. We seem to have stabilized research so that
renewal means a change of locus and costumes while
plots and paradigms carry the old familiar scores. We
are running out of costumes and out of time as the cultures of the world seek similar goals: achieving the
dreams of the early Utopian technocrats and raising
the standard of living for all as the quality of life
(for all) declines.

Any culture we choose to learn about, no matter
how exotic, is not encapsulated by an event horizon.(2) It is not unanalyzable and although its constituents form sets of internal relationships; these
are not bounded, and it is reaching out.

Any culture displays the spectrum of human possibilities for personality-variation. The investigator might well work more on the participatory aspect of his role as participant-observer. As he or
she becomes accepted, as well as accepting, understood
as well as understanding, Blake's observation will
make sense: If it were not for the Poetic and
Prophetic character, the Philosophic and Experimental
would soon be at the ratio of all things and stand
still, unable to do other than repeat the same dull
round over and over again. (Erdman 1970).

Notes

1. Acknowledgments: This paper was presented in part at the annual meeting of the American Anthropological Association, November 20, 1976, Washington, D. C. The Symposium was entitled Ethnographic Models in Meso-American Research.

2. As a star collapses and increases in density, its surface becomes stronger and the space-time around it becomes increasingly curved. As a consequence of this, the star reaches a stage where nothing, not even light, can escape from its surface. For this reason it is called a black hole. At this stage it is said that an event horizon forms around the star, because no signal can get away from it to communicate any event to the outside world. (Capra 1975).

Selected References

Adorno, T. W., Else Frenkel-Brunswik, Daniel J. Levin-
son and Nevitt Sanford. The
Authoritarian Personality. New
York: Harper.

Bateson, Gregory
1973   Steps Toward an Ecology of Mind.
New York: Ballantine.

Bidney, David
1953   Theoretical Anthropology. New
York: Columbia University Press.

Capra, Fritjof
1975   The Tao of Physics. Berkeley:
Shambhala.

Erdman, David (ed).
1970   The Poetry and the Prose of
William Blake. New York:
Doubleday.

Foster, George
1967   Tzintzuntzan, Mexican Peasants in
a Changing World. Boston: Little,
Brown.

Freud, Sigmund
1956   Character and Anal Eroticism (1908)
in: Collected Papers. vol. II.
London: The Hogarth Press.

Fromm, Erich
1941   Escape from Freedom. New York:
Rinehart.

1947   Man for Himself. New York:
Rinehart.

1951   The Forgotten Language. New York:
Rinehart.

1970   Social Character in a Mexican
         Village: a Socio-psychoanalytical
         Study. Englewood Cliffs, New
         York: Prentice-Hall.

Garfinkel, Harold
1967   Studies in Ethnomethodology.
         Englewood Cliffs, New York:
         Prentice-Hall.

Gonzalez-Pineda, Francisco
1961   El Mexicano, Psicologia de su
         Destructividad. Mexico, D. F.,
         Editorial Pax-Mexicano.

Levi-Strauss, Claude
1949   Les Structures Elementaires de la
         Parente. Plon: Paris.

Lewis, Oscar
1951   Life in a Mexican Village:
         Tepotztlan Restudied. Urbana:
         The University of Illinois Press.

Malinowski, Bronislaw
1944   A Scientific Theory of Culture and
         other Essays. Chapel Hill: North
         Carolina.

Potter, Jack M., May N. Davis and George M. Foster
1967   (eds.) Peasant Society, A Reader.
         Boston: Little, Brown.

Radcliffe-Brown, A. R.
1952   Structure and Function in Primi-
         tive Society. Glencoe, Illinois:
         Free Press.

Redfield, Robert
1930   Tepotztlan - a Mexican Village.
         Chicago: University of Chicago
         Press.

1956   Peasant Society and Culture.
         Chicago: University of Chicago
         Press.

Ricardo, David
1817   Principles of Political Economy
         and Taxation

Romano, Octavio
    1968   The Anthropology and Sociology of
                    the Mexican-American El Grito.
                    11:13-26.

Romanucci-Ross, Lola
    1966   Conflits Fonciers a Mokerang,
                    Village Matankor del Iles de l'
                    Amiraute. In L'Homme: Revue
                    Francaise d'Anthropologie.
                    6:32-52.

    1973   Conflict, Violence and Morality in
                    a Mexican Village. Palo Alto,
                    California, Mayfield Publishing
                    Co. (National Press Books).

    1975   Italian Ethnic Identity and its
                    Transformations. In De Vos, George
                    and Romanucci-Ross, Lola (eds.).
                    Ethnic Identity: Cultural Con-
                    tinuities and Change. Palo Alto,
                    California, Mayfield Publishing Co.

    1976   With Margaret Mead in the Field:
                    Observations on the Logics of
                    Discovery. In Ethos. 4:4:439-454.
                    Winter, 1976.

    1978   Melanesian Medicine: Beyond Cul-
                    ture to Method. In Culture and
                    Curing. Morley and Wallis, eds.
                    London: Peter Owens, Ltd.

Rorschach, Herman
    1942   Psychodiagnostics, A Diagnostic
                    Test Based on Perception. Berne:
                    Hans Huber.

Tax, Sol
    1953   Penny Capitalism: A Guatemalan
                    Indian Economy. Institute of
                    Social Anthropology Publications
                    No. 16, Washington, D. C., Smith-
                    sonian Institute.

Wolf, Eric R.
    1955   Types of Latin American Peasantry.
                    In American Anthropologist.
                    57:452-471.

1959   Sons of the Shaking Earth.
Chicago: University of Chicago
Press.

THE AFFINITY BETWEEN DAVID BIDNEY'S CONCEPT OF CULTURE

AND THAT IMPLIED BY HUMANISTIC PSYCHOLOGY

Arthur J. Newman
University of Florida

Bidney's Humanistic Conception of Culture

An always-convenient point of departure in describing the intellectual tradition of humanism is the classical observation of Protagoras that "man is the measure of all things." This, coupled with Alexander Pope's proclamation that "the proper study of mankind is man," underscores the point that he who would understand man holistically must do so by employing constructs and modes of inquiry derived from and predicated upon this-worldly experience. The humanists' insistence that homo sapiens is a part of nature is conjoined with the apparently paradoxical contention that man is equipped, by virtue of his creative, rational capacities, to challenge and transcend his environment. This notion that man ought to be regarded as, in part, the efficient cause of his own behavior is nicely captured by Corlis Lamont in his Humanism as a Philosophy:

> Within certain limits prescribed
> by our earthly circumstances and
> by scientific law, individual human
> beings, entire nations and mankind
> in general are free to choose the
> paths that they truly wish to follow.
> To a significant degree they are
> the moulders of their own fate
> and hold in their hands the shape of
> things to come [1949:136].

The humanist regards human nature as intrinsically ethical and intellectually worthy. Man is emphatically not innately evil or depraved, but as Jean Paul Sartre puts it, chooses what he is to become. This conception of human nature, when related

69

to the aforementioned beliefs that human behavior is
understandable within a largely naturalistic context;
and man is, in part, the creative cause of some of his
own behavior--leads the humanist to conclude that man
is capable of ameliorating social conditions inimical
to his welfare. This reasoned optimism is nowhere
better reflected than in the Enlightenment insistence
on the perfectability of mankind.

.   A concept of culture, consistent with humanistic
tenets is to be found in the anthropological philosophy propounded by David Bidney. In the revised
edition of his Theoretical Anthropology, Bidney writes,
"[Culture is] the totality of the arts of living
experienced by man individually and collectively in
interaction with his ecological environment to promote
survival and the enjoyment of life" (1967:xxx). In the
earlier version of this work Bidney states, ". . .
Human culture may be understood to comprise, in part,
the art of self-cultivation or self-conditioning, with
a view to the development of human capabilities in
relation to a given environment" (1953:77). For our
purposes, perhaps the most noteworthy observation is
that Bidney regards culture quintessentially as an
active human process. Culture is not regarded as
something--whether a body of ideas, a superstructural
manifestation of economic laws, or whatever--which
supervenes upon the hapless human creature. Nor is it
properly regarded as merely a logical construct.
Rather, culture is, in its most significant sense, a
process initiated and sustained by the proactive,
creative human being. This is not to suggest that
Bidney disregards cultural products--whether ideational
or material--as delimiting socio-cultural forces. He
clearly acknowledges the impact of such forces
(1953: Ch. 3). However, he unequivocally insists that
such products are rightfully regarded when conceptualized as having been derived from and predicated
upon human invention.

According to Bidney's theoretical position,
culture cannot be explained exclusively through
historical interpretation--as in the tradition of A.
Koeber's earlier writings--nor exclusively through
psychological deduction--as is the case with some neo-
Freudian psychological anthropologists. The historical
and the psychological are both necessary, although not

sufficient, perspectives for understanding human culture. The historical is crucial as man is admittedly
highly conditioned by apparently super-organic factors
which seem to evolve independent of human intervention.
But, the human condition while thereby conditioned, is
not wholly determined. To understand comprehensively
some of the crucial determining variables, the anthropologist must look to a psychology which subsumes the
notion that man is, in part, the free, creative agent
of some of his culturally manifested behavior. An
ethno-psychological perspective which draws upon the
heuristic power of history and psychology is an inval-
uable analytic posture for a holistic anthropological
understanding both of cultural evolution and contemporary sociocultural milieux.

Bidney's distinction as a humanist is forcefully
pointed up by his assertions that man can transcend
his environmental manifold.

> Man is not only a part of the order
> of nature but also a being who, through
> his self-reflective intellect and cre-
> ative imagination, is able to transcend
> the cosmic order of nature by setting
> up for himself norms of conduct which
> do not apply to the rest of nature
> [1953:9].

The point is eloquently articulated in the classic
essay, "The Varieties of Human Freedom." In this
essay Bidney refers to "normative or moral freedom"
[described as a type of human freedom which] "pre-
supposes the power of human reason to conceive
rational ideals not necessarily derived from a given
culture and to motivate action for the practical
realization of these ideals. Normative freedom is
metacultural in the sense that it serves as a moulder
or norm of individual perfection which transcends the
requirements of a given culture" (1963:12).

Bidney's conception of culture is unabashedly
highly normative. One can--the anthropologist
should--through careful comparative, historical analysis, distinguish those cultural conditions which
conduce to the commonweal from their opposites. This

71

is apparent from several vantage points, one of which is his conception of sociocultural integration. Bidney writes: "Normatively, a culture is integrated teleofunctionally if its adherents are enabled to lead a happy life which gives maximum scope for individual participation in the advantages of social life" (1953:394). In this context, to draw upon Sapir, the culturally genuine can be distinguished from the culturally spurious.

Form yet another perspective, one can take note of the normative dimension of Bidney's conception of culture. He insists that one can apply the afore-mentioned metaculturally valid standards of ration-ality to given cultural phenomena in order to ascer-tain whether such phenomena are functioning (or more accurately, dysfunctioning) as cultural survivals (1953:369). According to this interpretation--one at odds with some functionalistic positions--a cultural survival is something which, while rationally and morally defensible at the time of its inception, evolves to a condition of impeding the ongoing devel-opment of a morally wholesome sociocultural milieu. In this context, as in others, Bidney insists upon the crucial importance of appreciating the origin of cultural phenomena and of conceptualizing anthropology as a comparative, historical area of inquiry in which the anthropologist not only can, but should make reasoned value judgments of given cultural conditions.

The Humanistic Psychologists' Conception of Culture

The spirit of Bidney's conception of culture is cogently reflected in the writings of prominent humanistic psychologists. While a perusal of the major statements of proponents of this genre of psychology does not turn up a crisp definition of the concept of culture, there are some solid explanatory--if not descriptive--clues. In his Toward a Psychology of Being, Maslow writes:

> A teacher or a culture doesn't create
> a being. It doesn't implant within
> him the ability to love, or to be cur-
> ious, or to philosophize, or to sym-
> bolize, or to be creative. Rather it
> permits, or fosters, or encourages or

72

> helps what exists in embryo to become
> real and actual . . . the culture is
> sun and food and water; it is not the
> seed [1962:161].

According to this position, humanness is neither derived from nor fully dependent upon culture. Rather,
culture is rightfully regarded as a matrix of conditions which enhance or impede the process of becoming
human. As Maslow puts it, "A society or a culture
can be either growth-fostering or growth-inhibiting.
The sources of growth and of humanness are essentially
within the human person and are not created or inven-
ted by society, which can only help or hinder the
development of humanness. . ." (1962:211).

As is the case with Bidney's position, the key
undergirding contention--one the humanists insist
is borne out by empirical analysis-is that human behavior, while profoundly conditioned by the cultural
environment, is not wholly attributable to the impact
of external (cultural) forces. Man is possessed of
the creative capacity to challenge and transcend the
social forces that impinge on him. (It is noteworthy
to observe that the first article of the first issue
of The Journal of Humanistic Psychology is entitled
"Health as Transcendence of Environment.") Carl
Rogers observed that man

> is a figure who, though he may be
> alone in a vastly complex universe,
> and though he may be part and parcel
> of that universe and its destiny, is
> also able in his inner-life to
> transcend the material universe;
> [he is] able to live dimensions of
> his life which are not wholly or
> adequately contained in a descrip-
> tion of his conditionings, or of
> his unconscious [1963:89].

The humanistic psychologists take pains to insist that
this supercultural process can be interpreted within
a wholly naturalistic context.

The humanistic conception of culture can be
brought into sharper focus by contrasting it with

73

that adopted by the widely acclaimed behaviorist, B. F. Skinner. In his Beyond Freedom and Dignity Skinner insists again and again that all human behavior can be attributed to and explained by the impact of environmental forces. Toward the end of the volume, he observes: "Although cultures are improved by people whose wisdom and compassion may supply clues to what they do or will do, the ultimate improvement comes from the environment which makes them wise and compassionate (1971:171). The contrast between the Skinnerian notion of culture as part of a totally deterministic manifold and that of Maslow and Rogers, who contend that culture, while a powerful moulder of human behavior, can be attributed to and explained by the impact of environmental forces. Toward the end of the volume, he observes: "Although cultures are improved by people whose wisdom and compassion may supply clues to what they do or will do, the ultimate improvement comes from the environment which makes them wise and compassionate (1971:171). The contrast between the Skinnerian notion of culture as part of a totally deterministic manifold and that of Maslow and Rogers, who contend that culture, while a powerful moulder of human behavior, can be challenged and creatively changed, is best illuminated by examining their respective conceptions of human freedom. For those of a Skinnerian persuasion, human freedom-- in the sense of man's having the capacity to be the creative cause of some of his behavior--is a chimera, something we ought best to be beyond. Man is emphatically not free, but is everywhere in (environmental) chains. The humanists insist, on the other hand, that part of the very definition of humanness is the attribute of creative causality. Like Bidney, they do not contend that the process of behaving freely cannot be referred to determining agents. Rather, that man himself, as efficient cause of his own behavior, is sometimes among these agents. This freedom, this indisputable datum of the human condition manifested at times by a transcendence of cultural bounds is eloquently discussed by Rogers:

> It is this inner, subjective, existential freedom which I have observed. It is the realization that "I can live myself, here and now by my own choice."

74

It is the quality of courage which
enables a person to step into the
uncertainty of the unknown which he
chooses himself. It is the discovery of meaning from within oneself,
meaning which comes from listening
sensitively and openly to the complexities of what one is experiencing.
It is the burden of being responsible
for the self one chooses to be. It
is the recognition of a person that
he is an emerging process, not a
static end product [1969:269].

Like Bidney, the psychological humanists do not
contend, at least in principle, that post hoc analysis
might not identify those determining variables responsible for a given instance of "free" behavior. What
they do deny is the possiblity of scientifically pre-
dicting precisely how a human agent will respond when
confronted with a given problematical situation. As
the educational philosopher Paul Nash puts it:

But not all causes compel us to act
in a certain way: they may be
necessary but not sufficient causes.
Only a sufficient cause compels an
effect. Causal explanations of human
behavior may be sufficient explanations
when we are talking about things that
happen to an individual, but they are
only necessary (and insufficient) explanations when we are talking of
deliberate choices and actions--where
responsibility, blame, praise, reward,
and punishment are considered appropriate. In other words, we have not
discovered any sufficient causes of
action that can be called free . . .
[1966:218-19].

As we've observed, Maslow contends that one can
label as morally deficient those cultural milieux
which impede man's ability to engage in free, deliberate choice and expression. Or to put the matter
differently, those cultures which frustrate the
process of human growth--as described by John Dewey--

75

are thereby defective.[1] As Maslow acknowledges, this
highly normative conception of culture is rooted, in
part, in Ruth Benedict's notion of cultural synergy,
a concept strikingly akin to Bidney's notion of teleo-
functional integration. As she put it in an unpublished lecture:

> I shall speak of cultures with low
> synergy where the social structure
> provides for acts which are mutually
> opposed and counteractive, and of
> culture with high synergy where it
> provides for acts which are mutually
> reinforcing . . . I spoke of society
> with social synergy where their insti-
> tutions insure mutual advantage from
> their undertakings, and societies with
> low social synergy where the advantage
> of one individual becomes a victory
> over another, and the majority who
> are not victorious must shift as they
> can [1964:156].

The highly synergistic culture reflects a condition
necessary for encouraging and permitting the satisfaction of those natural biological and psychological
needs definitive of man qua man. These basic human
needs are described by Maslow in a hierarchical order
of ascending importance for human self-fulfillment.
The basic biological needs lie along the base of the
hierarchy and the need of self-actualization at the
pinnacle. The notion that the "better" cultures are
those which provide for maximization of human need
satisfactions quite clearly removes the humanistic
psychologist from an endorsement of cultural relativism, a position repudiated by Bidney by virtue of his
insistence on the validity of metacultural ideals.
The contention that human biological and psychological
propensities are universal is predicated upon cross-
cultural empirical evidence (Rogers 1969:252-255).
The logical inference is that the cultural anthropologist (and sociologist and others) ought to be armed
with a "universal moral yardstick" by which they can
rightfully engage in a comparative enterprise which
distinguishes the culturally good from its counterpart.

There exists a close correspondence between the

concept of culture explicitly developed by Bidney and
that implied by the humanistic psychologists we have
examined. Both positions are one with the note of
reasoned optimism sounded by the Enlightment philosophers. Both provide fertile soil for the educator
who would hope to root his philosophy of education
in a base which justifies the insistence that, despite
the distressing crush of contemporary socio-cultural
infirmities, the student should hopefully and eagerly
look to himself or herself as a potential creative
contributor to the betterment of the human condition.

Some Implications

Undoubtedly the contrast between the humanistic
conception of culture and that propounded by those of
a Skinnerian persuasion is intellectually exciting.
Does the controversy, however, have any practical import? It would appear that one's conception of culture is indeed profoundly significant in myriad socio-
cultural contexts, not the least of which is that
embraced by the institution of education.

A crucial component of an educator's philosophy
of education is her/his notion of human nature. It
makes a great deal of difference for policy and practice whether or not the child is regarded as a creature possessed of an inner, indeterminate freedom
which permits her/him to engage creatively in adapting to or changing the environment. Bidney's anthropological philosophy clearly embraces this notion of
student freedom; the functionalistic position advocated by those in the Skinnerian camp just as clearly
deny it.

The humanistic educator is inclined to insist
that culture is not a ready made constellation of
values to be absorbed by the student. Rather, following Bidney, Maslow, and others, she/he contends that
all cultural phenomena ought to be examined critically.
A healthy skepticism is the order of the day.

Those teachers who subscribe to a humanistic
conception of culture are probably wary of any clarion
call which too harshly sounds a "return to basics" tune.
In all likelihood they would suspect that the demand
for more classroom emphasis on fundamental skills too

77

easily shades into an insistence that we ought to get
back to the "tried and true" values and attitudes of
yesteryear.

It is imperative that teacher preparation programs
involve the prospective educator in a searching probe
of such critical matters as concept of culture. To
the lasting credit of David Bidney, his richly compelling theory provides us with an illuminating
beacon whose brilliant radiance will aid us immeasure-
ably as we seek direction for the future.

NOTES

[1] According to Dewey, ongoing socio-cultural growth
inheres in the expansion of a pool of interests (artifacts, ideas, customs, art forms--and all else suggested by Tylor), numerous and varied--alternatives
in the sense suggested by Linton--as well as unimpeded
access to this pool by all.

REFERENCES CITED

Benedict, Ruth
    1964 in Maslow, Abraham, Synergy in the Society
    and in the Individual. Journal of Individual
    Psychology 20:156.

Bidney, David
    1953 Theoretical Anthropology. New York: Columbia
    University Press.
    1963 The Varieties of Human Freedom in The Con-
    cept of Freedom in Anthropology. The Hague:
    Mouton.
    1967 Theoretical Anthropology. Schocken Books.

Lamont, Corliss
    1949 Humanism as a Philosophy. New York:
    Philosophical Library.

Maslow, Abraham
    1962 Toward a Psychology of Being. Princeton:
    D. Van Nostrand Co.

Nash, Paul
    1966 Authority and Freedom in Education. New
    York: John Wiley and Sons, Inc.

Rogers, Carl
       1963 Toward a Science of the Person.   Journal of
       Humanistic Psychology III.
       1969 Freedom to Learn.   Columbus: Charles E.
       Merrill.

Skinner, B. F.
       1971 Beyond Freedom and Dignity.   New York:
       Alfred A. Knopf.

II. CROSSING THE BOUNDARIES OF UNDERSTANDING:

ANTHROPOLOGY'S ENCOUNTER WITH SOCIAL CHANGE

The human world is one in fact, inasmuch
as the cultural phenomena of any society
and ultimately world society are functionally interdependent. But the character,
or quality, of that unity, whether it is
to be a world of common humane values fit
for civilized man to live in, or whether
it is to be a world of social entropy,
shaken by perpetual crises, is a question
of value which we of this generation are
required to answer.

(From Theoretical Anthropology, 1953, p. 449)

THE RELIGIOUS ASPECT OF LANGUAGE
IN NATIVE AMERICAN HUMANITIES

Dell Hymes
University of Pennsylvania

I. INTRODUCTION

My topic requires me to think about three terms,
"religious," "linguistics," "humanities," and I have
trouble with each of them. I have had to think about
what to mean by each. The study of language as part
of the religious character of Native American humanities is not much cultivated, and there is no established tradition on which to draw. And each term means
enough to make one want to think it through. So I
apologize for a roundabout introduction, taking up the
three terms in turn.

Humanities

The question here is what relationship I, as a
non-Indian, have to the subject. The answer I can
give is this.

When we think of the humanities as part of
scholarship, we think in terms of a distance between
ourselves and something human that we value and wish
to understand. We ask how that distance can be crossed
so that we can appreciate and learn, even though we
cannot participate directly in what is studied. We
hope to participate imaginatively, and must do so, in
a way true to the lived experience we approach, if
analysis is to be at all adequate.

So it was when the humanities arose in the Renaissance. Classical antiquity was recognized as irremedi-
ably separate, as a source of valued knowledge, and as
requiring special study to be known. In subsequent
centuries the humanistic impulse extended to the world
as a whole. The antiquities and traditions of the many
peoples of Europe, the Orient, Africa and the New World

83

were addressed. Anthropology itself, although now often thought of as a social science, grew up in large part out of a humanistic impulse, an impulse in which language had a central part. Languages were seen as markers of identity and boundary between groups, and as manifestations of mental life. Much of the work of the early leaders of American anthropology was devoted to the recording of texts as "monuments," in the old phrase, of cultures without writing then of their own.

As all of us know, the relation between scholars and members of other cultures has greatly changed. It is no longer possible to think in terms of obtaining and preserving material for an audience that does not include members of the culture in question or their descendants. It is no longer possible to think of humanistic inquiry as wholly from the outside. Every people has members whose role as students of their own traditions must be given primacy.

Perhaps humanistic inquiry has always had a sociopolitical dimension at its root. A great Cambridge historian of the classical tradition and its beneficiaries, R. R. Bolgar (1954), says as much about the successive waves of "renaissance" in the Old World since the fall of classical Greece and then of classical Rome. Those who paid for scholarship had interested motives, such as political legitimacy. Certainly we cannot escape the sociopolitical dimension of cultural inquiry today. In a given case, sociopolitical considerations may even dominate considerations of advancement of knowledge. Who does the work may be as important as what the work is. I would hope that we would agree that a world in which knowledge of each people was the exclusive property of that people would not be a world we want. Ignorance may breed favorable illusions, but is more likely to breed prejudice and fear. Each people has something to gain from adequate knowledge of others. It is inequity in the sharing of knowledge, exploitation, not sharing itself, that must be abolished. Without sharing there cannot be adequate insight into the range and potentiality of our human nature, nor adequate appreciation of the place of our own cultural tradition.

Anthropology, folklore, linguistics, and other fields have often enough abused their privileges and responsibilities; yet as against some scientific approaches, these fields, at their best, honor an ideal of knowledge that we need. They recognize that members of a culture themselves have knowledge of their way of

life that is essential to any understanding of it.
They do not so lose themselves in awe of scientific
rigor as to forget this. Recognition of this fact is
a basis for respect and humbleness. At the same time,
one must be aware that individual members of a culture
do not in the nature of things have complete or impar-
tial knowledge. Men know different things than women,
children than adults, each individual to some extent
than each other; each of us is influenced by our own
interests and self-conceptions. No individual can
fully say what he or she is and does. Moreover, we are
all prone to state ideals as if they were descriptions,
and there are patterns to the whole of an activity that
no one person may be placed to see. Both membership
and a certain distance are needed for adequate perspective.

All this is familiar, but the continuing inequities
with regard to sharing of knowledge, and to participation in the production of knowledge, require that it
not be taken for granted. As to my own relation to
knowledge of Native American languages: in Oregon,
where my wife and I work, we do so with approval and
support of Indian people and in ways that make some
contribution to the community. There are at present no
people able to do this work themselves, although in the
case of Sahaptin, the language with which my wife works,
it has been possible to begin to prepare some. In a
few years no one will speak the language I have studied,
Wasco, and I see it as my responsibility to bring together and make available all that has come to be known
about it. There is little interest in this task among
younger people, but I hope that some day there will be.
In the meantime, what I know of the language and of the
skills of a philologist are of some service. Indeed,
after twenty-five years of concern with myth texts, I
have been able to discern a pattern in them that was not
seen before and that makes it possible to bring out
their value as literary art. My hope is that such phil-
ology can show younger people reason for interest and
pride in these texts.

In a number of cases, indeed, the contribution that
work with language can make is to the understanding of
texts and patterns of meaning that are ancestral rather
than active. A participant in one Native American tradition can use such work for understanding of traditions
not his or her own. In this regard there is a very
great deal to do. Despite the long history of atten-.
tion to Native American languages, there are very few
works that integrate and make available what is known

85

in ways that are useful. Attention has waxed and waned according to trends in scholarly fields and the acci- dents of personal dedication. Although many linguists think that work with Native American languages has been determined by the nature of the materials, and use this notion to account for such things as an emphasis on the phonology of languages in American linguistics (because of the need to record), the opposite is the case. An analysis of the history of the study of Native American languages shows that the successive interests of scholars and officials have determined the work--collection of vocabulary lists under Powell, grammatical sketches under Boas, phonemic analysis later on, and so forth. The materials of the language have not had much sus- tained attention for their own sake. Perhaps this situ- ation will change as the study of the languages comes to be based more and more on the work of Native American scholars and the interests of Native American communi- ties. Perhaps "The Americanist tradition, having begun as the study of languages of a fading past and far west, will find fruition as the study of the languages of citizens." (Hymes 1976a: 17; see ch. 12). Of all the humanities, none should have greater pride of place in the United States than Native American, but as we know, there is still a great way to go to ensure sustained attention through chairs and institutes of the sort en- joyed by many other subjects.

Language

I use the term "language," rather than "linguistics," because "linguistics" does not seem adequate. If we had to limit ourselves to what the profession of linguistics has to say about religion, there would be little to say. Few linguists concern themselves with the religious im- plications of language. Some aspects of contemporary linguistics do have great importance for religion--the study of speech acts, for example, which can include study of acts of invocation, propitiation, and the like (see Ravenhill 1976, Foster 1971, 1974), and the study of grammatical categories and semantic presuppositions, which can include study of the particular world view of those who use a language (discussed below)--but the re- ligious implications of language are not much taken up. Some aspects of language that are essential to religion are badly neglected--the uses of the voice that are called "paralinguistic" especially. These uses of the voice may be essential to distinguishing and understand- ing forms of religious speech (cf. Crystal 1976, Samarin 1972, Tedlock 1976), but they remain relatively peri-

86

pheral, if not ignored, among the main body of linguists.

The term "language" is preferable also because language, or a particular language, may be part of what religion means to people. Current linguistic theory does not take account of the fact that language, and particular languages, do not mean the same thing to everyone, everywhere. Language may be central to some, peripheral to others, generally or in certain respects. A particular language may be inseparable from what it means to be a person or a member of a group in some cases, in others, not. But when we ask what language, or a particular language, means to those who use it, we ask a question that currently would be called "socio-linguistic" or part of the "sociology of language." Much the same is true when we ask in what ways a language may be not only a manifestation of the nature of language in general, but also something shaped by the experience and history of the people who have used it. Linguistic theory is interested primarily in the light that Tewa, say, sheds on universals, or recurrent types, or language, not in the light that it sheds on the Tewa. The latter interest would likely be called part of "linguistic anthropology" or "ethnolinguistics."

Someday everything that has to do with language may be considered part of linguistics. For now it is better to talk about "language" without worrying about what part of "language" is "linguistics."

Religion

The term "religion" ("religious character") is the most difficult of all, and I have no claim to a right to define it, beyond a need to be clear about what sense I can give it for myself. It is difficult to agree on what "religion" should mean within the context of Western civilization, let alone on how it can be used for Native American cultures without distortion. Certainly there are things that everyone would include within "religion": prayers, rites and beliefs involving other than human powers. Disagreement comes as to how much to include, as to the boundary: is "religion" to be limited to institutions and organized faiths such as the Western world knows in the form of churches? Is "magic" to be included? Is "world view?" Disagreements over boundary become disagreements over essence. Let me pass by technical arguments of the kind that occur in theology, anthropology, sociology, and the like with regard to the proper distinctions among terms such as "rite," "cult," "myth," "ceremony," "magic," and the like, and go to

87

what seems the major issue. Is "religion" to be defined
so as to seem limited to certain stages of human history,
increasingly displaced by secularization, surviving as
at best a peripheral or residual phenomenon? Or is
"religion" to be defined so as to seem an essential aspect of human life, one that may take many forms? Put
in terms of language: does talk relate to religion
just when used in the setting of a church or rite, just
when it employs such terms as "prayer," "God," "soul,"
"sin," "power," "mana," "manito," "orenda," and the
like? Or can talk relate to religion even when no terms
that are patently religious are used? Are there kinds
of talk, genres and functions of talk, that are religious, even without a special religious vocabulary, if we
can discern the cues?

    If "religion" is limited to rites and ceremonies
of an obvious sort, and "religious language" to talk in
such settings and with such terms, then the task is easy.
There is a certain literature on "sacred language,"
"ceremonial language," and the like, of which a little
can be said from a linguistic standpoint (cf. Newman
1955, and references following it in Hymes 1964: 403;
cf. also again the papers by Foster). I shall try to
sketch a more difficult task, because it seems to me
more adequate to the situation of Native American humanities. I shall try to indicate how one might conceive
of "religion" as a pervasive and permanent category of
human life, as a basis for considering language in religion.

    Clearly, "religion" is a pervasive aspect of life
among Native American peoples. Many people have observed that Western categories of the "supernatural,"
standing over against the "natural," do not do justice
to Native American conceptions of the world, of its
constituent forces (cf. Hallowell 1960). Guardian
spirit quests, rites of initiation, demonstrations of
power, ceremonies of thanksgiving, are salient, but not
the whole story. The world of the society is pervasive-
ly potentially an occasion for encounter with experience
of the sacred, of the other than human persons and powers
with whom the world is shared. If we accept a conception of "religion" as "the human enterprise by which a
sacred cosmos is established," and accept that every
society is continuingly engaged "in the never completed
enterprise of building a humanly meaningful world"
(Berger 1969: 26, 28), then a radical distinction between "sacred" and "profane" within Native American
worlds seems inadequate. Such a distinction is of
course to be made, but it appears a relative one. To

88

make use of a linguistic notion, one seems to need to recognize two levels of distinction. Within the accepted world, there are spheres of the sacred set off against the profane, but the accepted world itself is colored as a whole by the sense of the sacred. Human beings appear involved with other powers of the world in mutual maintenance and renewal. The everyday world appears as the result, worthwhile and intended, of the preparatory acts of all its various powers.

The most striking thing about Native American conceptions of the world, indeed, seems to me to be the difference from societies in which the past is considered a Golden Age from which there has been a falling away, and in which the future is envisioned as a paradise to compensate for the way the world is. The world-building imaginations of Native Americans posited the past age as an age that had to be shaped, corrected, overcome, to produce the proper world in which one lives. Nothing more strongly suggests that material poverty (as judged by standards of industrial civilization) may go together with human and spiritual richness. To be sure, social theory would speak of a society that attributes human achievements, such as controlled use of fire, to other than human powers (e.g., the trickster Raven), as cognitively "alienated"; its members interpret their world in ways that conceal the human making of that world. In terms of interpersonal relations and the roundedness of lives, however, one may have to speak of some such societies, Native American societies, at least, as far less alienated than our own. The cognitive test of alienation considers the meaning found in the world in terms of its adequacy for individual character and identity. On the latter test, traditional Native American societies would score very high. That fact seems related to their view of the world as potentially meaningful throughout (hence the proliferation of myth endings that explain the features of a place or creature--the significance is not so much the particular explanation, which can vary, but the constant function the explanations serve. The variability (which induced folklorists in the past to think such explanations unimportant in explaining myth) shows the vitality of the function. The multiplicity of explanations show how vitally the world was, through narrative, an explainable world).

The sacred coloring of the world as a whole is obvious, if we include mythology within the sphere of religion. There is good reason for such inclusion. The formal recitation of myths can itself be seen as a

89

rite. The limitation of such recitation to the winter season, the sacred season, can be seen as giving to formal myth recitation the character of a world-renewal rite. (I believe this to have been implicitly the case among Chinookan peoples.) The myths could be entertainment, character analysis, morality, critique, all in one, but in important part they are accounts of the formation of the order of the world out of disorder. The morality and character analysis they provide is implicitly instruction in the maintenance of that order. The time of telling is one in which success in maintenance of that order is being tested and validated. No sources of food could be had except what had been accumulated during spring, summer, and fall. Success in obtaining food is clearly associated with a right relationship to the persons and powers with which one shared the world. And the formulas with which myths formally ended among Chinookans all variously refer to weather, to the coming of good weather, and hence the ending of the winter in which no new food could be obtained. The telling of the myths would seem to validate past success (since the people are alive in winter with the food obtained) and to help ensure it (by calling for a shortened period in which the obtained food must be relied upon). (This interpretation seems supported by a favorite story in which the violation of a tabu prolongs the winter in a single village.)

Certainly myths and tales were central to the enterprise of building a humanly meaningful world (what Berger calls "cosmization"). The well-known impossibility of sharply sorting such narratives into categories according to the presence or absence of "supernatural" actors or actions; the actual continuum among narratives from most remote to most recent times; together with the points just made, all these things seem to show that myths participate in the religious character of the world, and help to show that world as having a religious character throughout.

If we use the term "cosmos" for a "meaningful world," then the relationship can perhaps be drawn as follows. Our common tendency is to think of the "sacred" as marked qualitatively, sharply set off in kind from the secular or profane. The world itself is often seen as secular or profane, and as having no inherent meaningfulness. The Native American traditional world is inherently meaningful, a cosmos, and while the "sacred" is set off from the mundane (mundane is a better word, here, I think than profane), especially with certain persons, settings, acts, objects, the contrast is one of _intensity_ rather than of absolute difference in quality, in kind. In diagrammatic form:

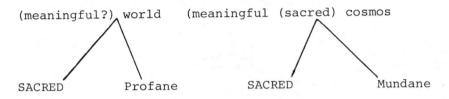

(meaningful?) world   (meaningful (sacred) cosmos

SACRED   Profane   SACRED   Mundane

    Such a conception of the pervasive scope of "religion" in traditional ways of life implies the relevance to religion of general norms of verbal conduct and of general patterns of meaning in language. In particular, if "religion" is inseparable from "world view," then whatever sheds light on world view may shed light on the religious character of life. Let me pursue this theme with some observations on verbal conduct and discourse, and a lengthier discussion of grammar. After that, I shall take up verbal conduct again in relation to non-traditional lives and to the question of "religion" as a permanent category.

II. EVIDENCE OF LANGUAGE

Verbal conduct

    Ethnographies may partition a way of life into chapters on economics, kinship, government, life cycle, alongside religion, but specific patterns of verbal conduct seem to unite them all, at least among Chinookan peoples. Thus, a formal speech event is constituted by a second speaker repeating words of a first to an audience (see ch. 8). That pattern can be traced in all the major speech events of the society, whether patently religious (the guardian spirit quest and its revelation at the end of life), only implicitly so (formal myth recitation in winter), or only secondarily so (formal name-giving, in which the surrounding powers are addressed, but in which the focus is on kinship and family and validation through gifting).

    Again, there is a traditional rhetorical organization of narrative in terms of three aspects of action that can be called "onset, ongoing, outcome" (Hymes 1976b, see ch. 9). Myths that account for the constitution of the present order of things through transformations wrought by Coyote share this pattern with historical legends, personal narratives, and quite _ad hoc_

91

accounts of recent happenings.

Again, the values that underlie such myths as that of the origin of death are found in accounts of recent reservation activities as well. The ethos is one and the same. In the myth of the origin of death, Eagle and Coyote return from the place where the souls of the dead had gone, Eagle carrying the sack containing the souls. Coyote pesters Eagle to let him carry the sack. Eagle refuses, knowing full well Coyote's character, but finally consents. Coyote soon lags behind, surreptitiously opens the sack to hear what the souls are saying, and of course they escape and return whence they had come, so that death is permanent in the world. Similarly, in the Kathlamet Chinook Sun's myth, which I believe reflects a thinking through in terms of myth of the historical destruction of the people, the Sun at first refuses to give the chief who has gotten to her house the shining thing that fascinates him, but after he continues to insist, finally consents (leading to his wreaking disaster unwillingly on all his people). The same phrase is used, "her heart became tired" (cf. ch. 13). (The phrase occurs with the same force in Clackamas narratives as well.) Now it would seem that Eagle could not be wise and noble, the Sun not wise and supportive, despite the fact that each is clearly viewed that way, why consent to something one knows will result in something bad? It is not possible to hear such points discussed today and perhaps never was --literary criticism may hever have been an avocation among Chinookans--but it is possible to sit with people and hear a recent political event discussed in terms that justify the action of a chief, because people kept after him and finally "his heart became tired." A request from those with whom one shares obligation cannot be permanently refused by a responsible person.

In sum, a study of ways of speaking among Chinookan people could find some things to set apart as specific to myth (cf. Hymes 1958), religion, and the like, but the things that unite the way of life are striking and important. (Cf. the way in which the Zuni pattern of "raised up" speech can be traced from formal prayer to everyday conversation (Tedlock 1976), and cf. Ravenhill 1976: 37).

A study of discourse about phenomena considered intrinsically religious, because "supernatural," would lead to the same conclusion, I think. Wascos still do discuss such things as the powers of "Indian doctors," the albino elk (i-ilmix) that cannot be shot, and the

92

like. These phenomena indeed "stick out" from everyday
life, but do not, I think, stand over against it (as
many would take religious phenomena to do). Many things
"stick out" in our lives, as remarkable and worth telling about, but we do not on that count alone consider
them as set apart--or if we do, then the amazing feats
of the athletes, musicians, teachers and friends we
have known are candidates for our personal "religions."
The tone in which Wascos discuss curing powers and the
like is matter-of-fact, even skeptical. The evidence
of the senses counts. The grandmother one remembers
oneself as saying correctly that someone was about to
arrive, as swallowing bullets, as turning water into
blood, had genuine power. The claims of others, not
validated by one's own eyes or the credibility of the
teller, bespeak only "bullshit artists." There are
such things as invulnerable white elk because one's
brother, a sure shot, was only twenty yards away when
he fired, and when he looked up, the elk away in the
distance, unharmed; yet the brother could not have
missed. A carful of girls, chatting about school, may
casually observe that they are passing the place where
so-and-so was chased by "stick-men." And so on. The
roster of beings and abilities in the world may have a
makeup different from that allowed by empirical science; the first origins of those beings and abilities
may seem to have had to be in numinous or extraordinary
experiences (though I myself am not so sure); but the
attitude taken toward those beings and abilities admits
of skepticism, evaluation of evidence, discrimination.
By and large, it is not separate from the sources, the
persons, associated with it; it is not separate from
the social world.

Grammar

A comprehensive conception of religion seems to
be essential if grammar is to contribute to understanding. In some cases a separate code may be used in
ceremonies--songs from a neighboring tribe, a special
vocabulary in the kiva--but by and large the grammar
that underlies religious uses of language is the same
as the grammar that underlies other uses of language.
Now if grammar is thought of as only an external orna-
ment or decoration, or as only trivially different from
one people to the next, then this point has no special
significance. But if grammar is thought of as reflecting and shaping the orientation of those who use it,
and as significantly different from one people to the
next, then two things follow. An examination of the
grammar of a language may contribute to our understand-

93

ing of its users; and in the Native American situation, that understanding will be relevant throughout their world. The grammar will contribute to understanding of a world view that embraces whatever might be set apart as "religion" together with the rest of a way of life.

Such a statement raises questions that have been much discussed in connection with the work of Benjamin Lee Whorf on the language of the Hopi (and, marginally, of the Shawnee); of Dorothy Demetracopolou Lee on the language of the Winto; and of Harry Hoijer on the language of the Navajo. Let me try to sketch briefly a reasonable view of the controversy. First, Whorf himself should not be understood as having proposed that a language in and of itself creates the world view of its users. In his most careful exposition of his ideas (Whorf 1941) he specified only connections between a language and the rest of a culture, and only where the two had developed together over a period of time. In other words, he saw a language and other aspects of a way of life as mutually influencing each other, as cohering. Such a position is inescapable, it seems to me. When we find a language changing its grammatical categories over time, from a focus on one aspect of experience to another, it is impossible to understand the change except as a product of change in what the speakers of the language have come to select and emphasize in reporting experience. When we observe that one language elaborates distinctions of tense, another of aspect; that one language has many distinctions with regard to person, another few, it is impossible to imagine how the differences arose except as a result of choices made by speakers of the language. A language, then, embodies evidence of such choices. Where the results of the choices, the particular grammatical categories, processes and words, are productive, activly available, one can reasonably infer an orientation or outlook from them.

Participant maintenance. Wasco is an example of this. A number of different features of the language share in common the expression of an orientation that can be called "bipolar." By "bipolar" is meant a definition of situations in terms of relationships between two poles. Thus there is a set of verb-like inflections of kinterm stems which literally are to be translated as "you-RELATIONSHIP-me." m-n-a-mut "I am your uncle" is literally "you (m) uncle (mut) me (n)"; g-n-a-gikal "I'm her spouse" is literally "she (g) spouses (gikal) me (n)"; and so on. The productive patterns of formation of new themes and idioms in verbs

94

make use of the person-marking prefixes of verbs to
state meanings in terms of relations between whatever
is signified by the prefixes. Certain recent grammatical developments, involving post-positions taken over
from Sahaptin, imply relations between terminals or
poles. The most striking single example perhaps is an
acculturational word, that for "window." It is not
borrowed from another language, nor is it coined in
reference to "glass" or "opening." It is derived from
a verb construction that literally means "they-two
(diminutive, i.e., the eyes) see each other by means of
it" (i-s-x i-l-u-qmit). The most profound example perhaps has to do with the elaboration of distinctions of
tense. Wasco has potentially 10 distinctions of tense:
first of all, the future, the present, and four pasts
(immediate, near, distant remote), and secondly, a
nearer and remoter distinction within the future, the
distant and the remote pasts, and the present (where
the effect is an immediate past continuing into the
present). The distinction between nearer and remoter
depends upon the interaction between the tense prefixes
as such (the first six mentioned) and two morphemes
that occur within the verb just before the stem. This
interaction is a puzzle. When the future tense prefix
occurs with one of these two morphemes, the morpheme
-t- signifies the remoter future, the morpheme -u- the
nearer future. Just the opposite is the case with the
past tense prefix. With it the morpheme -t- signifies
the nearer past, the morpheme -u- the remoter past.
How can this be? Obviously enough neither -t- nor -u-
can in itself mean "remote" or "near"; their significance can be either, depending on the tense prefix with
which they occur.

If one assumes that there is an explanation, a
system here, the answer can be found by considering
where the morphemes -t- and -u- have come from. They
are in origin markers of direction. In verbs that expressly state direction, they still mark direction
only. Thus with the verb stem -i- "to travel," the
imperative m-t-i means "Come!" (you (m)-this way-
travel), and the imperative muit means "Go!" (you(m)-
that way-travel). (The t at the end occurs as a marker
of present state.) In verbs that do not expressly
state direction, the morphemes -t- and -u- have become
indicators of relative time by some sort of semantic
shift, or metaphor. For a marker of direction or space
to become a marker of time is not in itself at all unusual. But how did it come about here?

The only answer that makes consistent sense has

two parts. First, it is necessary to recognize that
the morphemes -t- and -u- were never just markers of
direction. They did not and do not mean just "this
way" and "that way." Rather, they mark direction between two poles; then mean "from there to here" and
"from here to there." Second, it is necessary to infer
that the metaphorical extension from space to time was
made on the basis of the pole or terminal nearest the
present in each case. For an event in the present or
future, the starting point is the closer, the ending
point the more distant. That fits the fact that -u-
(from here to there) signifies the exact present and
the closer future, while -t- (from there to here) signifies the less immediate present and the remoter future. For an event in the past, the starting point is
the more distant, the ending point the closer. That
fits the fact that -u- (from here to there) signifies
the remoter pasts, while -t- (from there to here) signifies the closer pasts.

   To summarize in two tables, one for the direc-
tional force (A) and one for the temporal force (B) of
the two prefices:

		Starting point	Ending point
(A)	t	there	here
	u	here	there
(B)	t	far	near
	u	near	far

(This analysis draws on my paper of 1975d; see especially pp. 322-6).

   In sum, a variety of productive linguistic patterns go together to indicate an orientation toward bipolar relationships. These patterns are distinctive in
their specific traits, yet at the same time they suggest, together with other features of the language (such
as the abundance of person-markers and the centrality
of person-markers to the working of the grammar) that
in its own way Chinookan manifested the general world-
view that Redfield (1952) called Participant maintenance, a relation to the world, not of one-way control
and exploitation, but of mutual dependence. One might
even suggest that the world view had an "I-Thou" character. And one can go on to notice that in their interpretations of Wintu, Navajo and Hopi, Lee, Hoijer
and Whorf each find in a different way an orientation
of the same general character. The languages can be

seen to contrast at the level of particular cognitive
orientations and foci, such as Navajo emphasis on motion, Hopi on preparedness, Wintu on immutability of
essence vs. transiency of form, Wasco on perfectivity
vs. imperfectivity. (Hopi, for example, "does not in
any way formalize as such the contrast between comple-
tion (perfective) and incompletion of action" (Whorf
1936 LTR 51)). They can be seen also to share some
particular orientations. Lee's account of the expression in Wintu of the relationship between self and
other (Lee 1944: 185) fits such expression in Wasco:
"a coordinate relationship," associated with a "respect
for essense or quality," and "intimacy between self and
other," as against coercive, aggressive or forcing relationships. Beyond these particular contrasts and
agreements in orientation there appears to be a general
outlook, one which Lee describes in Wintu in terms of
the relation between particular and generic, and associates with (Lee 1944: 187):

> "the attitude of humility and respect to-
> ward reality, toward nature and society.
> .....The Wintu·' relationship with nature
> is one of intimacy and mutual courtesy."

Hoijer, having described three broad speech patterns in
which Navajo emphasizes movement, specifying its nature,
direction and status in considerable detail, goes on to
find in the relationship of subject, action and goal in
the Navajo verb (including verbs concerned with motion)
a parallel to Kluckhohn's inference of a cultural premise that "Nature is more powerful than man" (Hoijer
1951: 120 (in Hymes 1964: 148). As for Hopi, Whorf
mostly emphasizes the specific elaborations of Hopi
with regard to expression of categories, such as punctual vs. segmentative aspect, various modalizers, dur-
action, intensity and tendency of events. Perhaps what
Whorf says about the relation between manifested and
manifesting in Hopi (Whorf 1950, LTR 59-61) and the
character of preparation (Whorf 1941: LTR 148-152) can
be seen as also involving a view of the world in which
human beings participate as a part and partner.

These remarks are suggestive, not definitive.
Much more work needs to be done to warrant confident
conclusions. Methodologically, the great need is to
compare the grammars of languages within a coordinate
frame of reference; to establish equivalence between
different labels and formulations, to make sure that
not too much is being read into particular phenomena,
that the terms of description are not so vague and vast

as to accomodate anything. In short, structural re-
statements in terms of the purpose of discovering cognitive orientations and world views, and controlled
comparison within a consistent frame of reference are
required.

One reason we do not have such information now
is that the interest in Whorf was overtaken by a different view of language. Accounts such as those just
cited (by Whorf, Lee, Hoijer) came to the fore in the
late 1940s and early 1950s in the context of a climate
of opinion in which anthropology was a prominent factor
in linguistic work, and analysis of grammatical categories an accepted concern. By 1960 there was under
way the dominance of a climate of opinion in which the
most prominent factor in linguistic work was psychology
and analysis of syntax the overriding concern. Psychology and syntax of course can and sometimes have
gone together with an interest in world view. But this
time round the concern was with what laboratory experiment transplanted to the field could show, not with
interpretation of grammars and texts, and a new mood of
denying the importance of specific differences among
languages, and of denying psychological consequences of
differences among languages, was to the fore. Work of
the kind I have sketched has stayed about where it was
twenty years ago.

I think that the field of Native American Humanities has an interest in taking up this kind of work,
and thus an interest in challenging the academic outlook that has put this kind of work in the shade, indeed, into disgrace. It seems to me that the dominant
tenor of recent linguistic theory has been a flight
from individuality and particularity. The leitmotifs
have been formalism and universality. I do not question the importance of formal analysis or of universal
aspects of language, but it seems to me that they are
inadequate to our purpose. A dedication of understanding of languages as part of humanities entails a concern with whatever modes of interpretation can shed
light, be they formal or not most of all, it entails a
concern with what is specifically realized in a given
language or text, not just with what is latently and
potentially possible in language as such. This is as
much as to say that one's goal must be less a contribution to linguistic theory, and more a contribution to a
language, tradition, and community. (In ch. 12 I try
to show a historical and philosophical basis for this
view.)

98

The deictic center. Having indicated the contribution that Whorf's kind of concern can make, I must go
on to show its limitations. But before doing that, I
should like to show a further example of the contribution that grammatical analysis can make, if undertaken
in the appropriate perspective. Twice I have had the
experience of finding that a formal puzzle in grammar
has opened up an aspect of world view, indeed, the same
aspect in two quite different languages. Some years
ago I was puzzled by the relation between two affixes
in the Tonkawa language of Texas. As analyzed by Hoijer, there was a joining of a "future" and a "past"
affix which he called "future of the past." Without
giving details, let me simply say that the linking of
the affixes turns out to make perfect sense, once one
abandons the assumption that time is being handled in
terms of a linear se uence. The underlying contrast is
not in terms of a sequence from past through present to
future, but in terms of a center and a periphery. The
center defines a sphere more immediate in space and
time. The marker that seems in English translation to
give rise to a "future of the past" does not mark
either "future" or "past" as such, but falling outside
the central sphere, hence, either "future" or "past"
(as determined by other things). The underlying semantic conception is not one of a line but of concentric
spheres (see Hymes 1967e).

The analysis of the remoter and nearer tenses in
Wasco has led to a parallel discovery. Again without
giving details, let me just note that one is led to
discover a recurrent distinction between location at or
in the sphere of a temporal reference point, on the one
hand, and location beyond the sphere of the temporal
reference point. The distinction recurs throughout the
elaborate Wasco system of tenses. The distinction explains the samenesses and differences in form among the
several tense prefixes (all those containing -a(l) have
to do with location beyond the sphere). (See Hymes
1975d; 327-8).

One is led through analysis of grammatical relationships to inference of a conception of the seasonal
round, year and world (the Chinookan word for "year" is
also the word translated as "world," namely wi-lx). The
ten discriminations of tense are organized first of all
in a major contrast between perfective and imperfective
(completed vs. now-continuing). The completed or perfective part is further divided into reference to the
present day (action today vs. action yesterday) and
reference to the preceding part of the present year

99

(within or beyond the season vs. within or beyond the
year, or seasonal round as a whole). In tabular form
(drawing again on Hymes 1975d: 325):

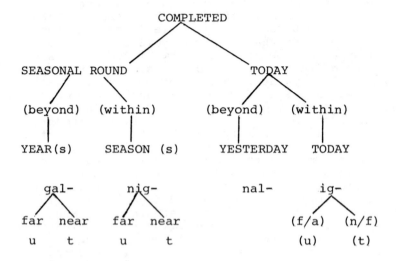

COMPLETED

SEASONAL ROUND   TODAY

(beyond)   (within)   (beyond)   (within)

YEAR(s)   SEASON (s)   YESTERDAY   TODAY

   gal-   nig-   nal-   ig-
far   near   far   near   (f/a)   (n/f)
u   t   u   t   (u)   (t)

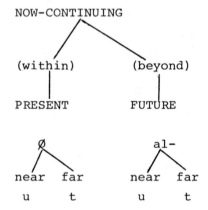

NOW-CONTINUING

(within)   (beyond)

PRESENT   FUTURE

     ∅   al-
near   far   near   far
 u   t   u   t

(The parentheses under *ig-* indicate certain variations
and imcomplete extension of the *u/t* pattern of time
marking to it.)

This organization of temporal reference into
spheres of a central here and now vis-a-vis a peripheral there and then may recur widely in the grammars

and outlooks of Native Americans. It occurred to me
recently that it might be implicit in the organization
of space among a people such as the Acoma of New Mexico.
The Acoma are said to distinguish six directions,
north, south, east, west, above, and below. Perhaps
there is actually more than one level of distinction,
such that the preferred pattern number of four is consistently observed. It is noteworthy that "below" is
organized into four worlds, and that "above" is organized into four skies. The four usual cardinal directions seem parallel. May not north, south, east and
west be the four subdivisions of a location that can be
called "circumference," just as the worlds and skies
are subdivisions of the locations "below" and "above"?
There would then be three locations having fourfold subdivisions, together with the fourth superordinate location, the center itself, the location of the Acoma. In
diagrammatic form:

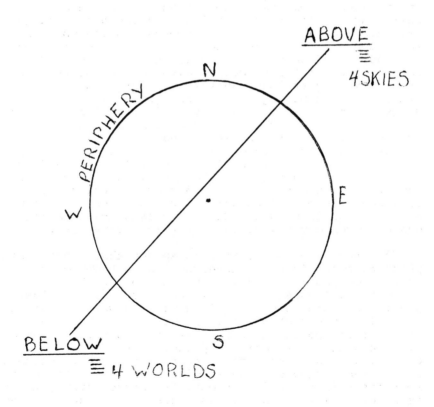

III. CONCLUSION

Let me return now to the limitations of this kind of analysis, limitations that apply also to Whorf. It was Whorf's belief that once an orientation or world view had been formed in a language and culture the language would play a central, crucial role in transmitting and maintaining it. Language, he thought, was more an integrated system than the rest of culture; language would thus be slower to change, more constraining. All such analysis runs afoul of a sociolinguistic critique, because it takes for granted the function of language. It implicitly assumes that each people has a single language, and that the single language has the same role everywhere, such that it shapes outlook in the same way. The facts are quite different. Many peoples have more than one language, and whether they have one language or more than one, their way of life may allocate differing roles to language. In the one group language may permeate the socialization of the child and the learning of things; in another language may have a marginal role, and emphasis being upon observation, practice, and demonstration. One group may provide verbal accounts for everything it does and has, another feel little concerned with such accounts. One group may be garrulous, another taciturn. And so on. True, it might be argued that any group will use language to the minimum necessary to implant its implicit orientations. But what if one of the languages it uses is used only in certain situations, such as at work and not at home? Is learned only in school or in adulthood? One quickly sees that the function of language affects the chance language has to shape outlook, and that one cannot predict a person's world view or outlook solely from analysis of a language the person uses. Independent evidence is needed. Not every language is a language of world view, at least not for every user.

Thus it would be rash to assume that the semantic patterns found in Wasco determine the outlook of the handful of people who still know Wasco. Perhaps they do, but the language is little used among these older people; all are multilingual, having known at least one other language most of their lives. From the productivity of the patterns that attest to a bipolar orientation, and to an emphasis on perfectivity (of which more below), we can be sure that recent traditional speakers shaped the language in these directions, that these directions reflect their outlook. As argued above, there is no other way to explain the presence of the patterns. But the presence of such patterns in the speech of

102

people who seldom have occasion to use them, and whose dominant language is English, probably is not strong evidence that the outlook has been maintained along with recollection of the words, or even that it was firmly ingrained when they first acquired the language.

In sum, analysis of language can shed light on past orientations and outlooks. The effect of language on present orientations and outlooks has to be investigated in the light of present patterns of the use of language.

Patterns of the use of language, indeed, should be investigated not only as a control on inferences from language, but also as a source of evidence in their own right as to world view. Earlier I indicated some patterns of use that were consistent throughout several spheres of traditional Wasco culture. Let me develop this theme to show further that a comprehensive view of the relation of language to culture is necessary.

In the discussion of the elaboration of tenses in Wasco I mentioned perfectivity, that is, a concern with the completeness (vs. the incompleteness) of actions. This concern is pervasive in Wasco. It first struck me when I attempted to elicit the way to say the future tenses for each of the verbs in the language from Philip Kahclamet. He would not say the verb until he was satisfied that the action was certain to occur. The future was not subjective, optative, or the like, but perfective, a commitment. Later I began to see that the dimension of perfectivity occurred in many parts of the language, and also that it occurred in the major speech events of the culture. In the naming of an individual, the quest for guardian spirit power, and the recitation of myths, an event of explicit disclosure was accompanied by a period in which explicit disclosure was forbidden (cf. ch. 8). Outside the formal event, to be sure, a certain part could be quoted, but the whole could not be disclosed. The period in which explicit disclosure was forbidden was the period of uncertainty as to outcome. For myth, it was the portion of the annual cycle devoted to economic activity; for individual naming, the period until resumption of a name would validate its title-like quality; for guardian spirit experience, the period until the end of life when what had been foretold would be seen to have come true. In Wasco, in short, perfectivity became a major aspect of both grammar and the use of grammar.

103

This discussion of language, its use, and orientations that may link both, shows, I hope, that language should be considered together with the rest of a culture in any attempt to discover world view. In the context of a view of the religious aspect of a traditional way of life as pervasive, I hope that such an "ethnolinguistic" approach to language has been shown to be valuable to understanding of the religious character of Native American humanities. Yet a further question remains. It has to do with the kind of situation just discussed. Most Wasco people today cannot be said to participate in much of a traditional way of life, or at least not in a traditional religious way of life. A few are Shakers. Most of the older people at Warm Springs Reservation are Presbyterian. Wascos, by and large, have long taken the lead in economic adaptation and advancement in relation to the surrounding society. None but the oldest use the language. Is there nothing to be said, then, about the religious character of Wascos in the future, as Native Americans, apart from whatever interest they may take in what is known of their ancestral way of life? About others in such a situation?

It is possible to develop a perspective from which "religion" is a permanent category of human life, and so relevant to individuals, whether or not they take part in what is saliently religious. I can say nothing specific about language among Wascos or other Indian people in terms of this perspective, but think it is important to become able to do so. I have met and known a few individuals who embody an orientation, a spirit, that I can only think of as religious, and as stemming from Native American tradition, even though the persons in question do not take part in ceremonies. (One's sphere is athletics, especially long-distance running; the other's embraces public administration and education.) To understand the linguistic aspect of the religious orientation of such people would be to shed light on the religious situation of many people in the modern world and to illuminate the nature of religion itself.

The perspective depends on a view of religion as a human creation. Religion is understood as an outcome of the human drive to find meaning in the world, to conceive the world as a meaningful whole. This is the process that Berger (1969) calls "cosmization." I want to agree with that view of the source of religion, but to avoid a common consequence. I want to avoid the conclusion that religion is a stage of human thought

104

superseded by science. The way to avoid the consequence, I think, is to avoid the assumption that the
existence of religion depends on the existence or pos-
tulation of a kind of experience that its participants
cannot analyze or understand as human in origin. One
can grant that many religious practices and beliefs
have been superseded by science and rational explanation, but still understand the category of religion itself as an inescapable and permanent part of human life,
as part of continuing efforts to conceive a meaningful
world.

For many writers, such as Berger, the sacred is
defined as a quality of mysterious and awesome power,
other than man and yet related to him, a quality which
sticks out from the normal routines of everyday life as
something extraordinary (and potentially dangerous).
Certainly this quality does exist in religion. And
from this point of view it is true that different religions may find a different proportion of the sacred
in reality. As compared to Catholicism, for example,
Protestantism can be seen as involving an immense
shrinkage in the scope of the sacred, divesting itself
as much as possible of mystery, magic, and miracle
(Berger 1969: 26, 111). Native American peoples might
have differed among themselves in the extent of the
sphere of the sacred, yet certainly all would have regarded that sphere as far more pervasive than it is in
urban Western life.

It seems to me that the essential quality that
should be identified with the "sacred" is not this
quality, however important it is in many cases, but the
quality of transcendence. The experiences and emotions
of transcendence may be dramatic or serene, extraordinary or satisfyingly expectable. It is the fact of
transcendence that counts.

The question of the sacred takes on a different
quality from this point of view. It becomes possible
to accept the sacred as a quality of life that is at
the same time open to rational understanding. One can
understand its roots in human lives, in the necessity
for a meaningful world, without denying its validity.

The essential thing, I think, is to consider the
location of the transcendent in relation to the one, or
those, for whom it is transcendent. That which is
transcendent has a source and base in something outside,
or of greater scope than, those for whom it is transcendent. Commonly we think of such a source or base as

105

extra-human and extra-empirical. But even from the
standpoint of humankind as a whole, a conception of
the world as an eternal realization of natural law; a
conception of the survival of the earth as a suitable
habitation; a conception of the suitable survival of
humankind--such conceptions could be transcendent of
any one generation of inhabitants of the earth. It is
similar from the standpoint of particular societies or
other parts of humankind. To be sure, such empirical
sources of transcendence are possibilities that some
have recognized, but far from all. The situation is
different with individuals. Something answering to
"religion" may be necessary for every society. In the
terms we are using it certainly is necessary for every
individual. Every individual must "go beyond the evidence" of transitory reality and experience, as it
were, if he or she is to have faith in the orderliness
and meaningfulness of life. And the basis of that
faith is open to evaluation in empirical terms; indeed,
it seems commonly to include a great proportion of
transcendence with such a basis. The sense of self, of
identity, with reference to origins in the past and to
hopes for the future, that sustains most individuals,
while often enough conceived as extra-human and extra-
empirical in basis, very often is thoroughly close to
hand.

A sense of origins in the past and of hopes for
the future are the two essential dimensions of rational
religion, according to Santayana, who dubbed them
"piety" and "spirituality" (the one being loyalty to
necessary conditions, including those of one's origins,
the other being devotion to ideal ends (Santayana 1951:
276)). It is possible of course to analyze the conditions of faith in experience, of a sense of an orderly
world, of the relations of a self or identity to a
world, purely as problems of cognition and epistemology.
The question of transcendence is then a question of how
human beings constitute worlds out of experience. When
one considers how persons relate a sense of the ongoing-
ness of an orderly world to a past and a future, in
terms of a willingness to live, to hope, to sacrifice,
then one has a dimension of attitude that seems to be
transcendent in a religious sense. The quality of the
attitude may not be one of awe or excitement at mystery,
miracle or magic (it may or may not be), but it will be
a quality of reverence, commitment, resistance to violation, that can well be seen as partaking of the sacred. I take Erving Goffman's analysis of "The nature
of deference and demanor" (1956) to show just such a
presence of a sacred quality (which he calls "ceremon-

106

ial") in the obligations a person has to others and can expect from others in everyday life. The specific rights and duties between persons, indeed, may reveal, just as much or more than grammar, fundamental orientations toward the world.

There may be great variation among personal worlds, but in each may be found something that answers to a personal seasonal round, a personal calendar of meaningful anniversaries on which happen the events that give order and purpose to life, a personal series of places, objects and acts that involve piety and spirituality, propitiation and invocation, transcending the senses and the self. The categories one uses to describe the world of a tribe or village as having a religious, ceremonial, sacred dimension, can all be applied to the life-worlds of persons.

This is not to say that lack or loss of such a world is impossible. The point is that such a world is not necessarily missing when one does not go to church, or synagogue, or longhouse. Such a world is missing only when there is nothing known to the person for which they would sacrifice, no aspect of their world whose demise they would not wish to live beyond, nothing outside themselves in which they see something of themselves surviving. Such a person indeed lives in a meaningless world, or at least a world whose meaning has nothing of the sacred.

From this standpoint, it is easy to understand how "little" things can sometimes be so violently upsetting. Little habits, infringements, violations, may in fact be violations of a personal world's sacred character. And some of the aspects of life we least regard may appear in a new light as of major importance. The etiquette of everyday life, of the ways in which people visit, take turns in talking, teach and learn, may not be seen as "culture," and certainly not as "religion." Yet the meaningfulness of a world, the meaning of much that is sacred in the larger sense, may inhere in such things. A reservation on which old myths are no longer told, old dances only rarely performed, spirit quests no longer successful or even undertaken, might still have the quality of a sacred traditional world if the relations among persons, and the relations between persons and the rest of their world, were maintained. God's redness need not depend, from this point of view, on the scientific standing of traditional medicines, and may depend very much on the survival of a social ordering of life.

What are the implications of all this for "language"? The first consequence is that the religious character of a world view may not depend on language in the sense of grammar. There seems to be good evidence for this from different parts of the world. In southern Africa, for example, the Ngoni people have largely given up the Ngoni language, but maintain their identity through maintenance of distinctively Ngoni ways of using language. Warm Springs Indian children may go to school using only English, yet bring traditional Indian ways of speaking with them. They may still maintain traditional understandings of when one should speak and when remain silent; when it is appropriate to demonstrate competence in something publicly; how to tease and joke; what is permitted and what is required in gatherings; what is respectful to old people.

This last is important to mention because people may not think of such conduct as "culture," let alone as "world view" or "religion." All of us, when we think of maintaining traditions, tend to think of the humanities in the sense of "high culture" of specialized arts and ceremonies. I want to suggest that the ceremonies of everyday life should be thought of as well. Where Native American people can maintain traditional ways of showing respect, of giving and obtaining information, of teaching, of enjoying, through language, something of the character of their world view may be maintained. And if a religious character is pervasive in the traditional way of life, then something religious may be maintained as well.

A second consequence is to suggest that a nontraditional language can serve as a means of expression for a traditional religious outlook. Not necessarily, of course. Something religious is often felt to be inseparable from a specific linguistic form. The linguistic form has to be intact for the religious meaning to be present. Where this is so, then maintenance of the religious character of a way of life depends on maintenance of the associated language. But it is possible to think of religious meanings as not dependent on a single language. Christians have come to think this way of Hebrew, Aramaic (Christ's own language), and Greek. There is thought to be a single religious message in all three. Indeed, Christians have come to think this way of all languages. The message of the religion is thought to be translatable into every language. In its own way this is an expression of belief in the creative potentiality of every language, in every language and language itself as inherently adequate to mediate God's word.

Some Native Americans may wish to think in this way about the many different Native American languages. They may wish to emphasize what is common to the religious outlooks of Native American peoples, and what is therefore not dependent on a particular language.

Such a view leaves open the possibility that Native American languages as a group may differ in important ways from some other languages. Perhaps the common elements of world view give rise to common features of language that non-Indian languages do not share. Whorf's contrast of Hopi to "Standard Average European" certainly implies such a possibility (Whorf 1941).

The question would then arise: are English (and Spanish and French) inherently unable to express a Native American world view, and its religious character? I do not know for certain, but I think the answer is "No." More exactly, the answer is: it depends on what is done with English (Spanish, French). The English of some Native Americans already may carry over semantic features of an Indian language. What may appear to the superficial observer as mistakes in English may in fact be expressions of what linguists call a "substratum"--the persistence of a new language of characteristics of the community's first language. Styles of use of language, patterns in the organization of narrative, patterns of humor and perspective, certainly have carried over into the English of many Native Americans. George Wasson of the Coos is an authentic narrator of Coos myths to whom the stories were transmitted by his grandmother in English. Larry George of the Yakima employs Yakima style in either Yakima or English. At the same time the English of some Native Americans on some occasions, and of others perhaps on all, reflects little or nothing distinct from the English of non-Indians.

The general conclusion to draw would seem to be this: where a language has been part of a way of life for many generations, undoubtedly it will reflect that way of life. Its grammatical categories and relationships, its words and ways of joining words together in speech acts and styles, will express and facilitate that way of life. This does not mean that another language cannot come to express and facilitate that way of life; but it can do so only insofar as the people are able to make it their own. The people may interpret

109

and select and group together the possibilities of
another language in ways that are at least compatible
with their outlook. Where English (or Spanish or
French) has become a language of a Native American
people, they must have a right and voice in what it is
to be for them. This applies both to features of language proper--pronunciation, vocabulary, grammar, and
to features of the ways language is used, which express
and facilitate a way of life and outlook too.

For many Native American peoples, the crucial
question about language may be whether or not the traditional language can be maintained. There are other
Native Americans who now do not have a traditional language. Some of them may wish to learn a surviving language, such as Navajo, because it is Native American;
others may wish to study what is known of their own
ancestral language; others may remain entirely with the
use of a non-Indian language. The first priority obviously is to maintain native religion and language
together wherever possible. There is also need to make
what can be known accessible to those who must approach
it as young adults through study (as young Chinookans
today must). And there is need to consider the ways in
which those Native Americans who use no Native American
language may still express and participate in the religious character of a Native American outlook. Native
Americans have made great contributions to the world,
through discoveries of medicines and foods. It is they
who made the New World habitable for humankind. Perhaps they will make it sayable in all its languages as
well.

FOOTNOTE

This paper was prepared for a consultation on "The Religious Character of Native American Humanities," sponsored by the Program of Religious Studies, Arizona State University, and held April 14-16, 1977. I want to thank Dr. Sam D. Gill, director of the program, for inviting me, and members of the consultation for their comments, particularly Elizabeth Brandt, Donald Bahr, Emory Sekaquaptewa, and Grace McNeley.

REFERENCES

Berger, P. L. 1969. The social reality of religion. London: Faber and Faber. (Published in New York as The sacred canopy (1967)).

Bolgar, R. R. 1954. The classical heritage and its beneficiaries. London: Cambridge University Press. (New York: Harper Torchbooks, 1964).

Carroll, J. B. (ed.). 1956. Language, thought and reality: Selected writings of Benjamin Lee Whorf. New York: Wiley; Cambridge: M.I.T. Press.

Crystal, D. 1976. Nonsegmental phonology in religious modalities. In Language in religious practice, ed. W. Samarin, pp. 15-25. Rowley, Mass.: Newbury House.

Foster, N. K. 1971. Speaking in the longhouse at Six Nations Reserve. In Linguistic diversity in Canadian society, ed. R. Darnell, pp. 129-154. Edmonton: Linguistic Research.

Goffman, E. 1956. The nature of deference and demanor. American Anthropologist 58.473-502. (Reprinted in his Interaction ritual: Essays on face-to-face behavior (Garden City, N. Y.: Anchor Books, 1967), pp. 47-96.

Hallowell, A. I. 1960. Ojibwa oncology, behavior and world view. In Culture in history ed. S. Diamond (New York: Columbia University Press, 1964), pp. 49-82).

Hoijer, H. 1951. Cultural implications of some Navajo linguistic categories. Language 27: 111-20. (Reprinted in Language in culture and society, ed. D. Hymes (New York: Harper and Row, 1964), pp. 142-8).

Hymes, D. 1958. Linguistic features peculiar to Chinookan myths. International Journal of American Linguistics 24: 253-57.

Lee, D. D. 1944. Linguistic reflection of Wintu' thought. International Journal of American Linguistics 10(4): 181-7.

112

Newman, S. S. 1955. Vocabulary levels: Zuni sacred and slang usage. Southwestern Journal of Anthropology 11: 345-354. (Reprinted in Language in culture and society, ed. D. Hymes. (New York: Harper and Row, 1964), pp. 397-403.

Ravenhill, P. L. 1976. Religious utterances and the theory of speech acts. In Language in religious practice, ed. W. Samarin, pp. 26-39. Rowley, Mass.: Newbury House.

Redfield, R. 1952. The primitive world view. Proceedings of the American Philosophical Society 96: 3-36.

Samarin, W. 1972. Variation and variables in religious glossolalia. Language in Society 1: 121-130.

Santayana, G. 1951. Reason in religion, (The Life of Reason, or the Phrases of Human Progress, III). New York: Scribner's Sons. 2nd ed. (First published, 1905, 1933).

Tedlock, D. 1976. From prayer to reprimand. In Language in religious practice, ed. W. Samarin, pp. 72-83. Rowley, New York: Newbury House.

Whorf, B. L. SEE ABOVE AFTER CARROLL, and also add the following:

---. 1950. An American Indian model of the universe. International Journal of American Linguistics 16.67-72. (LTR 57-64).

Whorf, B. L. (Papers by Whorf reprinted in Carroll (ed.).....are indicated by "LTR" together with their pages in that collection).

---. 1941. The relation of habitual thought and behavior to language. In Language, culture and personality, Essary in memory of Edward Sapir, eds. L. Spier, A. I. Hallowell, and S. S. Newman, pp. 134-159. Menasha, Wisconsin: Bantam Books, for Sapir Memorial Publication Fund. (This volume reprinted Salt Lake City: University of Utah Press, 1960). (LTR 134-159).

Whorf, B. L. 1974. When words become deeds: An analysis of three Iroquois longhouse speech events. In Explorations in the ethnography of speaking, ed. R. Bauman and J. Sherzer, pp. 354-367. New York and London: Cambridge University Press.

---. ed. 1964f. Language in culture and society. New York: Harper and Row.

---. 1966b. Two types of linguistic relativity. Some examples from Amerindian ethnography. In Sociolinguistics, ed. W. Bright, pp. 114-58. The Hague: Mouton. (Chs. 7, 8)

---. 1967e. The interpretation of a Tonkawa paradigm. In Studies in Southwestern ethnolinguistics, D. Hymes, pp. 264-278. The Hague: Mouton.

---. 1975d. From space to time in tenses in kiksht. International Journal of American Linguistics 41(4): 313-29.

---. 1975b. Folklore's nature and the Sun's myth. Journal of American Folklore 88. 345-69. (Ch. 13)

---. 1975a. Breakthrough into performance. In Folklore performance and communication, ed. D. Ben-Amos and K. S. Goldstein, pp. 11-74. The Hague: Mouton.

---. 1976c. The Americanist tradition. In American Indian languages and American linguistics, ed. W. L. Chafe, pp. 11-33. Lisse: The Peter de Ridder Press. (Ch. 12)

---. 1976b. Louis Simpson's "The deserted boy." Poetics 5: 119-55.

---. 1977. Discovering oral performance and measured verse in American Indian narrative. New Literary History 8: 431-458. (ch. 9)

---. (ed.) 1976. Language in religious practice. Rowley, Mass.: Newbury House

---. 1936. The punctual and segmentative aspects of verbs in Hopi. Language 12.127-131. (LTR 51-56).

HUMANISTIC APPROACHES IN APPLIED ANTHROPOLOGY

D. M. Warren
Iowa State University

Abstract

It is argued that humanistic approaches in applied anthropology can greatly facilitate communications between indigenous societies and directed change agents, enhancing the possibility for viable development. These approaches include the formalization of indigenous knowledge systems, an understanding of indigenous strategies for problem definition and solution, the viable involvement of local populations in the design and implementation of development projects, and a knowledge of the history of the local population in order to understand the dynamic processes which have influenced and affected it.

Assumptions and attitudes underlying Western definitions of and strategies for development programs are traced to nineteenth century social scientific and folk beliefs stemming from unilineal evolutionary models, beliefs which are still maintained through common twentieth century dichotomies such as the "traditional" and the "modern."

1. Introduction

The roots of humanistic approaches in applied anthropology can be traced to Sir A. B. Tylor who, in Primitive Culture, described the discipline of anthropology as a "reformer science" designed to further cultural progress and to reduce the prejudices and myths which exist between members of various races and cultures. Dr. David Bidney, nearly a century later, echoed similar desires when he wrote, "Instead of posing as an impersonal natural scientist whose objective is only to understand the world of culture, [the anthropologist] may well participate in changing his cultural world, and especially that of less developed peoples, with a view to achieving more rational and life-enhancing ideals and values" (Bidney 1967:xl).

I view applied anthropology as important and functional in the two areas expressed by Tylor and Bidney; these include teaching and study to reduce ethnocentrisms, as well as the application of anthropological knowledge and theory in domestic and international development. Many of the excesses and failures of educational programs and directed change projects may be viewed in terms of two inabilities of the change agents - whether they be teachers or social and technical scientists - both being based on Euro-American attitudes engendered in large part by unilineal evolutionary epistemological models developed in the nineteenth century, models maintained to a considerable degree to the present time. These inadequacies are (1) the inability of the agent of change to formally describe and define local knowledge and belief systems (in many cases the inability to even recognize these systems as valid and worthy of being formalized), and (2) consequent to this, the attitude which, assuming local populations to be basically inept, disregards local populations as capable of participating in the definition of problems and the implementation of solutions in developmental projects.

The paternalistic attitude which still frequently prevails assumes a primitive (superstitious, passive, irrational) mind, poorly-developed language and knowledge systems, and hence inabilities to make rational decisions. It is my belief that until the humanistic tenets which regard human beings as conscious, rational creatures capable of making viable and creative decisions regarding the improvement of their own life

styles (progress, if you like) are accepted by developmental agents, directed change programs will remain in
the coercive mold. The humanistic approach to planned
change is based on the premise that many difficulties
in innovative programs involve differential perceptions of the problem as perceived by the local population and the change agent, and hence a lack of communication which ultimately leads to program failure.

A humanistically-oriented applied anthropology
must be based on a knowledge of indigenous epistemological systems and social organization, a conscious
effort to define problems from the indigenous viewpoint and hence the establishment of local involvement
in change programs from their onset. It must also
be concerned both with the ethics and values of the
local population and with those upon which the external change agent operates in attempting to design a
program of implemented change. This approach involves
the role of the change agent as a communications
facilitator between local populations and national and
international agencies and provides the local population with an opportunity to increase the available options for change, thus enhancing its freedom of choice.

It is felt that recent developments in the study
of ethnoepistemological systems through the techniques
of ethnoscience may provide the bases for a fundamental
shift in (a) the attitudes held by many developmental
agents regarding local populations, (b) the role of
indigenous populations in developmental projects, and
(c) the structure and design of developmental projects.

An applied anthropology based in humanism would
also be involved with theoretical concerns such as more
precise definitions of universal norms and trans-
cultural absolutes, as well as an improved understanding of ethnocentrism and cultural relativism. The
improved knowledge of one's own culture through the
formalization of local knowledge systems (as folk
taxonomies, for example) increases one's awareness of
its nature and the limitations which it imposes upon
the individual.

It is proposed in this essay to describe certain
assumptions and attitudes underlying development, then
to indicate humanistic approaches in applied anthropology which should improve the nature and outcome of
planned change programs. These approaches include the

117

understanding of indigenous knowledge systems, which
can be formalized through ethnoscientific techniques,
the value and role of these knowledge systems in development projects, and the importance of the diachronic framework in better understanding the mechanisms for stability and the change processes which influence these knowledge systems. Such studies can
provide us further insights into the underlying assumptions and definitions of the term "development"
itself.

2. Assumptions Underlying Development

2.1. Unilineal Evolution and the Primitive Mind

The role of the Western social scientist over the
past century in elaborating and supporting the Western
popular and folk models, attitudes, and beliefs about
non-Western peoples can prove to be a useful, if not
an embarrassing, exercise. The basic relationship between the Westerner and non-Westerner was formalized
and given academic credence by nineteenth century
scholars such as Sir E. B. Tylor, frequently regarded
as the father of modern anthropology. Tylor, interested in "reform," "progress," and the "advancement of
civilization," described "the science of culture [as]
essentially a reformer's science" and stated that it
would be useful in exposing "the remains of crude old
culture which have passed into harmful superstition,
and to mark these out for destruction" (Tylor:539).
He felt that the so-called "savage," although capable
of reason, was misled by ignorance, limited knowledge
and a rudimentary intellect. This situation could
be improved through Western education, a civilizing
force which would assist the "savage" to climb the
unilineal ladder of evolution more quickly. This unilineal ladder, designed through comparative historical
cultural reconstruction, presumably showed the progressive development of mankind by means of a vertical
classification, the stages of savagery, barbarism, and
civilization.

John Lubbock (Lord Avebury) summarized the academic and lay attitude towards the non-Western world
by remarking that "it would be easy to fill a volume
with the evidence of excessive stupidity recorded by
different travellers" (565). Herbert Spencer noted
that the "savage," like the Western child, could
neither distinguish between "useless and useful facts"

118

(102) nor concentrate on the abstract or complex. Westerners, he said, "forget that discriminations easy to
use, are impossible to those who have but few words,
all concrete in their meanings, and only propositional
[sic] forms in which to combine these words." "By
such undeveloped grammatical structures, only the
simplest thoughts can be rightly conveyed...[and] we
learn that among the lowest men inadequate words in-
definitely combined are also imperfectly pronounced"
(149). Mental differences between those at the polar
extremes of the unilineal evolutionary ladder - the
"savage" and the "civilized" - were posited to be very
marked. The "primitive" or mythopoeic mind of the so-
called savage was due, supposedly, to undeveloped
languages. Frequently Lubbock and Spencer compared the
intellectual endowment and capacity of the "savage"
with the intellectual ability of European children.

Although most scholars and many laymen today would
regard such statements as unfortunate manifestations of
the past, many of these ideas are maintained today as
a cultural residue at both the covert and overt levels.
That they live on in many current school textbooks as
well as in the attitudes of many teachers is evident
from recent studies presented by Kohl, Kozol, and Rosenfeld. One also finds Herbert Spencer's nineteenth
century theory of the biological determinism of intelligence ("uncivilized" man has a simpler nervous
system) rearing its head again through the recent
publications of Shuey, Jensen, and Eysenck among others
(Warren 1976c:308). The fact that nineteenth century
attitudes live on is evidenced by recent statements by
other Western academicians: (1) "No matter how low
(in a socioeconomic sense) an American white may be,
his ancestors built the civilizations of Europe; and
no matter how high (again in a socioeconomic sense) a
Negro may be, his ancestors were (and his kinsmen still
are) savages in an Africa jungle" (Garrett 1962:984);
(2) a statement by Kiev (1972) about "the limited development of the African brain" (48); (3) a statement
by Carothers (1972) that "the stage of cerebral development reached by the average African was (and apparently is) that of the average European boy of between 7 and 8 years of age" (124).

2.2. The Traditional-Modern Dichotomy

Although the nineteenth century terminology from
unilineal evolution, used to explain racial and cultural differences, has lost much of its force in

119

twentieth century academia, other terms have been substituted. Hymes has noted that "The common coin has
been 'developed' vs. 'underdeveloped,' or 'modern' vs.
'traditional.' I submit that these are equivalents to
the 'civilized' and 'primitive' of a preceding era,
still a polar evolutionary model, combined often enough
with the notion of a center of diffusion to less fortunate peoples" (Hymes 1969:29).

Inkeles and Smith, in their massive study of change
in developing countries, characterize the "traditional"
individual in terms which appear very similar to nineteenth century depictions of the "primitive" person.
The "traditional" individual has a "passive acceptance
of fate and a general lack of efficacy; fear of innovation and distrust of the new; isolation from the outside world and lack of interest in what goes on in it;
dependence on traditional authority and the received
wisdom of elders and religious and customary leaders;
preoccupation with person and especially family affairs
to the exclusion of community concerns; exclusive
identification with purely local and parochial primary
groups, coupled to feelings of isolation from and fear
of larger regional and national entities; the shaping
and damping of ambition to fit narrow goals, and the
cultivation of humble sentiments of gratitude for what
little one has; rigid, hierarchical relations with sub-
ordinates and others of low social status; and under-
valuing of education, learning, research, and other
concerns not obviously related to the practical business of earning one's daily bread," qualities "extremely common in individuals, and exceptionally pervasive
across cultures and settings, in the countries of the
less-developed world" (Inkeles and Smith:315).

Leslie, like Hymes, has criticized the uncritical
usage of the traditional-modern dichotomy. "Western
social scientists interested in modernization processes...have neglected indigenous scientific traditions, apparently assuming that the only scientific
knowledge and institutions relevant to modernity are
Western. This Western-science ethnocentrism is consistent with the tendency to assume that modernity is
categorically antitraditional, and that we are modern
while they are traditional" (Leslie 1974:71).

In section 3.3 I present material which indicates
-the alarming superficiality of this dichotomy.

120

2.3. Involvement of Indigenous Populations in the Development Process

Because the term development itself currently implies the concept of progress and an upward movement toward a Western-based model - just as it did for Tylor, Lubbock, and Spencer - the communication process between the West and the non-West tends still to be unidirectional. Directed change programs emerge from and are based on Western knowledge systems, and problem definition and problem solution, despite the occasional rhetoric for grass-roots participation in development, is a function of these same Western knowledge systems. The Westerner (as well as the third world student who has been trained in Western or Western-oriented formal educational systems) usually assumes that indigenous knowledge systems are either non-existent or very primitive (Warren 1976c:309).

Illich has observed, "There is a normal course for those who make development policies, whether they live in North or South America, in Russia or Israel. It is to define development and to set its goals in ways with which they are familiar, which they are accustomed to use in order to satisfy their own needs, and which permit them to work through the institutions over which they have power or control. This formula has failed, and must fail" (Illich 1969:24).

More recently the World Bank has expressed "the need to involve local people in planning, in making decisions and in implementation" (The World Bank 1975:9) of rural development programs. "One particular advantage [for this] is that the problems of the community, as perceived by its residents and those imputed by local officials tend to be more easily reconciled" (The World Bank 1975:7), especially in view of the fact that "several countries have found that rural people have perceptions of needs and possibilities which are generally different from those of 'rational' officials" (The World Bank 1975:37). For the viable involvement of local populations to take place, however, there is need "for greater insight into the characteristics of target groups and the dynamics of traditional societies" (The World Bank 1975:75).

3. Humanistic Approaches in Applied Anthropology

3.1. Indigenous Knowledge Systems and Ethnoscience

There is then, the necessity to encourage indigenous participation in development as well as a need to understand differential perceptions of problems. It appears that humanistic approaches to applied anthropology can provide the mechanisms sought to effectively involve local populations in the development process. The mechanisms - communications facilitators between local populations and change agents - include the formalization of indigenous knowledge systems and the understanding by the change agents of these systems as well as the structure of the indigenous decision-making bodies which utilize them. Likewise the development of these knowledge systems across time must be delineated by the applied anthropologist. I will discuss these mechanisms in section 3.

My interest in indigenous knowledge systems began several years ago when I taught high school science in central Ghana, and it expanded when I returned to conduct research for a doctoral dissertation on a rather typical anthropological subject, that of culture change. I was interested in how the "traditional" Bono of Central Ghana defined, classified, cured, and prevented diseases. I accepted M. J. Field's findings that the Bono ultimately believe that all diseases are caused by spiritual forces. Assuming this to be accurate I hypothesized that those Bono who had become "modernized" through the study of Western science, would exhibit significant changes in the way they defined, classified, and dealt with disease. A new category, "naturally-caused disease," for example, might be substituted for the "traditional" term, "spiritually-caused disease," resulting in a concomitant shift away from traditional to Western-trained healers.

My research included two complementary components. The emic component, based on ethnoscientific techniques, was designed to explicate the indigenous Bono lexical units, semantic features, and classificatory relationships for defining diseases, relating these to sets of symptoms, and linking these to strategies for healing and disease prevention. The etic component, in which the research design is based on Western or anthropologically-derived categories, definitions, and classification systems, included the collection of oral

122

histories, census interviews, analysis of hospital records, and participant observation.

Several striking data emerged early in the research which indicated that the hypothesis, as influenced by Field's research, was simplistic as stated and that the entire problem of culture change was far more complex than I anticipated. I found, for example, that:
(1) The "traditional" indigenous disease classification system was highly complex, and the majority of the 1266 disease names isolated were classified by indigenous healers as naturally-caused; those classified as spiritually-caused included a limited number of disfiguring diseases, or those which could not be linked in terms of causation to the breaking of social norms. It was clearly evident that Field's study was incomplete.
(2) My emically-oriented interviews and questionnaires given to Bono secondary and middle-school students and to hospital personnel provided data which clearly indicated that Western education had far less impact upon the "traditional" taxonomic system than I had expected, and, moreover, there did not appear to be conflict between the system learned in the schools and the indigenous system.
(3) Census interviews (conducted with 4266 of the 12,068 inhabitants of Techiman Township, the capital of the Techiman-Bono Traditional State) indicated the presence of a large, stable, non-Bono population with numerous interethnic marriages. Representatives of 65 ethnic groups from eight West African countries, who spoke an inventory of 87 different languages, were interviewed.
(4) Oral histories collected from the chiefs in charge of the ethnic associations indicated that these interethnic contacts between Bono and non-Bono had been maintained, in some cases at least, for many generations, if not centuries.

Given these many ethnic groups interacting over such a long period of time, I had to face the problem of defining the "traditional" Bono base from which I intended to measure change. It seemed to me that either this area of Ghana was rather unique, or many of the ethnographic studies which I had read in graduate school conveniently glossed over the problem of change prior to that which occurred as a result of contact with the West. Perhaps a part of this portrayal of "traditional" cultures as existing in vacuo and in

123

a relatively static state is due to the handy and frequent use of the "ethnographic present." Once the dynamic state of a pre-Western-contact culture is neglected, it becomes an easier task to describe the
Western-contact period as one in which a relatively
stable or static culture becomes fraught with conflict
due to the impingement of Western society upon it.
This then can lead to the facile and sometimes inju-
dicious utilization of such sets of dichotomous terms
as the modern and the traditional, the developed and
the underdeveloped, the civilized and, the primitive.

Such portrayals, which inadequately describe the
complexity of the change situation, may be due to an
ahistorical approach. Through the utilization of arch-
ival material, particularly that written in vernacu-
lars, as well as the collection and analysis of oral
historical data, one can add to such studies a dynamic
component which is more challenging, more accurate,
and certainly far more useful in a wider academic context.

My own ethnoscientific studies on Bono medicine
(Warren 1974, 1975b, 1976d), aesthetics (Warren and
Andrews), and religion (Warren 1974, 1975c), as well
as Fink's study of Bono mathematics, indicate that in-
justices have been done the Bono and other non-Western
societies by neglecting to deal with the symbolic
richness and complexity of their cultural and knowledge
systems. Frequently the non-anthropologist reading
such accounts is left with the idea that the group
being described is "primitive," and that any complexities described probably were the result of contact with
Westerners.

3.2. Indigenous Knowledge Systems and Development

Another fruitful exercise in understanding "development" is the attempt to delineate the cultural
and academic premises and assumptions upon which me-
thodologies for data collection and interpretation are
based. An attempt at outlining the assumptions underlying "development" planning has been presented by
Hirabayashi, Warren, and Owen, Jr. We found an enormous amount of rhetoric in the West about the necessity
to provide mechanisms to stimulate an interest by local
groups in their own development, while only rarely
finding as project components the understanding and
utilization of indigenous knowledge systems, indigenous

124

decision-making bodies, and indigenous formal, informal, and nonformal educational systems. The importance of the incorporation of indigenous systems in development projects to make the projects viable through mechanisms which assure two-way communications and dialogue has been expressed in a number of recent studies (see, for example, Knight; Richards; Warren 1975a, 1975b, 1976c; Warren, Klonglan, and Beal; Warren and Meehan).

These studies have indicated that the failure of many development projects is due to the following: (a) the project design is usually based upon Western epistemological assumptions; (b) personal relationships and communication between the change agents and the local populations tend to be hierarchical and unidirectional; (c) project design still utilizes as supporting material studies written by Westerners from an etic perspective (one finds, for example, health delivery system projects in Central Ghana being based on Field's description of Bono disease belief systems, resulting in very inefficient utilization of local and external resources); (d) the tendency to continue to think and plan as if the dichotomies of the nineteenth century represent reality. These dichotomies are perpetuated by studies mentioned earlier in this essay, such as that of Inkeles and Smith.

3.3.   Ethnoscience and the Diachronic Framework

Development and directed change programs involve the processes of and mechanisms for cultural dynamics. A knowledge of the history of the society involved in such programs can provide change personnel with critical insights into past and future acceptance or rejection of innovations. Historical and comparative linguistic studies can improve our knowledge of the movements and cross-cultural contacts of a society. Content analysis of published vernacular materials can add diachronic depth to folk taxonomies and other classification systems. Such depth can provide clues to the stability of knowledge structures over time, the introduction and acceptance of new ideas and material items, and strategies for dealing with new problems such as the arrival of a new disease. Indigenous terms for change processes and concepts can be isolated from texts written in the indigenous language, and occasionally these terms are found in a context providing insights into pre-colonial development strategies.

Although some materialist-oriented anthropologists such as Harris (1968) have decried the possibility of placing ethnoscientific studies in a diachronic framework ("The linguistic model...is inherently incapable of making discoveries about the content of history and the nature of historical processes," (603-604)), this appears to be too extreme a position. There are, of course, limitations, but such studies can provide useful insights for determining the stability of a given indigenous knowledge system. I have found that the cross-generational approach can provide, in an era supposedly marked by severe conflict between "traditional" and "modernizing" forces, significant data on change. One finds in both synchronic and diachronic studies far more evidence for flexibility and accomodation by societies in their intersocietal dealings than for conflict (see, for example, Brokensha; Warren 1974).

One can deal with change in taxonomic systems of knowledge (which are typical of ethnobotanical, ethnozoological, and ethnomedical systems) through the careful pursual of early vernacular materials including vocabularies recorded by Europeans. One finds evidence of inter-societal contact and the diffusion and adoption of ideas in the form of borrowed lexical items, such as the Mande words incorporated into the Akan language, perhaps as many as five centuries ago (many of these deal with trade, such as yoma, camel; ɔpɔnkɔ, horse; adaka, box; kotoku, sack; bɛtɛ, pouch; tawa, tobacco, sɛbɛ, amulet; kramo, Muslim) (Wilks, 1962).

Fortunately the ethnoscientist interested in adding historical depth to synchronic studies of knowledge systems is trained in linguistics. Without such training a wealth of vernacular materials can be overlooked. I have compiled a bibliography listing more than 1600 items written in or about Akan (Twi-Fante), the earliest being a vocabulary recorded in 1479 by Fosse (see Warren 1976a). The name Twi alone, however, has been spelled at least 46 different ways over the past five centuries (Akĩ, Akyĩ, Chi, Chii, Chwee, Cĩ, Ekwi, Etwi, Kwĩ, Kye, Kyi, Ochi, Octhi, Odjii, Odschi, Oji, Okui, Okwi, Okyi, Otchi, Otci, Otji, Otschi, Otshi, Otshui, Otsuĩ, Otwi, Otwyi, Otyi, Tchi, Tci, Ti, Tiji, Tji, Tjwĩ, Tjwi, Tschwi, Tshe, Tshĩ, Tshwi, Tswi, Twi, Twi, Twi, Twii, Tyi). Other names also exhibit such wide fluctuations in orthographic representation (such as Ashanti found as Zandere, Atschati, Asjanti, Asandre) (see Warren 1976a:xv-xvi).

126

An appreciation of orthographic variations, and
the linguistic principles underlying them, helps keep
the ethnoscientist from falling into the procedure followed by some researchers who pick a given orthographic
form of a vernacular word and compare this with what
might appear to be a cognate in another language.
Meyerowitz used this technique frequently in tracing
the Bono-Akan first to Timbuktu, then to Carthage, and
finally to Ancient Egypt. Tait criticized this as
"identifications of forms from a modern language with
ones that were first recorded by Arabic writers from
a language not their own, from that translated into
Friench, and then from French into English. At no
point was any form treated by aphonetician" (Tait
1955:194). This procedure also allowed Meyerowitz to
make unwarranted and self-serving translations, such as
"The Bono-Takyiman...further recall that their ancestors, before they settled along the Niger, lived
farther north in the 'White Desert' or Sarem, 'the
country of the sand' which we call the Sahara" (1958:
17), whereas sarem (sare, grass; mu, in) means only
savanna. She also assumed that the same name spelled
more than one way represented different kings in a
given chronology (e.g. Kwatin, Koratin, Kwaaten, Kwaten)
(for critical detail on the abuse of such "historical"
methods see Warren, 1970; 1976d).

The utilization of early vocabularies has been
scrutinized most carefully by Hair in his Sierra Leone
studies; he feels that "concentration on the linguistic
evidence provides a sound and rigorous first stage in
the investigation of ethno-history" (72-73), and that
"while the early vocabularies provide some evidence of
language change, they give more evidence of continuity.
There is no reasonable doubt that the languages of the
early vocabularies are close ancestral forms of the
present-day languages, at least in their broad features" (74).

Alland, Jr., in his Abron ethnomedical studies in
the Ivory Coast stated that "written documents should
be the best source of information on disease history"
(108) and that "the collection of disease vocabularies
in particular language family areas might be used as
an index of relative age for specific conditions. Disease terms which are widely distributed and are not
cognate with the language of recent colonizers would
provide some indication of antiquity. Borrowed disease terms might indicate recent introduction...If a

127

linguistic area is large, the zone of cognates might
also prove interesting, showing a geographic distribution limited to part of an area. The existence of native terminology in one zone and borrowed terminology
in another might indicate that a particular disease has
spread only since the period of colonization" (111-112).

It has been possible to add centuries of depth to
many extant Akan lexical items, including disease
terms, through the perusal of vocabularies in Fosse
(1479), Marees (1602), Müller (1673), Petiver (1697),
Tedlie (1879), and 24 other sources all published prior
to Koelle's extensive work (1854).

In terms of the current concept of "development"
and the implicit assumptions held by many Westerners
that "we thought it up," it is very interesting to
note that a content analysis of century-old works written in Akuapem-Twi, including dictionaries, provides
us with a series of words or categories used by the
Akan themselves to differentiate the Akan innovators
from the "traditional" Akan. Among the more than
twenty culture change concepts isolated are bɛteani
(civilized, cultivated, refined), kɔdaafuom (uncivilized, rustic, boorish), nkɔanim (progress, improvement;
cf. nkɔso), anibue (civilization), and okuraaseni
(rustic) (see Warren 1976a:248-249 for details). My
recent survey of early vocabularies of the Efik, Yoruba,
Hausa, and Igbo languages also revealed similar terms
in those languages at an equally early period.

There are also extensive early vocabularies for
terms denoting creativity, innovativeness, and aesthetics (see Warren and Andrews), indicative of a necessity and desire to communicate about change processes
which were indigenous, and certainly not introduced by
the West. Even our understanding of Akan concepts and
definitions of "time" (see Warren 1976a:247-251, for a
summary of nearly 150 terms) makes it easier for the
Westerner dealing with oral history to understand
"discrepancies" which do not fit into Western expectations.

Wilks, in his massive tome (1975) on nineteenth
century Asante, has shown, in part through a survey of
Arabic manuscripts, that the Asante had equivalents to
five-year development plans, hired foreign advisors
and consultants, were eclectic and open to innovations,
had a sophisticated and complex bureaucracy and diplo-
matic corps, and were, for all purposes, highly

"developed" long before the British arrived in Kumasi.

My ethnohistorical data (see Warren and Brempong) indicate a similar complex state for the Bono. Ethnic and market associations have great historical depth; they are decision-making bodies with generations of experience which national planners could utilize for advice, but tend not to do so as they do not fit neatly into the "modern" paradigm.

Conclusions

Further collaboration between anthropologists and historians, particularly in ethnoscientifically-oriented planned change endeavors, should allow us better theoretical perspectives on culture change as an ongoing, dynamic process which can be understood through changing linguistic patterns. This should provide us insights into the role these knowledge systems and decision-making bodies played in the past and continue to play, and how development programs might utilize and work through these structures which arose as human groups defined and came to grips with their own social and physical environments. Perhaps then we will better understand the necessity for Westerners to utilize dichotomous sets of terms such as primitive-civilized, traditional-modern, and developing-developed, and how our Western-oriented perceptions have influenced our own current efforts to improve the quality of life for ourselves as well as for various other peoples around the world.

Footnote

[1] Some of the ideas and materials in this essay were presented at the Annual Seminar for the Advanced Study of Communication, The East-West Communication Institute, The East-West Center, Honolulu, July 1975 (see Warren 1976c), and in a paper entitled "The role of history for the ethnoscientist," presented at the annual meeting of the African Studies Association, Boston, November 1976. I have benefited greatly from comments and criticisms received during these presentations, many of which I have incorporated within this essay. I would like to thank Robert E. Welch and Bonnie J. Harmon in particular for critical comments and helpful suggestions used in the writing of this essay.

References

Alland, Alexander, Jr.
1970   Adaptation in cultural evolution: an ap-
        proach to medical anthropology. New York:
        Columbia University Press.

Bidney, David
1967   Theoretical anthropology. Second edition.
        New York: Schocken Books.

Brokensha, David
1966   Social change at Larteh, Ghana. Oxford:
        Clarendon Press.

Carothers, John C.
1972   The mind of man in Africa. London: Tom
        Stacey.

Eysenck, H. J.
1971   The I.Q. argument. New York: The Library
        Press.

Field, Marjorie Joyce
1970   Search for security: an ethno-psychiatric
        study of rural Ghana. (First published in
        1960). New York: W. W. Norton & Co.

Fink, Deborah
1974   Time and space measurement of the Bono of
        Ghana. M.S. Thesis. Ames: Department of
        Sociology and Anthropology, Iowa State
        University.

Fosse, Eustache de la
1897   "Voyage a la Cote Occidentale d'Afrique en
        Portugal et en Espagne (1479-1480)." Ed. R.
        Foulché-Delbosc. Revue Hispanique (1897):
        174-201. (list of 14 Fante words on p. 182;
        original manuscript is in Biblothèque Valen-
        ciennes).

Garrett, Henry E.
1962   Racial differences and witch hunting. Sci-
        ence 135:982-984.

Hair, P. E. H.
1975   From language to culture: some problems in
           the systematic analysis of the ethnohistori-
           cal records of the Sierra Leone region. In
           The population factor in African Studies, R.
           P. Moss and R. J. A. R. Rathbone, eds., pp.
           71-83. London: University of London Press
           Ltd.

Harris, Marvin
1968   The rise of anthropological theory. New
           York: Thomas Y. Crowell Co.

1976   History and Significance of the emic /etic
           distinction. Annual Review of Anthropology
           5:329-350.

Hirabayashi, Edward, Dennis M. Warren and Wilfred Owen,
Jr.
1975   That focus on the 'Other 40%': a myth of
           development. Third World Review 2(2):60-67.

Hymes, Dell
1969   The use of anthropology: critical, politi-
           cal, personal. In Reinventing Anthropology,
           Dell Hymes, ed., pp. 3-79. New York: Ran-
           dom House.

Illich, Ivan
1969   Outwitting the "developed" countries. The
           New York Review of Books 13(8):20-24.

Inkeles, Alex and David H. Smith
1974   Becoming modern: individual change in six
           developing countries. Cambridge: Harvard
           University Press.

Jensen, Arthur R.
1973   Educability and group differences. New
           York: Harper and Row.

Kiev, Ari
1972   Transcultural psychiatry. New York: The
           Free Press.

Kohl, Herbert
1967   36 Children. New York: Signet Books.

Koelle, S. W.
1854   Polyglotta Africana. London: Church Mis-
        sionary Society.

Knight, Gregory C.
1974a   Ecology and Change: rural modernization in
        an African community. New York: Academic
        Press.

1974b   Ethnoscience: a cognitive approach to Afri-
        can agriculture. Paper presented at the
        S.S.R.C. Conference on Environmental and
        Spatial Cognition in Africa.

Kozol, Jonathan
1967   Death at an early age. New York: Bantam
        Books.

Leslie, Charles
1974   The modernization of Asian medical systems.
        In Rethinking modernization, John J. Poggie,
        Jr. and Robert N. Lynch, eds., pp. 69-108.
        Westport, Conn.:   Greenwood Press.

Lubbock, John (Lord Avebury)
1913   Prehistoric times as illustrated by ancient
        remains and the manners and customs of mod-
        ern savages. 7th ed., revised. London:
        Williams and Norgate. (1st ed., 1865).

Marees, Pieter de
1912   Beschryvinghe ende historische verhael van
        het Gout Koninckrijck van Gunea anders de
        Gout-Custe de Mina genaemt Liggende in het
        deel van Africa. 's-Gravenhage: Martinus
        Nijhoff. (First published in 1602).

Meyerowitz, Eva
1958   The Akan of Ghana: their ancient beliefs.
        London: Faber and Faber.

Müller, Wilhelm Johann
1673   Die Africanische auf der Guineischen Gold-
        Cüst gelegene Landschafft Fetu, Wahrhafftig
        und fleissig aus eigener acht-jahriger
        Erfahrung, genauer Besichtigung und unabläs-
        siger Erforschung beschrieben, auch mit
        dienlichen Kupffern und einem Fetuischen
        Worterbuche geziehret. Hamburg: Michael
        Pfeiffer.

132

Petiver, James
    1697   A catalogue of some Guinea-Plants, with
            their native names and virtues; sent to
            James Petiver, Apothecary, and Fellow of the
            Royal Society; with his remarks on them.
            Philosophical Transactions [of the Royal So-
            ciety of London] 19:677-686.

Richards, Paul
    1975   'Alternative' strategies for the African en-
            vironment: 'Folk ecology', as a basis for
            community oriented agricultural development1
            In African Environment: problems and per-
            spectives, Paul Richards, ed., pp. 102-114.
            London: International African Institute.

Rosenfeld, Gerry
    1971   "Shut those thick lips!" A study of slum
            school failure. New York: Holt, Rinehart,
            and Winston.

Shuey, A. M.
    1966   The testing of Negro intelligence. New York:
            Social Science Press.

Spencer, Herbert
    1877   The principles of sociology. Vol. I. New
            York: D. Appleton and Co.

Tait, David
    1953   Akan traditions of origin. Man 53(10):11-12.

    1955   History and social organization. Transac-
            tions of the Gold Coast and Togoland His-
            torical Society 1(5):193-210.

Tedlie, Henry
    1819   Materia medica and diseases. In Mission
            from Cape Coast Castle to Ashantee, with a
            statistical account of that kingdom, and
            geographical notices of other parts of the
            interior of Africa, by Thomas Edward Bow-
            dich, pp. 370-380. London: John Murray.

Tylor, Sir Edward Burnett
    1871   Primitive culture. London: John Murray.

Warren, Dennis M.
    1970   A re-appraisal of Mrs. Eva Meyerowitz's work
            on the Brong. Research Review (University
            of Ghana) 7(1):53-76.

1974   Disease, medicine, and religion among the Bono of Ghana: a study in culture change. Ph.D. dissertation. Bloomington: Department of Anthropology, Indiana University.

1975a   Epistemology and development: perspectives derived from the Bono studies in Ghana. Paper presented at the African Studies Association annual meeting, San Francisco.

1975b   The role of emic analyses in medical anthropology. Anthropological Linguistics 17(3): 117-126.

1975c   The Techiman-Bono of Ghana: an ethnography of an Akan society. Dubuque: Kendall-Hunt Publishing Co.

1976a   Bibliography and vocabulary of the Akan (Twi-Fante) Language of Ghana. Bloomington: Indiana University Publications.

1976b   Ethnoscience in rural development. In Proceedings of the West Africa Conference on Natural Resources Management in Arid Regions, pp. 177-189. Tucson: The University of Arizona.

1976c   Indigenous knowledge systems for activating local decision-making groups in rural development. In Communication for group transformation in development, pp. 307-329. Honolulu: The East-West Center.

1976d   The use and misuse of ethnohistorical data in the reconstruction of Techiman-Bono (Ghana) history. Paper presented at the American Society for Ethnohistory annual meeting, Albuquerque.

Warren, Dennis M. and Joseph Kweku Andrews
1977   An ethnoscientific approach to Akan arts and aesthetics. Working papers in the traditional arts, No. 3:1-42.

Warren, Dennis M. and K. O. Brempong
1974a   Techiman Traditional State; part I; stool and town histories. Legon: Institute of African Studies, University of Ghana. (vol. I of three vols. for part I).

134

1974b   Techiman Traditional State; part II; deity histories. Legon: Institute of African Studies, University of Ghana. (vol. I of three vols. for part II).

Warren, Dennis M., G. E. Klonglan, G. M. Beal, et. al.
1975   Active indigenous involvement in rural development and nonformal education: a collaborative model for human resources development. Mimeographed. Ames: Department of Sociology and Anthropology, Iowa State University.

Warren, Dennis M. and Peter Meehan
1977   Applied ethnoscience and a dialogical approach to rural development. Anthropology and Humanism Quarterly 2(1):14-16.

Wilks, Ivor
1962   The Mande loal element in Twi. Ghana Notes and Queries No. 4:26-28.

1975   Asante in the nineteenth century: the structure and evolution of a political order. London: Cambridge University Press.

World Bank
1975   The assault on world poverty: problems of rural development, education, and health. Baltimore: The Johns Hopkins University Press.

CULTURAL FREEDOM AND CONSCIENTIZATION
AS SOCIO-ECONOMIC CHANGE FACTORS

Ronald J. Duncan
Inter American University

For many years David Bidney used anthropology to
talk about freedom. The value of his work comes into
perspective when this concept of cultural freedom is
compared with the work of Paulo Freire on socio-economic change in Third World countries. His The Concept
of Freedom in Anthropology (1963) and Freire's Cultural
Action for Freedom (1970a) and Pedagogy of the Oppressed
(1970b) have the common proposition that formal social
change efforts need not be oriented at "developing" the
people themselves but should be oriented toward removing
the barriers that prevent people from producing autochthonous change that is self-generated and culturally
relevant.

Cultural Freedom and Anthropology.

Breaking with cultural determinists, Bidney developed a theory of culture that included human freedom.
He posed the problem of culture and freedom in the
following terms:

Culturally, the struggle for freedom may be
viewed as, in large measure, the struggle for
the removal of arbitrary restrictions and the
extension of the privileges of the minority to
the majority. Progress in freedom always means
new possibilities for the exercise of freedom
through participation in community values and
exploration of new possibilities for action
and enjoyment. (1963:23)

He defines four basic types of human freedom:
natural freedom, cultural freedom, normative freedom,
and metaphysical freedom. They are defined as follows:
"By natural freedom I mean the conscious power to
initiate independent action without coercion or restraint
by some other force." (1963:12) This is an id-like, raw

137

freedom that exists integrally within the action capacity of a person.

"By cultural freedom I refer to the system of historically acquired rights and privileges prescribed on the authority of a given society." (IBID.) In each society acceptable forms of behavior exist. These forms of behavior are arbitrary and changeable; they permit certain kinds of behavior to people and deny others.

"By normative or moral freedom reference is made to action directed by rational ideals and conforming to rational laws or principles...Normative freedom is meta-cultural in the sense that it serves as a model or norm of individual perfection which transcends the requirements of a given culture." (IBID.)

"By metaphysical freedom I refer to the autonomous, sui generis, power of choice and decision of will as irreducible conditions for the exercise of natural, cultural and moral freedom." (IBID.)

Cultural freedom is our focus. When we are interested in social change, we are talking about the freedom of people to alter the arbitrary forms of behavior (i.e. culture) by which individual behavioral systems and social organization are ordered. In every society behavior is arbitrarily formed, permitting the members of that society to perform certain behaviors by denying others. Social change is the process of altering cultural freedom; it is an altering of cultural barriers to permit new alternatives of behavior for people.

Conscientization and Self-generation of Behavioral Modifications.

Freire used the term "conscientization" in a political sense as a process of building consciousness and will to deal with a problem common to the conscientized group. (Freire, 1970a:51) In this article the term "conscientization" is used in a more general behavioral sense as being the cultural process of evaluation of information and the subsequent formulation of action. "Cultural system" is used here to refer to the organization of cultural components known to and used by members of a society, and "cultural process" is used to refer to individual formulations of behaviors in the actual operation of culture.

Normative freedom is the capacity to by-pass the restraints of traditional, arbitrary forms of behavior in favor of new, more desirable alternatives. People push against undesirable restraints in their existing

138

cultural system in a continuous effort to eliminate them.

Agitation for change is stimulated by the discovery of information about existing alternatives. (Bidney, 1963:23) A man who knows more can want more. Substantive information (knowledge that something else exists) and processual information (knowledge of how it can be acquired) are both necessary ingredients for effective social change. Both substantive and processual information may be either true or false, and accordingly can lead to either success or failure in the social change effort.

Information is a key component of cultural freedom. Substantive and processual information can provide the initial stimulus for social change; concrete alterations of the cultural system constitute the realization of that change. This is the mechanism for the self-generation of behavioral modification. The capacity for change is an integral dimension of behavioral systems. Human groups have always had to contend with changing social and physical environments, and forms of behavior have had to change to adjust accordingly. The problem of social change is not one of persuading people to change. Change occurs as a natural expression of every behavioral system. The problem of social change is one of removing barriers to the existing readiness for change.

The traditional idea that people have to be motivated to participate in change has been developed by George Foster in the "image of the limited good", which suggests that peasants cannot effectively participate in social change because of the limitations of their "cognitive orientation." (1967:304f)

In sharp contrast to Foster's conceptualization, black peasants from the Cauca Valley in Colombia conceptualize the reason for their limited participation in the national economy as "denied good." (Duncan, 1974; 1975a; 1975b) According to them, "the problem" was not one of not being able to understand social and economic change or not wanting change, the problem was one of denied access to the resources of the larger society.

Various informants said that the possibilities for participation in social change in their community were inhibited because of systematic denial to them of training programs and non-access to the means of modern agricultural production. They blamed collusion by government and commercial agricultural interests for their situation. (Duncan and Friedemann ms: 187-188) These people are

139

conscious of their problem, and they are convinced of the needed solution. Their conceputalization of the problem is based on little information, so it does not necessarily include all of the elements for a balanced holistic solution. In Freire's terms their conceptualization will be limited by the structure of thought of their class. (1970b:22f)

Conscientization alone cannot produce social change. It must be linked with other facilitating elements in the larger political and economic system. However, the existence of possibilities for change without conscientization is not sufficient to produce change. Both are integral to change.

Conscientization and Formal Social Change.

There are two key dimensions of conscientization as a part of formal social change. One is the elaboration of the information delivery system to "free-up" and facilitate a more rapid turn around between people's felt needs for social change (normative freedom) and the concrete information needed to set in motion the processes to realize that change (cultural freedom). The second dimension is the need that information be available to many people simultaneously. Then, as each individual makes his or her interpretation of that information and adjusts his or her own behavioral system, the individual can be simultaneously adjusting to the same process going on in other individuals. In that way, the behavioral modification of each individual will be socially relevant and will for a longer period of time be viable in the boiler of social and ecological demands.

Freire's concept of conscientization refers to both dimensions mentioned here. His definition is, "Conscientization refers to the process in which men, not as recipients, but as knowing subjects, achieve a deepening awareness both of the socio-cultural reality which shapes their lives and of their capacity to transform that reality." (1970a:51)

The concept of cultural constraints on the decision-making process as used in this article is formulated by Freire as the "culture of silence." He says, "The fact is that the 'culture of silence' is born in the relationship between the Third World and the metropolis. It is not the dominator who constructs a culture and imposes it on the dominated. This culture is the result of the structural relations between the dominated and the dominators." (1970a:57f)

Peasant communities are dependent communities and in their role as receptors of rural development efforts in the 1970's they are once again in a dependent status. In commenting on the dependency of peasants Redfield said, "The culture of a peasant community...is not autonomous. It is an aspect or dimension of the civilization of which it is a part. As the peasant society is a half-society, so the peasant culture is a half-culture." (1956:40)

Peasants live in a "half-culture", a "culture of silence". That means that peasants have formulated their arbitrary forms of behavior (culture) in a dependent or subordinant status and that those forms of behavior are structured by the demands and restrictions of the stronger urban or metropolitan society. Members of the urban society have the cultural momentum and cultural leadership and have the dominant roles in relationships with members of peasant communities. Both urban and peasant people are frequently unaware of this unconscious structuring of their behavior. (Bidney 1963:23)

Conscientization is the process of elaborating critical consciousness of the structural factors in society and culture that influence the formation of behavior. The elaboration of critical consciousness requires augmenting the available information in a social context. As the concerned people contribute to the interpretation and analysis of that information, socially correct and acceptable interpretations should emerge. These new interpretations do not change anything in and of themselves, but they provide the bases for the actual realization of change.

Conscientization is a process of expanding the information base of the group in a context of mutual evaluation and interpretation of the new information. Any media can be used in this communication process although visual communication is frequently used with non-literate groups, including photography (LaBelle 1975:22) and film (Duncan 1975b). Conscientization must be an unrestrained process, free of control from the dominant, urban culture; it is a process in which equal collaboration exists between the urban and peasant halves of the society.

Conscientization is the process of adjustment of the arbitrary forms of interpretation of what can be done and what cannot be done in society; it is the reprogramming of cognition; it is a re-adjustment of the arbitrary terms of cultural freedom for the group of affected people.

At the same time that the cognition is being repro-

141

grammed, the program is being made up. There can be no
abstract programming process separate from the adjustment
process. Reinterpretation of what can and cannot be done
culturally are constantly being checked with the interpretations of other people and being cross-checked within
the individual's cognitive system with other items of
information. Cognition works by ingesting many separate
items of information and restructuring itself by accepting
those that work and rejecting the others.

    In this way a focus gradually emerges. Conscienti-
zation leads to specific content foci in the reinterpretation of cultural freedom. The peasant decides his new set
of rules for what can be done and what cannot be done,
and in this way the form of the new cultural freedom is
established. As Freire suggests,

> The fundamental role of those committed to
> cultural action for conscientization is not
> properly speaking to fabricate the liberating
> idea, but to invite the people to grasp with
> their minds the truth of their reality...
> Consistent with this spirit of knowing, scien-
> tific knowledge cannot be knowledge that is
> merely transmitted, for it would itself be-
> come ideological myth, even if it were trans-
> mitted with the intention of liberating men.
> (1970a:76f)

    That is to say that in the process of conscientization,
peasants should participate in the formulation of the content of formal social change. Without conscientization
two fallacies may develop in formal social change. One
that has been mentioned previously is the imposition of
scientific or political plans by representatives of the
dominant society that are not applicable to the local
community. The imposition of such plans by the dominant
society might come from either the left or the right.
Imposition from the outside is a fallacy in the social
change process; the suggested changes will have less
relevance to the local people and be less useable for
them.

    The second fallacy is that without conscientization
a peasant will evaluate formal social change in terms of
short term personal gain without consideration of the
wider social or time frameworks. Working in a southern
Italian rural community, Banfield formulated the local
rules of behavior. He found the general rule to be,
"Maximize the material, short-run advantage of the nuclear
family; assume that all others will do likewise." (1958:83)

One of the specific examples is, "In a society of amoral familists; no one will further the interest of the group or community except as it is to his private advantage to do so." (IBID.)

Freire also suggests that without conscientization the peasant will continue utilizing traditional cognitive structures that reflect the dominant-dependent structure in which he lives. That means reacting in terms of immediate, personal gain. Freire's conceptualization of this process is:

> But almost always, during the initial stage of the struggle, the oppressed, instead of striving for liberation, tend themselves to become oppressors, or 'sub-oppressors'. The very structure of their thought has been conditioned by the contradictions of the concrete, existential situation by which they were shaped. Their ideal is to be a man; but for them, to be a 'man' is to be an oppressor.
> (1970b:22)

In summary, conscientization includes the elaboration of the information delivery system to "free up" and facilitate a more rapid turn around between people's felt needs for social change (normative freedom) and the concrete information needed to set in motion the process to realize that change (cultural freedom). It is also necessary that that information be socially available to many people at the same time so that as each individual makes his interpretation of the information, and as he makes cognitive adjustment in his own behavioral system to that information, it will be simultaneously adjusted to the same process going on in other individuals.

Critical self consciousness of cultural restraints on the social change process is important for social change professionals. Office-based planning for social change may be an exercise that only incidentally relates to the real people of the local community. Formal social change can be realized more effectively if the dominance of the traditional heirarchical social structure is minimized to permit participation of local people in the decision-making processes that affect their future well-being.

In social change programs, representatives of both halves of the urban-peasant society confront each other with their conflicting cognitive frameworks. Professionals are culturally prepared to represent and perpetuate the dominant social, economic, and cultural systems. That

143

behavioral baggage complicates interaction with peasants in the way necessary to realize formal social change. Professionals should adjust the restraints of their own cultural freedom to permit effective participation for peasants and to accept them as being culturally integral to the overall analysis of the peasant situation. (Stavenhagen 1971:337)

Conscientization and cultural freedom.

Conscientization is the process by which information about new possibilities is introduced into the behavioral system, in other words the process by which culture freedom is adjusted. It is the process of deciding the cultural freedoms that are acceptable to a group. Knowledge is one element of freedom, and freedom means power to create some kinds of changes.

Bidney's use of the concept of cultural freedom is very close to Freire's concepts of conscientization and liberation. Both Bidney and Freire are seeking a humanistic explanation for human alternatives for social change. As their concepts are used to evaluate formal social change programs, it becomes clear that such programs are more effective in maintaining the present socio-economic system that facilitating freedom for change.

Bidney, like Freire, suggests that the participants in the social change process can best make the decisions about how social change is to affect them; conscientization leads to cultural freedom. Bidney is convinced of the basic value and inevitability of freedom as a factor in social change. He says,

"I am convinced...that the concept of freedom is not ethnocentric in principle, and that it is one of the great and enduring values of the contemporary world, with cross-cultural validity and application. The people of the world have now become conscious of their own power and of their natural right to participate in all that is highest and best in the cultural achievements of mankind." (1967:xxxv)

144

REFERENCES

Banfield, Edward
1958. The Moral Basis of a Backward Society. New York:
The Free Press.

Bidney, David
1963. The Concept of Freedom in Anthropology. The Hague:
Mouton and Co.
1967. Theoretical Anthropology. Second, augmented
edition. New York: Schocken Books.

Duncan, Ronald J.
1974. Villarrica: an anthropological diagnostic of
social change. Manuscript. Cali, Colombia:
Universidad del Valle. 142 pages.
1975a. Comment. On Image of Limited Good, or Expectation
of Reciprocity? By James R. Gregory. Current
Anthropology. Vol. 16,No. 1, March,1975.Page 86.
1975b. Anthropological Film as Conscientization Film.
Conference on Culture and Communication. Temple
University. March, 1975. 14 pages.

Duncan, Ronald J.& Nina S. Friedemann.
Ms. Villarrica: Cana y Proletariado Rural en
Colombia. 230 pages.

Foster, George
1967. Peasant Society and the Image of the Limited Good.
in Peasant Society. Jack M. Potter,et.al., editors.
Boston: Little, Brown and Company. Pages 300-323.

Freire, Paulo
1970a. Cultural Action for Freedom. Middlesex,England:
Penguin Books, Ltd.
1970b. Pedagogy of the Oppressed. Middlesex, England:
Penguin Books, Ltd.

La Belle, Thomas J.
1975. Liberation, Development, and Rural Nonformal Education. In Council on Anthropology and Education
Quarterly. Vol. VI, No. 4, pages 20-26.

Mead, Margaret
1964. Review. Of The Concept of Freedom in Anthropology.
American Anthropologist, Vol. LXVI,pages 1402-3.

Redfield, Robert
1956. The Little Community. Chicago: Phoenix Books.

Stavenhagen, Rudolfo
1971. Decolonializing Applied Social Sciences. Human
Organization. Vol. 30, Number 4, pages 333-344.

PUBLIC TERRITORY - HOME TERRITORY
PLANNING AND REALITY IN PERI-URBAN DAR ES SALAAM

Edwin S. Segal
University of Louisville

This paper is concerned with the planning and implementation
of social change. It draws on observations made during 1973-74
in the peri-urban area of Dar es Salaam, Tanzania, and focuses on
the relationship between the initial, formal plans for a residential community and the actual community based on those plans.
The data presented here reflect two types of adaptations: 1) North
American techniques are applied by Tanzanians to a Tanzanian
context, a fairly deliberate process; 2) The people of the community, by virtue of the ordinary activities of their daily lives,
modify and reorder their environment, a less self-conscious process. These observations have implications for both future planning efforts, and for humanistically oriented anthropology.

In this paper I have restricted my attentions to physical
structures and their spatial arrangements. This was done largely
because territoriality is a dimension of human life whose literature has a high noise to signal ratio. Yet, on one level, human
life is, at base, a matter of exerting control over the space in
which living occurs.

When we talk of the conditions of life, or definitions of
human value, one important, but largely neglected, source of information is the ways in which people arrange themselves in space.
If anthropology and anthropologists are to make meaningful contributions to the betterment of human life styles and life
chances, we need to know something about the impact of such
efforts on the infra-structural aspects of human cultures.

Frames of Reference

Territoriality

All behavior requires an appropriate setting. Proper spatial
loci are often crucial for defining the propriety of particular
behaviors. Definition and control of territory involves both
creation of boundaries and their closure (Lyman and Scott 1970).

147

Boundaries, by their very existence, imply access restrictions. Examination of who is granted access to a particular territory, and for what purposes, reveals the extent to which these creations of human activity reflect a variety of cultural values. This is most clearly seen in the use of special sites for special events (Kuper 1972). War memorials, convention centers, school campuses, synagogues are all clear instances of norms, values, and beliefs expressed by territorial boundaries.

There is no sound theoretical reason for assuming that only special sites physically manifest these non-material cultural facets. House forms are physical devices perpetuating and facilitating expression of norms and values. These structures are condensed, visible embodiments of the "relative importance attached to different aspects of life and the varying ways of perceiving reality" (Rapoport 1969:47).

Houses, house forms, and their spatial arrangement are commonplace parts of any society. The basic perspective of this paper assumes that the ordinary houses people live in, the ways they are arranged in space, and the ways in which spaces not physically occupied by houses are divided into public and home territories form a condensed physical expression of a culture's norms and values.

Territories are defined by their boundaries. Any particular territory also has its own special features. Roughly, these can be referred to as being fixed, semi-fixed, or informal (Hall 1966). Fixed features are those regarded as unchangeable and unmovable; semi-fixed features are actually movable, but usually treated as fixed; informal features are (as with informal norms) those features for which there are no overtly stated boundaries.

The inhabitants of contemporary Western residential areas tend to treat the layout of house plots and roads as fixed features. This is congruent with the formal and informal cognitions of the residents. The fixed plot boundaries are often manifested in the erection of hedges, children's play patterns and in the ways in which sub-urban lawns are mowed.

On the other hand, the fixity of the boundary between home and public territories is considerably less in the United States than in some other European cultures. This is most especially true of the boundary between a front yard and the public sidewalk. The suburban front yard is often unfenced and easily invaded, without any apparent threat, by a number of temporary and permanent residents. Mail and newspaper carriers, children,and others cut across front yards with impunity. The spatial threshold, analogous to the various distance limits defined by Hall (1966), is that point for which one needs permission to cross.

148

In the suburban United States it stands at the physical house threshold. In the similar English residential area it tends to be some distance from the house itself, marked by an actual fence (Rapoport 1969). These differences exist in spite of the fact that in both cases formal legal control over the area in question belongs to the householder. The feature, the boundary, is fixed, but to the extent that it is violable, it is also movable.

In the United States there is a maxim about knocking before entering. In Tanzania, people call "hodi" three times while ·approaching the house. The approach begins at about ten yards and ends no closer than one to one and a half yards, a clearly perceived, but usually unmarked, threshold.

Socialization and Behavior

A second important frame of reference for this paper centers on modes of behavior and the ways in which they are learned. Spatial arrangements are created by deliberate, as well as less conscious, activities. Distinctions among types of behavior and the ways in which they are learned add a significant dimension to understanding some aspects of this case study.

Behavior can be seen as falling into one of three modes: formal, informal and technical (Hall 1959). Formal modes are learned by precept, by deliberate teaching. Informal modes are learned by modeling and imitation. Technical modes are also learned by overt teaching, but the difference is that where formal modes are primarily concerned with explanatory norms (why a thing ought to be done), technical patterns are concerned with instrumental norms (how a thing ought to be done).

Planning activity is almost entirely technical, while the initial implementation of plans, at least as observed in this instance, takes place on both formal and technical levels. Secondarily, though no less important, creating a reality from the plans also involves informal modes of behavior. I have called the informal mode secondary on the grounds that it is manifested in a temporally secondary position. Only after plans are laid and houses are built can people live in them and create interactional networks of residents and spatial modifications.

A good portion, if not all, of these modes of expression are first learned in ways that may also be termed informal (Hall 1959: 73-74). Developing through imitation of everyday models, they come to constitute internalized patterns that exist (to borrow Hall's phrasing) out-of-awareness. One simply comes to expect that houses will have a particular shape, that people will respect the often unmarked, but well-known, boundaries between

149

public and home territories.

Any technical activity is informed by the formal and informal norms of the cultural tradition of which it is a part. In the international world of development planning the technical activities are often derived from one culture's patterns. The implementation of the technical planning then takes place in a different culture. The "clash of cultures" that results is most often a confrontation between a set of technical norms on one side and a different set of formal and informal norms on the other.

People moving through their living space do not consciously plan to do so as an expression of a particular normative order. That people can, at times, derive this structure from their own material remains is amply demonstrated by Griaule's studies of the Dogon (1956). However, deducing symbolic systems solely from material remains is hazardous. The problem is especially acute in the archaeological context (Douglas 1963), but is also serious in more contemporary settings.

The patterns of social life that constitute the informal domain have something of a ritual nature. They become most visible when the rituals are disrupted; tacit conventions become overt under conditions of crisis and perceived social breakdown (Harré 1970). In the contemporary world other conditions also disrupt social liturgies. Planned development (sometimes called modernization) is a primary source of such disruption.

The Data

The data discussed here deal with a planned residential area and the modifications made in those plans by the inhabitants. None of the modifications result from conscious communal, or individual, decisions. They are part of a general process of converting normally designated public territory into home territories of various sorts. In this sense these data refer to creation, closure and maintenance of boundaries; that is, territorial control.

The site for the study is a small peri-urban residential section of Dar es Salaam, Tanzania, known as Block 45. This area lies between two larger ones, Kijitonyama and Mwananymala. Kijitonyama is Area 16 of the Dar es Salaam Master Plan, and is totally surveyed and laid out. The original drawings were done by Project Planning Associates of Toronto in 1968. Mwananymala is an older area, apparently partially the result of uncontrolled urban settlement. No dates are available for development of the original plans.

150

The exact formal status of Block 45 is not clear. The Ministry of Water Development and Power considers it a part of Mwananymala. Both the residents and TANESCO (Tanzania Electric Supply Corporation) consider it a part of Kijitonyama. This confusion of formal identity leaves the residents of Block 45 free to develop independent community structures, unconstrained by the demands or requirements of either adjacent area, or government agencies.

The area was totally surveyed and laid out some time between 1968 and 70. The layout was not prepared by Project Planning Associates, but some of the planning criteria they set out in the Master Plan seem to have been utilized in Block 45.

The plans are the result of a transfer of technical norms from the originating technicians to a second set of technicians. Since the first group was composed of external consultants, their knowledge of Dar es Salaam and its environs was almost entirely technical. The second group, the personnel of the Dar es Salaam Town Planning Office, applied a set of cultural filters (based in part on formal and informal norms) to the selection of criteria used in their preparation.

Block 45 lies about 8 kilometers from the city center, along Bagamoyo Road. It is across the street from the Village Museum and a graveyard complex (German and British war graves, Ismalia and Hindu cemetaries). It is bound on the east by the road and on the west by a proposed park, as well as part of the Mwanaymala residential area. The northern boundary is Block 44 of Kijitonyama and the southern border is Mwananynala A, as well as some upper income housing along Bagamoyo Road.

The original drawings (Figure 1) divided Block 45 into three sub-blocks: a,b, and c. Each has a slightly different character, imparted by the original plans. These lodge primarily in the varying plot sizes and their implications for differences in income level, residential density and the kinds of construction and other uses that can be accommodated by a given piece of land.

Sub-block b contains the largest plots, averaging 2,604 square meters. Sub-block c contains both the smallest plots, averaging 372 square meters, and the largest number of them (over 400). Sub-block a contains plots averaging 744 square meters.

During the eight months of the study, Block 45 was the scene of continuous activity: expansion of agricultural land, clearing of land for other purposes, house construction, fence and hedge construction, and all the other ordinary activities of daily life. The data for this study consist of observations of these events and of the daily movements of people through the area.

151

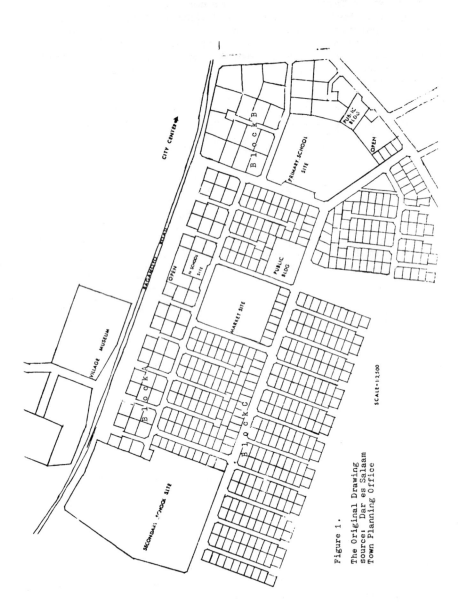

Figure 1.

The Original Drawing
source: Dar es Salaam
Town Planning Office

152

Most of the houses in Block 45 are single family dwellings; the
area's population is approximately 2,500.

In the following, reference is made to hedges, bush land
and shamba (garden) land. Hedges, as a category, take in fully
grown hedges, those that are partially grown, or are just being
started, as well as various kinds of wood or wire fences. All
land not under active use has been considered here as bush land.
No distinction is made between dense overgrowth, light overgrowth, and the relatively open grassy spaces that occur. The
only shamba land specifically considered here is that outside of
occupied house plots. Most people in Block 45 who have the room
on their own land also turn some of it to agricultural purposes,
raising everything from cassava to bananas and papayas.

Block 45 represents a clash between the planners' technical
vision of appropriate spatial arrangements and the more informal
one produced by the activities of daily life. The plans present
a physical structure quite different from that created by the
people. The original plans provided for house plots and roads,
as well as special use areas. If any provision for sidewalks or
other boundary devices was made, it was included, unmarked, in
the projected road beds. Since most people in Dar es Salaam
do not own automobiles, it is not surprising that a residential
area should be planned without specific attention to special
pedestrian paths. However, their absence gives the residents
almost total responsibility for defining their own boundaries.
The only formal ones are surveyor's markers placed at plot
corners.

In the absence of formally defined and demarcated boundaries, residential redefinition of both land use and control constitute an illustration of the degree to which the planners'
cognitions were at variance with the cognitions of those for
whom they planned.

Several techinical aspects of both land tenure and house
construction in Dar es Salaam form a significant backdrop to
the process of boundary closure, as it was observed. All land
is owned by the state. A person wishing to erect a house
applies to the Ministry of Lands, Housing and Urban Development for a plot. The assignment is accomplished by granting
long term rights of occupancy on a first come, first serve basis.

The first step in house construction is to mark out the
assigned plot boundaries. This is usually done by stretching
a cord between each of the existing corner markers placed by
the surveyors. Houses are then constructed in a more or less
central location.

Up to this point it is clear the potential resident views

153

a particular plot as being as much a fixed feature as did the planners. However, after a house is built and its occupants become part of the settlement, different patterns emerge. This is also true in regard to those areas designated by the planners as fixed feature public spaces,e.g.: open land, school, and market sites, and road beds.

These variations appear in two major areas, the arrangement of roads and the use of land not formally designated as someone's literal home territory. The roads indicated on the original drawing (Figure 2) were never actually constructed in their full planned width, and in some cases, not formally constructed at all. The planned roads are of three widths, 9.15 meters (30 feet), 12.2 meters (40 feet) and 18.3 meters (60 feet). Their arrangement and widths indicate a vision of traffic patterns whose major component is vehicular, flowing around Block 45, with secondary streams going through it, and tertiary ones going into it.

The roads and paths actually created by the movements of people and cars partially follow the layout, indicating the extent to which fixed feature planning can constrain and direct movement. They also deviate from the plans, indicating informally expressed needs and cognitions not dealt with by the technical planning. Taking the roads and paths by themselves, the most salient features of life in peri-urban areas ignored by the planning are: most people living in Dar es Salaam do not have continuing access to cars, generally do not utilize peripheral traffic patterns, and do not have the same view of land tenure and the fixity of boundaries.

All of this is most concisely summed up in the creation of roads and paths facilitating a through traffic pattern, one which closely corresponds to that found in areas of spontaneous housing (Segal 1974) as well as more traditional coastal villages (Georgulas 1967). This is even more obvious since many of the paths and roads cut across someone's assigned plot.

The roads and paths constituting the major traffic arteries (Figure 3) are, with one exception, those designed as medial in width, and with no exceptions the major roads are those roughly perpendicular to Bagamoyo Road, the link with the city proper. Even where the original road did not go entirely through the settlement, it now does so. This spatial orientation toward the major highway is mirrored in the orientations of individual houses, which with few exceptions, face a road or path.

The planned road structure seems to have been designed to avoid contact between residents as they _drive_ from house to road. On the other hand, people in Block 45 socialize with their neigh-

154

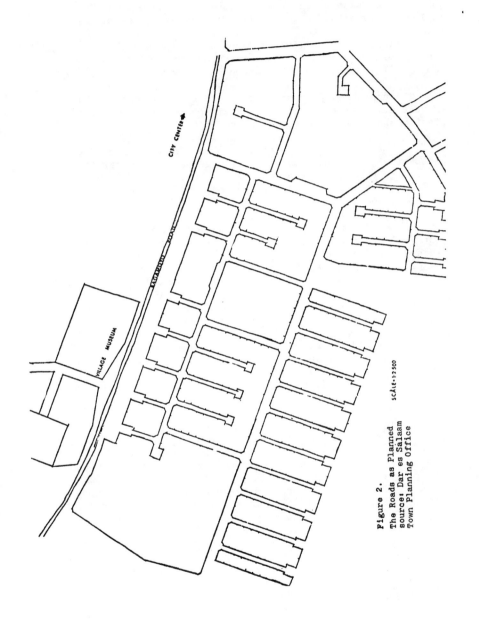

Figure 2.
The Roads as Planned
source: Dar es Salaam
Town Planning Office

bors, often _walking_ in groups, as they go to the bus stop, or just the roadside to catch a ride, or to walk to work. Interestingly, even the vehicular traffic follows these patterns.

Vehicular traffic follows the lead of pedestrian traffic, but the planning seems to have assumed that pedestrian movements would conform to the planned car flows.

The unplanned footpaths are perfect evocations of values expressed in spatial terms. They are patterned, spontaneous creations of the inhabitants of the area.

The original plans contained no provisions for specific pedestrian paths that could not also be used for cars. In addition , the original plans divide the area into five clearly demarcated subregions. One is sub-block 45b and three make up sub-block 45c.

Blocks 45a and 45b have, on the average, relatively large plots (744 and 2,604 square meters, respectively). The density planned for block 45c is approximately twice that of 45a, and the plots are arranged in units of from eighteen to twenty plots. Visual examination of the planned layout makes it clear that easy pedestrian access of one resident to another is severly restricted, especially if we assume, as the planners seem to have done, the fixity of plot lines.

However, the pattern of existing paths (Figure 4) tends to split these long blocks into smaller ones, and to increase the access of one plot to another. This pattern, while distinct from the original plans, is still somewhat constrained by them.

If the paths are taken as indicators of sub-unit boundaries and the same is said for the planned roads, then it becomes clear that the planners had little idea of the size of the sub-units within which most house-centered interaction would take place. Ironically, had the original plans been drawn so as to place minor boundaries between units approximating a TANU 10-cell, they would have come considerably closer to the spontaneously created arrangement as it existed in 1973-74.

The original plans for this small area divided it into three distinct kinds of territory: special purpose public, general purpose public, and home territories. Since the expected special uses (i.e., schools, public buildings, and a market) have not been implemented, all the public territory has, by default, become general purpose.

By creating their own roads and paths the residents, es-

156

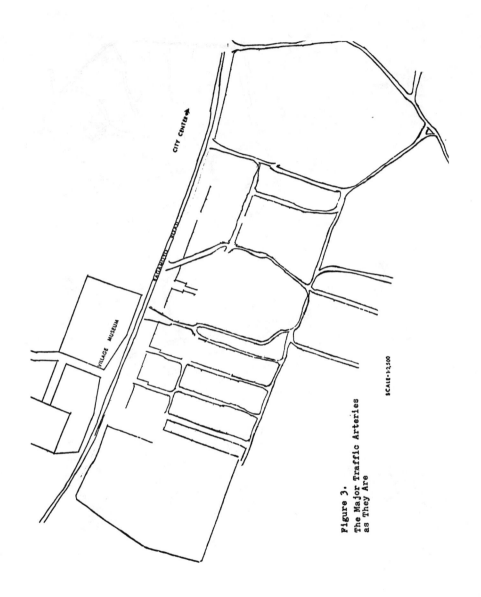

Figure 3.
The Major Traffic Arteries
as They Are

157

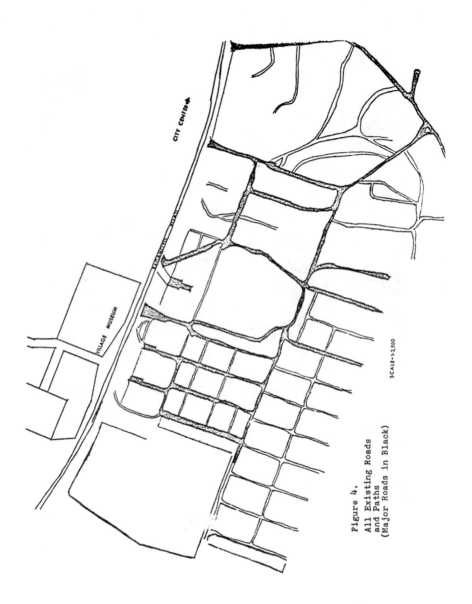

Figure 4.
All Existing Roads
and Paths
(Major Roads in Black)

SCALE·1:2,500

CITY CENTER

VILLAGE MUSEUM

pecially those of Block 45c, converted sections of formally
planned home territory into de facto public territory. They
also converted some public territory into home territory. This
was accomplished largely through erection of hedges and plant-
ing mashamba (gardens).

The extent to which the inhabitants of Block 45a and 45b
did not restructure the planned layout seems related to several
factors. Primary seems to be the relatively larger plot sizes.
It is not so much the plot size per se that seems to be significant as it is the implications of larger plots for the economic
level of the people who are likely to live there.

Larger plot means higher ground rents. This, of course,
means that in spite of the government's policy of awarding
rights of occupancy without regard to economic level, only
relatively wealthier people will be able to afford these plots.
In addition, these larger plots are already arranged into
groups of smaller sub-units. The modifications occuring in
Block 45c have already been built into other areas.

Finally, the generally higher economic level of the residents of Blocks 45a and 45b is reflected in larger houses, the
greater extent of electrification and indoor running water.
There also seems to be an association with a greater tendency
toward separating one home territory from another, indicated
by the fact that virtually all the plots in 45a and 45b were
fenced.

On the other hand, even where paths have divided large
house groupings into smaller ones in Block 45c, there is
little of this kind of boundary creation. Essentially, it
seems that the combination of small plots and minor boundaries
is sufficient to create small groups of interacting neighbors.

Summary and Discussion

The data reported here do not constitute a complete description of even this aspect of Block 45. However, they are
sufficient for delineating some potential directions for humanistically oriented applied anthropology.

Other animals occasionally engage in behavior that may
have repercussions leading to extinction. Human beings are
capable of foreseeing (guessing) such possibilities and taking
action to change the course of events. It is incumbent on
those who have the requisite knowledge to participate in the
process of consciously creating the kinds of cultural worlds
in which we wish to live.

Bidney (1967) beginning with a concept of culture stres-

sing the satisfaction of needs and the realization of potential-
ities in relation to ecological environments, arrives at the position that it might be possible, at some point in time, to evaluate particular cultures, determining the extent to which they
genuinely do, or do not, satisfy the needs and aspirations of
their participants. This evaluative potential is fraught with
ethical, as well as practical, problems.

One of the lessons of the large body of literature falling
under one form or another of the rubric, ethnoscience, is that
each cultural universe is different from each other, in spite
of common humanity. This means that definitions of goals, needs
and aspirations in themselves differ. This line of argument
leads to a worldview stressing the uniqueness of all cultural
groups and the impossibility of any general prescriptions for
directed change.

By recognizing that anthropologists are also culture
bearers, Bidney's position also leads in the direction of asserting the significance of anthropological activity in the universe
of interacting cultural worlds. He suggests that the anthropologist...
> may make significant contributions to contem-
> porary societies by suggesting new ideals and goals
> of culture, new utopias for the realization of pos-
> sible cultural alternatives not found anywhere at
> present (1967:xl).

That is, the anthropologist becomes a mover, participant and innovator in the process of cultural evolution and change.

One of the characteristics of the contemporary world is to
be found in the large number of professionals involved in the
process of development planning, modernization direction, or some
similar activity. Often these activities take place without
close attention to what already exists. Planning often ignores
the cultural and infra-cultural contexts within which it is supposed to occur. It is precisely at this point that the anthropologist's special expertise is most relevant.

More than building new worlds and utopias, which are being
built with or without the anthropologist's participation, there
is a vital function of bridging the gap between the new cultural order and the past. People faced with changing conditions
often seem to feel that they must make a polar choice: to move
to the city or stay in the country, to accept a government program or reject it, to be modern or traditional. These choices
are such that whatever decision is made, a certain level of
anomie and dissonance is bound to result. The urban migrant
finds, in addition to many benefits, unemployment, underemploy-
ment, and commodity shortages. Government programs bring both

160

benefits and taxes. Modern is the new way, and it is good, but the traditional ways are comfortable and predictable. One vital role of the anthropologist is centered on ensuring that transitions will be made with a minimum of cultural disruption and distortion.

Tradition is powerful; it provides a sense of continuity and meaning. This is crucial when a people is faced with the invasion of ideas and artifacts from another culture. The dominant tendency in the contemporary world has been in the direction of an increase in societal scale (Wilson and Wilson 1945). By and large this has taken the form of increased interactions between peoples, and among members of a larger world community. Chagga coffee growers in Tanzania, as participants in a contemporary cash crop system, are in direct contact, via networks of transportation and communication, with people well beyond the traditional (roughly 19th century) range. Indirectly, via these commercial activities, they are in contact with the rest of the world. Programs and policies seeking to enhance their capability for achieving their goals must be cast in terms meaningful to them.

The literature on development programs is instructive in this regard. In discussing the Farmech project in Lesotho in the early 60's Wallman (1969) notes that after a great deal of trial and error, misunderstanding and mistrust, the project finally proved to be partially successful because it found a familiar cultural pattern to use as its base.

The project was meant to introduce mechanized agricultural techniques, a goal described by both the planners and their clients. The stumbling point was the need to develop a means for controlling the distribution of a limited number of tractors and of assessing charges for their use. Not until charges were based on criteria familiar to the Sotho did the project begin to show some success. In this case, the people were not willing to put up with the disruption and loss of cultural autonomy that would have resulted from adopting alien and poorly understood standards of measurements.

While dealing with housing programs in Ibadan, Onibokun makes the point even more strongly.

> The importance of local sociocultural issues... suggests that any policies and programs formulated for dealing with housing and social problems in the emerging nations can only be effective if these policies and programs are sensitive to the historical and cultural character of the city concerned. ... it is 'intellectually inadequate

161

and strategical'/ fatal' to assume that
solutions +ↄ urban problems in one continent or city can be exported without change
to another continent or city. The problems
of a city are the products of the culture
and heritage of its inhabitants (1970:138).

Although Onibokun's perspective is urban, as is my own in this
paper, this warning also has relevance well beyond urbanization.

The anthropologist's expertise and training are suited to a
guidance role that takes account of precisely these factors. A
certain level of disruption occurs during any period of socio-
cultural change, but it can be minimized; too many development
projects go wrong, or at the least, astray.

The general lessons for applied anthropology are clear. If
we are to participate, even in a small way, in Bidney's vision of
the creation of new cultural systems, it is necessary to build
these new alternatives on existing bases. Planned progra- that
ignore cultural and infra-cultural variables like the social construction of space will be modified by the people so th . they
will fit into the cultural world in which they exist.

In the case discussed here, the observed modifications have
not seriously damaged the initial goal, providing adequate housing. This is largely the result of the partial coincidence of
traditional coastal village patterns and the planned layout.
However, if a similar layout is used in an area with a radically
different sense of village spatial organization, the end result
may not be so salutory. Some of the dimensions of this problem
are suggested, for a rural context, by Brain's (1967) description
of the Tanzanian village of Bwakira Chini. Interaction between
planners and those for whom they plan is crucial for the success
of any program of directed change. Especially important in this
regard is the need to be aware of the informal normative and value patterns of those whose needs are being met.

In some ways, the materials presented here fit a variant of
the general distinction between emic and etic approaches to culture. However, that framework tends to oversimplify the dynamics
of what has actually occurred. The general consensus that an
etic approach is associated with external, alien observers and
an emic approach with an insider's view is well summarized in
a recent textbook (Plog and Bates 1976). Emic and etic are taken
as contrasting the anthropologist's and native's views of phenomena.

In the case discussed here, while it is true that Project
Planning Associates can be seen as an external element, their
proposals were more congruent with what happened than were the

162

plans drawn by the Dar es Salaam Town Planning Office. The dynamic is the partial transfer of ~n etic construct, so that it becomes part of the emic consʹ⊥uct of a group whose perspectives then do not fit the emic views of a second group. Both the planners and those for whom they planned are cultural insiders, but with different emic views of the situation.

All of this reduces to the very simple notion that good heart, a sincere desire to help in creating a new utopia, is not enough for successful active planning, and neither is the power to create change by fiat. Involvement with the people and their ways, formal, informal, and technical is central. Without this most development programs will surely go astray. With it, success is not guaranteed, but the probabilities are increased. And no one can ask any more.

FOOTNOTES

1. Research was carried out with the cooperation of the Min-
    istry of Lands, Housing and Urban Development. I wish to
    especially thank Mr. Z.W. Haule, Director, and Mr. R.
    Catchpole, Consultant, both of the Ministry's Planning Unit,
    for invaluable help and support.

164

BIBLIOGRAPHY

Bidney, David
    1967   Theoretical Anthropology, second edition. New York,
           Schocken.

Brain, J.L.
    1967   Patterns of Change and Continuity, Program of East
           African Studies, Occasional Paper No. 27, Syracuse
           University.

Douglas, Mary
    1972   Symbolic Orders in the Use of Domestic Space, in P.J.
           Ucko, et al, Man, Settlement and Urbanism, Cambridge,
           Mass.

Georgulas, N.
    1967   Settlement Patterns and Rural Development in Tangan-
           yika, Program of East African Studies, Occasional
           Paper No. 29, Syracuse University.

Griaule, M.
    1956   Conversations with Ogotemmeli, Oxford University Press

Hall, Edward T.
    1959   The Silent Language. Greenwich, Conn., Fawcett.
    1966   The Hidden Dimension, Garden City, Doubleday.

Harré , R.
    1970   Foreword in Lyman, S.M. and M.B. Scott, A Sociology
           of the Absurd. New York, Appleton-Century Crafts.

Kuper, H.
    1972   The Language of Sites in the Politics of Space.
           American Anthropologist 74, 3, 411-425.

Lyman, S.M. & M.B. Scott
    1970   A Sociology of the Absurd. New York, Appleton-
           Century Crafts.

Onibokun, G.A.
    1970   Sociocultural Constraints on Urban Renewal Policies
           in Emerging Nations: The Ibadan Case. Human Or-
           ganization 29,2,133-139.

165

Plog, F. & D.G. Bates
    1976   Cultural Anthropology.   New York,   Knopf.

Project Planning Associates
    1968   National Capital Master Plan, Dar es Salaam, United
           Republic of Tanzania.   Toronto, Canada.

Rapoport, A.
    1969   House Form and Culture.   Englewood Cliffs, N.J.,
           Prentice & Hall

Segal, E.S.
    1974   Peri-Urban Settlement Patterns: Policy Implications.
           Research report prepared for the Ministry of Lands,
           Housing and Urban Development, Dar es Salaam, Tan-
           zania.

Wallman, Sandra
    1969   The Farmech Mechanization Project, Basutoland
           (Lesotho), in Brokensha, D. and M. Pearsall, The
           Anthropology of Development in Sub-Saharan Africa.
           The Society for Applied Anthropology, Monograph 10,
           14-21.

Wilson, Godfrey and Monica Wilson
    1945   The Analysis of Social Change.   New York, Cambridge
           University Press.

UTOPIAN SOCIETIES AND THE CHARISMATIC INDIVIDUAL

Jon Wagner
Knox College

Anthropologists have long maintained that the self-knowledge of our species required study of the greatest possible range of cultural forms and developments. In actual practice, this principle has often been translated as a directive to study those primitive and traditional societies which the other social sciences and humanities tend to ignore. This substantive specializa'* justifiable though it may be, can create biases ᴧᴨ the anthropological view of cultural phenomena -- precisely the result which the cross-cultural approach was ostensibly designed to avoid.

One result of the focus on traditional societies may be seen in the relative lack of attention given by anthropologists to the visionary aspects of culture change. Studying societies which view life as essentially unchanging and change as inconsequential, societies which typically have achieved relatively stable adaptations to their environments, we see change in a peculiar light. We may view change as something which "normally" occurs by imperceptible increments, moving toward conditions which individual persons never envisioned, much less aspired to. Rapid change, such as that brought on by intercultural contact, is thought of as abnormal. This conception of culture change is reinforced by the evolutionary approach, with its emphasis on long time spans and material determinants. As useful and important as this perspective is, it can lead us to ignore humankind's capacity for envisioning radical social innovations and deliberately putting these visions into practice.

Throughout America's history, utopian visionaries, both domestic and imported, have been busily constructing experimental societies. These American utopias, which numbered no less than two hundred in

the nineteenth century and several thousand during
the communal revival of the early 1970's, are but one
expression of the growing instability of the modern
world and the increasing tendency to offer visionary
solutions to the human problems which existing social
arrangements cannot solve. Some of the American experiments were remarkably "successful" and others
were dismal "failures," but nearly all of them attempted significant social innovations. Careful
study of such experiments could provide valuable information relevant to the evaluation of social alternatives and the understanding of change processes.
Anthropology, which cut its teeth on studies of traditional societies, may reap particular benefits from
the study of utopias. Not only do such societies
help to round out the spectrum of human cultural
variation, but they also provide excellent settings
in which to examine certain processes of cultural and
social innovation which may be relatively submerged
in traditional societies but dramatically expressed
in experimental utopias.

In the following pages I propose to discuss two
recurring themes of American utopias: (1) reliance
on the ideas of a particular individual, and (2) the
organization of these ideas into ideologies which
form bases for innovative social systems. These will
be illustrated with examples from historical American
communes and from the author's field work in a contemporary communal society, and the implications for
culture change will be considered.

Max Weber's now-famous concept of "charisma" is
a useful tool for dealing with the visionary-utopian
facets of culture change. Unfortunately, the term
"charisma" has passed into popular usage since it was
introduced into the sociological lexicon. To most
laymen the adjective "charismatic" describes a person
with leadership qualities based on personal magnetism,
forcefulness, or attractiveness of personality. This
popularization of the concept of charisma, however,
ignores many of its more subtle and significant features. For Weber, charisma is one of the several
possible sources of "legitimation" of social patterns,
the other important ones being reason and tradition
(1968:46). In defining charisma, he wrote:

> The term "charisma" will be applied to
> a certain quality of an individual whereby
> he is set apart from ordinary men and treated

168

as endowed with supernatural, superhuman, or
at least specifically exceptional powers or
qualities. These are such as are not specifically accessible to the ordinary person,
but are regarded as of divine origin or as
exemplary, and on the basis of them the individual concerned is treated as a leader
(1968:48).

More recently, Edward Shils has further refined the
concept of charisma, using it to refer to

...the quality which is imputed to persons,
actions, roles, institutions, symbols, and
material objects because of their presumed
connections with "ultimate," "fundamental,"
"vital," order-determining powers (1968a:386).

The charismatic person is not just likeable or
persuasive; he is a spokesman for some vision of life
which he and his followers believe to be rooted in the
transcendent, the ultimately good. Such persons are
often visionaries in the literal sense, for they may
derive their perception of ultimate human reality from
divine revelation or some "altered" consciousness in
which important new perceptions or understandings are
acquired. Even an inspired, spontaneous breakthrough
of insight or understanding may qualify, if the content of that understanding addresses the question of
ultimate good. In any case, the charismatic vision
is derived from extraordinary sources and is concerned
with a basic definition, or redefinition, of human
purpose. Furthermore, it presents a view of human
life which is not strictly derived from observation,
but which relies heavily on imagination.

Although some persons may be temperamentally
disposed to charisma, charismatically based social
movements are the products of cultural "crises." As
Bidney has pointed out, cultural crises may stem from
problems of survival or they may reflect conflicts
among cultural values (1967:355; cf. Shils 1968a:389).
In either case, a cultural crisis exists when a substantial segment of society is unable to embrace a
conception of the good life that is internally coherent and practically approachable. When such a
situation exists, the stage is set for a redefinition
of values, which may come from a charismatic visionary. Weber and Shils both recognize the connection
between charisma and crisis situations, and Wallace's

169

famous article on "revitalization movements" (1956) makes explicit references to Weber in this regard.

Not all visions of human good are charismatic; the true charismatic vision is transcendent and radical. A charismatic ideology distinguishes between the petty, proximate, or socially institutionalized "good" and the ultimate purposes of human life, it defines the two as being in conflict with on another (temporarily, at least) and it demands a commitment to the ultimate or transcendent good. Thus, the appeal of the charismatic vision is not usually in its immediate adaptiveness or promise of tangible rewards. Indeed, its appeal may be enhanced by the demands it makes upon individual believers in the name of higher good. The charismatic leader never lived who rallied support by openly advocating the course of least resistance.

The charismatic vision is in certain respects both revolutionary and reactionary. It is reactionary insofar as it attempts to embrace timeless, primeval sources of human morality and purpose -- to turn away from decadent society and return to the fountainhead of all human values. It is revolutionary in its unequivocal rejection of prevailing social institutions and cultural patterns as valid avenues to the "good." It relies on the appeal to needs or goals which are not tied to specific social arrangements but are presumed to be inherent in the human condition. In the context of charismatic ideologies, existing laws and codes handed down by tradition tend to be regarded with suspicion and often hostility (Eisenstadt 1968:xix; Weber 1968:24,51).

Despite the rejection of immediate benefit or advantage as a motivating force, the charismatic vision also has an important adaptive dimension. It is teleological by nature, advocating a course of action which is ultimately expected, even promised, to lead its followers out of crisis and into an age of unprecedented goodness and satisfaction. Thus, the radical surgery which separates ultimate human good from its cultural or conventional encrustations is therapeutic in its intent. Much of charisma's importance for cultural development stems from the fact that, however mystical its overt justification, it usually attempts a logical diagnosis of problems (from its own premises) and an equally logical solution. If the crisis-generating problem is perceived, for ex-

170

ample, as thirst for property or a lack of intimacy, a new code of conduct will be proposed which counteracts the presumed source of evil.

From the viewpoint of the charismatic visionary, social institutions and values--products of tradition and petty self-interest rather than moral inspiration--are among the main obstacles to higher good. Yet, charisma, if it is to outlast the visionary who originates it, must itself become "routinized." Weber writes:

> In its pure form charismatic authority has a character specifically foreign to every-day routine structures...If it is not to remain a purely transitory phenomenon,...it is necessary for the character of charismatic authority to become radically changed...It cannot remain stable, but becomes traditionalized, or rationalized, or both (1968:54).

Shils' definition, quoted above, allows for the location of charisma in groups, offices, institutions, or even objects, but it can be argued that charisma normally originates with individual vision and that these other loci of charisma are simply milestones along the path to routinization. Charisma is a response to social routine that is no longer able to serve human needs; it is intelligible in terms of the routine order it opposes, and its ultimate fate is to lose its radical and visionary qualities and, if successful, to become part of a new routine order.

Consistent with the traditional belief that the ultimate source of human good is supernatural, most charismatic visions have been religious in character. Although religion is not a necessary element of charisma, charisma requires some sort of ideology which clearly defines the good, how it is to be known, and its relation to history and human action. Such ideologies, which form the core of the charismatic vision, tend to be closed, dogmatic and righteously belligerent. It is this factor, coupled with the desire to follow a new lifestyle, which often leads the followers of a charismatic visionary to form their own community.

If the charismatic vision discussed here were simply an individual's way of "escaping" from the stress of cultural crisis by retreating into fantasy,

171

it would have little importance for culture change; however, charisma is more than a quality of individual vision. As already noted, it can be taken as a manifesto for social change. The charismatic visionary becomes a leader by communicating his vision to others and convincing them that the vision is worthy of their support. The followers of a charismatic leader are, in certain respects, more important and interesting than the leader himself, since it is they who have the potential to translate individual vision into social practice. The followers of a charismatic visionary may become a political faction within the larger society, or they may embrace a new religion or sect which coexists with the existing social order and is "overlaid" upon their daily lives. In extreme cases, the charismatic vision may become the basis of a new lifestyle for its followers and provide the foundation for a separate society. When this happens, a visionary alternative social system or "utopia" has been formed.

It would, of course, be loading our case to include charisma in the definition of utopia. Utopia, as it has usually been understood, is a conception of a perfect, or at least superior society which breaks sharply with traditional social forms and for which there is no immediate historical precedent. There is no reason why a utopian society could not be based on orthodox moral concepts and planned by a committee, and the participants recruited by placing a newspaper advertisement offering a comfortable salary. Indeed one modern commune, Twin Oaks, is ostensibly based on the scientific principles of psychology as articulated by Professor B. F. Skinner, and it works by an apparently uninspired system of regulated material rewards (Kinkaid 1973). Furthermore, there is no a priori requirement that a utopia be small and intimate, or socialistic. As it happens, though, the utopian societies in the United States has usually been charismatically based, small communities structured along socialist lines. This confluence of traits is no coincidence, and while the peculiarities of Euro-American history may have contributed to this association, much of it probably stems from the dynamics of charisma itself.

The charismatic system of thought, with its emphasis on the perfection of human morality and its promise of salvation from moral crisis and anomie, exhibits an extraordinary need for comprehensiveness,

172

closure, and certainty. This characteristically results in a dogmatic ideology which aims at the resolution of all ambiguities and renders the basis for
all judgements perfectly "clear." Such a system is
unassailable from within, since faith is a more valuable attitude than critical doubt. All "outsiders,"
those who doubt or criticize the ideology, or even
those who simply fail to commit themselves to it, are
regarded as liars, villains, or victims of false consciousness. This leads to what Shils (1968b) has
called "aggressive alienation," a situation in which
alienation from the mainstream of society comes to be
seen as a virtue. Persecution by outsiders may even
be welcomed as proof of the ideologues' status as a
righteous minority in a corrupt world, and as a rein-
forcer of group cohesion. This is amplified by the
charismatic attitude toward the routine rules and
principles by which society defines morality, since
the charismatic vision considers such rules misguided
and often virtually demands their breach.

Equally important is the fact that the charismatic vision demands not only intellectual assent but
active participation in a plan of action. The charismatic vision must be lived; it must make demands on
the individual. Society, with its malevolence and
corruption, must be actively refuted. This may be
done by attempting to resist and change society from
within, or it may be done by forming a separate community (cf. Weber 1968:51; Shils 1968b:70).

The charismatic community may be a community of
the spirit, or it may take the form of a physically
separate, relatively independent social system. In
forming a separate community, the charismatic group
does not necessarily abandon its ideal of triumph
over the corrupt world, but may see such triumph as
the inevitable result of their successful example, or
as the outcome of an Apocalypse.

While the universality of the process described
above must be a subject for future research, it is
certainly applicable to the formation of many utopian
communes in the United States. In fact, the author
first became interested in the process while doing
field work in a contemporary communal society, and
was struck by the commune's similarity to other historical and contemporary examples.

173

"Haran" is a pseudonym for a contemporary Mid-western commune studied by the author in 1972-73. The commune provides an excellent illustration of the extent to which sweeping personal innovations may become established as cultural and social forms in a utopian society. Haran was founded in 1965 by a non-denominational minister known to his followers as "Samuel." Samuel had experienced a series of revelations and supernatural experiences during his youth and early manhood which had made it increasingly clear to him that he was to be a prophet of God. Prior to his founding of the commune at the age of about fifty, he had developed a complex theology based on the concept of opposition between the male and female principles of the universe. Samuel teaches that the female principle or the "woman mind" is the tendency of humans toward selfishness, ignorance, carnality, competition, war, and capitalism. The male principle, of which God is the ultimate expression, is the uplifting force of selfless spirituality and brotherly love. History is seen as a conflict between religious truth based on the revelations of prophets, and the degeneration of revealed truth into decadent social institutions, including established religion, at the hands of women and "woman-minded men." Progress, both on the social and the personal level, is seen as a process of rejecting the domination of "woman mind" and acquiring the spiritual "wisdom" of brotherly love which will provide peace of mind, health, strength and immortality, and will teach women their "proper place."

Samuel had succeeded in winning some converts and followers prior to the founding of the commune, but his radical theology was kept within bounds by his responsibilities as pastor of a "non-demonina-tional" Protestant congregation. Although the command to start a commune came from the voice of God, the reasons for doing so were well considered. Samuel, true to his charismatic character, had decided that no set of beliefs is valid "unless it is lived." The only way to do this was to separate the believers from the corrupt outside world which the Haran people now call "Scag." Acting on the divine command to "come out of Her" -- to leave the woman-minded world and create a utopia based on God's "wisdom" -- Samuel selected a wooded valley and moved there with his followers. In this "Valley of God," the people formed a social system based on Samuel's visionary principles of good and evil. The life-

style, morals, and even peculiarities of speech that
they adopted reflected their determination to conquer
the evil of "carnality" or "the woman mind" and to
achieve the "wisdom" envisioned by the prophet Samuel.
In 1972-73, when the author resided in Haran, this
community of ninety men, women, and children had
created a stable and well-integrated society and culture based on Samuel's visions.

Greed and competition are regarded in Haran as
products of the "beast" or "woman" mind, and the community has made every effort to minimize these impedi-
ments to wisdom. Thus, the community is organized on
an egalitarian basis. Inspired proverbs state that
"All work is honorable," but that "He who does not
work, neither shall he eat." Everyone, including Samuel himself, works long hours in the community's logging and sawmill business, subsistence farming, women's domestic chores, or other designated tasks.
Everyone, including Samuel, shares the same plain but
adequate fare of housing, clothing, food, and minor
personal luxuries. Competition or acquisitiveness,
from the seeking of material privileges to the desire
for status and "pre-eminence," is discouraged.

Worry is seen as the result of ignorance and selfish desire, and is the source of both disease and
death. Therefore, the members of the commune value
peace of mind above strife, and they have developed
attitudes and proverbs to support this. Apparent mis-
fortune is met with the statement that all things are
predestined by God to work for His chosen people. Personal crises and annoyances are dismissed with the belief that all things are sent by God to teach his individual followers and to guide them in their inevitable progress toward personal perfection.

Because Samuel's teachings reject all that is institutionalized (and particularly formalized religions) as products of the "woman mind," the people of
Haran are careful to avoid the adoption of acknowledged laws or codes of conduct, except for the abstract principles of patriarchy and brotherhood and
the rules and patterns necessary to accomplish vital
tasks. The people eschew prayer, ritual, and formal
worship in favor of unstructured religious reflections and experiences. Even the all-important religious teachings of the Prophet are communicated in unplanned and unstructured conversations which they
call "raps."

175

Vanity and luxury, too, are avoided as manifestations of the "woman mind." For this reason clothing,
living quarters, and general esthetic tastes are deliberately "primitive" and homespun. Men wear work
clothes and are unshaven, women dress in simple
skirts or pants, and the people are housed in log
cabins of their own construction. No flush toilets
exist in the community despite its million-dollar-per-
year logging business. Even the economic base itself -- logging and subsistence farming -- was chosen
for its compatibility with the self-image of virile
simplicity.

The most important social innovation, from the
viewpoint of the Haran people themselves, is the escape from woman's rule, and the establishment of
"patriarchy" and "brotherhood" as organizing principles. Woman is competitive by virtue of her "beast"
nature, but man is competitive only through the influence of the "woman mind" which permeates society.
As an antidote to this rule of ignorance, patriarchy
is the domination of man over woman, of age over
youth, and of wisdom over ignorance. In practice,
this means that Samuel is the benevolent "head" of
the male brotherhood, and the men are the "heads" of
their respective families. Women are expected to
obey their husbands and other men, and are restricted
to traditional, servile "women's work," particularly
domestic duties. They have no ackowledged voice in
community decisions and, unlike the men, are denied
official partnership in the community's business oper-
ations. In conversations among the men, women are
held to blame for many of the commune's day-to-day
problems as well as the general degradation of the
human race.

"Brotherhood" is another important concept underlying Haran's society. The men, who call themselves
"brothers," consider themselves a close-knit group
united in opposition to the outside world and to the
influence of the "woman mind" from within. The lifestyle is deliberately arranged so that the brothers
work, eat, sleep and live in close proximity, encouraging fraternal intimacy and forbearance while
reducing the divisive effects of female influence
within the private family (there is no corresponding
notion of "sisterhood"). Childrearing, too, is
structured so as to maximize the child's contact with
a large circle of adults and minimize the influence
of the mother: children sleep with their parents but

176

spend their waking hours under the general supervision of the whole community. Every expression of selfish individualism, whether it be privilege-seeking, engaging in disputes, or shirking one's duty, is stigmatized. Men are expected to show their virility by forsaking such behavior, and women and children are simply held to proper conduct by the "rule" of their "father figure" (the husband/father or Samuel himself).

Perhaps the most surprising facet of Haran's unique culture is the complex set of myths, proverbs, and other verbal arts that support it. These come mostly from Samuel's own revelations and inspired reflections, but some have been embellished with information obtained from members' "regressions," trance journeys into the primeval past under Samuel's guidance. A narrative related by Samuel tells of a beginning time when the earth did not turn, and when all humans lived at the fringes of a single continent. At that time there were few women, and men attached no importance to them except as breeders; the women were sexually shared or, as Samuel put it, "communally owned." Men were wise, able to communicate telepathically, were free from strife and disease, and lived for centuries. Later, when women increased in number, men fell under their influence and became carnal, ignorant, and plagued by disease and death.

Dozens of proverbs revealed to Samuel are used to illustrate religious discussions, to help settle disputes, to criticize wrongdoers, to justify behavior, or simply to enliven conversation. Some examples are "Man is caught in the trap he sets for his brother," "No 'woman' can hear or tell the truth," and "No two 'women' can be friends." The first might be used to discourage competition, the second to dismiss opposing views, or the third to encourage the settlement of disputes among the men.

An even more unique form of verbal art is the inspired etymology. According to Samuel's teachings, the primeval language has left "seed" meanings in modern words that the inspired "man of wisdom" can discern. "Evil," for example, means "Eve-ill" (woman's carnality); "Woman" means "whoa, man" or "woe man," and so forth. Even the words "MATERialism" and "HERd" have hidden connotations. These etymologies, like the proverbs, are used in support of the community's values and in interpreting or justi-

177

fying everyday actions.

It is very important to emphasize that the beliefs and norms described here are not simply those
of one man. While nearly all of Haran's culture has
its origin with Samuel, it constitutes a world view
and lifestyle that is shared by virtually every member of the community. The men say that the "truth"
embodied in Samuel's teachings is the main source of
their own motivation to participate in the community.
Even the women, who constitute a minority, nominally
accept Samuel's teachings and say they are happy to
have found their rightful place in a superior community. The children, too, express a devotion to Samuel's teachings in their behavior and their statements. Nor is the acceptance passive; the daily behavior of the Haran people studiously follows the
precepts of the charismatic vision.

One of the remarkable features of Haran, in view
of its idiosyncratic origins, is its functional unity
as a sociocultural system. The ideology is a self-
reinforcing cognitive system that validates the social order and discourages those sorts of behavior --
competition, nuclear family bonds, and selfishness --
which might be threatening to the community, while
reinforcing the cooperative solidarity vital to the
commune's existence. An ethnocentric conception of
the outside world as "Canaanites" headed for Apocalyptic destruction contributes to the internal cohesion of the community, as does the religiously-
based emphasis on hard work and sacrifice. The promise of health, perfection, peace of mind and even immortality to those whom God has chosen, coupled with
the grim fate envisioned for those beyond the pale,
encourages each individual to identify with the group
and internalize its values. Although Samuel attributes his ideas to revelation, his talent for social
design is remarkable. The community's viability is
reflected both in the high morale and esprit de corps
and in its material success. After only seven years
of existence, the commune of ninety persons (they
have deliberately limited population growth) owned
nearly a million dollars in assets.

In sum, Haran exhibits a social system, lifestyle and world view as complex and cohesive as most
traditional cultures; yet it was conceived mostly by
one man, in a relatively short period of time, and on
the basis of mystical, charismatic visions. Such an

extreme case is unusual, and it may well be transitory. Nevertheless, it is part of the spectrum of human social events which anthropology purports to
study, and it represents a class of phenomena which
deserves to be taken into account in our formulations
of culture theory.

The seminal importance of the individual visionary is made particularly clear by an examination of
nineteenth century American utopias. One of the best
comparative sociological treatments of these is to be
found in Kanter's Commitment and Community (1972) in
which the 30 best-documented utopias of the last century are divided into successful and unsuccessful
categories (based on whether or not they survived for
at least 25 years). Of the nine "successful" utopias
listed by Kanter (Shakers, Harmony Society, Amana,
Zoar, Snowhill, Saint Nazianz, Bethel-Aurora, Oneida,
and Jerusalem) all but one can be clearly associated
with the influence of a single visionary founder.
The lone exception, Amana, is set apart not but the
absence of charismatic leadership but by the presence
of a series of inspired visionary leaders spanning
the society's existence and influencing various
stages of its development. Kanter's "unsuccessful"
utopias also signify a general, if somewhat less
clear-cut, tendency toward personal visionary influence. Many, like Bishop Hill, Jasper Colony, New
Harmony, or Bethel-Aurora, show a straightforward relationship between the ideas of a single founding visionary and the ultimate character of the community's
intellectual and social life. A number of others
show a slightly more complicated pattern wherein the
community was influenced by some visionary not personally involved in the founding of the community.
For example, four of Kanter's 20 "unsuccessful" groups
were founded on the ideas of the Fourier, a French
utopian writer who never set foot in America; three
more on this list were founded on the ideas of Robert
Owen (apart from Owen's own venture at New Harmony);
Communia was led by Wilhelm Weitling but based on the
ideas of Karl Marx; and the community of Preparation
was a schismatic development of the Mormon Church,
which in turn had been founded on the earlier visions
of Joseph Smith. Many of these, like Preparation,
had their own particular founders whose ideas further
influenced the community. Kanter's sample of 29
utopias contains only one--Northhampton--for which no
specific personal visionary inspiration is mentioned.

179

The picture for contemporary communes is less clear, since the revival of communalism has been in full swing for only about ten years. While there are some contemporary communes, like Twin Oaks, which tend to resist the idea of charisma, it also appears that some of the most successful communes, including Stephen Gaskin's "Farm" and Haran, are those which manifest the visions of a single prophet/founder. Even Twin Oaks, which eschews both personal leadership and transcendent inspiration, bears the stamp of its prophet (B. F. Skinner's Walden Two is acknowledged as the "inspiration" of the community) and of its founder, Kat Kinkaid.

In sum, an examination of American Communal Utopias shows that Haran is far from unique; these ventures, particularly the most successful ones, are often the product of personal charismatic inspiration to the same degree, and in many of the same ways, as Haran. Typically, the founder of such a utopia was the source of most of the social and cultural features which characterized the group; to put it differently, the group and its social life was largely a projection of the thinking of the charismatic leader. Some of these leaders, like the Shakers' Ann Lee or the Harmonists' Father Rapp, derived their ideas initially from direct revelation of supernatural truth. Others, like Oneida's John Humphrey Noyes, proposed ideas that were innovative and religious in character, but based on radical re-interpretations of existing religion rather than direct revelation. Even such leaders as Robert Owen, whose ideas were predominantly secular in origin and scope, were charismatic in their advocacy of a new order based on the fundamental principles of human morality with which they felt themselves to be in close contact.

The utopian societies created by charismatic leaders transformed the individual deviance and eccentricity of charismatic persons into self-contained subcultures and miniature societies. Individual revelations and theological speculations became established religions, often complete with their own myths, vocabularies, rituals, and social values. These cultural ideas were manifested in radically innovative forms of social organization. The Shakers, for example, established a stable social order based on communal production and consumption of goods and an egalitarian, celibate relationship between the sexes. The Oneida colony also instituted a communal economy,

and they abolished the existing family order and its
accompanying roles in favor of a system of group
marriage and a nonsexual division of labor. Many of
the fundamental principles of social organization in
the outside world--market exchange, kinship, marriage, and sex roles--were utterly transformed or
abandoned in these experimental societies. Behavior
and emotions which were acceptable or even virtuous
in the outside world, such as competitiveness, personal friendship or love, and the desire for privacy,
became cardinal sins for the utopians.

If the visionary utopians failed to achieve
their inflated dreams of heaven on earth or Apocalyptic triumph, we are not thereby entitled to dismiss them as irrelevant to cultural development.
Not only did some of these communities survive for
many generations as alternative societies in their
own right, but they left an imprint on the American
consciousness which is out of proportion to their
modest size (and, in some cases, duration) and material influence. Even though the developing capitalism, individualism and materialism of nineteenth-
century American was rather inhospitable to the message of these idealistic, spartan communalists, the
utopias provided annoyingly successful models of alternative social arrangements. Not only socialism
but group marriage, planned birth control, and sexual equality, all considered radical by many today,
were practiced over a hundred years ago in American
utopias.

Awareness of these options persisted in our cultural inventory, and with the rebirth of communalism
in the past decade, the interest in these early experiments has reached unprecedented levels. It remains to be seen just how effective this "second
sowing" of utopianism will be in influencing the
mainstream culture, but communities like Haran are
currently receiving their share of positive attention
from the news media. It is important to realize,
however, that radically innovative utopias are often
far from becoming societies in their own right. They
derive their motivations and commitment in large part
from the belief that they act in accordance with a
higher truth than that underlying "straight" society.
Their institutions exist as responses to the outside
world, and are in that sense dependent upon it for
meaning. If the utopian society is an important step
in the transformation of charismatic innovation into

181

socially shared behavior and belief, the creation of
such an entity by no means insures that the innovations will eventually become part of the larger society. In fact, the reverse is often true. Since
charisma is by its very nature dependent on freshness
of vision, usually on the part of an outstanding individual, the charismatically-based utopian society
is a rather unstable entity. Historically, the
charismatic societies of American have usually undergone one of two fates; either they flourished for a
period of a few years or decades and then disappeared,
or they became rigidified and withdrawn, losing the
vital innovative quality which created them and re-
tiring into a self-imposed orthodoxy and isolation.

    It would be counterproductive to claim too much
for the charismatic vision in culture change -- or
too little. Haran and other utopian societies indicate that the individual visionary is not only a
leader but a cultural innovator, whose visions may
lead to new lifestyles which are viable at the level
of the small community. But what is the ultimate effect of these small utopias? The intensity of vision
and commitment that gives them their vitality is difficult for them to maintain, particularly after the
original leader dies. It is even more difficult to
communicate the charismatic vision into the larger
society without considerable reduction of intensity.
This is what Weber meant when he said that charisma
tends to become "routinized." A positive interpretation of this phenomenon, however, might use the metaphor of a "pill" becoming dissolved and diluted so
that its contents may enter the bloodstream. But we
must also recognize that the "body" can reject the
medicine entirely.

    Turning attention to such subjects as charisma
and utopia does not necessarily constitute a retreat
into a purely emic, idealist perspective on cultural
phenomena, nor must it lead to individualistic re-
ductionism. What is suggested here is the further
study by anthropologists of those relatively un-
charted regions where individual creativity and cultural necessity interact with one another. The influence of the charismatic individual on a complex
society is unlikely to be simple or direct; it is
more likely to take place through a series of cultural "reverberations," of which the utopian society
is one form. If these "reverberations" follow identifiable patterns, the study of these patterns should

182

prove interesting to any student of culture change.

There are several lines of inquiry which future researchers might pursue: (1) Under what specific conditions do charismatic leaders tend to arise? (2) What patterned relationships exist between the sociocultural milieu and the specific content of charismatic idealogy? (3) What circumstances govern whether a charismatic innovator will become the founder of a utopian society? (4) Is the formation of a utopia the only, or the most effective, avenue from charismatic vision to large-scale social realization? (5) Under what circumstances will the utopian society influence culture change in the larger society? In regard to this last question, such factors as perceived need, psychological and cultural compatibility, and political-economic adaptiveness of the charismatic innovations should prove relevant variables.

The utopian society has been treated here as the immediate manifestation of the individual, visionary, and teleological input to cultural change. As such, it is relevant to cultural theory as an antidote to an overly "superorganic" view of culture change which tends to give the individual and all consciousness (visionary or otherwise) a passive role. It is especially appropriate to our own cultural milieu, characterized by the presence of cultural crises and the need for rapid and effective solution of cultural problems. In such times as these, charismatic movements are likely to arise in profusion with or without our approval or understanding. While the transcendent moral message, the power to generate commitment, and the adaptive teleology of the charismatic vision may have great value, it is also possible that its tendency toward dogmatic, nonrational idealogies and Apocalyptic self-righteousness can lead to tragic demagoguery. Thus, the charismatic and visionary side of culture change embodies the best and the worst of the human potential. Our responsibility as students of cultural development is not to define it out of existence but to understand appreciatively its patterns, possibilities, and limitations.

REFERENCES CITED

Bidney, David

    1967   Theoretical Anthropology. New York: Shocken Books.

Eisenstadt, S. N.

    1968   Editor's Introduction to: On Charisma and Institution Building (Selected Papers of Max Weber). Chicago: University of Chicago Press.

Kanter, Rosabeth M.

    1972   Commitment and Community: Communes and Utopias in Sociological Perspective. Cambridge: Harvard University Press.

Kinkaid, Kathleen

    1973   A Walden Two Experiement: The First Five Years of Twin Oaks Community. New York: William Morrow & Company, Inc.

Shils, Edward

    1968a   Charisma. International Encyclopedia of the Social Sciences 2:386-390. New York: Macmillan.

    1968b   Ideology. International Encyclopedia of the Social Sciences 7:66-76. New York: Macmillan.

Wallace, Anthony F. C.

1956   Revitalization Movements. American
             Anthropologist 58:264-281.

Weber, Max

1968   On Charisma and Institution Building.
             (Selected papers, S. N. Eisenstadt,
             ed.) Chicago and London: University
             of Chicago Press.

TRADITION AND CHANGE IN EDUCATION
IN RIO GRANDE DO SUL, BRAZIL

Malvina Rosat McNeill, Ph. D.

Introduction

In the 1930's a group of Brazilian educators, inspired by
ideas current in the United States and in France, began a reform
movement that would make the educational system of Brazil more
democratic (McNeill:1970, 5-8).

Education was no longer to be considered a privilege of
the social elite but a means of developing both the human
potential of the country and its economic resources. To join
the modern nations Brazil had to educate all of its population.

However, this movement met with serious obstacles. During
the Vargas dictatorship of the 1930's and forties the reform
leaders -- they called themselves "pioneers" -- were dismissed
from their positions of influence, and in the 1950's some
bishops of the Catholic Church and politicians launched an
attack on the new orientation as being of Communist inspiration.
This "conspiracy against public education" spread over various
states, confusing the issue, weakening the position of those
interested in modern education, frightening some local educational authorities, helping to hold back the movement. Eventually the issue died out but many years and much effort had
been wasted.

Features of the traditional Brazilian elementary education
were the long, compact curriculum, demanding early proficiency
in verbal skills, and the final annual examination that selected and eliminated children as early as the first grade.

From the administrative point of view the system was
centralized, homogeneous, authoritarian. High schools and
universities followed the models established in Rio de Janeiro.
Some more freedom was allowed to the States to organize elementary education, and the Secretariats of Education, in the
State capitals, became administrative centers.

187

Curricula were almost alike from State to State and within States. Teachers, programs and books coming from the capitals were unsuited to the local populations, inhibiting regional initiative and development. In Rio Grande do Sul the final examinations were organized by the Secretariat of Education and all children were examined the same day. The administration of such centralized system was difficult, relying heavily on rigid, formal communication from the heads of government to the schools, and a lack of participation or acceptance by teachers and parents.

This study focuses on one attempt to modify the selective character of the schools, initiated by a suggestion of the Federal educational authorities to the Rio Grande do Sul Secretariat of Education, and on the process of its implementation.

The Problem

In 1958 The Centro de Pesquizas e Orientação Educacionais (CPOE, Center of Research and Educational Supervision), Secretariat of Education, Porto Alegre, Brazil, introduced a new grouping policy, namely, age grouping and consequently, automatic promotion. The desired result was to end the failure of about 50 per cent of first graders and to reduce a correspondingly high drop-out rate. For those falling behind required standards "rehabilitation classes" would be organized. These innovations constituted the "Reforma do Ensino Primario" (Reform of Elementary Education) hereafter referred to as Reforma.

The starting point for this study was the realization that, parallel with the Reforma, achievement rates in the State capital's first grades had decreased. (Pacheco and Santos, 1965:5).

Assumptions and Method

One of the basic assumptions of this study is that a school system is a cultural institution that expresses widely shared values more or less transmitted without awareness, and that these values have to be scrutinized and clarified if the humanistic orientation implied in the very existence of schools is to be maintained. This process of analysis is especially pertinent when a desirable change is to be introduced.

Another fundamental belief is that an elementary school system has a structure, that all its parts are interdependent, and that a change in one part entails other changes not always clearly anticipated.

It is also assumed that a sudden change in a school system necessarily creates a conflict between the already established ways of thinking and doing things in the classroom, and the new ones proposed, and that in order to become effective the new orientation has to be perceived as having a value greater than the previous one. At any point of this process the value attributed to previous beliefs and practices, in addition to the force of long standing habits, could generate strong resistance against the proposed innovation; it would then be expected that a program of increased communication between the various parts of the system would be maintained until the desired outcome would become evident.

The planning of this study thus included the following broad questions: 1) Were the new objectives, assumptions, premises and procedures clearly spelled out; 2) Were the current procedures and premises shown to have different and less humanistic objectives; how were classes organized; 3) What new means of communication were established between the Secretariat of Education and the teachers; and, 4) What was the situation in the schools in 1969.

To a large extent this study was inspired by Bidney's humanistic anthropology and by his position regarding cultural values. They are "Facts" to those who investigate them, and in the sphere of human culture and society the scientific observer cannot avoid studying value phenomena (Bidney 1967:416). Suggestions also came from Bidney's interdisciplinary approach -- the methods of natural and social sciences as well as the philosophic method are not incompatible or mutually exclusive and that the educational field is most appropriate for the investigation of normative modes of human conduct. The problem under consideration is a limited one, however it seems to the writer that the experience of Rio Grande do Sul will emphasize the importance of an objective search for those normative aspects of a culture which may interfere with the initiation and establishment of humanistically desirable change.

Following another of Bidney's suggestions, an attempt was made to relate the introduction of the new grouping policy in Rio Grande do Sul to some historical and psychological events that had an impact on that initiative.

Other methodological ideas came from Arensberg's (1965) anthropological interaction theory, from Atwood (1964) who provided an example of the usefulness of this approach in the study of educational innovations[1], and from Miles (1964) whose proposed agenda for such studies was closely followed. The extent to which our effort approaches the methodological standards set up by these authors will be judged by the reader. The attempt was

189

made to catch relevant data and relevant interaction of factors rather than look exhaustively for details.

Part of the problem was to reconstruct the development of the new grouping idea from its introduction in Rio Grande do Sul to its implementation in the school system.

A variety of techniques were employed in collecting data which required a field trip to Porto Alegre, the capital of the State of Rio Grande do Sul. For the historical aspects, educational journals and CPOE publications immediately prior to and after 1958 were perused; basic documents, statistics and available evaluations were analyzed, and persons who had been involved with the innovating process were interviewed. A sample of the current school situation concerning promotion and drop-out rates, the rehabilitation classes, and the principals' and teachers' opinions about the new system were gathered in Porto Alegre, in twenty-four "Grupos Escolares" (Elementary Schools, hereafter referred to as Grupos Escolares); these school buildings were rated according to a check list; their twenty-four principals were interviewed, 144 of their teachers were given a questionnaire to answer, and approxiamtely 40 supervisors were collectively interviewed at one of their regular meetings. In addition, a brief analysis was made of the Reforma objectives as staged in five available documents, of the implementation procedures as described in CPOE publications, and of some key concepts and how they were understood.

Accordingly, this paper is divided in three sections. Part I includes an educational description of Rio Grande do Sul, the Reforma background and implementation, and the results of various evaluations; Part II includes the examination of the new data; in Part III analysis is made of the Reforma's stated objectives, concepts and implementation procedures, and the opinions which principals and teachers have formed of them.

The substantive aspects of the Reforma itself, that is, of the value of homogeneous or ability grouping versus age grouping are not discussed even though the subject at different times has provoked intensive, controversial discussions. A considerable amount of research has been done on the United States and elsewhere regarding the educational and social consequences of ability grouping. While some authors believe that ability grouping "at best can be ineffective, at worst harmful" (Goldberg and Passow:1966), others assert that it "tends to reflect, emphasize and exaggerate the divisions that exist in society as a whole" (Yates:1966) and that children in the lower group generally come from lower classes and rarely rejoin their age group peers (Daniels:1961).

In the 1950's the controversy had calmed down (Morganstern: 1966) but in the 1960's the problem was again subject to extensive scrutiny (Yates:1966, Goldberg and Passow:1966, Thelen:1967), and the very concept of "homogeneous group" was considered of doubtful validity.

At the present time age grouping, per se, as the only criterion for promotion is again under criticism.

There seems to be sufficient evidence to show that together with grouping an appropriate selection of content, materials and methods of teaching is what produces educational benefits.

Part I, The State of Rio Grande do Sul. The Reforma do Ensino
    background

Together with São Paulo, Paraná and Santa Catarina, Rio Grande do Sul forms the Brazilian region called the South; Rio Grande do Sul is the southern-most state, bordering on Uruguay and Argentina. The state's population was estimated at more than six million (Anvario Estatistico 1967:37) 94 per cent white, mostly of Portuguese, German, Italian and Eastern European origin. The predominant religion is Catholic.

Porto Alegre, the State Capital, a port on the Guaiba river, is, together with the surrounding communities, the center of the state's industry; the greater Porto Alegre population is estimated at more than one million. Livestock, agriculture and industry, respectively, form the state's economy. (Sperb: 1967).

From the educational point of view Rio Grande do Sul is one of the most progressive states. In 1974 (Anuario de Educacao 1966:686-687) there were 13,747 elementary schools staffed with 38,855 teachers, and with an enrollment of about one million pupils. Elementary education is a state responsibility even though the counties have their own educational systems subsidized by the state and following the state's educational policies.

State appropriations for elementary education, in 1964, amounted to NC (New Cruzeiro) $960,642, a higher per capita expenditure than São Paulo even though lower than Minas Gerais and other states with smaller elementary school systems.

Schools function six days a week from March first to December fifteenth with a vacation period in July, the academic year having 200 days. There are five grades in the majority of the schools, some have kindergarten and a sixth grade. Traditionally, schools have two four hour sessions daily; however, in certain areas, with a growing population and lack of means to enlarge their facilities, many schools have had to expand their capacity

191

by increasing the number of sessions, thus reducing to three hours the time a pupil attends classes daily.

Teaching standards for all schools are set by the State Department of Education's "programs" (curricula). The standards for teacher education are also set by the State Department of Education even though most of the normal schools are private (Anuário de Educação 1966:688).

The highest educational authority in the State is the Secretary of Education, head of the Secretariat of Education, in Porto Alegre, the administrative center of all State educational activities, except for universities. Public higher education is a Federal responsibility. Within the Secretariat, the Centro de Pesquisas e Orientação Educacionais, commonly known as CPOE is the division in charge of, among other programs, Curriculum, organization, supervision of elementary education, and educational research. The CPOE has been responsible for the advancement of education all over the State since its creation in the forties.

For Supervisory purposes CPOE has divided the State into 19 "Delegacias Regional de Ensino" (Regional Educational Offices) which establish and maintain communication between the central administration and the region's Grupos Escolares. Periodically the heads of the Delegacias meet in Porto Alegre for instructions which they transmit to the Supervisors, Principals and teachers in their region. Communication between the Secretariat and the teachers is otherwise made in the form of "comunicados", "instrucoes", "oficios", (communiques, instructions, official notes) distributed through the Delegacias. Those agencies, in general, are understaffed and do not have transportation facilities for their personnel.

The Federal Government has no jurisdiction over the State elementary system. However, one of the Ministry of Education divisions, the "Instituto Nacional de Estudos Pedagogicos" (from here on referred as INEP) was founded in order to exert a leadership role on the country's elementary education and has actually had a great influence on most of the nation's state systems. Among its many educational activities INEP organized in-service education programs for teachers from all over the country, distributes model types of curricula, promotes educational research, and publishes the "Revista Brasileira de Estudos Pedagogicos", an excellent educational journal. Relationship between INEP and CPOE, as well as between CPOE and the country's educational administrators have been characteristically formal but cooperative.

The "Reforma do Ensino" Background

As mentioned in the Introduction, selectivity at all levels including the elementary grades has been traditionally a characteristic of Brazilian education but in the thirties a new concept of the objectives of elementary education was introduced in the country and great concern for the school's efficiency began to appear in the states most sophisticated educationally. In São Paulo, a review of statistics for the 1917 - 1936 period showed that 30 to 40 per cent of the children were failing every year in the state capital's elementary schools; in other cities promotion rates were still lower. In 1954 another survey showed that the situation continued to be more or less the same (Almeida Junior 1957).

The Local Context

A similar concern existed also in Rio Grande do Sul. In 1956 CPOE surveyed the failures, drop-outs, repeaters, and the number of years a repeater actually spent in school (Boletim 1958:8). In the first grade only 52 per cent of pupils were promoted.

A first attempt to improve the situation in this period was made in 1956 with the introduction of a new grouping procedure (Boletim 1956+1957:13-18). Ability grouping had been customary in the first but not in other grades. Beginning school children were grouped according to their "maturity level" as measured by a widely known maturity test (Lourenço Filho: 1950); in the following grades however children of different ages and achievement levels including repeaters were put together unless a sufficient number of repeaters justified the organization of a separate class for them.

Just prior to the beginning of the 1956 school year instructions were sent to the schools to group children, from second grade on, according to their grades in mathematics, initially, then in language arts and finally according to the mathematics-language arts average grade. Children with 50 points or more on a 100 point scale would be grouped in a "Regular Class", those with lower grades in "Special Classes". Regular classes were further divided, grouping children with above 75 and below 75 points.

This is what had been done when the Reforma was started in 1958.

The Latin-American UNESCO Regional Conference on Free and
Compulsory Education

Pointing to widespread concern about the educational situation in Central and South America, in April 1956 a Latin American UNESCO Regional Conference on Free and Compulsory Education
was held in Lima, Peru. The Brazilian group, consisting of INEP
staff members and other educators invited by INEP, proposed that
all Latin American countries revise their elementary school
promotion policy; selection of children at the elementary level
should be eliminated. Schools were not educating the largest
part of the population, and together with the human waste to
have a child repeating a grade was economically wasteful (Re-
comendações, RBEP 1956:158-178). The Brazilian delegation, says
Almeida Junior, Director of Public Education in São Paulo, did
not dare to propose the adoption of automatic promotion "for fear
that it would provoke a reaction among Brazilian teachers as
strong as that of the proclamation of the Republic". The delegation realized that such a proposal would sound too radical to
the traditionally "tough" Brazilian teachers; they hoped for
automatic promotion in Brazil but felt that teachers should "be
prepared" to accept the idea. They also realized that other conditions had to be achieved before automatic promotion could be
introduced without harmful results.

On September 19, 1956 some of the members of the Brazilian
delegation to the UNESCO conference were together again at the
First State Meeting on Education, in Ribeirao Preto, São Paulo.
On this occasion Anisio Z. Teixeira, Director of INEP, made a
speech emphasizing the value of the common public school as an
instrument for promoting social reform, a point which he had
been proclaiming for a long time; Horace Mann in the United
States and Sarmiento in Argentina, were cited as examples of
great men who, contrary to violent social reform had however
implemented social change through the public schools. In his
speech Almeida Junior introduced to the teachers the concept of
automatic promotion.

Meantime the idea seemed to have gained momentum. In a
December 1956 graduation speech at the "Instituto de Educacao"
in Belo Horizonte, Minas Gerais, President Juscelino Kubitscheck
pointed to the calamitous consequences of selection at the elementary school level, advocating among things the automatic promotion system (Kubitscheck:1956). In 1956 the Director of INEP
proposed a national plan for "a modest educational system" which,
however, would provide all Brazilian children with public, free,
education from 7 to 13 years of age; again, automatic promotion
was part of the plan. In São Paulo and Rio Grande do Sul, states
with the highest literacy rates in the country, only 50 and 34
per cent of the children, respectively, were achieving a fourth

grade level education (Teixeira: 1956).

In May 1958 INEP, assuming its leadership role, sent to the Secretariat of Education in Porto Alegre, a proposal to provide assistance — technical and financial — to the State for the purpose of reorganizing its school system, specifically in regard to the grouping of children by age and to the adoption of a "flexible system of promotion". The objective of this reorganization was to keep children 7 to 13 years of age in school, to reduce drop-outs, avoid repeating, and to provide children with a long enough school day to make possible their "integral education" (INEP:1958a). (The meaning of "integral" here probably was to combine practical and social with book learning.)

This proposal encountered a favorable climate of opinion in the Secretariat of Education in Porto Alegre, already aware of State educational problems, and was accepted. However a counter-proposal was elaborated by CPOE, the Division which would have to implement INEP's suggestions, and two clauses of the INEP proposal were slightly, but significantly, modified; first, in the second clause, it specified that grouping would be according to age and learning ability; and second, in the third clause, INEP technical assistance would be accepted if requested. (CPOE: 1958). Two items proposed by INEP, the "daily schedule" and "integral education" were not included. The expression "automatic promotion" does not appear in these documents.

On December 10, 1958 CPOE presented to the Governor a document entitled "Exposição de Motivoa" (Statement of Purposes) explaining that the low efficiency of the school system was due to the current promotion system, and asking for an executive order to replace it by an "age and achievement classification system". The Governor's Decree No. 9950 promulgated on December 31, 1958 established both the new system and a five year time limit, or 14 years of age, for a child to be in elementary school. The draft for this Decree was prepared by CPOE. The expression "automatic promotion" was avoided and some CPOE officials assert that automatic promotion was never intended. However, children were actually "promoted", at least nominally, at the end of each academic year.

By the end of 1958 (INEP:1958b) INEP sent a report to the International Bureau of Education, Geneva, in which the Brazilian elementary education reform, "planned by INEP", is described as consisting of a program for six grades with a vocational emphasis in the last two years, with children being grouped by age; the reform objectives, says the report, were to reduce the high rate of failures, to group children according to their psycho-social development, and to open in the schools vacancies previously held by repeaters. "Automatic promotion" is

195

not mentioned.

The National Context

Cultures are not integrated wholes (Bidney 1967:460) and various ideologies co-exist at a given time in different parts of a society. In traditional Brazil the beliefs about the educational system had been unchallenged for centuries even though the upper class would go abroad for a better education. The introduction of the idea of modifying the school system to educate all children produced a strong negative reaction, a moral crisis, and the movement started by INEP was seen as a dangerous sign with alarming political implications. Some INEP officials were publicly accused of being inspired by "communist ideas". In the House of Representatives (Dec. 14, 1956) Federal representatives accused the INEP director of "being an authentic Marxist intellectual", "a follower of John Dewey (who is) recommended and applauded by Russia". This accusation was based on excerpts from the Ribeirão Preto speech on social reform through the public schools mentioned above.

The Brazilian Education Associate published a statement dismissing the accusation and defending both Dewey and the INEP director (ABE:1956). In the first place, it said, Professor Teixeira's speech was a "valuable appeal to be listened to by the whole nation" and nothing in it was "incompatible with ideals already adopted for a long time by the Western democracies"; secondly, "there was no relationship between Dewey's educational principles and methods and the doctrine of economic materialism". However, the controversy was further stimulated by a 1957 book by Professor Teixeira, Educacao Não é Privilegio; in this book the class bias of the Brazilian educational system and its incompatibility with a democratic regime as well as the need for a greater number of public elementary schools were once again pointed out.

A strong reaction came from some high Catholic Church authorities (Memorial:1958); the Archbishop of Porto Alegre and all the Bishops of Rio Grande do Sul addressed a "Memorial" to the President of Brazil condemning the emphasis of INEP as being of "socialist inspiration" and as such something "to be suppressed". The activities of INEP were said to be a menace to the democratic regime, and the emphasis on public education was also interpreted as an "intent to eliminate the country's private educational institutions", mostly Catholic; the Archbishop and the Bishops did not see it as "fit for a governmental institution to preach social revolution through the schools". The issue assumed national proportions when the Bishops of Minas Gerais joined those from Rio Grande do Sul in subscribing to their accusations against INEP.

196

As an answer, Professor Teixeira, Director of INEP, published a list of items he was "for" and "against" in education, pointing once more to the millions of Brazilian children out of schools, something the country could ill afford, and to the need for public, universal education. Support on behalf of Professor Teixeira came from nationally known groups of educators, scientists, university professors, and also from some left of center Catholic circles (Apoio:1958).

Rio Grande do Sul educators from the Secretariat of Education did not give public support to the INEP director even though the agreements to initiate the Reforma were being negotiated. Actually, the position of the CPOE Director was indirectly expressed in an address to a group of normal school psychology teachers (Palestra:1958) in which Dewey's view of "education as a social process" was considered inadequate and contrasted with "Thomas Aquinas' beliefs"; education was said to be an "individual -- not a social -- process". These words suggest that at least some CPOE staff members were not clearly in favor of the INEP Dewey inspired ideas but more in harmony with the position of the Catholic hierarchy in Rio Grande do Sul at the time.

Within the emotional context created by these conflicting positions and accusations the "Acordo" between INEP and the Secretariat of Education was signed, and the Reforma started in Rio Grande do Sul in May, 1958.

Implementation of the Reforma

This section gives samples of the type of actions taken to implement the Reforma during the first two years as recorded in CPOE publications. While most of the references are from the CPOE "Boletins" some of the data were collected during interviews with school personnel.

Launching the New Policy

While the official documents authorizing the Reforma were in preparation a "pilot project" was started in 33 Grupos Escolares in Porto Alegre; the schools had been chosen on the basis of the supervisors' information regarding their physical facilities, quality of the teaching staff, and their receptivity to new ideas. On May 30, 1958, 10 A.M., at the CPOE office, and on June 17, 2 P.M. at the "Pontificia Universidade Catolica" (Catholic University)[1] the principals of the 33 chosen schools were told by the CPOE director about the Reforma, the new grouping criterion, and the importance of securing the teachers' cooperation in the reorganization of classes. A "general plan" dated May 19, 1958 (Boletim 1958:71-84) was prepared. An Introduction tells of the research and studies made in the preceding

197

years designed to "reorganize classes, revise curricula, improve methods of teaching, evaluate results of learning and change the grouping procedures"; there is no mention of ultimate objectives or of the agreement with INEP. The words "failure" and "repeaters" should not be used to spare the children the feelings of inadequacy. Rehabilitation class children should have a "reduced curriculum" only. Instructions for a new classification and grouping of children were attached to the plan. A chart showed how many groups of children could be organized considering age and ability level: five of first graders, four of second, six of third graders, and eight of both fourth and fifth graders. Each of these groups was designated by a symbol, a combination of letters and numbers referring to age and grade level, and maturity or achievement level.

In December 1958 a report was sent to INEP listing the difficulties encountered in this pilot project: first, age and ability grouping from first to fifth grade had not been possible since there were not enough teachers, school rooms, furniture and teaching materials; elementary level educational facilities for pupils 14 years of age or older did not exist in the city. Secondly, parents were not accepting the new system.

In spite of these difficulties in the Grupos Escolares selected for the "experiment", the new idea was extended to all state elementary schools; on December 4 (Boletim 1958:86-89) instructions were sent to all school principals for the organization of classes the following academic year starting March 1959; the "rigorous observation of the instructions: about the new classification system was emphasized. Problems and results of the pilot project in Porto Alegre were not mentioned.

On December 31 the Governor's Decree No. 9950 was promulgated, making the new system official. On February 1st, following gubernatorial elections, the CPOE director resigned. The Reforma plan was not changed and the December 1958 instructions were sent again to all school principals (Boletim 1959:70-73). On June 5 (Boletim 1959:135) the Delegados were asked about the number of schools functioning under the new system since "it had come to the knowledge of CPOE that only a reduced number of schools were following the new instructions".

Presumably in consequence of an answer to this question (there is no available evidence of this answer) an "intensive course (workshop) about the Reforma" was organized in Porto Alegre for all elementary school supervisors, during the July 1-15 period; and from July 22nd to 24th all Delegados also met in the Capital to discuss the problems of the Reforma inauguration (Boletim 1959:51). Their opinion was that conditions in their regions were far from optimal; there was a limited number

of teachers having normal school education, few supervisors, and
no means of transportation for carrying out supervisory activities. Under these conditions they believed the Reforma should
be extended only "gradually".

Three months later, on October 30 (Boletim 1949:154) the
Delegados were "asked" to indicate which schools in their region could adopt the "Reform".

New instructions about the classification system, with a
new set of symbols, were sent to the schools on December 7
(Boletim 1959:177-183); four pages of examples show the teachers
how to "classify" children during the following academic year.
Children from regular classes A and B would continue in the next
grade A and B respectively; but those who had been in classes
C, D, and R (rehabilitation classes) should be classified with a
specific set of symbols indicating the grade in which they
should be according to their age, that in which they actually
were, and how well they had performed in the final examinations.*
The instructions specified that the words "suficiente and
insuficiente" should be used instead of the previous "promoted"
and "failed"; children classified as "suficiente" would not be
grouped together with the "insuficientes"; the word "repeater"
should not be employed any more. This new terminology contituted
the "new evaluation system" part of the Reforma.

A new classification Chart (Boletim 1959:199-203) much more
elaborate than the first was sent to the schools showing the
great variety of possible combinations of ages, grades and levels
of achievement.

By the end of 1959, 157 schools -- 80 in Porto Alegre and
77 in the interior of the State -- with a total of 64,582 pupils
were organized according to the Reforma (Revista do Ensino 1960:
11-13). CPOE had promoted meetings, seminars, workshops, and
"missoes pedagogiacas" in which 4311 teachers, supervisors and
Delegados participated.

During 1960 the task of expanding the Reforma to the interior of the State continued. In April the first seminar for
supervisors was held in Porto Alegre (Boletim 1960:146); in a
10 day, seven hour a day program, 19 subjects were taught.

The classification charts continued to be sent to the
schools, slightly increased year after year. In the 1958 chart
48 groups of children can be organized; in the 1959 chart there
are 93 such possibilities. In the schools surveyed for this
study, children were classified according to 101 combinations of
symbols. The practical difficulties of administering such a
system are not mentioned in CPOE publications even though the

pilot project had clearly indicated them.

Evaluations

There seems to be a tendency (Miles:1964) not to evaluate
innovations on a systematic basis, and, because of the infre-
quency of it, "substantive failure...often goes unnoticed". The
Rio Grande do Sul experience is no exception to this trend.

A complete description of all phases, conditions, and difficulties encountered in the implementation of the Reforma, and
an evaluation of all its education outcomes does not seem to have
ever been done. However, while the collecting of data for the
present investigation was in process, some surveys were located;
the 1958, 1959, 1960 and 1961 school statistics had been published in the CPOE "Boletim", three comparative statistical analyses had been undertaken and mimeographed also by CPOE, the "rehabilitation class teachers" opinion had been surveyed, and the
professional competence of first grade teachers had been examined.

The following are summaries of these studies in chronolog-
ical order.

* * * * *

The first attempt to assess the effects of the new grouping system was made in December 1958. Results obtained from May
to December in the thirty-three Grupos Escolares included in the
pilot project were compared with the achievement of children
from schools operating under the older system. Results in favor
of the pilot schools were considered "very small" but "encouraging", suggesting "the superiority of the new system" (Suple-
mento 1960:10).

In 1960 a more extensive statistical analysis was made comparing 1960 with 1959 data and pointing to the inferiority of
some of the 1960 results (Boletim 1960:207-210). Among first
graders only thirty-three per cent had been promoted; third and
fourth grade percentages were also inferior to those in 1959;
only second and fifth grades reversed this downward trend. The
word "failed" continued to be used. Twelve hypotheses were
raised to explain these results. Among them were the teachers'
insecurity about the new system. In addition too extensive curricula, too short a school day, lack of teaching materials,
teacher mobility, lack of adequate lunch programs, lack of medical and dental assistance are also indicated as causes of failure. With the exception of the first, all other problems were
permanent conditions of the school system.

In 1963 two different studies were made from distinct sets

of assumptions and independently of each other. There is no optimism in these analyses; on the contrary, both assume that there
is something wrong with the Reforma. The first one (Silva:1963)
is an opinion survey of the rehabilitation class teachers in the
pilot project schools; 77 per cent considered the rehabilitation
classes more difficult to manage, and felt professionally incapable of dealing with these children; 85 per cent of them believed that "very little" of the Reforma objectives had been a-
chieved.

The other 1963 study made by a group from outside the Secretariat of Education provides only incidental appraisal of the
Reforma (Pacheco and Santes: 1965). The focus of this investigation was the first grade teachers and their professional adequacy. This report starts by pointing out that promotion rates
in the 1961 Porto Alegre first grades were inferior to those in
1956. Teachers had no knowledge of fundamental principles of
learning, had no assistance either from the school itself or from
supervisors, and were not familiar with recent literature published for them in Porto Alegre. While positive results achieved
with children were interpreted by the teacher as resulting from
her own proficiency, negative results were attributed to the
children's difficulties, their socio-economic background and the
multiple session system; prediction of achievement was found to
be closely related to class classification; teaching materials
were scarce and there was no organized plan for their utilization.

The study also reveals that there were three rehabilitation
classes for every four regular, and that principals had the tendency to assign first grades to the younger, inexperienced,
teachers.

In 1966 a comparative study of school achievement during the
1960-1965 period was prepared (CPOE:1966). "Suficiencia" in 1965
was lower than before, especially in the first and fourth grades;
the drop-out rate in the first grade was higher than in previous
years, in remedial classes higher than in regular ones and the
number of remedial classes had increased considerably. Many
questions raised about these low results were answered by pointing again to the multiple session arrangement and to the
teachers' mobility. Only 39 per cent of the schools had two regular sessions; 53 per cent had three, and 4 per cent had four
daily two-hour periods of classes; in addition only 54 per cent
of the first grade classes had had only one teacher during the
academic year, 36 per cent had had two, and 9 and 1 per cent had
had three and four teachers respectively. Many suggestions are
presented in this report.

In 1967 more statistics about the rehabilitation classes
outcomes in 1964, 1965 and 1966 were compiled (CPOE:1967). Re-

sults are given by type of rehabilitation class, not by grade. A
new terminology was introduced, some R. C. children had been "rehabilitated", some had had "normal achievement". The children's
socio-economic level was found to be either low (64 per cent) or
middle-low (17.5 per cent); less than three per cent were in the
high and middle-high brackets. The teachers' opinions about
their classes confirmed a previous report; they considered the
work to be difficult, 82 per cent saying that their normal school
programs did not include any specific preparation for these
classes; in addition, they said they had only "some" or "little"
and "too general" supervision.

In spite of their differences in approach, focus and method,
these reports repeatedly point to the growing failure of the
schools in Porto Alegre, attributing it to a variety of problems.
However the grouping system was never accused.

The 1963 and 1967 teacher complaints are practically the
same which indicates that conditions have not changed since the
beginning of the decade; actually, there is no indication that
these reports prompted any modification of existing conditions,
or that they had been taken into account for programs in normal
schools and workshops, or even that they had had wide distribution among teachers. As mentioned before, some of these reports
exist only in manuscript form and others had limited circulation.
None of them suggests the elimination of the classification system.

Part II, Examination of the New Data; The Classification System;
        Characteristics of the Schools; School Population and
        the Teachers.

As mentioned in the Introduction, our objectives were quite
different from those of the above described evaluations. Our
purpose was to investigate the Reforma itself, its historic-
cultural background, its conceptualization, introduction in the
school system and its methods of implementation. For these two
latter objectives we went to the schools in Porto Alegre. Also,
some other characteristics of the school system would be investigated, such as the actual material conditions of the schools,
the socio-economic characteristics of the school population, the
preparation and personal satisfaction of teachers, the contact
between children in regular and rehabilitation classes, all factors that influence the results of teaching.

The choice of the schools to be surveyed was made in consultation with a group of 12 psychologists, social workers and
educators in the Secretariat of Education who surveyed the schools.
The objective was to have a full representation of the Porto
Alegre schools. The sample consists of three downtown schools,

202

six located in industrial areas, fourteen serving different residential zones, and one on the city periphery serving a region which includes some small subsistence farms -- a total of 24 out of 156.

None of these schools serve a homogeneous area from the socio-economic point of view; while on the main streets there are good, well-built residences, in the back streets houses are dilapidated and some families even live in shacks. All 24 schools surveyed are within a three block distance from public transportation. In 1967 the enrollment in the 24 schools was 15,455, 8,520 in regular classes and 6,935 (45 per cent) in rehabilitation classes. Of these, 1,437 graduated from fifth grade.

The Classification System Used

In 1967 there were two types of regular classes for every grade, A and B, and three basic types of rehabilitation classes designated as C, D, and R; class C is for those who failed one or more subjects; class D for 8 and 9 year old children who are in the first grade but are illiterate; and class R for older children. Age grouping actually is rigorously followed in the regular classes and with the younger children; older children of various ages in general are grouped together. In the 144 R.C. of the sample 101, different combinations of symbols were in use.

Of the 101 combinations used, only 55 indicate age-ability homogeneous grouping, the actual objective of the classification system. The other 47 combinations indicate a heterogeneous combination of age and ability. The CPOE in 1958 and 1959 actually suggest heterogeneous combinations, recognizing that the schools do not have facilities for only homogeneous groups. The fact that this suggestion makes official the continuing practice of heterogeneous grouping in 46 per cent of the classes does not seem to have been perceived as defeating the initial objectives of the classification system.

In 1964 about 50 per cent of the children all over the state were in R.C., the proportion varying from 48 - 30 per cent in Porto Alegre to 66 per cent in the sixth education region (CPOE: 1964). In the 24 schools studied the proportion was 45 per cent.

Material Conditions of the Schools

The buildings in which the 24 sample schools operate point to overwhelming financial problems of the Secretariat of Education. Twelve of the 24 schools are wooden frame buildings, "emergency solution" to overcrowded schools since the beginning of the decade. There is no insulation or sound proofing devices. Extremes of temperature are acutely felt, and the voices of children and teachers are heard from every classroom.

Classifications Used in the 24 Schools Sample

		Total
First Grade	- 1A^{13}, "1st grade," 2DM^1, 3CM^1, 4CM^1	5
Second Grade Level	- "2nd grade," 2ABMR, 2CD, 2BM, 2BMR 2DM, 2DM^a, 2CM, 2(3RM^2) 3CR^2, 3R^2, 3BM^2, 3CRM^2, 3RM^2, 3R^2, 3CM^2, 4RM^2, 4CRM^2, 4R^2, 4C^2 (2O)5CM^2, (2O)5RM^2, 5R^2, 5C^2, 6C^2, 5x6RM^2 6R^2	34
Third Grade Level	- "3rd grade," 3B^b, 3D, 3DM, 3ABR, 3BC, 3RCM, 3BRM, 3CDM 3^O(4°CRM^3), 3^O(4CR^3), 4RM^3, 4CM^3, 4R^3, 4CR^3, 4C^3, 4°x6^{O}R^3, 4RCM^3, 4°R3a, 4RMC^3 3^O(5CR^3), 5R^3, 5RM^3, 5CRM^3, 5C^3, 5RM3ab, 5RC^3 6RCM^3, 3^O(6°CR^3), 6R^3, 6C^3, 5°x6^{O}RM^3	32
Fourth Grade Level	- 4°C, "4th grade," 4AB, 4DM, 4(5R^4) 5CM^4, 5C^4, 5R^{4b}. 5CRM^4, 5RM^4, 5RC^4, 5R^4, 5°x6^{O}RM^4 6RM^4, 6R^4, 4^O(6RM), 6CRM^4, 6CR^4, 6C^4, 6CM^4.	20
Fifth Grade Level	- 5RC, "5th grade," 5C, 5DM, 5CM, 5BR 6R^5, 6CR^5, 6CRM^5, 6R^{5a}	10
T o t a l		101

Six buildings are rented family houses, mostly in poor condition. The other six are masonry buildings actually built for educational purposes but only two were relatively new and have gymnasiums. Sanitary installations in most of the buildings are few, not functioning properly or not functioning at all. All schools have kitchens, 10 with wood-burning stoves. Most schools have a snack program which in general means milk distribution but some give the children a soup prepared on the premises.

The classrooms have rows of individual desks facing the teacher; in two of the schools there are desks with two seats. At the end of the school day, which may be of four, three, or even two hours, teachers and children carry their books and materials home so as not to interfere with the successive groups which utilize the same room. Teaching materials are few. First graders do not have a reader, daily lessons being prepared by the teachers. Rehabilitation and regular classes are in the same condition. However, only 10 teachers spontaneously mentioned these problems as being drawbacks to the Reforma objectives.

Socio-Economic Level of the School Population

Public elementary schools in the Rio Grande do Sul used to be considered "democratic" in the sense that children were representative of all strata of society. Grupos Escolares had prestige among middle and upper class groups, were considered better than private schools, and in addition were free, a significant factor for the great majority of middle class families usually living on very limited budgets. Within the decade of the sixties the situation changed considerably in Porto Alegre and in 1967 about half of those enrolled came from very low socioeconomic groups.

In half of the 24 schools surveyed children came from a very low socio-economic group with fathers earning minimum salaries -- less than U.S. $35 a month. In five schools they were mostly from middle class families, the majority of the fathers being professionals, businessmen and civil servants. And in two schools skilled worker fathers predominate. Five schools did not have this information.

Some of the teachers' comments about their pupils's socio-economic situations are very revealing. The reason for absenteeism of children in 70 instances was said to be their poverty: either they lacked adequate clothing, school materials such as pencils, notebooks and books, or they had to stay home taking care of younger siblings; some girls were sleep-in servants and were absent on "cleaning days"; some boys had to do seasonal work on farms or in gardens; an additional reason was that some lived in flooded areas where their homes were isolated for periods of time. Teachers from three schools mentioned that many of their pupils had been abandoned by their parents and lived with their god-parents or on the charity of strangers.

Contact Between Regular and Rehabilitation Class Children

The majority of R.C. children have only casual, non-organized contacts with their more fortunate school contemporaries;

fifty teachers said that there was no contact between them and ninety-four answered that some contact existed "at entrance and leaving time" and "at recess time". However, in nine of the 24 schools there was no recess period because of their running three sessions, and three schools had all R.C. children in one session, all regular classes in another. Thus in more than half of the schools R.C. children are kept in two distinct "tracks", in a "de facto" intellectual segregation which is also, as suggested above, class segregation. Such an undesirable outcome certainly was not intended at the UNESCO conference.

Teacher Preparation and Job Satisfaction

Regarding professional background, 85 teachers graduated from the Porto Alegre normal schools and "Institutos de Educacao", 53 from schools in 28 different cities in the state, and 6 came from other Brazilian states. Most of them did not have training other than normal school; 25 were university graduates (from the "Faculdade de Filosofia"), 2 had the School Administration program and only one mentioned having had the CPOE Intensive Course for Rehabilitation Classes. Also, as found in previous surveys, 80 of the teachers (55 per cent) stated that they did not have speical training to teach R.C.

When asked about the classes they would like to teach, 115 (79 per cent) said they would prefer regular classes. The R.C. children were perceived as having many overlapping problems such as lack of interest (69 per cent), lack of discipline (35 per cent), malnutrition, poor health (20 per cent), absenteeism (40 per cent), parental indifference (65 per cent); a too extensive curriculum (27 per cent), and a shortage of teaching materials (59 per cent) were additional factors explaining the general dislike for rehabilitation classes.

Principals were also asked about their teachers' professional adequacy; 20 of them (83 per cent) said that "teachers are not prepared to teach R.C. and don't like them", confirming what teachers themselves said. Class assignment is thus done on a rotation basis; "as a matter of justice", as one of the principals put it, the "poor" and "good" classes should not be assigned always to the same teachers.

In addition to all these problems teachers were unhappy about their salaries. In Rio Grande do Sul teacher salaries are low, even by Brazilian standards, ranging from U.S. $35 to $65 per month after 25 years of work. However, since teaching is still one of the professions widely accepted for women -- there are no male teachers in the elementary schools -- most of them are from a middle socio-economic level and their salaries are a small supplement to the family income.

206

Disliking the rehabilitation classes, they move from one
school to another hoping for a regular class. That this is done
during the school year, ignoring the additional burden to the
schools, only points to a concept of administration less than
optimal at the Secretariat level.

Part III, Comments on the Reforma Objectives, Concepts and Implementation Procedures

As the reader has already understood, the situation of the
schools in 1968 was disastrous and a new "status quo" had been
established without the hopeful results of the 1958 pilot project. Some older principals and teachers had uneasy feelings,
but those who had been hired recently had found the school system already organized, separating children by age and achievement level, more strictly than in 1956.

In the following pages a brief analysis is made of the most
obvious elements in the Reforma that, in retrospect, were responsible for its failure.

As mentioned before, at the UNESCO Conference in Lima, Peru,
INEP officials were afraid that Brazilian teachers would not
accept automatic promotion; the system was selective but an attempt should be made to change and to educate all Brazilian
children. Apparently, to avoid a confrontation with CPOE, INEP
only proposed "a flexible system of promotions" and age grouping.
Both of them were new.

The concept of age grouping, strictly speaking, was foreign
to Brazilian schools even though children are expected to enroll
in the first grade at seven years of age. However, age variety
in every class is common. Rural areas do not have either the
necessary number of schools or means of transportation and children remain illiterate for a long period of time, going to school
at different ages.

With families moving to the city the custom is perpetrated
and children have been grouped according to grade level, not age.
Automatic promotion was a totally foreign idea, not easily acceptable. Schools had to educate and promotions were both a
reward and an indication of the children's intellectual development. Teachers, parents and children themselves knew what it
meant to have finished elementary school. Every society's form
of organization has the defects corresponding to its virtues
(Bidney:1967), and in Rio Grande do Sul selectivity was the price
to be paid for the clarity of purposes of the schools. The expression "automatic promotion" was carefully avoided in the Reforma and some CPOE officials asserted that it was never intended. However, children were automatically promoted. A combina-

207

tion of age grouping plus grade level and automatic promotion was
the compromise worked out by the educational authorities as a solution to the problem of selectivity versus democratization. In
addition, INEP authority was not antagonized. The result was
that those "promoted" to a rehabilitation class rarely or never
would rejoin the regular class, an advantage that repeaters had
always had. A clearly separated, two track system was started,
maintaining the previous selectivity and establishing intellectual segregation.

An examination of the documents in which the Reforma objectives are stated reveals that they do not represent a unified
body of purposes and policies carefully planned; they rather
point to a hesitancy in establishing new objectives as well as
maintaining independence from INEP's leadership.

This is not to say that INEP's educators would know how to
make the Brazilian system of education more democratic. It is
one thing to point to the ideal direction for the resolution of a
problem and quite another to indicate the practical steps to
bring about the desired change (Bidney:1967:434). The existing
cultural situation could make it impossible to proceed immediately with the establishment of a more humanistic system. How much
the national movement of opinion against INEP's approach to education influenced CPOE's attitudes and decisions was not investigated. However, the sequence of events strongly suggests such
a relationship. With the introduction of the combined age-ability criterion for grouping, CPOE educators clearly indicated
their belief in the efficacy of the selective grouping system
and in the advantage of keeping apart the fast from the slow
pupils.

The "Planejamento Geral do Reforma" (Boletim 1958:71-79) is
CPOE's most extensive statement of objectives and procedures.
The objectives do not refer to social change but to "the pupils'
emotional adjustment", and, in second place, to "the recovery of
those who had a late start in school or who fell behind". The
elimination of repeaters and drop-outs is not mentioned.

The objectives of the R.C. are also described as being "the
structuring of the child's personality...", "the solution of the
pupils' personal problems..." Other objectives of the R.C. imply
conflicting assumptions about the possiblities of the children in
these classes. They are assumed both to be able to learn only
a "minimal" part of the regular curriculum (Ibid"74), and to advance rapidly and rejoin the regular classes (Ibid:76).

Evaluation is described as "the study and interpretation of
all changes in the child's global behavior" (Ibid:75), but the
judgment about the R.C. child's achievement is to be made only

208

on the basis of written examinations organized by CPOE (Ibid:76).

The "Planejamento" thus does not represent an ideal point of view and the guidelines for change in that direction. However, this was the basic document repeatedly sent to the schools and nationally distributed, in 1960, in the educational journal Revista do Ensino. CPOE was proud of it.

The Government's Decree 9950 which made the Reforma official -- and that was prepared by CPOE -- does not determine either that selectivity should be reduced or that all children should be educated. It establishes the classification system.

The Rehabilitation Concept

According to one CPOE official interviewed the number of R.C. children joining the regular classes is not known. Only the 1959 statistics mention this item in absolute numbers.

Our data from the 24 schools shows that the word "recuperacao" is actually used with more than one connotation, sometimes in the same school. In some schools it has the intended meaning of making up the grade; in others it means "to repeat the grade successfully"; a third connotation is "to skip a grade". Fourth grade children at times are give an enriched program and encouraged to try the high school entrance examinations. If they pass they are said to be "recuperados". The word has still another meaning at the CPOE itself: those children who successfully repeat a grade are designated in the statistics as having had "normal achievement" (CPOE:1967).

Obviously statistics are either ambiguous or meaningless. For instance, 14 of the principals said they did not have "recuperados" in their schools, declaring that they opposed any attempt to R.C. children making up the grade, that this was impossible. One principal reported 121 "recuperados" and seven said that in 1967 they had had 20, 4. 27, 3, 10, 7 and 13 respectively. Clearly they were referring to different things.

The Drop-Out Rate

Similar difficulties were encountered with the number of drop-outs. In Rio Grande do Sul school statistics have two enrollment figures, the "general", that of March first -- the beginning of the school year -- and the "real", which indicated the actual number of children attending school at the end of the year. Some of the schools in the sample provided only the "real" enrollment at the end of 1967 with no indication of the number of those eliminated during the year. Some others provided the numbers of those promoted as the "real" enrollment.

Regarding the fifth grade, some schools supplied the number of regular fifth grade level children while others gave the number of those who were in school for five years but actually were in the fourth grade.

Feelings of Frustration

One of CPOE's expected positive consequences of the Reforma was the elimination of feelings of frustration which presumably all "repeaters" had in the past. Unfortunately R.C. children were not interviewed and most teachers did not seem to know if their pupils were aware of being in an R.C. Only 17 clearly expressed that children knew who are the "advanced" and the "poor" students; one stated that R.C. children want to hide their grade level, telling others that they are in regular classes and are called "liars"; another told of children saying "I am stupid, I can't learn, I am not promoted as others are."

Principals believed that R.C. children are as aware that they are not at the same level of the regular children as repeaters used to be. For one of them this is actually one of the Reforma problems: "Children know they were not really promoted, are frustrated and don't believe in the teacher any more." Another said: "the (System) creates distrust between child and teacher"; still another, "it creates great confusion in the child."

The Black Children

In Porto Alegre schools, as in Brazil in general, color segregation never existed either in law or in practice, and the word "race" is not used for identification purposes. Many public schools only have records in terms of the children's sex; of the 24 Grupos Escolares surveyed only 14 supplied information on the pupils' color and two explained that they did not make a distinction between children by color.

However small and inaccurate the available figures might be they suggest that the drop-out rate among black children is greater than among whites, that the number of fifth grade graduates is still smaller, that there are more black children in R.C. than in regular classes and that they are in the lowest socio-economic class.

Of the 729 black children reported enrolled 253 were in regular classes and 476 in R.C., a proportion of 65 per cent, 20 per cent more than for the total enrollment. In addition, the great majority of black children leave school before the third grade; out of 729 only 49 were enrolled in third, fourth and fifth grades all together, and of these only 30 graduated, a proportion of 4 per cent over the total black children's enrollment.

210

School #11 with the higher percentage of graduates -- and seemingly, accurate statistics -- reported one black child in the
fifth grade while there were 39 in the school. If the statistics
show anything at all it is that, in spite of the total racial integration of the schools, there is a greater drop-out rate among
black children, more of them are in rehabilitation classes and a
very few actually graduate from elementary school

More of the Principals', Teachers' and Supervisors' Opinions

Among the principals interviewed 54% said that the Reforma
objectives have not been achieved; the drop-out rate is, they
said, practically the same as before, the concept of "repeaters"
did not disappear, and very few pupils are actually rehabilitated.
Thirty-five per cent said that age grouping is good. Two saw the
Reforma as a success. One of them, a young, new appointee, said
without qualification that "all the Reforma objectives have been
achieved", despite the fact that in her school more than 70% of
the children drop-out before the fifth grade.

In relation to their experience with the Reforma 13 of those
interviewed were already principals in 1958; they all said they
had received the CPOE instructions and had been present at the
orientation meetings but considered them "not satisfactory" and
"too few". Some of their most expressive comments were as follows: "We only received instructions about the classification
system"; "the supervision was insufficient"; "the meetings were
only with the principals, not with the teachers"; "teachers were
confused, one fourth grade teacher followed two curricula even
though hers was a regular class"; "until now teachers don't know
either the Reforma objectives or how to classify children".

All the 11 principals who were not yet on the job in 1958
said they don't know how the Reforma started but that the CPOE
instructions are filed in their schools. Their answers are not
very different from those of the older principals: "There is
the classification but not the rehabilitation"; "it is only a
label"; "it is deceptive for the children and their parents".

Among the R.C. teachers 45 per cent were strongly against
the Reforma, the others either did not answer the question or
gave non-commital answers. Some of the characteristic negative
answers follow: "two curricula in one year is impossible"; "it
does not avoid either frustration or repetitions"; "it is an
illusion for parents and children"; "the child does not make any
effort and is promoted"; "the child does not know his own level".

The supervisors interviewed confirmed most of the teachers'
and principals' answers. Some of them had been teachers when
the Reforma started and some of their comments were as follows:

211

"In the school where I was working as a teacher, the news of the Reforma was given very casually; I heard that the third grade was under a new system". "Teachers do not want rehabilitation classes"; "It is a privilege to teach a regular class and R.C. are given to new teachers."

During the interview one of the supervisors said: "We don't talk about the Reforma any more", and most of her colleagues agreed. One explained: "The new classification is something for the principal and the secretary to know; teachers receive their classes already organized and are told of their level." Giving support to this assertion another said: "One of the problems is that new teachers know nothing of the Reforma; the normal schools do not teach it and, as a matter of fact, even the "Curco de Administração" (School Administration program) does not teach it either. "In some localities neither teachers nor principals know the classification system."

In an individual interview a CPOE official deeply involved with the analysis of the Reforma results rather bitterly declared, "I don't believe there has been a reform."

P.S. While this study was in process in Porto Alegre a new Secretary of Education ordered the elimination of the classification system. A few years later, another Secretary of Education eliminated the CPOE itself.

Conclusions

The experience of Rio Grande do Sul is an example that cultural values are facts -- observable, effective factors -- especially in the field of education, a normative endeavor par excellence. The analysis of the difficulties of introducing a democratic, humanistic concept of grouping children into the selective and bureaucratic educational system of Rio Grande do Sul, Brazil, points to the difficult task of changing values and the complexity of establishing educational policies which will help in the process of change. A cultural ideal accepted only by a few courageous persons at the top adminstrative level may never filter down to the classroom practices unless all the phases of the transformation of ideas into practice are clearly spelled out, understood, accepted by a majority, and critically examined periodically.

NOTES

[1]Following Miles (1964) the term innovation is used there meaning "a deliberate, novel, specific change which is thought to be more efficacious in accomplishing the goals of a system."

[1]This information is registered in CPOE's Registrar of Meetings.

[*]A symbol such as 3CMR[2] indicates a second grade child (exponent 2) with a poor first grade achievement (c) of 10, 11, or 12 years of age (M for mixed ages) who should be in the third grade (the first 3).

REFERENCES

ABE.
1957 "A Associacão Brasileira de Educacao e o Ensino Pablico." ("The Brazilian Education Association and Public Education") Revista Brasileira de Estudos Pedogógicos, Vol. 27, pp. 162-170.

Almeida Junior, A.
1957 "Repetencia ou Promoção Automitica?" ("Repetition - or Automatic Promotion?") Revista Brasileira de Estudos Pedagógicos, Vol. 27, pp. 3-15.

Anuario Brasileiro de Educacao 1964
1966 (Brazilian Education Yearbook") Vol. 1, Rio de Janeiro: Ministerio de Educacao e Cultura, Instituto National de Estudos Pedagógicos.

Anuirio Estatictico do Brasil 1967.
1967 ("Brazilian Statistics Yearbook") Vol. 28, Rio de Janeiro: Fundacao IBGE, Instituto Brasileire de Estatistica

Antunha, Elza Lima Goncalves.
1962. "Promoção Automitica na Escola Primaria." ("Automatic Promotion in Elementary School.") Pesquisa e Planejamento, Vol. 5, pp. 97-110.

"Apoio a Dr. Anisio"
1968 ("In Support of Dr. Anisio") Revista Brasileira de Estudes Pedagógicos, Vol. 29, pp. 68-84.

Arensberg, Conrad M.
1965a "The Community Study Method." In Conrad M. Arensberg and Solon T. Kimbal Culture and Community. New York: Harcourt, Brace and World, Inc. pp. 28-47.

Arensberg, Conrad M.
1965B "Behavior and Organization: Industrial Studies." In Conrad M. Arensberg and Solon T. Kimbal Culture and Community. New York: Harcourt, Brace and World, Inc. pp. 301-324.

Atwood, M.S.
1964 "Small-scale administrative change: resistance to the introduction of a high school guidance program." In Mathew B. Miles editor, Innovation in Education. New York: Teachers College Press, Teachers College, Columbia University.

Ballinger, Stanley E.
1965 The Nature and Function of Educational Policy: An Introductory Essay. Bloomington, Indiana: The Center for the Study of Educational Policy, Department of History and Philosophy of Education, School of Education, Indiana University, 46 pp.

Bidney, David
1967 Theoretical Anthropolgoy, New York: Schodken Books.

Boletim do Centro de Pesquisas e Orientacão Educacionais
1956-1957 Ponto Alegre: CPOE, Secretaria de Educacao e Cultura, p.255.

Boletim do Centro de Pesquisas e Orientacão Educacionais
1958. Porto Alegre: CPOE, Secretaria de Educacao e Cultura, p. 347.

Boletim do Centro de Pesquisas e Orientacão Educacionais
1959 Porto Alegre: CPOE, Secretaria de Educacao e Cultura, p. 611.

Boletim do Centro de Pesquisas e Orientacão Educacionais
1960. Porto Alegre: CPOE, Secretaria de Educacao e Cultura, p. 491.

Boletim do Centro de Pesquisas e Orientacão Educacionais
1961-1962 Porto Alegre: CPOE, Secretaria de Educacao e Cultura, p. 653.

CPOE
1958a "Termo de Acordo Especial Celebrado entre o Ministerio de Educacao e Cultural (MEC) par Intermedio do Instituto Nacional de Estudos Pedagógicos INEP), e o Governo do Estado do Rio Grande do Sul, para Cooperacao no Plano de Reforma do Ensino Primirio."

CPOE
1958B "Exposicão de Motives." (Statement of Purposes) Porto Alegre: Centro de Pesquisas e Orientacao Educacionais. Secretaria de Educacao e Cultura. 5 pp. Unpublished copy.

CPOE
1964 Reforma do Ensino Primirio. Classes Regulares e de
Recuperação. (Reform of Elementary Education. Regular
and Rehabilitation Classes.) Porto Alegre: Centro de
Pesquisas e Orientacao Educacionais. Secretaria de Educacao e Cultura. Unpublished.

CPOE
1966 "Estudo Comparativo do Rendimento Escolar 1960-1965."
(Comparative Study of School Achievement 1960-65.) Porto
Alegre: Centro de Pesquisas e Orientacão Educacionais.
Secretaria de Educacao e Cultura. 28 pp. Mimeographed.

CPOE
1967. "Avaliacao dos Resultados da Aplicacão de Reforma
do Ensino Primirio." (Evaluation of the Reform of Elementary Education.) Porto Alegre: Centro do Pesquisas e
Orientacao Educacionais. Secretaria de Educacao e Cultura, 14 pp. Mimeographed.

Daniel, J.C.
1961 "The Effects of Streming in the Primary School. Part
I. What Teachers Believe." British Journal of Educational Psychology Vol. 31, pp. 69-78

Departmento de Educaco Primariea
1968. "Numero de Classes Vospertinas e de Sento Ano em
Funcionamento." Porto Alegre: Divisio de Controle da
Rede Escolar, Departamento de Educacao Primaria, Secretaria de Educacao e Cultura. Personal Communication.

Fortes, Amyr Borges
1958 Aspectes Fisiograficos. Demogrificos e Economicos
do Rio Grande do Sul. Porto Alegre: Livraria do Globo
S.A. 75 pp. 43 mapas e 8 quadros.

INEP
1958a Termo de Acordo Especial Celebrado entre o Minis-
tario de Educacao e Cultura (MEC) por Intermedio do
Instituto Nacional de Estudos Pedagógicos (INEP), e o
Governo do Estado do Rio Grande do Sul, para Execucao
do Plano de Regularizacao da Matricula. Escolar Primeria,
par Idade. (Terms of the Special Agreement between INEP
and Rio Grande do Sul State Government to Introduce Age
Grouping in the Elementary Schools.) Porto Alegre: Con-
tro do Pesquisas e Orientacão Educacionais Secretaria de
Educacao e Cultura, 3 pp. Documento nao publicado.

INEP
1958b. "Relatorio do Bureau International d'Education." (Re-

port to the International Bureau of Education.) Revista
Brasileira de Estudos Pedagógicos, Vol. 31(74), p. 195-206.

Kubitscheck, Juscelino
   1956 "Reforma de Ensino Primirio com Base no Sistema de
   Promocão Automitica." (Reform of Elementary Education
   Based on Automatic Promotion) Revista Brasileira de
   Estudos Pedagógicas, Vol 27, 00. 141-145.

Lourenco Filho, M.D.
   1948 O Teste ABC. Rio de Janeiro: Editora Melhora Mentos.

McNeill, Malvina Rosat
   1970 Guidelines to Problems of Education in Brazil, A
   Review and Selected Bibliography. New York: Teachers
   College Columbia University.

"Memorial dos Bispos do Rio Grande do Sul sobre of Ensino Oficial."
   1958 (Statement by the Bishops of Rio Grande do Sul on
   Oficial Education.) Revista Brasileira de Estudos
   Pedagógicos, Vol. 29, pp. 64-48.

Miles, Mathew B.
   1964a "Educational Innovation: The Nature of the Problem."
   In Mathew B. Miles editor, Innovation in Education. New
   York: Teachers College Press, Teachers College, Columbia
   University, pp. 1-46.

Miles, Mathew B.
   1964h "Innovation in Education: Some Generalizations."
   In Mathew B. Miles editor, Innovation in Education. New
   York: Teachers College Press, Teachers College, Columbia
   University. pp. 631-982.

Moreira, J. Roberto
   1947 "A Educacao Elementar em Face do Planejamonto Eco-
   nomico." (Elementary Education and Economic Planning").
   Revista Brasileira de Estudes Pedagógicos Vol. 28 (67)
   pp. 155-168..

Morgenstern, Anne, editor.
   1966 Grouping in the Elementary School. New York,
   Pitman Publishing Corporation.

Pacheco, Graciama and Santos, Olga M.
   1965 As Classes de Alfabetizacao Atraves do Parecer das
   Professoras. (First Grade Classes from the Teachers'
   Point of View.) Porto Alegre: Centro Regional de
   Pesquisas Educacionais, Instituto Nacional de Estudos
   Pedagógicas, Ministerio de Educacao e Cultura.

216

"Palestra Inaugural."
  1958   (Inaugural Speech.)   Boletim do Centro de Pesquisas
  e Orientacao Educacionais.   1958.   Porto Alegre: CPOE
  Secretaria de Educacao e Cultura, pp. 118-121.

Pereira, Luis
  1958   "A Promocao Automatica na Escola Primaria."   (Automatic Promotion in Elementary School)   Revista Brasileira de Estudos Pedagógicos, Vol. 30, pp. 105-107.

"Primeiro Congress Estadual de Educacao em Ribeirao Preto."
  1956   Revista Brasileira de Estudos Pedagógicos. Vol.26 (65)

"Recomendacoes da Conferencia Regional Latino Americano sobre
Educacao Primaria Gratuita e Obrigatoria."
  1956   (Recommendations of the Latin American Regional Conference on Free and Cumpulsory Elementary Education.)
  Revista Brasileira de Estudos Pedagógicos, Vol. 26 (6),
  pp. 158-178.

Reforma do Ensino Primario
  (Reform of Elementary Education)   Porto Alegre: Suplemen-
  to no. 4, Revista do Ensino, 1960.   Secretaria de Educacao e Cultura, 16 pp.

Silva, Hilda
  1963   A Classe de Recuperação e o Professor.   São Paulo:
  Centro Regional de Pesquisas Educacionais, Instituto Nacional de Estudos Pedagógicos, Ministerio de Educacao e
  Cultura.   Curso de Especialistas em Educacao.   Unpublished
  manuscript.   35 pp.

Sperb, Dalila and others
  1967   Subsidios para o Planejamento Educacional no Rio
  Grande do Sul.   Porto Alegre: Centro Regional de Pesquisas Educacionais do Rio Grande do Sul, Instituto Nacional de Estudos Pedagógicos, Ministerio de Educacao e
  Cultura, 159 pp.

Teixeira, Anisio S.
  1957   "Bases para uma Programacao da Educacao Primaria no
  Brasil." (Basis for a Program of Elementary Education in
  Brazil.)   Revista Brasileira de Estudos Pedagógicos,
  Vol. 27 (65).pp. 28-46.

Thalem, Herbert A.
  1967   Classroom Grouping for Teachability.   New York: John
  Willey Sons, Inc.

Yates, Alfred, editor
  1966 The UNESCO Institue for Education. Hamburg. Grouping
  in Education. New York: John Willey Sons, Inc.

AGING, SOCIETY, AND PROGRESS

Marea Teski, Ph.D.
STOCKTON STATE COLLEGE

If we wish to consider the position of the old in human society, we must take a careful look at the evolution of culture as a whole and then at the development of our particular culture. If cultural evolution refers to changes in adaption between humans and their environment, and different adaptions tend to encourage different patterns of social relations, the understanding of any aspect of social relations is improved by understanding the development of culture. Every culture has a place in an evolutionary progression - both in terms of its own special history of development and in terms of human culture as a whole. Sahlins' (1960) terms "specific" and "general" evolution point out the two dimensions of change to which we can refer any particular body of data. The term "specific" has to do with the individuality of different cultures in forming their own patterns, while the term "general" carries with it some notion of progress - perhaps greater adaptability, or greater complexity which becomes part of the total human experience.

How does our original concern, the place of the old in society, relate to the question of progress? First of all we must distinguish two forms of progress. The first we have been discussing in relation to "general" evolution. It means the development of new forms of coping with the environment out of the old forms and implies the concept of increased efficiency. Leslie White's (1949) discussion of culture as a mechanism for harnessing increasingly powerful forms of energy is an example of this concept of progress.

There is also another sense in which we can use the word "progress." This is in an ideal, or normative sense - meaning improvement in an absolute way. When we use the word "progress" in this way we project for ourselves an image of what human society and life should be. We then measure our achievements against this image. At any point we can then say whether given social forms or practices are progress or not.

In discussing the position of the old in society, both uses of the word "progress" are significant. Their fate relates to the interaction of their culture with the environment and its potential for survival, and control over subsistence. It also relates to the values of the group - how they feel about human life and how they feel about weaker or helpless members.

Studies of primitive cultures, the development of the state, and the emergence of modern civilization out of older civilizations make clear how often the forms of culture are dictated by the necessities of nature. The development of horticulture in the ancient Middle East was probably a response to the need to find a food source for a rapidly increasing population. Harris (1977) suggests that the development of agriculture in both the Old and New Worlds occurred because a warming climate about 13,000 years ago caused much of the big game to become extinct. This big game had been the major food source for humans during the Pleistocene period and they had to find a replacement for it. Human activities are often a response to natural conditions, and large changes in human activities a reflection of major climatic alterations.

Social arrangements, like subsistence activities reflect the relationship between man and the environment. Simmons' (1945) survey of the place of the old in 71 societies shows, predictably, that in societies which are very close to subsistence level, the prospects for old people are not good. Actually, in such societies, few people survive into old age. If some do live to become old, their interests may well be sacrificed when conditions become difficult. It will be more important for younger people to survive to continue the group. The abandonment of old people in societies whose subsistence is difficult is a common feature of the anthropological literature.

Simmons' descriptions of the elderly in different cultures focus on their general, political, and civil activities. There is also consideration of older people's participation in religion and their use of magic. The functions of the family and comments about reactions to death in different cultures are also included.

Opportunities for old people to participate in daily activities are significantly influenced by climate, permanence of residence, subsistence activities, and the form of family organization. When conditions allow, old people seem to have a great deal to do. In the area of political and civil activities, Simmons finds that improved social stability and advances in the economy, and complexity of societies often give the elderly advantages. Under these conditions they have sometimes emerged as chiefs - especially in Africa, or Samoa. Age alone cannot give political position, but ability, initiative, being male, and other favorable social and cultural conditions plus age often result in important positions for rather old people.

Knowledge too, is important, especially in the areas of cultural lore, religion and magic. These were found to be important sources of prestige for old people cross culturally. Often the aged are seen as mediators between the society and the world of the supernatural. They are also sometimes seen as conservers of knowledge for the group. These functions, where they are considered important, give the old person an assured place in society.

As family members, the old are found to have small and useful chores to perform. As long as they are able to do these things they seem to have an assured place in the group. However, Simmons feels that his data indicate that the position of the helpless and decrepit old person is bad in every culture. He says:

> Thus even in societies where the aged
> have possessed firmly entrenched rights,
> the very decrepit have faced the threat
> of indifference, neglect and actual
> abuse. (1945:177)

At this point even families sometimes abandon the old person. This happens without regard for the ability of the society to provide for the helpless person. In all of the societies of Simmons' sample there seems to be the idea that at a certain point, the old person "should" die. If the person lingers on too long, neglect might hasten death. Exposure, or even the killing of such old people is reported. Suicide of old people is also reported. In suicide the elderly person agrees with society's judgement that he, or she should die and saves others the necessity of making sure that it happens. If an old person commits sui-

221

cide it gives that person a kind of heroic stature in some societies, for it shows that the welfare of all was put before personal considerations.

The ethnographic material reviewed by Simmons suggests that as societies progress in terms of more efficient control of the environment, the position of people who live to be old is improved. More effective management of subsistence resources makes it possible to feed more people who are not actively involved in subsistence activities. As societies become more complex, special positions suited to older members begin to become important. Experience in human relations counts and older people become administrators and teachers.

However, there seems to be no explanation for why the helpless old are in a precarious position even in societies which can well afford to maintain them. Simmons' material suggests that neglect and mistreatment of such elderly is the rule, rather than the exception even in more affluent cultures. To find the answer to why this should be we have to look more closely into both our "human nature" as genetically given and into the particular cultural traditions of whatever society we are considering. We must not be too quick to consider the position of the elderly as "caused" by the economic conditions of society.

Harlan (1968) attacks a fondly held misconception - the idea that traditional non-industrial societies value the old more than our society does. These societies are seen as linked with the past, not obsessed with fear of obsolescence, and cherishing of the old because they are living representatives of the past. Harlan observed the treatment of the aged in three Indian villages and discovered that their position was as precarious as that described by Simmons for the helpless old. In none of the three villages which he describes do the old have high status positions. Other variables such as caste, family, etc. are operative here, but the fact remains that age does not seem to command respect, or any special treatment. Information like this, along with Simmons survey, makes it clear that the treatment of the old in any society is a complex matter involving the deepest values, assumptions, and fears of the group. It must be investigated much more completely than has been done in the past.

Turning our attention to American society of the present, it is clear that our ideas and feelings about aging and the elderly are basic to our tendency to devaluate the older citizen. The society is in the position of having to change some of its values if it is to devote sufficient resources to the elderly. The concept of "productiveness" is central in this society and developed from the world-view which emerged during the Industrial Revolution. It leads to a devaluation of those who have retired, for they are seen as being "non-productive." Our view of productiveness goes much further than the idea of procuring basic subsistence, and involves much more. To be productive in this society, one not only works for money in order to live, but puts excess money back into the economy to keep it healthy. One must not only earn, but spend so that others may earn. If old people are devalued in the United States it is not only because they are not working, and working is important to our idea of productiveness, but also because they are not big spenders.

The 1975 report from the Senate Committee on Aging indicates that economic problems now make life difficult for a large proportion of the elderly people of the United States. We have about 22 million or more older people and this number increases daily. These people usually ! ·e less than half the income of their younger counterparts. In 1973, the median income for an older person living alone or with relatives was $2,725, and in the same year half of the families headed by an older person had incomes of less than $6,426. 3.4 million or about one sixth of the elderly population live in households with incomes below the official poverty level. These figures make it clear why the elderly are not big spenders! If pensions become more adequate as the proportion of the population over 65 increases, we may predict that the increased spending power of the old will gain for them more participation in the culture and higher status positions.

Once a society has passed the subsistence level its ideas about the role of the old in society become significant in determining how they are treated. However, we must realize that in most former societies - of all levels of affluence - there were relatively few older people. Therefore, the present situation in the United States where the elderly will form an increasingly large part of the population, is a new situa-

tion. We can consider the roles and statuses of the
elderly in other times and places, but the demographic
evidence shows, that we are entering a new phase of
industrial civilization and that new ideas, and new
solutions are required.

The question of how ideas emerge in a culture is
now significant, as we consider how cultures came to
think and believe certain things about the elderly.
Whitehead's concept of the way in which ideas and
activities interact in a cultural setting is most
lucid.

> We have been considering the emergence
> of ideas from activities, and the effect
> of ideas in modifying the activities
> from which they emerge. Ideas arise as
> explanatory of customs and they end by
> founding novel methods and novel insti-
> tutions. (1933:127)

Therefore, the human society reacts to the material
and social environment in building its culture. Societies are individually and collectively creative,
using the reflective capacity of the human being to
explain, criticize and reformulate concepts of why
things are as they are, and to formulate concepts of
how things should be. Ideas about things emerge from
the living and reflecting process.

In the United States our ideas about the elderly
in society are a product of our way of life and our
concepts about the importance of individual life, productiveness in the economy, and the relation between
the two. The way in which we think about individual
life and productiveness is also related to our thinking about progress. Progress, as we understand it in
our culture, relates to both: 1) progress as more
effective management of the environment, and 2) to the
idea of absolute improvement of all aspects of life.
The idea is a modern one and involves normative judgements upon forms of life, society and culture. Progress is important to the modern way of thinking about
history and social change. An affirmation of the possibility of improvement is implicit in many modern
writers from Vico to Marx. At times improvement of
material conditions of life alone is counted as progress in the absolute sense.

The fact that material and social improvement

seem to us to have occurred, is made the basis for predictions about the possibility of future improvements. Fulfillment, for modern thinkers is more often to be found in the future than in the past. Improvement of society and all of the conditions under which humans live is seen as a goal. Practices such as the killing, or abandoning of the old are deplored, because we see them as evidence of a lack of realization of the person-hood of the individuals so treated and evidence of "backward" societies. We tend to equate the existence of practices which we dislike, with the existence of harsh economic realities which "force" people to act as they do. Thus cannibalism, infanticide, abandonment of the old, the inhumane behavior of the Ik (Turnbull: 1972) and so on, may be attributed to causes outside human control. In fact, certain practices are tied to survival needs. But what can we say about the old in American society? What about the deplorable conditions under which many of them live? We can see why the traditional Eskimo family sometimes had to abandon the old during a hard winter, but why do some of our own elderly live in dreadful housing, or in parks and subsist on dog food?

In our thinking, progress is connected with the improvement of life on all fronts economic, social and political. It ties in with the idea that we are moving constantly toward attainment of some ideal. Whitehead expresses this idealistic conception of progress most clearly.

> Progress consists in modifying the laws of nature so that the Republic on earth may conform to that society to be discerned ideally by the divination of wisdom. (1933:53)

Progress and the normative definition of civilization are the same in Whitehead's scheme because both embody ideas of improvement.

> For civilization is nothing other than the unremitting aim at the major perfections of harmony. (1933:349)

Such concepts are built into American thinking about the future, with emphasis on the importance of technology in attaining the ideal society and perfections of harmony.

In the realm of the social, this culture likes
to think we are more humane than the societies of the
past. This is another aspect of progress. The old in
the society however, present us with a dilemma. They
are not productive in our current sense of the word,
and they are seen as having no future. We have little
interest in the past which they represent. Our definition of the person should not allow for the treatment of the old as "non-persons". Yet we are aware
that our devaluation of the old and our treatment of
some of the decrepit old makes them just that - "non-
persons".

Jules Henry describes the decrepit old as being
in the category of distorted people.

> The intact human being is sane in mind
> and body. This includes sight, sanity,
> hearing and continence. But a distorted
> one is insane, or blind, or deaf or in-
> continent and so on. Some people are
> distorted in several ways. The more
> distorted a person, the greater the ten-
> dency of others to withdraw from him.
> (1965:428)

People in our culture, according to Henry, are re-
volted in various degrees by distorted people, depending upon the state of the intact person and the
degree of distortion perceived in the distorted one.
Withdrawal of aid and comfort by others may increase
the degree of distortion - isolating the aged, or ailing person even more. Degrading measures such as re-
straining old people in bed, or in chairs are often
employed to reduce the amount of time which staff in
institutions must spend with them.

One might add that the more distorted a person is
perceived to be, the less human he is considered to be
and the less humanely he is treated. Age itself is
thought of as a kind of distortion in this society.
Great age and disabilities place an individual in the
"non-person" category which, of course, we deny exists. Storage until death in a mental hospital, or
nursing home may be for some, the finale of a devaluation process which begins with retirement from work.

Our assertion of the absolute significance of
individual human life in this culture requires that
lives which are not treated with respect be defined

226

as "non-lives". One often hears it said of ailing old people - "He's not really living!", or "It's no life!", or "I'd rather be dead!". The suggestion is that it would be better if such people were not alive. This idea leads to the helpless old sometimes being treated as if they are not really alive.

Further comment on the question of values and the aged in this society is provided by Margaret Clark (1968) in an article "The Anthropology of Aging". Focusing upon the problem of mental health and mental illness in old age, she examines significant values in American culture. She finds that certain key values such as aggressiveness, ambition and a desire for control, while helpful to younger groups are actually maladaptive for old people. Among the group which Clark studied, more old people who held these values are mentally ill than people who did not hold them. It is suggested that, although the culture is changing, some of the important values and expectations make it very difficult for the aged in America. The fatalism and resignation which are learned from childhood in some cultures are learned in old age here. The learning process is often full of pain. Our culture seems to provide few blueprints for how to grow old. The idea seems to be: not to grow old at all and since it is unavoidable, difficulty and suffering are also unavoidable.

Clark and Anderson (1975) continue this theme in another article "The Anthropological Approach to Aging". This article examines aging as a cultural, as well as a biological process. The view of self is seen as very crucial to a person's relative contentment in later years and the authors point out that here some culturally inculcated views breed despondency, feelings of futility, and even mental illness in the elderly. Views of the self are shaped largely by social expectations and they reflect social values.

Different cultures experience the biologically based "stages of life" differently. For example, it is open to cultural definition when manhood begins - at puberty, at economic independence, or some other time. Thus one may become a man at age 14,16,18,21, 25,30 or even later. Arensberg's The Irish Countryman (1937) shows that manhood may be delayed until 40 or 50 years of age when the "boy" finally takes over the family farm.

227

Clark and Anderson point out that in general, western civilization has a temporal definition of "youth", "old age" etc., which depends upon how many years a person has lived. This factor combines ironically with our technologically aided longevity, leaving us with people who are defined as "old" who may have 20-30 more years of life ahead of them. The authors are well aware of the bizzare quality of this situation, stating that it is absurd to have a segment of the population living for decades with no socially related tasks. These people, because they are defined as "old" have no function in the society other than self-planned leisure activities. Not having a social function they are sometimes treated as moribund, when they are not. They are treated as dying people over a span of many years.

The problem is not confined to complex societies. Clark and Anderson describe the sadness of old men among the Attawapiskat Cree Indians of northern Canada. Values in the group decree that everyone should be busy and have many activities. The old men are sad because they are unable to do as many things as they did when they were younger. They have only their memories of former activities.

In contrast Korean society is cited as an example of a comples society which cultivates positive feelings about aging. Attainment of age 60 brings additional prestige to an individual. This is a sharp contrast to our own society where loss of some prestige with aging is a fact of life.

Because the older person faces loss of prestige here, and must try to reject values of striving and control which are maladaptive, he is often left to develop his own values - outside the mainstream of society. It is in this regard that the ethnographic studies of retirement communities are very significant. Here, in communication with others their own age, the elderly can begin to deal with the devaluation which brings in the larger society, and try to articulate some values which are appropriate, and useful for their group.

Hoyt (1954) noticed the beginnings of a value system different from that of the general population emerging in a trailer park retirement community. Here the primary interests of the residents center around leisure and recreation. This creates a different

228

focus from that of the "outside" world, and Hoyt notes
that there is little carryover of status from working
life into retired life. The status which a person
creates for himself at the park is more important than
the status of the pre-retirement life. Leadership in
park activities is the main source of prestige.

Teski (1976) also asks the question of whether
new values were emergent in the process of living in a
retirement hotel. The 300 residents of a Chicago retirement hotel assess each other's social position on
the basis of how fully they participate in the hotel's
activities, and their own activities outside the
hotel. Former status here, as in Hoyt's trailer park,
is not as important, as present activities. However,
a closer look at the values expressed by the residents
shows them to be similar to those of the larger community. Leisure time activities are seen as a replacement for work and the residents "work hard" at
being busy. No resident leader would ever be caught
relaxing, or doing nothing. They were always involved
events, or going to, or coming from events. Being
busy is universally admired. Only the most depressed,
or senile people would admit that they had nothing to
do.

What was observed in this community was not a
change of values but a reapplication of the idea of
working hard to leisure time activities. Being active
shows that a person is worthwhile and not lazy. Residents worked hard at their social activities and
evaluated their fellows on the basis of how hard they
worked at them. There was no concept of a qualitative
difference in the world of work and the world of leisure activities. Ambition, striving and seeking to
gain control are an important part of this group's
attitude to their activities. Most of them had never
thought of changing their approach toward feeling good
about themselves.

Jacob's (1974) description of "Fun City," a retirement community of individual family houses suggests that leisure time activities are not enough to
give a sense of significance to the lives of retired
people. The "Fun City" people seem to be vaguely depressed and lacking a feeling of purpose. One gets
the sense that ennui pervades the community.

The emphasis on work in this culture is too much
a part of the past lives of the residents not to con-

tinue to be a value for them. Leisure has meaning truly only in contrast with work or, to use Clark's terms "socially related tasks." Lack of work makes people-consumers alone. The role of consumer, as we have already noted is an important one in American culture. Spending, like working, is a social duty. However, values from the past make spending, like leisure, less meaningful without work.

This and other materials indicate, that older people want to develop some framework in retirement, which can validate them as worthwhile people. Like younger groups they want to see themselves as doing something important. In the absence of socially significant tasks, other activities such as leisure activities may be substituted as a means of gaining prestige. The idea that it is good to be busy at a worthwhile task, may be replaced by the idea that "busyness" alone is valuable.

It seems obvious that what would be desirable is not so much teaching people to enjoy leisure time, but the assignment of valid and socially useful work to those, who are over 65 or 70 and wish to undertake it. More older people are returning to colleges and universities, and more would return to meaningful work as well, if it were available to them. For example, would it not be effective as well as humane, to provide employment as protectors of the environment to older people who wish to do this work? These citizens could inspect and report on parks, city streets, neighborhoods etc., keeping local and state governments informed about the state of the environment. Retired people could be gainfully employed close to their homes noticing and reporting on conditions which others might be too busy to see. They would be doing a great service to the whole community and to the next generation as well. They would feel themselves to be part of the community, not as parasites or isolates.

The size of a territory covered by an elderly inspector would depend upon that person's ability to drive, walk, or get around, and need not exceed what could be realistically undertaken. If we are concerned as a society with the deterioration of the environment, and the wasting of the later years of many older people, surely these two concerns could be merged in a meaningful and useful way.

230

Progress in general ability to cope with the
environment, and progress in the improvement of human
life are both significant values in this culture.
Surveying the condition of the old in many cultures we
have seen that their position is usually improved as
their cultures become more adept at utilizing the environment. However, as has been noted, beyond a certain point of material security, the treatment of the
old is mainly determined by the culture's definition
of the value of old age.

Our culture is well able to maintain old people,
even the helpless old, at a decent standard of living.
We cannot point to economic problems of the society
at large, as a cause for the poor conditions of life
of many of our helpless aged. Their position is
largely a result of a way of thinking about life and
productiveness, which gives little opportunity for
older people to have roles which are an important part
of the society as a whole.

Erikson (1963) defined the psychological tasks of
old age. Perhaps it is now time to define the social
tasks of the elderly and to begin to think of ways to
involve them in these tasks. Jobs in environmental
protection such as we have described could be one way
to make a beginning.

It is also time to examine the transgressions
against our stated values which take place when living
people are defined as dead by the way we treat them.
We are shocked at the thought of abandoning the old,
or burying them alive which has been done in other
cultures, but the outcomes are not very different from
what happens in our culture in the case of the helpless old person. As in many cultures, meaningful
activities and relationships are taken away from the
old when they are so old, or sick that it is "time" to
die.

Progress in the normative sense requires that we
reconsider ideas about what makes human life significant and when, and for how long a person is a person?
Definitions of productiveness and absolescence must be
reconsidered. Simmons found no society in which the
decrepit old were well-treated. This is an area in
which we could make culture history. As our population of elderly people increases we must take thought
for their welfare. It would be beneficial for all to
provide socially significant tasks for elderly people.

It would also be beneficial to assure that the end of
life for all of our people comes in a manner, that
shows full recognition of their individuality and
person-hood. If we were able to do this as a whole
culture, and to develop the values to support such
activity, it might well be the first time in the
history of culture, that such action was taken.

BIBLIOGRAPHY

Arensberg, C.M.
1937   The Irish Countryman. New York: Macmillan.
Clark, Margaret
1968   The Anthropology of Aging. In Middle Age
        and Aging: A Reader in Social Psychology.
        B. Neugarten Ed. Chicago and London: Uni-
        versity of Chicago Press. pp. 433-443.
Clark, Margaret and Barbara Gallatin Anderson
1975   An Anthropological Approach to Aging. In
        Introducing Anthropology. James R. Hayes
        and James M. Helslin Eds. Boston: Holbrook
        Press Inc. pp. 331-346.
Erikson, Erik H.
1963   Childhood and Society. New York: W.W. Norton
        and Co.
Harlan, William H.
1968   The Aged in Three Indian Villages. In
        Middle Age and Aging: A Reader in Social
        Psychology. B. Neugarten Ed. Chicago and
        London: University of Chicago Press.
        pp. 469-475.
Harris, Marvin
1977   Cannibals and Kings: The Origins of Culture.
        New York: Random House.
Henry, Jules
1965   Culture Against Man. New York: Vintage
        Books.
Jacobs, Jerry
1974   An Ethnographis Study of a Retirement Set-
        ting. Gerontologist 14 (1974).
Sahlins, Marshall and Elman R. Service Eds.
1960   The Evolution of Culture. Ann Arbor: Uni-
        versity of Michigan Press.
Simmons, L.W.
1945   The Role of the Aged in Primitive Society.
        New Haven: Yale University Press.
Teski, Marea
        Living Together: The Ethnography of a Re-
        tirement Hotel. Unpublished Manuscript.
Turnbull, Colin
1972   The Mountain People. New York: Touchstone
        Books.
White, Leslie
1949   The Science of Culture. New York: Farrar,
        Strauss and Giroux.
Whitehead, Alfred N.
1933   Adventures of Ideas, New York: Macmillan Co.

III. SYMBOLIC EXPRESSION AND HUMAN UNDERSTANDING

. . . man is not only a product of
cultural conditioning and cultural determinism - as modern anthropologists are
want to stress - but is also the originator
or author of his cultural systems, the self-
determined creator and efficient cause of his
cultural conditions and patterns.

(From Theoretical Anthropology, 1953, p. 14)

INTO THE ENDZONE FOR A TOUCHDOWN:
A PSYCHOANALYTIC CONSIDERATION OF AMERICAN FOOTBALL*

Alan Dundes
University of California, Berkeley

In college athletics, it is abundantly clear that it is football which counts highest among both enrolled students and alumni.* It is almost as though the masculinity of male alumni is at stake in a given game, especially when a hated rival school is the opponent. College fundraisers know well that a winning football season may prove to be the key to a successful financial campaign to increase the school's endowment capital. The Rose Bowl and other post season bowl games for colleges plus the Super Bowl for professional football teams have come to rank as virtual national festival occasions in the United States. All this make it reasonable to assume that there is something about football which strikes a most responsive chord in the American psyche. No other American sport consistently draws thousands of fans in the numbers which are attracted to football. One need only compare the crowd attendance statistics for college or professional baseball games with the analogous figures for football to see the enormous appeal of the latter. The question is: what is it about American football which could possibly account for its extraordinary popularity?

In the relatively meager scholarship devoted to football, one finds the usual array of theoretical approaches. The ancestral form of football, a game more like Rugby or soccer, was interpreted as a solar ritual--with a disc-shaped rock or object representing

* It is a pleasure to dedicate this essay to Professor David Bidney who taught me that there is no cultural data which cannot be illuminated by a judicious application of theory. I must also thank Nancy Nash and Stuart Blackburn for their helpful comments and suggestions.

the sun (Johnson 1929:228) and as a fertility ritual intended to ensure agricultural abundance. It had been noted, for example, that in some parts of England and France, the rival teams consisted of married men playing against bachelors (Johnson 1929:230-231; Magoun 1931:24,36,44). In one custom, a newly married woman would throw over the church a ball for which married men and bachelors fought. The distinction between the married and the unmarried suggested the the game might be a kind of ritual test or battle, with marriage signifying socially sanctioned fertility (Johnson 1929: 230).

The historical evolution of American football from English Rugby has been well documented (Reisman and Denny 1951), but the historical facts do not in and of themselves account for any psychological rationale leading to the unprecedented acceptance of the sport. It is insufficient to state that football offers an apropriate outlet for the expression of aggression. Arens (1975:77) has rightly observed that it would be an oversimplification "to single out violence as the sole or even primary reason for the game's popularity." Many sports provide a similar outlet, e.g., wrestling, ice hockey, roller derby, but few of these come close to matching football as a spectacle for many Americans. Similarly, pointing to such features as a love of competition, or the admiration of coordinated teamwork, or the development of specialists (e.g., punters, punt returners, field goal kickers, etc.) is not convincing since such features occur in most if not all sports.

Recently, studies of American football have suggested that the game serves as a male initiation ritual (Beisser 1967, Fiske 1972, Arens 1975). Arens, for example, remarks (1975:77) that football is "a male preserve that manifests both the physical and cultural values of masculinity," a description which had been applied, aptly it would appear, to British Rugby (Sheard and Dunning 1973). Arens points put that the equipment worn "accents the male physique" through the enlarged head and shoulders coupled with a narrowed waist. With the lower torso "poured into skintight pants accented only by a metal codpiece," Arens contends the result "is not an expression, but an exaggeration of maleness." He comments, further (1975:79) "Dressed in this manner, the players can engage in hand holding, hugging, and bottom patting, which would be disapproved of in any other context, but which is accepted on the gridiron without a second thought."

Having said this much, Arens fails to draw any inferences about possible ritual homosexual aspects of football. Instead, he goes on to note that American football resembles male rituals in other cultures insofar as contact with females is discouraged if not forbidden. A man has only so much energy and if he uses it in sexual activity, he will have that much less to use in hunting. warfare, or in this case, football. I believe Arens and others are correct in calling attention to the ritual and symbolic dimensions of American football, but I think that the psychological implications of the underlying symbolism have not been adequately explored.

Football is one of a large number of competitive games which involves the scoring of points by gaining access to a defended area in an opponent's territory. In basketball, one must throw a ball through a hoop (and net) attached to the other team's backboard. In ice hockey, one must hit the puck into the goal at the opponent's end of the rink. In football, the object is to move the ball across the opponent's goal into his endzone. It does not require a great deal of Freudian sophistication to see a possible sexual component in such acts as throwing a ball through a hoop, hitting a puck across a "crease" into an enclosed area bounded by nets, and other structurally similar acts. But what is not so obvious is the connection of such sexual symbolism with an all-male group of participants.

Psychologists and psychoanalists have not chosen to examine American football to any great extent. Psychologist Patrick writing in 1903 tried to explain the fascination of the game. "Evidently there is some great force, psychological or sociological at work here which science has not yet investigated" (1903:370), but he could offer little detail about what that great force might be. Similarly, psychoanalyst A.A. Brill's superficial consideration of football in 1929 failed to illuminate the psychodynamics of the game. Perhaps the best known Freudian analysis of football is the parody written originally in 1955 in the Rocky Mountain Herald by poet Thomas Hornsby Ferril, using the pseudonym Childe Herald, but the essay is more amusing than truly analytic. Actually, his interpretation tends to be more ritual than psychoanalytic. He suggests "football is a syndrome of religious rites symbolizing the struggle to preserve the egg of life through the rigors of inpending winter. The rites begin at the autumn equinox and culminate on the first day of the New Year

239

with great festivals identified with bowls of plenty;
the festivals are associated with flowers such as
roses, fruits such as oranges, farm crops such as cot-
ton, and even sun-worship and the appeasement of great
reptiles such as alligators" (1965:250). While he does
say that "Football obviously arises out of the Oedipus
complex," he provides little evidence other than men-
tioning that college games are usually played for
one's Alma Mater, which he translates as 'dear mother.'
Actually, a more literal translation would be nourish-
ing mother (and for that matter, alumnus literally
means nursling!)

    A more conventional psychoanalytic perspective is
offered by Adrian Stokes in his survey of ball games
with special reference to cricket. Stokes predictably
describes football [soccer] in Oedipal terms. Each
team defends the goal at their back. "In front is a
new land, the new woman, whom they strive to possess
in the interest of preserving the mother inviolate, in
order, as it were, to progress from infancy to adulthood: at the same time, the defensive role is the
father's; he opposes the forward youth of the opposition" (1956:187). Speaking of Rugby football, Stokes
proposes the following description. "Ejected out of
the mother's body, out of the scrum, after frantic
hooking and pushing, there emerges the rich loot of
the father's genital." According to Stokes, both
teams fight to possess the father's phallus, that is,
the ball, in order to steer it through the archetypal
vagina, the goal" (1956:190). Earlier, Stokes had suggested the ball represented semen though he claimed
that "more generally the ball is itself the phallus"
(1956:187). Folk speech offers some support for the
phallic connotation of a ball. One thinks of balls
for testicles. A man who has "balls" is a man of
strength and determination. To "ball" someone is a
slang expression for sexual intercourse (Rodgers 1972:
27; Wepman, Newman, Binderman 1976:178). On the other
hand, while one might agree with the general thesis
that there might be a sexual component to both soccer
and American football, it is difficult to cite concrete evidence supporting Stokes' contention that the
game involves a mother figure or a father surrogate.
If psychoanalytic interpretations are valid, then it
ought to be possible to adduce specific details of
idiom and ritual as documentation for such interpretations. It is not enough for a psychoanalyst to assert
ex cathedra what a given event or object supposedly
symbolizes.

I believe that a useful way to begin an attempt to understand the psychoanalytic significance of American football is through an examination of football folk speech. For it is precisely in the idioms and metaphors that a clear pattern of personal interaction is revealed. In this regard it might be helpful first to consider briefly the slang employed in general American male verbal dueling. In effect, I am suggesting that American football is analogous to male verbal dueling. Football entails ritual and dramatic action while verbal dueling tends to be more concerned with words. But structurally speaking, they are similar or at least functionally equivalent. In verbal dueling, it is common to speak about putting one's opponent "down." This could mean simply to topple an opponent figuratively, but it could also imply forcing one's adversary to assume a supine position, that is, the 'female' position in typical Western sexual intercourse. It should also be noted that an equally humiliating experience for a male would be to serve as a passive receptacle for a male aggressor's phallic thrust. Numerous idioms attest to the widespread popularity of this imagery pattern to describe a loser. One speaks of having been screwed by one's boss or of having been given the shaft. Submitting to anal intercourse is also implied in perhaps the most common single American folk gesture, the so-called digitus impudicus, better known in folk parlance as the 'finger.' Giving someone the finger is often accompanied by such unambiguous explanatory phrases as Fuck you! Screw you! Up yours! Up your ass! etc.

Now what has all this to do with football? I believe that the same symbolic pattern is at work in both verbal dueling and much ritual play. Instead of scoring a putdown, one scores a touchdown. Certainly the terminology used in football is suggestive. One gains yardage, but it is not territory which is kept in the sense of being permanently acquired by the invading team. The territory remains nominally under the proprietorship of the opponent. A sports announcer or fan might say, for example, "This is the deepest penetration into (opponent's team name) territory so far" (my italics). Only if one gets into the endzone (or kicks a fieldgoal through the uprights of the goalpost) does one win points.

The use of the term "end" is not accidental. Evidently there is a kind of structural isomorphism between the line (as opposed to the backfield) and the layout

241

of the field of play. Each line has two ends (left end and right end) with a "center" in the middle. Similarly, each playing field has two ends (endzones) with a midfield line (the fifty yard line). Ferril remarked on the parallel between the oval shape of the football and the oval shape of most football stadiums (Herald 1965:250), but I submit it might be just as plausible to see the football shape as an elongated version of earlier round soccer or Rugby ball, a shape which tends to produce two accentuated ends of the ball. Surely one of the distinctive differences between the shape of a football and the shape of the balls used in most other ballgames (e.g., baseball, basketball, soccer) is that it is not perfectly spherical. Support for the notion that a football has two "ends" is found in the standard idiom used to describe a kick or punt in which the ball turns over and over from front to back during flight (as opposed to moving in a more direct linear spiraling pattern). The idiom in question in an "end over end" kick.

The object of the game, simply stated, could be said to be: to get into one's opponent's endzone and at the same time to prevent the opponent from getting into one's own endzone. Structurally speaking, this is precisely what is involved in male verbal dueling. One wished to put one's opponent down, to "screw" him while avoiding being screwed by him. We can now better understand the appropriateness of the "bottom patting" so often observed among football players. A good offensive or defensive play deserves a pat on the rear end. The recipient has held up his end and has thereby helped protect the collective "end" of the entire team. One pats one's teammates' ends, but one seeks to violate the endzone of one's opponents.

The trust one has for one's own teammates is perhaps signalled by the common initial postural stance of football players. The so-called three point stance involves bending over in a distinct stooped positon with one's rear end exposed. It is an unusual position (in terms of normal life's activities) and it does make one especially vulnerable to attack from behind, that is, vulnerable to a homosexual attack. In some ways, the postural positon might be linked to what is termed "presenting" among nonhuman primates. Presenting refers to a subordinate animal's turning its rump towards a higher ranking or dominant one. The center thus presents to the quarterback--just as linemen do to the backs in general. Plimpton has described (1965:59) how

the quarterback's "hand, the top of it, rests up
against the center's backside as he bends over the ball
--medically, against the perineum, the pelvic floor..."
We know that some dominant nonhuman primates, for example, will sometimes reach out to touch a presenting
subordinant in similar fashion. In football, however,
it is safe to present to one's teammates. Since one
can trust one's teammates, one knows that one will be
patted, not raped. The traditional joking admonitions
of the locker room warning against "bending over in the
shower" or "picking up the soap" (which would presumably offer an inviting target for homosexual attack) do
not apply since one is among friends. "Grabass" among
friends is understood as being harmless joking behavior.

The importance of the "ends" is also signalled by
the fact that they alone among linemen are eligible to
receive a forward pass. In that sense, ends are equivalent to the "backs." In symbolic terms, I am arguing
that the end is a kind of backside! and that the endzone is a kind of erogenous zone. The relatively recently coined terms "tight end" and "split end" further demonstrate the special emphasis upon this "position" on the team. The terms refer to whether the end
stays close to his neighboring tackle, e.g., perhaps
to block, or whether he moves well away from the normally adjacent tackle, e.g., to go out for a pass.
However, both tight end and split end (cf. also wide
receiver) could easily be understood as possessing an
erotic nuance.

I must stress that the evidence for the present
interpretation of American football does not depend
upon just a single word. Rather there are many terms
which appear to be relevant. The semantics of the
word "down" are of interest. A down is the unit of
play insofar as a team has four downs in which to
either advance ten yards or score. A touchdown which
earns six points refers to the act of an offensive
player's possessing the ball in the opponent's endzone.
(Note it is not sufficient for the player to be in the
endzone. It is the ball which must be in the zone.)
In a running play, the ball often physically touches
the endzone and could therefore be said to touch down
in that area. However, if an offensive player catches
a pass in the endzone, the ball does not actually touch
the ground. The recent practice of "spiking" the ball
in which the successful offensive player hurls the ball
at the ground as hard as he can might be construed as

243

an attempt to have the football physically touch down
in the endzone. In any case, the use of the word
"touch" in connection with scoring in football does
conform to a general sexual symbolic use of that word.
The sexual nuances of "touch" can even be found in the
Bible. For example, in 1 Corinthians 7:1-2 we find
"It is good for a man not to touch a woman. Nevertheless to avoid fornication, let every man have his own
wife..." (cf. Genesis 20:6; Proverbs 6:29). Touching
can be construed as an aggressive act. Thus to be
touched by an opponent means one has been the victim of
aggression. The game of "touch football" (as opposed
to 'tackle' football) supports the notion that a mere
act of touching is sufficient to fulfill the structural
(and psychological) requirements of the basic rules.
No team wants to give up a touchdown to an opponent.
Often the team on the defense may put up a determined
goal line stand to avoid being penetrated by the opponents' offense. The special spatial nature of the endzone is perhaps indicated by the fact that it is not
measured in the one hundred yard distance between the
goal lines. Yet it is measured. It is only ten yards
deep, and, for example, a pass caught by an offensive
player whose feet are beyond the end line of the endzone would be ruled incomplete.

Other football folk speech could be cited. The
object of the game is to "score," a term which in
standard slang means to engage in sexual intercourse
with a member of the opposite sex. One "scores" by
going "all the way." The latter phrase refers specifically to making a touchdown (Rote and Winter 1966:
102). In sexual slang, it alludes to indulging in
intercourse as opposed to lesser forms of petting or
necking. The offensive team may try to mount a "drive"
in order to "penetrate" the other team's territory. A
ball carrier might go "up the middle" or he might "go
through a hole" (made by his linemen in the opposing
defensive line). A particularly skillful runner might
be able to make his own hole. The defense is equally
determined to "close the hole." Linemen may encourage
one another "to stick it to 'em," meaning to place
their helmeted heads (with phallic symbolic overtones)
against the chests of their opposite numbers to drive
them back or put them out of the play.

A player who scores a touchdown may elect to
"spike" the ball by hurling it down towards the ground
full force. This spiking movement confirms to all
assembled that the enemy's endzone has been penetrated.

The team scored upon is thus shamed and humiliated in front of an audience. In this regard, football is similar to verbal dualing inasmuch as dueling invariably take place before one or more third parties. The term "spike" may also be germane. As a noun, it could refer to a sharp-pointed long slender part or projection. As a verb, it could mean either to mark or cut with a spike (the football would be the phallic spike presumably) or to thwart or to sabotage an enemy. In any event, the ritual act of spiking serves to prolongate and accentuate the all too short moment of triumph, the successful entry into the enemy's endzone.

The sexual connotations of football folk speech apply equally to players on defense. One goal of the defensive line is to penetrate the offensive line to get to the quarterback. Getting to the offensive quarterback and bringing him down to the ground is termed "sacking" the quarterback. The verb sack connotes plunder, ravage, and perhaps even rape. David Kopay, one of the few homosexuals participating in professional football willing to admit his preference for members of the same sex, specifically commented on the nature of typical exhortations made by coaches and others. "The whole language of football is involved in sexual allusions. We were told to go out and 'fuck those guys'; to take that ball and 'stick it up their asses' or 'down their throats.' The coaches would yell, 'knock their dicks off,' or more often than that, 'knock their jocks off.' They'd say, 'Go out there and give it all you've got, a hundred and ten per cent, shoot your wad.' You controlled their line and 'knocked' em into submission. Over the years I've seen many a coach get emotionally aroused while he was diagramming a particular play into an imaginary hole on the blackboard. His face red, his voice rising, he would show the ball carrier how he wanted him to 'stick it in the hole.'" (Kopay and Young 1977:53-54). The term rape is not inappropriate and in fact it has been used to describe what happens when an experienced player humiliates a younger player, e.g., "That poor kid, he was raped, keelhauled, he was just destroyed..." (Plimpton 1965:195,339). Kopay's reference to jock as phallus is of interest since jock is a term (short for jockstrap, the article of underapparel worn to protect the male genitals) typically used to refer generally to athletes. Calling an athlete a jock or a strap thus tends to reduce him to a phallus. A "jocker" is used in hobo slang (Wentworth and Flexner 1967:294) and in prison slang (Rodgers 1972:155) to refer to an aggres-

245

sive male homosexual. (The meaning of jock may well
be related to the term jockey insofar as the latter
refers to the act of mounting and riding a horse.)

Some of the football folk speech is less obvious
and the interpretation admittedly a bit more speculative. For example, a lineman may be urged to "pop" an
opposing player, meaning to tackle or block him well.
Executing a perfect tackle or block may entail placing
one's helmet as close as possible to the middle of the
opponent's chest. The specific use of the verb "pop"
strongly suggests defloration as in the idiom "to pop
the cherry" referring to the notion of rupturing the
maidenhead in the process of having intercourse with
a virgin (Randolph 1976:9). In Afro-American folk
speech, "pop" can refer to sexual penetration (Wepman,
Newman, and Binderman 1976:186). To "pop" an opponent
thus implies reducing him to female victim status.
Much of the sexual slang makes it very clear that the
winners are men while the losers are women or passive
homosexuals. David Kopay articulates this when he
says, "From grade school on, the curse words on the
football field are about behaving like a girl. If you
don't run fast enough to block or tackle hard enough
you're a pussy, a cunt, a sissy." (1977:50-51). By
implication, if a player succeeds, he is male. Thus in
the beginning of the football game, we have two sets
or teams of males. By the end of the game, one of the
teams is "on top," namely the one which has "scored"
most by getting into the other team's "endzone." The
losing team, if the scoring differential is great, may
be said to have been "creamed."

It is tempting to make something of the fact that
originally the inner portion of the football was an
inflated animal bladder. Thus touching the enemy's
endzone with a bladder would be appropriate ritual
behavior in the context of a male homosexual attack.
However, it could be argued that the bladder was used
because it was a convenient inflatable object available
to serve as a ball.

If the team on offense is perceived in phallic
terms, then it is the quarterback who could be said to
be nominally in charge of directing the attack. In
this context, it may be noteworthy that a quarterback
intending to pass often tries to stay inside of the
"pocket," a deployment of offensive players behind the
line of scrimmage designed to provide an area of maximum protection (Rote and Winter 1966:130). A pants

246

pocket of course, could be construed as an area where
males can covertly touch or manipulate their genitals
without being observed. "Pocket pool," for example, is
a slang idiom for fondling the genitals (Rodgers 1972:
152), an idiom which incidentally suggests something
about the symbolic nature of billiards. The quarterback if given adequate protection, e.g., by his pocket" may be able to "thread the needle," that is, to
throw the football accurately, past the hands of the
defensive players, into the hands of his receiver. The
metaphor of threading the needle is an apt one since
getting the thread through the eye of the needle is
only preparatory for the act of "sewing." (Note that "to
make a pass" at someone is a conventional idiom for an
act of flirtation.) The receiver once the ball is in
his possession is transformed from a passive to an active role as he tries to move the ball as far forward
as possible.

While it is possible to disagree with several of
the interpretations offered of individual items of folk
speech cited thus far, it would seem difficult to deny
the overall sexual nature of much of football (and
other sports) slang. The word sport itself has this
connotation and has had it for centuries. Consider
one of Gloucester's early lines in King Lear when he
refers to his bastard son Edmund by saying "There was
good sport at his making" (I,i,23) or in such modern
usages as "sporting house" for brothel (Wentworth and
Flexner 1967:511) or "sporting life" referring to pimps
and prostitutes (Wepman, Newman and Binderman 1976).
In the early 1950s, kissing was commonly referred to
by adolescents as a "favorite indoor sport," presumably
in contrast to outdoor sports such as football. It
should also be noted that "game" can carry the same
sexual connotiation as sport (cf. Rodgers 1972:92;
Wepman, Newman and Binderman 1976:182).

I have no doubt that a good many football players
and fans will be sceptical to say the least of the analysis proposed here. Even academics with presumably
less personal investment in football will probably find
the idea implausible if not downright repugnant that
American football could be a ritual combat between
groups of males attempting to assert their masculinity
by penetrating the endzones of their rivals. David
Kopay despite suggesting that for a long time football
provided a kind of replacement for sex in his life and
admitting that football is "a real outlet for repressed
sexual energy (Kopay and Young 1977:11,53) refuses to

believe that "being able to hold hands in the huddle
and to pat each other on the ass if we felt like it" is
necessarily an overt show of homosexuality (Kopay and
Young 1977:57). Yet I think it is highly unlikely that
the ritual aspect of football, providing as it does a
socially santioned framework for male body contact--
football, after all, is a so-called "body contact" sport
--is a form of homosexual behavior. The unequivocal
sexual symbolism of the game as plainly evidenced in
folk speech coupled with the fact that all of the participants are male make it difficult to draw any other
conclusion. Sexual acts carried out in thinly dis-
guised symbolic form by, and directed towards, males
and males only, would seem to constitute ritual homosexuality.

Evidence from other cultures indicates that male
homosexual ritual combats are fairly common. Answering
the question of who penetrates whom is a pretty standard means of testing masculinity cross-culturally.
Interestingly enough, the word masculine itself seems
to derive from Latin "mas" (male) and "culus" (anus).
The implication might be that for a male to prove his
masculinity with his peers, he would need to control
or guard his buttock area while at the same time
threatening the posterior of another (weaker) male.
A good many men's jokes in Mediterranean cultures
(e.g., in Italy and in Spain) center on the "culo."

That a mass spectacle could be based upon a ritual
masculinity contest should not surprise anyone familiar
with the bullfight, Without intending to reduce the
bullfight to a single factor, one could nonetheless
observe that it is in part a battle between males in
which who penetrates whom is crucial. The one who is
penetrated loses. If it is the bull, he may be further
feminized or emasculated by having various extremities
cut off to reward the successful matador. In this context, we can see American football as a male activity
(along with the Boy Scouts, fraternities and other exclusively male social organizations in American culture) as belonging to the general range of male rituals
around the world in which masculinity is defined and
affirmed. Whether it is the verbal dueling tradition
of the circum-Mediterranean (cf. Dundes. Leach, and
Ozkok 1970) in which young men threaten to put opponents into a passive homosexual position, or the initiation rites in aboriginal Australia and New Guinea (and
elsewhere) in which younger men are subjected to actual
homosexual anal intercourse by older members of the

248

male group (cf. Dundes 1976), the underlying psychological rationale appears to be similar. Professional
football's financial incentives may extend the playing
years of individuals beyond late adolescence, but in
its essence American football is an adolescent masculinity ritual in which the winner gets into the
loser's endzone more times that the loser gets into
his!

* First published in Western Folklore, volume 37, 1978, pp. 75-88.
Reprinted here by permission of the Editor.

Bibliography

Arens, William
    1975   The Great American Football Ritual. Natural
           History 84(3):72-80. Reprinted in W. Arens
           and Susan P. Montague, eds., The American
           Dimension: Cultural Myths and Social Reali-
           ties. Port Washington: Alfred Publishing
           Co., pp. 3-14.
Beisser, Arnold R.
    1967   The Madness in Sports. New York: Appleton-
           Century-Crofts.
Brill, A.A.
    1929   The Why of the Fan. North American Review
           228:429-434.
Dundes. Alan
    1976   A Psychoanalytic Study of the Bullroarer.
           Man 11:220-238.   "   "
Dundes, Alan and Jerry W. Leach and Bora Özkök
    1970   The Strategy of Turkish Boys' Verbal Dueling
           Rhymes. Journal of American Folklore
           83:325-349.
Fiske, Shirley
    1972   Pigskin Review: An American Initiation.
           In M. Marie Hart, ed., Sport in the Socio-
           Cultural Process. Dubuque: Wm. C. Brown
           Company. Pp. 241-258.
Foster, George M.
    1965   Peasant Society and the Image of Limited
           Good. American Anthropologist 67:293-315.
Herald, Childe [Thomas Hornsby Ferril]
    1965   Freud and Football. In Wm. A. Lessa and
           Evon A. Vogt, eds., Reader in Comparative
           Religion. 2nd ed. New York: Harper and
           Row. Pp. 250-252.
Johnson, W. Branch
    1929   Football A Survival of Magic? The Contem-
           porary Review 135:225-231.
Kopay, David, and Perry Deane Young
    1977   The David Kopay Story. New York: Arbor
           House.
Magoun, Francis Peabody, Jr.
    1931   Shrove Tuesday Football. Harvard Studies
           and Notes in Philology and Literature
           13:9-46.
Marshall, George O., Jr.
    1958   Epic Motifs in Modern Football. Tennessee
           Folklore Society Bulletin 24:123-128.

Patrick, G.T.W.
  1903 The Psychology of Football. American Jour-
        nal of Psychology 14:368-381.
Pickford, R.W.
  1940 The Psychology of the History and Organiza-
        tion of Association Football. British Jour-
        nal of Psychology 31:80-931 129-144.
Plimpton, George
  1965 Paper Lion. New York: Harper and Row.
Randolph, Vance
  1976 Pissing in the Snow and Other Ozark Folk-
        tales. Urbana: University of Illinois
        Press.
Riesman, David and Reuel Denney
  1951 Football in America: A Study in Cultural
        Diffusion. American Quarterly 3:309-325.
Rodgers, Bruce
  1972 The Queen's Vernacular: A Gay Lexicon.
        San Francisco: Straight Arrow Books.
Rote, Kyle, and Jack Winter
  1966 The Language of Pro Football. New York:
        Random House.
Sheard, K.G., and E.G. Dunning
  1973 The Rugby Football Club as a Type of "Male
        Preserve": Some Sociological Notes. Inter-
        national Review of Sport Sociology 3-4(8):
        5-24.
Snyder, Eldin E., and Elner Spreitzer
  1974 Sociology of Sport: An Overview. The Soc-
        iology Quarterly 15:467-487.
Stokes, Adrian
  1956 Psycho-Analytic Reflections on the Develop-
        ment of Ball Games, Particularly Cricket.
        International Journal of Psycho-Analysis
        37:185-192.
Wentworth, Harold, and Stuart Berg Flexner
  1967 Dictionary of American Slang. New York:
        Thomas Y. Crowell.
Wepman, Dennis, and Ronald B. Newman and Murray B.
  Binderman
  1976 The Life: The Lore and Folk Poetry of the
        Black Hustler. Philadelphia: University
        of Pennsylvania Press.

CHANTS THAT DO NOT WOUND:
CONCEPT AND SENSATION IN KOLEDA

Nahoma Sachs
Princeton University

The village glistens in the moonlight, fields, rooftops, ponds, and paths covered with snow, frosted, dazzling. The general store, usually open for drinking in the cold evenings, is dark and empty. Even the animals sheltered in the great thatched barns seem to have postponed their shufflings and lowings for another evening. The air is crystalline, nostril-searing, motionless, the houses dark.

If you look carefully, however, you notice that here and there a door is quitely opened and closed again. Men reduced to small black shadows, packages under arms, fists deep in pockets, capped heads tucked forward against the cold, walk singly, quietly out towards their unlit bonfires. Finding each other there, they wait until they are twelve and then Ljube, young, lithe, eyes already burning as he pulls out matches, lights the hay. Other stacks, distant but within earshot, are beginning to burn, too. The men stand, enjoying the fire's warmth, and begin to pass the rakija (grape brandy) bottle, toasting before each takes his gulp.

"So zdravje."

"Aj, so zdravje." (With health.)

Blagoja, a man from the next fire, passes by on his way there. Lado, always quick to speak, starts to chant, his cronies joining in:

Blagoja odi po patče,   "Blagoja walks on the little path,
Da jadi lajna na lopatče, May he eat shit on a little shovel
Oo ooooo,   Oo ooooo,
Kolede kolede oo ooooo   Koleda koleda oo ooooo."

They chant in voices far deeper than their speaking voices, slowly, in monotone, ending with long, drawn-out, repeated salacious-sounding vowels--"Oo ooooo"--and earthy, hearty laughter.

253

A scant 200 yards away, the men at Blagoja's bonfire, having heard the attack, respond directly to Lado:

"Lado sedna na tikva,
Tikvata pukna,
Blagoja na sestra mu go lupna,
Oo ooooo."

"Lado sits on a pumpkin,
The pumpkin explodes,
Blagoja peels his (Lado's)
                    sister,
Oo, ooooo."

This is greeted with laughter by the males at both fires. Ljube, Lado's older brother, passes the bottle and initiates yet another chant intended to outwound these others:

"Blagoja sega niži,
Da deda mu za mu go leži,
Oo ooooo,
Kolede Kolede oo ooooo."

"Blagoja is now stringing
                    tobacco,
May his grandfather lay it
                    in him,
Oo, ooooo,
Kolede koleda oo ooooo."

Both groups in stitches, they drink some more and turn their attentions to other nearby bonfires and their denizens. The chanting and laughter continue late into the night as Koleda, the annual Macedonian winter solstice ritual, continues. By the time that the snow-laden sky begins to turn leaden, the Koledari are walking home, tired but still happy and high, a few last muted verbal thrusts passing between trudging celebrants.

The existence of similar rituals in East Slavic areas (Ralston 1872) indicates that Macedonians have probably been celebrating Koleda, their winter solstice ritual, since before their 7th centure migration to the Balkan peninsula. Although it is likely that Koleda was originally connected to the worship of some pre-Christian Slavic deity, contemporary Macedonians know nothing of this. The meanings of Koleda, then, can be understood directly from the ritual, the ritual texts, and from an understanding of contemporary Macedonian culture.

In this paper, I shall examine the contemporary meanings of Koleda by utilizing two avenues of inquiry: interpretation through symbols and through tropes. This will allow me to evaluate and compare the kinds of understanding gained from each in order to indicate, first, the contributions the analysis of tropes can make to the understanding of culture and, second, that the full panoply of meaning in any ritual or expressive form ranges wider than cultural conceptualization and its various behavioral embodiments.

I define the symbol as a term existing in sensory reality which stands for intellectual, emotional, and sensate meanings either singly or in combination. Its use directly denotes the

meaning(s) attached to it. A trope is a special symbolic term
which explains the nature or quality of one form or experience by
comparing it to another. It is used either for aesthetic or
stylistic reasons or, more relevant to Koleda, when there is no
term available in the language to denote the full set of meanings
in question. Often, tropes describe something ineffable which
either has no term or partakes of some experiential quality which
the relevant term does not express. Following David Sapir's
formulation, I use the term metonymy to indicate a trope which
"replaces or juxtaposes contiguous terms that occupy a distinct
and separate place within what is considered a single semantic
or perceptual domain," and synecdoche to refer to a trope which,
while drawing its terms from a single domain, is structured so
that one term includes the other (1977:4).

The men of Rosa, a farming village of 630 people located on
the Pelagonian plain, perform Koleda annually for six consecutive
nights before Eastern Orthodox Christmas. They have been taught
that, like a number of other rituals they perform, it will aid
crop and stock fertility. Many, however, say that they no longer
believe in the efficacy of such rituals and have stopped performing them; they still enjoy performing Koleda, however.

In fact, Rosan men stress how much they enjoy Koleda. It is
the only ritual which males of all ages perform not out of a
feeling of obligation but, rather, because it is fun. It is perhaps the sole activity in which the traditional, village-oriented
values of older men do not clash, as is usually the case today,
with those of younger, urban-oriented, upward mobile men.

The ritual activity which comprises Koleda begins one week
before Christmas Day. Males over age 6 gather in groups of at
least ten each evening of that week at pre-selected places outside the circumference of the village houses to chant what they
call either izvici, ejaculations, shouts, or rečenici, sentences,
at both individual members of other groups and entire groups.
Typically, the man or bonfire group which has been chanted to
responds in kind, aiming the returning chant at the original
chanter(s). Liquor is passed around during the ritual which ends
when the men tire or get too cold. There are neither winners nor
losers in this verbal competition.

Badnik, Christmas Eve, is the last and most important day of
the ritual. Early on Badnik morning, groups of children called
Koledari (Koleda celebrants) go from door to door chanting the
words of the two non-obscene Koleda greeting chants. They visit
only houses in their neighborhood, a number of groups performing
simultaneously in different parts of the village; they are given
small change or food in exchange for their chanting.

255

The Badnik evening Koleda is considered to be the culmination of the ritual. Females remain at home for it is said that the obscenities in the chants are unfit for their ears. The men of each neighborhood spend part of the week before Christmas building a large bonfire in a wide place which is not close to any dwellings; the location is chosen to prevent the spreading of obscenity to women and fire to buildings. Each bonfire consists of shocks of straw piled up with iron pitchforks and is at least ten feet high. On Badnik night the bonfires sketch an eerie circumference around the village.

Only on Badnik night do the Koleda participants bring home-made plum or grape brandy (rakija), ritual breads (kolacina), nuts, figs, and apples with them; these things must be brought, they say, at God's behest. Nothing having meat or animal fat is included since Badnik night marks the end of the Orthodox pre-Christmas Lenten period. The ritual participants' exchange of these comestibles with the other members of their group recalls similar exchanges usually made during funeral and death rituals (za duša). In the latter, the food which one person gives another to eat "for the souls" of the former's dead kin is transformed, by virtue of being eaten, into food available to them in the other world. To eat for another's dead souls is to impart a gift to his or her family. When adult Koledari perform comparable food exchanges, they symbolize their solidarity with the two-world cosmos and, by virtue of the fact that they exchange with each other--one does this most often with friends or kin--their mutual solidarity (Sachs 1975:passim).

When it is dark, the fires are lit. The chanters of each group stand around their own fire, chant at the members of the other groups, and are chanted at by the latter. Each man, when he pleases, initiates a chant. Since they are known by the entire group, the opening words are sufficient to cue the other members of the group to join in. Once having heard them the group begins to chant in unison.

Koleda week is the one week of the year when Yugoslav Macedonians, urban and rural, traditional and modernizing, with or without women, engage in ritual verbal abuse. Twenty-five short chants are used by the members of the Rosa Koleda group with which I worked extensively. These fall into two general types. The first consists of one chant which simply celebrates Koleda's coming and is also used by the children going from house to house in the morning. This chant consists of four obligatory lines of rhymed text, AABB, plus two obligatory formulaic end lines,

Oo ooooo,	Oo ooooo,
Kolede kolede oo ooooo,	Koleda, koleda oo ooooo,

256

and an optional opening line which is the same as the final obligatory end line. One chant, which because it is obscene, falls
into the second grouping, follows this structure as well. It is,
unlike the other obscene chants, a description of Koleda rather
than a taunt.

The second type, which includes most of the izvici is, in
Macedonian terms, obscene; it consists of direct and metaphoric
descriptions of micturition and defecation in public situations,
sexual acts between humans and animals, men and unmarried girls,
and men. The second type is typically directed as a taunt to men
within earshot: members of nearby Koleda groups, entire Koleda
groups, or passers-by.

This type consists of two obligatory rhymed lines, AA, and
may optionally include one or both of the ending lines given
above. In these chants, the first line typically begins with
either the name of the person or family at which the chant is
directed, or with the indefinite subject koj (whoever). Thus,
each chant is inflexible in its content except for its subject
and the end lines. Since many bonfires are within hearing and
seeing distance of one another, baiting goes back and forth between them, names of particular groups, men, or boys being inserted into the chants as they, in competition, escalate obscenity.

Nowadays the performance of Koleda is the one yearly occasion on which verbal and behavioral taboos relating to the Macedonian category mrsen (greasy=obscene) or bezobrazen (shameful=
faceless=obscene) are suspended for and by men. The unthinkable
and undoable are uttered in a context of drunken hilarity. In
discussing Koleda, all informants strongly stress the pleasure
they take in its performance and the absence of anger or loss of
face on the part of men who become the temporary subjects of
obscenity.

In order to understand Koleda, it is necessary to consider
the conceptual bases upon which the ritual operates today. To
begin with, the people of Rosa utilize the term mrsni to indicate
the scatological nature of texts, songs, or statements. The term,
however, is used in two other contexts which provide a frame for
understanding the nature of Macedonian obscenity. In everyday
life it is used to mean fat, fleshy, or carnal. Good meat, for
example, is mrsno, high in fat content, and much preferable to
lean meat.

The term extends also into Orthodox Christian Lenten practices. Rosanci say, "Ne mrsime sega" ("We are not eating fat
now"), to indicate their participation in Lenten abstinences from
meat, animal fat, and eggs. Like other Indo-Europeans, then,

257

Macedonians connect the obscene primarily with the sensate or carnal. Before the existence of the Socialist Federated Republic of Yugoslavia, eating meat during a Lenten period constituted the performance of a religious obscenity since carnality connotes the mixed pleasures of physical sensation: sex, micturition, defecation, and eating. Informants, however, do not feel that the term mrsni has similar meanings in the contexts of Lent and Koleda; they are conscious of no connection.

Koleda texts, then, are mrsni when they allude to sex, micturition, defecation and the eating of things termed inappropriate for human consumption. In everyday parlance, clipped reference to such activities occurs only in the sporadic and formulaic exercise of the Mediterranean temper in cursing. Like the anger it freely and immediately expresses, cursing tends to be short-lived and quickly forgotten. This contrasts strongly with the six nights which men devote slowly and lovingly to Koleda, when mrsni izvici, dirty ejaculations, are the focus of attention.

The structure of chanted interaction between members of different Koleda groups on the one hand and between the members of one group and passers-by on the other is related to the way Rosanci categorize their fellow villagers. Like other Orthodox Christians, traditional Rosanci live by a dual code of values which corresponds to their division of the universe into two contiguous worlds, the empirical sensory world and the world of God, the saints, and the dead (Campbell 1966:139-170). Christian values and the opposing Mediterranean honor-shame complex find different spheres of application in the realm of interpersonal relations and form the conceptual bases of social behavior and self-image for most of the villagers.

Rosanci today implicitly divide the human population of this world into three flexible categories which I have glossed as nuclear family, "strangers," and "friends." The first of these, until the dissolution of extended families between the world wars, consisted of all kin in the extended family, i.e., all people defined as consanguines or their spouses who shared one pocket and came under the rule of the domakin, the male head of house. Today the latter part of the definition still holds, but the three-generational nuclear family is the norm. Members within this grouping try to treat each other in accordance with Christian ethics: with trust, cooperation and, although it is seldom shown in public, affection.

The second social grouping conceptualized by traditional Rosanci, here called "strangers," consists of most people who are not kin: fellow villagers, acquaintances, some neighbors, and business associates. It is between people who categorize each other as belonging to this second group that relations based primarily on the concepts of honor and shame obtain. Interaction among "strangers" is characterized by mutual hostility, suspicion, distrust, and sometimes violence (Ibid:142). People so defined are, at best, strangers, at worst, enemies.

Interaction between "friends," the third group, falls between the relationships characteristic for the other two groups. Before the division of extended families, "friends" included only affines and families in god-parental relationships. Today kin who live in separate, economically independent houses and, sometimes, neighbors who, like godparents, are treated as spiritual kin (Chock 1974:33), are considered "friends" as well. Relations among "friends" are predicated upon varying mixtures of the Christian and honor-shame systems. Some "friends" whose relationships. with a nuclear family have been marked by no important disagreements are given cooperation, affection, and sometimes limited economic help, but the degree of support is smaller than that given to nuclear family members; equal return is usually expected, and some degree of distrust is always maintained towards "friends."

Village demography and visiting patterns symbolize the groupings delineated above and also indicate the primacy of the nuclear family as the basic social grouping. Each nuclear family's house and outbuildings are surrounded by a tall, straw-covered, mudbrick wall which constitutes a literal and symbolic barrier between the nuclear family and all others Most contiguous family compounds are composed of people who are patrilineal consanguines. The divided nuclear remnants of extended patrilocal families thus constitute neighborhoods within the village, and most casual visiting occurs within such neighborhoods or among "friends." "Friends" also visit each other on their respective familial Saint's Day Celebrations (slavas), namedays of individuals (imendenovi), funerals, weddings, and christenings. "Strangers" most frequently visit each other for business reasons. Since business is carried on primarily by domakins, they most often visit "strange" houses.

The categorization of any particular family as "friends" or "strangers" is not static. Confrontations, disputes, unexpected support, marriage, death, and displays of friendly behavior can redefine "strangers" as "friends" or "friends" as "strangers." The most frequent causes of redefinition are inheritance disputes in which the nuclear families of brothers become "strangers" upon their father's death because one or more feel they have received the smaller inheritance. Although such families still refer to each other as consanguineal kin, they behave towards each other as "strangers" and regard each other as enemies.

The demography of Koleda bonfires utilizes these categories of social proximity. Before the rapid urbanization of the 1950's

259

and 1960's cut the Rosan population in half, each Koleda group
tended to consist only of consanguineal kinsmen. Since a proper
bonfire compliment is considered to consist of at least ten men--
and the more the merrier--the men of as many as ten contiguous
households often gather to Koleda together today. These men are
either kinsmen or neighborhood friends.

The kinsmen and neighborhood friends gathered at one bonfire
chant at those gathered at other fires who are similarly related
to one another. Thus, just as men did not chant at consanguines
before urbanization, they do not chant at friendly neighbors and
consanguines today They direct their chants, instead, at strangers and friends from other neighborhoods, replicating symbolically the categorical division between those treated in terms of
Christian ethics and those treated also in terms of honor and
shame.

Social differentiation among Rosans is also manifested directly in terms of honor and shame; both of these concepts have
dual application: the honor or shame that accrues to any individual adult reflects upon the honor or shame of his or her nuclear
family, and vice versa. Furthermore, the characteristics of the
honorable man and the honorable woman oppose and complement each
other. Honor is a sex-linked quality inherent in the Macedonian
man by virtue of his maleness. Within the limits of fatalism,
the honorable man is confident of his ability effectively to deal
with those aspects of his environment which are defined as
humanly manipulable.

The Macedonian woman, to the contrary, has no intrinsic hon-
or. It is her social presentation of sexual modesty which constitutes her honor rather than the inborn existence of the latter
within her.

Although personal honor is derived from concepts of sexuality, other characteristics are also important in the attribution
of honor in Rosa, whether it is personal or familial. These include domestic cleanliness and hospitality, physical strength and
health, courage, and cleverness. These characteristics and those
relating to sexuality are preconditions not only for the attribution of honor, but also for the definition of men as good domakinci (heads of house) and women as good domakinki (female heads
of house). Domakinci must exhibit physical strength, manliness,
health, courage, and cleverness, while domakinki must exhibit
sexual modesty, strength, health, and cleanliness.

Familial honor is a quality equally common to all families in
Rosa until it is violated. Violation typically consists of at
least the social knowledge of a family member's unrequited seduc-
tion, rape, illegitimate pregnancy or loss of chastity, defamation, theft, drunkenness, fighting, infanticide, passive accep -

260

tance of verbal abuse, poverty and, in historical times, homi-
cide. Having honor is the social condition upon which positive
personal self-regard is predicated since, in this culture, self-
image is traditionally defined in social rather than psychological terms. The clear explanation provided by Campbell for the
transhumant Sarakatsani of Northern Greece fits Rosanci with one
modification; as fatalists they do not expect to achieve the
ideal unaided. Their quest for self-regard, as a result, is less
intense than that of the Sarakatsani:

> Self-regard is the inner necessity and obligation to achieve
> identity with the image of the ideal self. This image, of
> course, is a stereotype presented by society, there is little
> room for individual speculation, nor would it occur to most
> traditional Rosanci to question its traditional content.
> Self-regard is concerned with what must be positively
> achieved, that is, the ideal of a social personality with
> particular moral qualities but also certain material attri-
> butes....
>
> Self-regard is molested where a man is insulted or defamed,
> or believes himself to have been so treated....In such circum-
> stances the core of a man's social personality is touched, his
> manliness and prepotence are questioned....
>
> If self-regard is the need to achieve an identity with the
> image of an ideal self, shame is the emotion experienced by
> an individual when he clearly fails to do so. (Ibid:149.).

Thus, if one is dishonored, one has been shamed; and in Rosa, the
shame of the individual becomes the shame of the family.

The matter does not end there, however, for the attempt to
dishonor another is not necessarily equivalent to the success.
In Rosa, a man can deflect dishonor by counter-attaking in such
a way that village opinion sides for rather than against him.
This is most easily achieved when dishonor comes from defamation,
fighting, or the acceptance of verbal abuse, situations in which
the escalated riposte can reverse the direction of shaming with
relative ease. It is this pattern which is replicated in the
structure of Koleda chanting interaction with one important exception: The emotional concomitants to an everyday situation of
dishonor, being focused seriously upon anger, hostility, and
revenge, differ greatly from those consciously linked by informants with Koleda: pleasure and mirth.

Pavle Bentovski, in explaining to me why Koleda chants are
directed at men of other bonfires, clearly indicates the primacy
of the honor-shame complex to the ritual:

261

Look. We are doing Koleda here. They are doing it there,
at their bonfire. We want to make a joke. For pleasure.
I chant at Boge. He won't get angry at what I say. Even
when I chant about taking his sister. We don't get angry
at each other. He can return it in a different way, with
different words. We try to compete at wounding each other.
If we don't wound each other, there is no point to the chants;
there's no reason to koleda....The pleasure of the chants is
that each of us wounds another. We in our group know who is
in the other groups. If we sing about the Silofci family,
I know who is at their fire. I know who is in other groups
too. That is to say, I call people I chant to by name:
'Peco koledas near the bridge....'

   Were Pavle for example, to cast aspersions about Peco's
sister in a non-ritual context, Pavle's aggressive intention to
wound (narani) would be unambiguous and Peco's response, angry
and insulting. In Koleda, however, the wounds are all in fun
and no one may take offense. Whereas in non-ritual situations
which test honor the faces of combatants are suffused with
anger, they show broad smiles in Koleda. Ljube Dioski adds:

I wound someone at another fire and then some other friend
of mine will wound someone else there. There they will enjoy
it, because it's mrsni; it's about his sister.

Clearly, then, the emotions associated with the maintenance and
testing of male honor are inverted in Koleda and wounding, the
process by which one man can dishonor another and create dis-
cord, is transformed from a serious literal assault into a
symbolic jest; the pressure to assert one's honor is gone, at
least on Koleda nights.

   Each participant, however, most frequently wounds another
either by symbolically dishonoring his female kinswomen or by
attributing female characteristics to him. In doing so, he en-
acts a set of polarities which finds expression in most social
and ritual contexts in Rosa. On the innate, ascribed, intrinsic
level, honor is a positive quality which inheres to men. On the
behavioral level, male honor is expressed through manly assertive,
attention-garnering acts; male shame results from defamations of
various kinds. Modesty, and in particular, sexual modesty, is a
positive embodiment of honorable behavior in adult females. If
these qualities are permuted and combined with others by which
men and women are differentiated in Macedonia--women are implicitly evil and should act submissively whereas men are implicitly
good and should act dominantly--it becomes clear that the behavioral embodiment of honor in the sexes is arrived at both
through opposing definitions of their basic nature and through
opposing strategies of proper comportment. That which constitutes

262

honorable behavior for one sex is dishonoring to the other. The
resultant polarities may be schematized as follows:

INTRINSIC QUALITIES	MALE	FEMALE
	honor	
	good	vessel of evil

EXTRINSIC, BEHAVIORAL QUALITIES	MALE	FEMALE
	charismatic, attracting attention, assertive	demure, modest
	active	passive
	dominant	submissive
	above	below
	sexual, thrusting	chaste, virginal, receiving
	hot, fiery stirred up	cool, placid

   These male-female polarities explicate another element in
Koleda demography: the absence of women. Men, because their inherent honor protects them from being sullied, may perform chants
which are mrsni, bezobrazni. However women, evil by nature, are
already too contaminated to be able to perform a ritual in which
one delves into the carnal only to emerge with honor. Women have
no intrinsic honor with which to emerge. They sit in their
houses, the subjects of chants, vessels of evil.

   While sexual duality is taken seriously enough to prevent
the women from participating in the ritual, relations among men
based upon the honor-shame complex are simply made light of in
Koleda. This is because the bases of the two sets of attributes
differ somewhat from each other. The attributes of Macedonian
gender are considered to be inborn and immutable; male honor,
one of these traits, can thus be made light of precisely because
it is inborn. One can sully the untarnishable because it is pure
by nature, but one cannot dirty that which is already unclean
since there is then no way to purify it. By this typically
Macedonian logic women, as long as they are defined as intrinsically evil--and this, along with segregation in Koleda, is
changing in the cities though few inroads have been made in rural
areas--cannot participate in Koleda.

263

The constituents of the linked honor-shame and male-female
complexes form the implicit but inverted basis for the ritual
enactment of mirthful dishonoring. However, the ways in which
these cultural categories are enacted and elaborated through
the embodiment of obscene jest are best understood through consideration of some of the chants. The first two set the tone of
ambivalence which underlies the entire corpus and the ritual as a
whole:

1. Kolede kolede oo ooooo,
   Koledica varvarica,

   Opni pica na polica,
   Škripni ripni obidija,

   Što e ova bela medu nija?
   Oo ooooo,
   Kolede kolede oo ooooo.

Koleda koleda oo ooooo,
Little Koleda, little barbar-
   ian (fem),
Jump cunt, onto the shelf,
Scramble, jump, make the
   attempt,
What is the evil between them?
Oo ooooo,
Koleda koleda oo ooooo.

2. Koledica varvarica,

   E po nea Vasilica,
   Ednaš ni e vo godina,
   Kako cveče vo gradina,
   Oo ooooo,
   Kolede kolede oo ooooo.

Little koleda, little barbar-
   ian (fem),
And after it St. Basil's Day,
You come to us once a year,
Like a flower in a garden,
Oo ooooo,
Koleda koleda oo ooooo.

In both texts, Koleda is made diminutive and feminine and is
termed barbarian: something wild, uncivilized and, most important, alien. The first text continues by developing a sketchy
image of a pair of female legs scrambling onto a shelf, genitalia
visible in its frenzy. This part-person, a synechdoche representing a dehumanized portion of a woman-as-object, is characterized as having a seat of evil: the vagina. Just as the ritual is
alien and barbaric, the sexuality of woman is all this and evil
too. The first text, then, expresses the distance, repulsion,
and negativity which Macedonian men feel toward women. The
second text, by contrast, likens the female Koleda to a garden
flower which blooms only annually. Thus Koleda, transformed in
the first text into a woman is, both as festival and woman, a
flower in the second.

Many Rosan women are named after flowers, and most take
great pains tending their flower gardens. In fact, they pot those
shrubs which can survive the winter into old oil cans which are
taken indoors. The flower, within the province of women's work
(ženska rabota) and never tended by men, serves in the second
text as a symbol of the feminine. Koleda is a female symbol
which, at the same time, connotes the essentially evil nature of
the feminine, its alienness to men, and its specialness and
attraction. Koleda, then, represents woman as paradox.

264

The opening texts embody the male Macedonian ambivalence towards the feminine. Women are simultaneously attractive, desireable, and rare, and evil and alien. In a culture where the verbal communication of intimate experience between the sexes is a rarity, it is dismaying though not surprising to find such stereotypic notions developed and used by one sex about the other.

If this ambivalence is related to the basic Macedonian duality of male and female, it becomes clear that the male conceptualization of both men and women in Koleda can be seen as a somewhat Western version of the Taoist yin-yang duality (Granet 1975:48-50); although good and evil give valence to each pole--and this is the Western addition--each has inherent in it something of its contrasting member. For Macedonians, evil women are still special and attracting, and men can easily be made into women as well. Moreover, each member of the original male-female opposition is itself a duality. As the mechanism of Koleda makes clear, passive men have negative value; like women, men are themselves ambivalent, as the third text indicates:

3. Kolede kolede oo ooooo,   Koleda koleda oo ooooo,
   Koj go ima ke go tuci,   Whoever has it will shower
                                   it,

   Koj go nema ke go brici,   Whoever doesn't will shave
                                   it,

   Oo ooooo,   Oo ooooo,
   Kolede kolede oo ooooo.   Koleda koleda oo ooooo.

The image created in the text is an impressionistic and fragmentary one, its subject virility, tumescence. Those men having it will ejaculate the result with honor while those who do not will be shaven and hence shamed.

It is significant that the depilation of pubic hair is not practiced among Macedonian Christians; the only people in the area who are known to so depilate themselves are Moslem women. This act, a part of their religious hygiene, is a subject for mirth among Christian Macedonian men. Furthermore, Moslems in general fair poorly in the social stratification of Yugoslav Macedonia; they are generally accorded status higher only that that ascribed to Gypsies. Since the status of women and Moslems is lower than that of men and Christians, the chant says that a man who is not virile and hence must shave himself is assigned a doubly demeaning status, that of a Moslem woman. Lack of tumescence, then, in unmanning a man, transforms him into a woman, and one who shaves herself at that; thus, the texts treat male as well as female duality by indicating that some men can be unmanned, and that the best way to dishonor a man is to put him in a feminine role or position, a demeaning one which Macedonian men would ordinarily refuse to take for themselves.

265

The following Koleda texts exemplify the symbolism typical
of the genre:

4. Silofcite Koledari vika amin,

Da mu gevam gazum amin,

Oo ooooo.

The Silo family koledari say
    say amen
That I fuck his (a Silo
    member's) ass, amen,
Oo ooooo.

5. Jonče ima ovca roguša,
Da ja fteram na sestra mu
  doguša,
Oo ooooo,
Koleda koleda oo ooooo.

Jonce has sheep's horns,
That I force his sister to
  embrace me,
Oo ooooo,
Koleda koleda oo ooooo.

6. Cele kupi slama,
Da jadi ot pesot salama,

Oo ooooo.

Cele buys hay,
May he eat salami made of
  dogmeat,
Oo ooooo.

7. Koj odi po patče,

Da jadi lajna na loptače,

Kolede kolede oo ooooo.

Whoever walks on the little
  path,
May he eat shit on a little
  shovel,
Kolede kolede oo ooooo.

These examples illustrate the form typical of most Koleda
texts. The name of a male individual or the nickname of a lineage
--in these texts, Jonče, Šilofskite, and Cele--is inserted at the
beginning of any izvik by the individual who initiates its chanting. The men or lineages named are usually placed in a passive
or feminine position vis-a-vis the action described in the text.
For example, in the fifth text Jonče, complete with horns, does
nothing while his sister is taken by a member of the Koleda group
which is chanting. In other cases a man is described as actively
doing something which is in itself demeaning, such as eating salami made of dog meat. In yet other chants such as the seventh,
when no particular person or lineage comes to mind, someone described as performing a seemingly neutral act is demeaned by its
consequences.

Either the first example, demeaning only to women, or the
second, which is not demeaning to anyone, is generally inter-
spersed between chants of the type exemplified by 4-7, much as
Yugoslav oral narrative singers intersperse formulae between sections of relatively extemporized narrative (Lord 1964:30-67).
However, except for the variation of names inserted in the texts,
there is no extemporaneous composition during the ritual. Rather,
texts are gradually memorized by boys and young men as they participate in Koleda.

The content analysis offered below indicates the frequency of various types of subject matter in the collected texts. The 25 Koleda texts collected from one group of male Rosan kinsmen who customarily perform Koleda together focus on the themes listed on the chart below:

CONTENT ANALYSIS OF CHANT TEXTS

SUBJECT OF SONG TEXT	NUMBER OF TEXTS	%AGE OF SAMPLE
1. Texts which dishonor the man or family made the subject of a given group's Koleda chant through:	(22)	(88)
a. attribution of passive male homosexuality;	6	24
b. reference to a man passively doing nothing while a second man has intercourse with the former's sister;	5	20
c. a passive man is demeaned in an asexual manner;	3	12
d. reference to a man's active micturition, defecation, or their products;	2	8
e. reference to active sexual intercourse by males with animals;	2	8
f. a man performing an ordinary act must, as a consequence, eat meat considered inedible;	2	8
g. references to female genitalia	1	4
h. references to a man getting cursed as a result of his doing something innocuous;	1	4
i. reference to having or not having one's masculinity;	1	4
2. Texts with no references like the above;	1	4
3. Texts whose meaning was inadequately decoded;	1	4
TOTAL	25	100

The symbolism of the Koleda group extends the conceptualization of masculinity, honor, and shame. A male microcosm as it
chants, each Koleda group symbolizes the solidarity of males in
general; furthermore, it stands for the solidarity of males in
particular families and neighborhoods, since it is these who
koleda together. The bonfires around which the Koledari chant
are both the physical and the symbolic centers of the ritual;
Macedonian symbols for maleness or virility, they are phallic in
shape. The fire, furthermore, is another symbol of male solidarity, since it is the center around which each Koleda group unites.

However, male solidarity in Koleda is most clearly articulated in the textual treatment of dishonored men. A man can be
dishonored in jest by izvici that describe him as eating the
inedible, copulating with animals, or remaining passive while
another has his sister or even himself. The degree of mock sever-
ity of defamation depends entirely upon the degree to which he
is accused of being feminine, the greatest evil. The vilest
accusation, in Macedonian male terms, is that which attributes
passive homosexuality to a man for it symbolically turns him
into a woman, one whose sex automatically dishonors her, one
who can have no solidarity with men. This is more demeaning
than having one's sister taken since it is more personal.

8. Koj koleda pot vratika,   Whoever koledas at the door,
    Pop da mu go napika,   May the priest enter him,
    Oo ooooo,   Oo ooooo,
    Kolede kolede oo ooooo.   Koleda koleda oo ooooo.

The solidarity symbolized by Koleda coexists with its opposite: mock competition between single males and groups for
honor through attack and defamation. This is the focal activity
at Koleda, the one which is not to be taken seriously. Each text
that falls into the dishonoring categories listed above (i.e.,
88% of the sample) is directed by one man or group at some other
man or group who are jestingly dishonored by the performance of
the chant. The more passive and sexual the text is, the greater
the symbolic dishonor of its subject until he chants back in
retribution, returning the wound, and deflecting dishonor.

The 24 decipherable texts thus fall onto a spectrum between two general poles of meaning in Koleda: male solidarity
and honor, and male competition forhonor through aggressive
acts which dishonor other men. The more active and asexual the
text, the more it connotes male solidarity and honor; the more
passive and sexual it is, the more it symbolizes male competition
for honor and the attempt to dishonor others in order to achieve
greater honor for oneself. Thus, just as femaleness is itself
a polarity for Macedonian men, maleness, caught in the tension
between solidarity, and aggressive competition, is as well.

268

Unlike most traditional Rosan rituals, the performance of Koleda has not been modified through the exclusion of chanting or other ritual acts. This is so for a number of reasons. To begin with, even the recent input of socialist ideology encouraging the equality of the sexes and resulting in the desire for conceptual change in other areas of life has modified neither Rosan conceptualization nor behavior with regard to male sexual dominance. Young, modernizing men participate in Koleda with the same lustiness that typifies the behavior of their elders. Since the symbolism of Koleda is consistent with the conceptualization of males of all ages, there is nothing which keeps younger Rosans from participating in and thereby perpetuating the ritual.

Furthermore, they have no reason to shun the ritual, and cogent ones for participating. As individuals placed by traditional assumptions and rules at the bottom of the village male social hierarchy, young men enjoy Koleda because they are equal to older men during it.

Finally, for all male Rosans, Koleda is a special ritual context in which anyone can symbolically attack and dishonor any man not of his bonfire without risk of real retribution. Thus, Koleda functions as a vehicle for the free, relaxed, and risk-less expression of aggression. It is an enactment of cultural fantasy which, unlike the more painful reality it replaces, does not garner social disapproval and, perhaps, arrest. Koleda can serve this function for Rosan men because none of them have values which mediate against its performance and, in addition, because it suspends the hierarchical structure of ordinary male social relations so that groups and individuals have equal opportunity to heap extrafamilial calumnies when no one may take offense.

The Koleda ritual is thus typified by anti-structure, the temporary removal of the distinctions of social status, prestige, and honor upon which everyday social interaction is built. The members of each Koleda group share, instead, existential or spontaneous communitas, the recognition and acceptance of "an essential and generic human bond" (Turner 1969:96) because of which, to paraphrase Blake, the mutual laughter at each vice (Ibid:132) is the accepted form of interaction; this obtains both within Koleda groups and between any such group and those it takes as the subjects of its chants. Finally, it is a rite of reversal in which usually unpardonable behavior is lustily sanctioned and the normal, discordant, violent responses to such behavior are softened, mellowed, and inverted into chants.

Rosa is a village in which personal and familial defamation is an everpresent and unpleasant possibility which every man dreads to experience. His response to Koleda, however, is one of anticipation and then, enjoyment. The difference in attitudes

269

towards the two types of experience stems, of course, from the
fact that in Koleda one plays for fun, not for keeps. Dishonor
in Koleda, though omnipresent, is unreal. Like village age
stratification, its presence in Koleda lies in its irrelevance to
ongoing reality. Humor, in fact, makes communitas possible by
negating the implications of the contents of the texts. Peco
may have a dishonoring text chanted about and to him, but this
fact will influence neither others' opinion about him nor his
self-esteem. It is a relaxing situation for a Macedonian to find
himself in; he may do everything necessary to defame another, but
need not fear consequences; he may be defamed but, unlike in
everyday life, it is merely a joke. Because it is conceptualized
as funny rather than as serious, then, Koleda leads to no consequences worse than a hangover.

Although, in the end, Koleda is not really about honor and
shame at all--it concerns the relaxation and enjoyment caused by
their absence--its structure and contents tell a great deal about
both. As is the case with duality in general, inversion and
redundancy make the conceptual meaning of either half of an opposition iterative of the content of both halves.

The Koleda texts, thus, exemplify a special form of polysemy,
that in which two poles of emotional meaning are present; one,
the serious anger-producing honor-shame axis, is implicit while
the other, its riskless and humorous expression, is contextually
relevant. It should be noted, however, that the contextually
relevant meaning can function only in light of the implicit meaning which underlies it.

Most of the symbolism of contemporary Koleda, then, refers
ultimately to the nexus of male concepts and categories which
relates honor and shame, male and female, solidarity and competition. As such, it articulates an important portion of Rosan
male worldview and ethos, a segment as yet untouched by the
modernization, socialization, and Westernization which are slowly
changing the character of Macedonian cosmology.

The izvici, however, share another characteristic which
demands interpretation: their use of tropes and imagery. Given
the lexicon of mrsni terms available to and used by men both in
cursing and in the chants--pica, cunt; saka, desire sexually;
moca, urinate; lajna, shit; geva, jebi, fuck; kur, prick; gaz,
ass; madi, balls, to list the most obvious--the use of tropes
is clearly unnecessary to the communication of general concepts
which underlie Koleda. Instead of more frequent repetition of
these and other terms, however, Rosanci utilize a number of
tropes and images which do more than replace other kinds of symbols.

It is possible, to begin with, to relegate the use of tropes to Macedonian aesthetics in the sense that the words and phrases chosen for use in the texts accord with Macedonian preferences. However, as Gregory Bateson has aptly pointed out, style is by itself meaningful in that it too is a source for cultural information (1972:130-131). The third text, for example could just as well have been chanted in the following manner with little loss of meaning:

3a. Kolede kolede oo ooooo,   Koleda koleda oo ooooo,
    Koj go ima ke si jebi,   Whoever has it will fuck,
    Koj go nema toj e žena,   Whoever hasn't is a woman,
    Oo ooooo,   Oo ooooo,
    Kolede kolede oo ooooo, Kolede kolede oo ooooo.

The differences between the original Rosan text and my invention are subtle but present. The second line of text 3a is a more-or-less factual statement which conjures up a variety of possible images whereas that of text 3 results in a far more limited set, those pertaining visually and tactilely to ejaculation. The third lines give even clearer indication of the differential effects of tropes and other Koleda symbols. "Whoever doesn't will shave it" connotes the image of an impotent man, an image simultaneously funny and derogatory. Furthermore, it connotes a woman's shaven mons which, in cultural context, is both funny and absurd. In fusion, the two images clearly specify the visual elements associated with impotence by Rosan men and imply the feelings and values concomitant to them as well. By comparison, the altered line is matter-of-fact and visually less iterative. This indicates that tropes can attach new visual and evaluative images and qualities to concrete objects and acts. Unlike those discussed by Fernandez (1974), these qualities and images are not necessarily only inchoate concepts which already exist in a culture; rather, these tropes blend known, clear concepts with nonconceptual visual associations, sensations, and feelings: here, humor, shame, and the visual image of the shaven woman. These experiential meanings have not been rationalized by the process of conceptualization. In that such tropes apply the concepts, associations, and images from one domain of experience to another, they are capable of combining a different and more innovative array of referents than are symbols whose referents are more clearly codified by traditional usage.

Analysis of the following izvik indicates that tropes serve to externalize and express individually experienced sensations:

9. Sotir sedna na tikva,   Sotir sits on a pumpkin,
    Tikvata pukna,   The pumpkin explodes,
    Blaže na sestra mu go lupna, Blaze peels his (Sotir's)
    Oo ooooo.   sister,
                                 Oo ooooo.

271

The pumpkins grown in Rosa are green but otherwise similar in size and appearance to our own round, orange fruit. Although just what explodes is ambiguous--is it a pumpkin, an orgasm, or do Sotir's genitalia explode?--it is clear that what explodes is under him and therefore in contact with, equivalent to, or issuing from his genitalia. This violent metonym connotes the energy issuing from that part of a man; the English glosses for the verb pukna include firing, shooting, bursting, exploding, splitting, and breaking (Crvenkovski and Gruić 1965:296).

Equally energetic is the activity described in the third line, for instead of simply referring to intercourse, it describes Blaže's act with the verb lupna--to peel, pare, scrape, husk, or scale (Ibid: 1968)--thus evoling a simultaneously tactile and visual polysemous image in which the woman is passive and the man is exerting himself upon her violently, to the maximum. The tropes used here thus externalize, focus, and evoke not just acts, but the nature and intensity of sensate experiences. As such, their analysis adds to the conceptualization and categorization of honor, shame, male, and female a non-ideational sensory component usually lacking in anthropological analysis and interpretation. It indicates that Macedonian maleness, in addition to the characteristics already discussed, has associated with it a strong sense of the intensity of male libidinous energy, an aggressive energy which explodes and husks in Text 9 and which, elsewhere, emphatically catches (fati), pushes into (napika), forces (ftera), showers (tuči), and ejaculates (mija). This assertive intensity correlates well with the characteristics of the honorable man not by modifying them, but rather by extending them into the sphere of the sensate.

The corresponding extention of the nature of Rosan womanhood into the sensory also exists, although what is given in Koleda is, of course, the male conception of the matter. The first text provides the most extended image of the feminine in the Rosan cycle. It describes a seemingly disembodied pair of legs and loins attempting to scramble onto a shelf. The image is not of an individual, nor even of a type; it is an archetypal, synecdochic running vessel of evil, heaven and hell on legs. Unlike its male counterpart, its actions are uncertain and tentative; instead of forcing or pushing into, it scrambles, makes the attempt, seems almost to be running away. "Bela pica medu nije" (evil cunt between them) presents the image of something fleetingly and unclearly seen or understood. Being evil, it remains, so to speak, in shadow. This trope indicates that the Rosan male experience of woman is one in which her sexuality is distanced or amputated from her other characteristics. In this chant she is merely an evil, alien object seen running at a distance. And what runs is there to be chased and caught.

272

In the texts in which a man copulates with a woman or with
another man who is given the female role, the latter are always
described as if they were merely there, unprotesting, passive
receptacles:

Go jadi na Pop Kostadina;	May he eat Father Kosta;
Blaže na sestra mu go lupna;	Blaze peels his (Sotir's) sister,
Da ja fteram na sestra mu doguša	May I force his sister to embrace me,
Da me fati sestra mu za durov	May I catch his sister for my prick.

That is undoubtedly how they are usually experienced by Macedonian men.

The experiential, nonconceptual nature of the sensate meanings of Koleda is further exemplified by consideration of what
the chants do not communicate: the nature of feminine sexual sensations. Rosa is a village where feminine modesty precludes
heterosexual discussion of intercourse. This male genre cannot
extend our knowledge of women's sexual sensations as it does of
men's since communication, the only substitute for actual first-
hand experience, is culturally precluded. This indicates that
sensate tropes are expressive forms which, in the absence of
such communication, can metaphorize only their creators'
experiential knowledge; where communication of nonconceptual
experience does not exist, secondary experience derived from it
cannot form the basis for tropes. The tropes of Koleda, then,
specify the nature of images relating to male sensate activities
and in doing so concretely focus only male associations and pro-
jections.

The tropes of Koleda possess a number of important qualities
which are characteristic of tropes in general. To begin with,
they can express unconscious meaning. For example, although in
Koleda they express ideas, feelings, and sensations relating to
sexual sensation, Rosan men accept their sexual referents as
merely ideational. They do not consciously experience the sexual ideas encoded in Koleda symbols and metaphors as referring
to the physical sensations of intercourse. The fact that such
reference is clearly present in the texts indicates that tropes
do encode unconscious meaning.

Furthermore, their expression of sensate experience exempli-
fies another general characteristic of tropes: that they, more
than other kinds of symbols, express nonconceptualized internal
states by presenting images onto which individuals may project
their own experience and with which they may associate cultural
and personal sensate and emotional concomitants.

273

Finally, this analysis indicates that, because they apply
qualities from a known subject onto one which is, for their
creators, conceptually and verbally unexplored or in need of
reassessment, tropes are more conducive to the development of
new nonconceptual images and associations than are other kinds of
symbols. Indeed, the use of tropes in such situations may pre-
cede the development of new codified, culturally accepted symbols.

Koleda is a complex ritual in which men turn each other to
varying degrees into metaphoric women in a mirthful pseudo-con-
test for honor. Its interactive and textual symbols most clearly
represent the interrelation of the Macedonian male-female and
honor-shame polarities while its textual tropes clearly illumine
concomitant nonconceptual feelings, images and sensations. Where
both are available, the analysis of tropes as well as codified
symbols results in the interpolation of two complementary and
overlapping kinds of understanding, understanding which opens up
not only conscious feeling and conceptualization, but unconscious feeling and sensation to anthropological inquiry.

Bateson, Gregory

    1972 "Style, grace, and information in primitive art in
           Steps to an ecology of mind. pp. 128-152. New York:
           Ballantine Books.

Campbell, J.K.

    1966 "Honour and the devil," in Honour and shame: The
           values of Mediterranean society. Edited by J.G.
           Peristiany, pp. 139-170. Chicago: University of
           Chicago Press.

Chock, Phyllis Pease

    1974 Time, nature, and spirit: A symbolic analysis of
           Greek-American spiritual kinship. American Ethnolo-
           gist 1(1):33-48.

Crvenkovski, Dušan and Branislav Gruic

    1965 A little Macedonian-English dictionary. Prosvetno
           Delo: Skopje.

Fernandez, James

    1974 The mission of metaphor in expressive culture. Cur-
           rent Anthropology 15(2):119-146.

Granet, Marcel

    1975 The Religion of the Chinese People. Oxford: Basil
           Blackwell.

Lord, Albert B.

    1964 The singer of tales. Cambridge: Harvard University
           Press.

Ralston, W.R.S.

    1872 Songs of the Russian people. London: Ellis.

Sachs, Nahoma

    1975 Music and Meaning. Musical symbolism in a Macedonian
           village. Ann Arbor: Michigan University microfilms.

Sapir & Crocker

1977   The social use of metaphor: Essays on the anthro-
        pology of rhetoric. Philadelphia: University of
        Pennsylvania Press.

Turner, Victor W.

1967   The forest of symbols: Aspects of Ndembu ritual
        Ithaca: Cornell University Press.

1969   The ritual process. Chicago: Aldine.

INCA CONCEPTS OF SOUL AND SPIRIT

Glynn Custred
California State University, Hayward

Concepts of soul and spirit are found in one
form or another in all societies of the world where
they form basic conceptual elements which underlie
and support not only magic and religion, but in many
cultures such crafts as medicine, hunting, fishing,
agriculture and even mining and metallurgy. These
beliefs may also function on the ethical level to
organize and guide certain aspects of purely secular
and non-technological behavior.

Besides these social functions concepts of soul
and spirit also act as explanatory devices to orient
individuals and to reduce anxieties arising from
personal stress and natural catastrophies. These
beliefs, therefore, form a nexus of Man's social and
psychological natures, and represent one of his most
basic and most enduring conceptualizations.

For the sake of convenience this conceptual domain might be labeled pneumatology, a word which has
been used in Western philosophy and theology to refer
to theories or doctrines of soul and spirit. The
pneumatology of a given culture would therefore refer
to that culture's coherent body of belief in spiritual
essences, entities and forces, beliefs which appear
in both folklore and in social activities of all kinds.

Concepts of the human soul are of particular interest within pneumatology, and have received a great
deal of attention from both historians and ethnologists. In fact such concepts reveal Man's earliest
attempts at psychological explanation, and form the
basis of his earliest medical theories. Ideas of
soul, therefore, as they appear in their rich variety
around the world, present the humanistic anthropologist with an insight into Man's many and varied attempts at understanding his own, often puzzling human

277

nature.

This paper, however, is not concerned with soul concepts in general, but rather with the conceptualization of soul as it existed in the southern Andes of Peru just prior to and shortly after the Spanish conquest. Unlike comparable civilizations in the Old World, Andean culture never produced a system of writing. The intellectual edifices constructed by Andean thinkers, therefore, have been either lost to us entirely, or are visible only in shadowy form through the writings of sixteenth and seventeenth century Spanish clerics.

The only direct information which has come down to us on Andean pneumatology is found encoded in the words of the Quechua language as they were used in appropriate contexts within the dictionaries and the didactic Christian literature of the early colonial period. A glimpse at the pneumatology of Inca Peru, therefore, depends heavily upon the reconstruction of the semantic domain which these terms realize. To borrow a phrase from the classical philologist Bruno Snell "once these words are grasped with greater precision in their meaning and relevance, they will suddenly recover all their ancient splendor" (Snell 1953:1).

Unfortunately all the ancient splendor of the Quechua vocabulary, especially within this particular domain, is not entirely recoverable, since the Quechua language was purposely altered by Spanish missionaries during the colonial period in an effort to forge it into an instrument suitable for transmitting the Christian doctrine. Any attempt at reconstructing the pre-hispanic meanings of Quechua words, therefore, must take this fact into account.

There are only a few texts out of the meager colonial Quechua literature which are relevant to an investigation of pre-conquest pneumatology. The first texts a dictionary and a grammar of the language published in 1560 by the Spanish priest Domingo de Santo Tomas. This grammar and lexicon are the first ever written for Quechua, and appeared less than thirty years after Pizarro and his troops first marched into the Andean heartland from the sea. These documents are especially valuable since they reflect the language at a time when major lexical changes had only just begun. Other documents important for the

278

present project are an anonymously authored dictionary
published in 1586, and a comprehensive lexicon published in 1608 by the Spanish priest Diego Gonçalez
Holguin. Also of interest are the Quechua sermons of
Francisco de Avila published in Lima in 1648.

Of these documents the most useful for present
purposes is the Gonçalez Holguin dictionary. Unlike
the other two lexicographers, who simply listed
lexical entries and glosses, Gonçalez Holguin took
pains to list the major derivations and inflexions
of basic Quechua words, and to present them in the
contexts of illustrative phrases and sentences. These
contexts of occurrence, therefore, show us the principle patterns of collocation which Quechua terms
could contract with one another, thereby revealing the
semantic ranges which they covered. In turn these
semantic ranges reveal the underlying conceptualizations which the lexicon realized in the ecclesiasti-
cal standard language of colonial Quechua.

In order to reconstruct pre-hispanic semantic
domains, it is therefore necessary to recognize the
Spanish loan words and loan translations appearing in
Quechua. In this way we can isolate the lexical
substratum which underlay colonial standard Quechua.

In all the colonial documents, except those of
Santo Tomas, the Spanish word anima is used to express the idea of soul. In his dictionary, and in a
sermon appended to his grammar, however, Santo Tomas
used the Quechua terms camaquenc and songo inter-
changeably, and together in the same slot, to express
the concept of soul. And in his dictionary he glosses
alma and anima 'soul' with the term çamay along with
songo and camaquenc. Santo Tomas also translates the
Spanish term espiritu as çamay. Obviously none of
these words came close enough to Christian doctrine
to warrant their continued use during the colonial
period, thus the introduction of the Spanish term
anima into the lexicon. A reconstruction of Inca
pneumatology, therefore, must concentrate on the distribution of the Quechua terms songo, çamay and
camaquenc.

The 1586 dictionary however, states that camaque
(appearing in the first person possessive form
camaquey) means 'my creator', and is not used exactly
in the sense of soul (no se dice propriamente por el
anima), and Gonçalez Holguin does not even list this

279

form in his 1608 dictionary. It is not certain which
dialect Santo Tomas was working with, therefore it is
possible that he was employing a local term for some
soul aspect which may have been labeled differently
in other dialect areas. With no further occurrences
of this term, however, further comment would be sheer
speculation. The hard data thus lie with the terms
songo and çamay.

The Inca Concept of Soul

An analysis of these terms in the light of contemporary linguistic and ethnographic data suggests
the following Andean conceptualization of soul. The
central idea is that of a body soul labeled sonqo
(variously sonqo, soncco and sonco in the colonial
literature).[1] The body soul accounts for 1) the
animation of the body and of the nutritive processes,
2) consciousness and intelligence, 3) the personality
or the characters and temperaments of individuals,
4) temperamental differences between men and women
and 5) behavioral differences between human beings and
animals. Samay (çamay, zamay) referred to a breath
soul which accounted for the life of the individual,
and which linked man to the spiritual beings residing
within the physical environment. There also appears
to have been some idea of a free soul, that is the
notion of the individual, or some characteristic of
the individual, in an extraphysical form. Unlike the
European unitary free soul concept, however, which
plays a central role in Christian doctrine, Andean
free souls appear to have been of a dual nature, and
were subordinate to the body soul. Furthermore, they
may have varied both lexically and conceptually from
place to place throughout the Andes.

Sonqo: The Body Soul

The term sonqo was used in three related senses
in the sixteenth century: 1) heart of wood, 2) heart
of fruit (this sense was listed only in the 1586
dictionary) and 3) heart of a person or an animal.
In the latter sense it was more precisely defined by
all three lexicographers as 'heart, innards or stomach'
(corazon, entrañas or estomago). Gonçalez Holguin goes
on to say that sonqo also means 'conscience, judgement

280

or reason, memory, volition (or will) and understanding'. The Spanish term entrañas 'innards' comes closest to capturing the general meaning of sonqo since entrañas denotes those internal organs necessary to life, while connoting the essence of the person and strongly implying that these essential organs are the seat of feeling or emotion. As the distribution of sonqo reveals, however, this similarity in meaning is only superficial.

As an organic system sonqo accounts for the animation of the body as seen in the beating of the heart, and in the nutritive processes which take place in the stomach and the intestines. Other terms are encountered for liver (cucupi) and for lungs (çurca or challa challa), words which were not collocated with sonqo in any context. For this reason, and since no separate terms seem to have existed for stomach or heart, it would appear that the sonqo performed only these two vital functions which were conceptually merged into a single organic complex.

The term ñati appears as an apparent synonym of sonqo in the Gonçalez Holguin dictionary as seen in the phrase tucuy ñatyhuan (tucuy 'all' - huan 'with' - y 'my') which was glossed as 'with all my soul (alma), or will or innards' (entrañas). Ñati sonco, however, is translated as 'the interior of my soul (alma)' implying a part to whole relationship where ñati may represent one organ within the heart-digestive complex labeled sonqo. If this interpretation is correct, then we see in this semantic relationship an indication of a purely physical seat of psychological manifestations. The term ruru 'kidney' may also have been thought of as a part of the sonqo since it appears in the same context as do sonco and ñati as listed by Gonçalez Holguin under the Spanish phrase entrañas mias. Soncoy, rurulla or ñatiyñatilla (-y 'my', -lla 'delimiter') are the terms so listed, each carrying an affective connotation.

The sense of sonqo as physical organs is further revealed in such phrases as sonconannay 'stomach ache'; ccaymak sonco 'an upset stomach which causes a loss of appetite' (estomago desabrido que no gusta de la comida) and soncopllican 'lining of the internal organs' (redaño o tela de las entrañas).

In the sense of consciousness sonqo appears in phrases like soncco ppittin 'to faint', literally

281

'to tear the sonqo apart'. This implies that the
physical organs of heart and stomach as a single complex organ performed the functions of both vital and
psychological processes. The term ppittin means
literally 'to split apart what was a whole'. To
'come to' or 'regain consciousness' is soncota
hapicupuni literally 'to catch for oneself the sonqo'.
Also to regain one's senses or reason is soncoy
chincayninmantan caucarini literally 'I revive after
loosing my sonqo'.

    Sonqo also carries the meaning of reason or
sanity. A kollasoncolla or llullusonccollarac huahua
is a child who does not yet have full use of reason,
and llullo sonccohuarmarac or mana soncoyoc, literally
'still an immature sonqo child' and 'not a possessor
or sonqo', describe someone ignorant or who does not
use good sense. Also huarmay soncco cay, literally
'to be a child sonqo', means 'ignorance', while soncoy
huican is 'lacking sanity' (faltando juyzio).
Sonccocta chincachicuspa, literally 'to cause oneself
to lose sonqo', refers to someone who drinks until
he passes out, and an unconscious drunk is said to be
a soncconchincascca, literally 'one who has lost his
sonqo'. Conversely the verb for recovering from in-
sanity is sonccoya cupuni, and to be in full command
of one's faculties is soncoy camacani, literally 'I
command my sonqo'.

    Sonqo refers to intellect and understanding on a
more refined level as well. For example, Francisco
de Avila in his sermon against idolatry appeals to
the reason of his listeners to turn away from the
worship of nature to the adoration of the true God.
"The man of understanding" (soncoyocc runa, 'the
sonqo possessing man'), he writes, "who looks at the
sun, (and) thinks and says, this sun, whose creation
is it, where does it come from?" In contrast to this,
people of 'little understanding' (poco entendemiento)
are called pici soncco runalla (pici 'little'). And
in his 1608 dictionary Gonçalez Holguin translates
çatisca soncoyoc, literally 'possessor of a filled
heart', as one who is 'wise and prudent, and who is
experienced and versed in all things'. Also sonco
çapa (çapa 'augmentative') is translated in Spanish
as sabio, or 'wise one'.

    As seen from the examples above sonqo meant both
the physical organs of 'heart and stomach' and the
configuration of cognitive traits which form the
'mind'. In fact Gonçalez Holguin glosses rational
soul (anima racional) as sonccoyoc alma, literally

282

'the soul-possessing sonqo'. There is, however,
another word in Quechua which more precisely lexi-
calizes the concept 'mind', or mental activities.
This term is yuyu. Gonçalez Holguin lists yuyak
(-k 'agentive') and yuyayniyoc (-niyoc 'possessor')
as synonyms of sonccoyoc alma, 'rational soul'. He
also defines the verb yuyani as 'I remember, I think,
I am careful, or I have charge of something'. The
noun yuyana is defined as 'imagination', and a yuyay
runa is 'someone of understanding, a man of intelligence and caution, an adult in full possession of
his reason'.

The many derivations of yuya, and the contexts
in which they appear, further clarify the meaning of
yuya as 'mind' and 'mental or cognitive activities'.
For example, yuyaynicama means 'in conformity with
my feeling or judgement'; mana alli yuyayta acturcconi
'to do away with bad thoughts', and yuyaycuni 'to be
thoughtful with one's self'. Yuyachipuni is 'to
remind someone of some thing'. To completely remember
is yuyarccupuni, and yuyaynipi is 'to have something
in my memory'. These are only a few of many such
phrases. Yuya co-occurs with sonqo in a large number
of contexts throughout Gonçalez Holguin's dictionary
in an apparent relationship of synonymy. For example
'to understand or apprehend deeply' is yuyaman or
soncoyman (-man 'to'). 'He who is versed in all
things and understands all that he explores' is hamu
hamu soncoyoc or yuyayniyoc (hamu 'wise'). To faint
can be either soncco ppittin or yuyay ppittin, and
to regain consciousness soncoyta or yuyayta ñitticuniy
hapipuni. Also 'to repress thoughts' is yuyayta or
soncoyta nitticuniy, and 'to carry in the memory' is
either soncoypi or yuyapi apaycachani. A host of
other examples could be given to illustrate this point.

On closer examination, however, the semantic
relationship between sonqo and yuya appears to be one
not of synonymy, but rather one of part to whole.
This is seen in the occurrence of yuya as a modifier
of sonqo, but never the other way around. For example
yuyak soncoyok michay or yuyacpa sonccon is 'an
intellectually precocious person', literally 'a
possessor of an intellectual sonqo early'. And yuyac
soncoy, literally 'my thinking sonqo' is glossed
'I have an opinion'.

This form, in fact, is only one of several where
an adjective modifies sonqo. In such constructions

283

the latter term often has the meaning of 'general
capacity or ability'. For example yachaypac soncoyoc
is the 'capacity to know', literally 'the possessor
of a sonqo for knowing' (yacha- 'know', -y 'nomina-
lizer', -pac 'for'). Also the phrase 'to be possessor
of sonqo' soncoyoc cay means 'general capacity or
ability'.

Sonqo is also used in the sense of natural inclination and thus describes the character or temperament of a person. Paccariscca soncco means both
'natural inclination' and 'natural ability', or the
endowment we are born with. Mana alli paccarisca
sonccoyoc is glossed by Gonçalez Holguin as 'a person
with bad inclinations' or a bad character. More
specifically one who is inclined to lie, or a born
cheater, is llullaycuc sonco (llullu 'lie').

The term sonco may also be used to express not
only the inborn temperament of individuals, but also
the changeability of their moods, as well as their
different tastes. Someone in a bad mood is said to
be ysa soncco, literally 'two sonqo' (-lla 'delimiter')
(see Gonçalez Holguin under the entry de mala gana).
Someone who likes to change clothes often is astacuk
sonco, a person who likes to drink is akamansoncco, a
lady's man, or a man fond of women, is huarmiman
soncco, someone who is dedicated to gambling is a
chuncayman soncco, and many more.

The use of sonqo in phrases describing personality traits, especially those for virtues and vices,
are to be regarded with some suspicion if our task
is to separate colonial usage from pre-colonial
semantic content. The reason for this is stated
by Gonçalez Holguin in his introduction, where he de-
plores the lack of Quechua terms for Christian vices
and virtues, and states that he will rectify this
lack in his dictionary. Since sonqo however forms
the base of a number of phrases describing almost all
other personality traits, not just those essential to
Christian preaching, we might be safe in assuming that
the Spaniards were merely expanding an Andean concept,
not creating a new one. For example, to be discontent
is marayak soncco; compassionate, mayhuapayak soncco;
impatient, cucuc mana muchu pucuk soncco; and to be
timid or a coward, llaklla soncco.

Besides individual character differences, sonqo
was also used to describe ideal differences between

men and women. Karisoncco, literally 'man hearted' is glossed 'animated and valorous'. A karisoncco huarmi, literally a 'man hearted woman', is one who is masculine in her ways (veronil), and an effeminate and weak man is said to be huarmi pissisonco literally 'a small sonqo, like a woman'.

The sense of 'basic essences' of individuals and of the sexes, as illustrated in the examples given above, also holds for animals as well. Gonçalez Holguin says that sonqo is the heart of people or animals. Another term, however, puyhuan, was also used for animal heart. A beastly person, he writes, is a puyhuansonccoyok runa, literally 'a person with an animal heart sonqo'. Presumably puyhuan referred only to the corporal organ, while sonqo, when used in the context of animal, meant 'essence' or some aspect of soul (see Gonçalez Holguin corazon). For example, when describing the trait 'animal-like'(bruto como un animal) Gonçalez Holguin lists llama sonccoyok as one of his definitions. This literally means 'possessor of a llama sonqo'. And in his 1560 sermon Santo Tomas contrasts the souls of animals, which are mortal, with those of human beings which are immortal in his explanation of the soul, angels and demons. The term sonqo was used for soul in each case.

Sonqo, however, was also used in the more restricted sense of human soul, or perhaps more precisely in the sense of essence or core of attributes which makes us human. This is seen in Gonçalez Holguin's Quechua glosses for those Spanish terms describing 'animal' or 'animal-like' (bruto, bestial, brutez, animales bruto and bruto como un animal). In each of these entries either sonconnac 'without a soul' or mana soncoyoc 'not having a soul' together with tahuachaquiyoc 'four footed' is used within the Quechua definitions.

Looking back on the phrases given above, as well as at the many other contexts of sonqo not listed here, the question immediately arises as to where that semantic line must be drawn between literal and metaphoric use. In many cases it appears we are dealing with purely metaphoric meaning, and among those metaphoric phrases it is not clear whether the metaphors were native creations or whether they were Spanish neologisms. However, given the sheer weight of numbers of collocations involving sonqo (this could be the most frequently used noun in the Gonçalez Holguin

dictionary) and given evidence from other cultures
around the world (Hultkrantz 1953), including the
early history of our own culture (see Snell 1953;
Onians 1973; Van Peursen 1966), it is quite reasonable
to assume that most of the contexts of sonqo found in
the colonial Quechua literature do indeed indicate
belief in a literal merger of mind, temperament and
emotion with the corporal organs of the heart and the
stomach. In fact many of the metaphors which were
undoubtedly used may have been based on a firm belief
in the sonqo body soul as described above. The best
evidence in support of this theory, however, comes
not from sixteenth century lexical data, but rather
from contemporary ethnographic evidence.

In the high altitude llama and alpaca herding
zones of Chumbivilcas (department of Cuzco) the
Quechua-speaking peasants perform a certain ritual on
specific occasions in behalf of their domesticated
animals. This ritual consists of the burning of an
offering containing pieces of llama or alpaca fat,
corn kernels, coca leaves, and seeds, pieces of soap
stone and incense. The smoke from the offering is
said to supply the hill spirits with their nourishment. If these offerings, or payments as the peasants
call them, are not made, the hill spirits will have
no other recourse than to eat the hearts of the animals in order to sustain their own lives. The word
used for heart is sonqo. The loss of sonqo resulting
from this, say the peasants, causes sickness, loss of
fertility and even death. Hill spirits can also eat
the sonqo of humans in cases of ritual lapses, thus
resulting in sickness and other forms of harm. What
we see in this ritual, therefore, is a belief in the
soul-like essence of the internal organs which 1) is
linked to the spirit world, and 2) which accounts for
the vitality and proper behavior and functioning of
men and of animals. This contemporary belief is consonant with our analysis of the colonial lexical data.

The reason why such contemporary evidence weighs
so heavily in this reconstruction of pre-hispanic soul
beliefs is the fact that traditional Andean symbolism
and ritual, as they focus on production activities,
have changed very little in form, function and manner
of performance since the sixteenth century (Custred
1973). It is therefore safe to assume that the structure of ideas contained within these rituals, and
which rationalize and support them, has likewise undergone little if any major alterations.

Samay: The Breath Soul, or Spirit

Santo Tomas glossed the Spanish terms espiritu o
soplo, 'spirit or breath', as çamay in his 1560
dictionary. He also lists the term çamay, together
with camaquenc and songo, as a definition of both
alma and anima, Spanish synonyms for 'soul'. He does
not, however, use çamay in his sermon. In the 1586
dictionary the term zamay is defined as 'rest, recreation, breathing and to take courage'. The Spanish
verb resollar, 'to breathe heavily' is glossed zamani
(-ni 'I') and the noun huelgo, 'breath', is defined
as zamay.

Gonçalez Holguin glosses breath (huelgo) as
çamay, and respiration as çamay or çamarcuy.
Çamayccurcuni huazrata means 'breathe in through the
mouth', çamayccucuni cincaycucuni is 'breathe in
through the nose', and çamarcuni is defined as either
'to breathe out', or as 'the odor of the breath'.
The term çamaycuni means 'to give one's breath the
odor of what one has eaten or drunk', çamarccuni is
'to evaporate and lose force and smell', çamaycuhuan
means 'to give myself the fume or the vapor of
chicha', and the phrase 'fumes from the mouth or from
the pot' (baho de la boca, o de la olla) is glossed
çamaynin, çamarccuynin. In the same entry Gonçalez
Holguin contrasts çama- with the term huapci which
refers to 'vapors which rise from the earth'.

This strictly physical sense of samay however is
only one of the meanings it may have. Another is that
of 'inspire' or 'to influence' as in çamaycuni mana
allin soncoyta which is glossed by Gonçalez Holguin as
'infect others with bad habits', literally 'breathe
out my bad songo'. The 1586 dictionary glosses
zamacuni as 'to let the vigor of the soul flow in, or
to breathe in' (infundir el alma dalle vigor o in-
suflar). And the term zamasca runa, literally
'breathed in person' is translated 'sorcerer'
(hechizero). Gonçalez Holguin defines çupaypa
çamaycuscan, or simply çamasccan, as 'sorcerer', or
'one inspired by the devil' (çupay 'devil'), and
çupaypa çamayninmi tucuni as 'I am inspired by the
devil'. Conversely çamaycuni is translated as 'God
infuses the soul (alma), and in it graces or virtues,
or light or good inspirations'.

With only this to go on it is not clear whether
'inspiration' is a literal or an extended meaning of

287

samay. However in the light of both contemporary
Andean beliefs and rituals, and historical and ethnographic data from elsewhere, it is clear that the
Inca term samay did indeed label a concept which
equated spirit with wind and breath. The Spanish use
of this term to mean inspiration in a Christian sense,
therefore, reveals a Spanish adaptation of a native
Andean pneumatological belief.

Among the contemporary Quechua-speaking peasants
of southern Peru the breath plays an important role
in those rituals associated with the spirits of the
hills and the earth. Besides the herding rituals
discussed above, burned offerings are also made on a
number of other occasions, especially at the beginning
of the agricultural cycle (in many places before every
agricultural activity), and before the construction
of houses and other buildings (Custred 1979). In the
provinces of Canas, Canchis, Espinar and Chumbivilcas
in the department of Cuzco, for example, each person
present at the ritual performance must blow on the
offering before it is burned. In this way he participates in the required payment of resources to the
nature spirits in a direct and personal manner. The
life breath, so to speak, becomes a part of the smoke
which rises up to the hills for their sustenance.

The Peruvian anthropologist Jorge Flores says
(personal communication) that near the mountain of
Ausangate in southern Peru the belief prevails that
everyone personally interacts with the hill spirits
to some degree. There is, however, a member of each
family who is thought to be in closer communication
with the spirits than his kinsmen. There are also
shamans (ponqo) within many communities who are
thought to enjoy facile communication with the hills,
and who receive their shamanic powers from the hill
spirits. Ponqos and family specialists alike are
said to be samayoq runa, literally 'people possessing
breath'. In fact, the way people commune with hill
spirits is by taking deep breaths. Breathing in,
therefore, is the means by which information and power
is received from the spirits. Breathing out, in the
context of ritual offerings, is the means by which
men place themselves, in some measure, into the offering made to the spirits, payments which are required for successful human enterprises.

Samay, therefore, is not only the 'life force'
which animates individuals (their breath souls), but

also a linkage, or a bonding agent between man and the animating forces of his environment. In this sense we are dealing with a classic version of the concept of spirit, or pneuma. The modern term samayoq runa, provisionally translated above as 'people who possess breath', is better translated as 'people who possess spirit', and the term samasqa as it appears in the colonial dictionaries (zamasca, çamascca) would be better translated as 'those having received the spirit'. Since all native religious practices were considered by the Spaniards to be demonically instigated, and thus all native practitioners were said to be sorcerers (hechizeros), it is easy to see why the sixteenth century lexicographers recorded this native belief in the first place, and why it appears in the contexts we find it in. Wind, as well as breath, is believed by contemporary peasants to have spiritual qualities. Winds are associated with the hill spirits and the windy month of August is the time when these spirits are said to revive (kausarinku). Winds blowing from certain places on the landscape are also thought to bring illness.

Belief that air is "spirit", and that the breath of individuals is a soul aspect, is not unique to the Andes. For example wind and breath are associated with spiritual characteristics in the pneumatologies of many native North Americans. Among the Hopi there exists a belief in a systematic "panpsychism" in which the entire universe is endowed with the same breath. Animals, minerals and men all share this breath spirit. The Pueblo Indians connect the breath of man with the wind and the clouds. It is believed among the Pueblos that the breath is a unitary soul, which constitutes the surviving principle of Man. After death individuals, it is said, become cloud beings. The Zunis say that the rain or snow is the breath of the dead, and that dancers in the rain dance are asking the dead, who have become clouds, to send down their breath. Other Pueblos, those of New Mexico, believe that the person's breath flows together and merges with winds and clouds after the death of an individual. Similar conceptualizations are also encountered among the Haida, the Tsimshian, the Sauk as well as among other Indian groups (Hultkrantz 1953: 185-186, 183).

The association of breath, clouds, smoke and spirit is also characteristic of the soul beliefs of many South American lowland peoples. The Waika of the

upper Orinoco, for example, believe in two souls, a
shadow soul and a free soul. The latter is within
the body, and is released after death through cre-
mation, when it rises to heaven in the smoke of the
funeral pyre. The word for this soul is the same as
that for cloud. If the body is not burned, the soul
must wander the earth in search of another means of
reaching heaven (Zerries 1961: 345-346).

Among the Apapocuva-Guarani of central South
America there also exists a concept of dual soul. One
of these is the breath soul which originates from a
godhead in the sky, or in the west, and which enters
the body at birth. Also the Shipaya of the Brazilian
Amazon believe in a breath soul which leaves the dying
through the mouth. This soul after death resides
within hills or cliffs, leaving only the "husk" of the
soul on the earth's surface as a ghost (Zerries 1961:
342-344).

The association of breath, wind, vapor, etc. with
soul and spirit is not only found among native American peoples, but also in the ancient Near East and
the eastern Mediterranean as well. For example the
term ruah in ancient Hebrew was sometimes used as
wind, or blast, sometimes as breath and sometimes as
a vapour. In the book of Genesis this term also has
the sense of 'spirit' as in the first chapter, second
verse of Genesis: "And the spirit (ruah) of God
moved upon the face of the waters". It was also the
breath of God which infused life into Man, thereby
giving him a soul. "And the Lord God formed man of
the dust of the ground, and breathed into his nostrils
the breath of life (ruah); and man became a living
soul" (Gen.2:7).

In ancient Hebrew the term nepheš meant soul.
Based on the meaning of the root from which this term
is derived it appears that nepheš was connected with
the breath of life. The nepheš therefore appears to
have been a breath soul which accounted for the ego
in life, and which passed to some neutral and
shadowy place, sheol, after death.

In Homeric Greece breath, along with blood, seems
to have been considered an important soul aspect.
The term thumos is used in contexts of both breath and
of consciousness and emotions, thus indicating the
merger of the two (Snell 1953; Onians 1973: 48, 59-60).
General perception also seems to have been associated

with breathing in. An analogous conceptualization
also characterized ancient Hindu thought (Onians 1973:
73-75).

In the classical world the dual spiritual-cor-
poral concept of air, wind, breath, vapor and smoke
did not end with the rise of Platonism, a philosophy
which distinguished ideal essences from corporeal
objects. This was especially true in Greek medicine.
And even the neo-platonic hermetic literature retained
the notion of a corporeal spirit, or pneuma. Robert
Verbecke, in his history of the concept of pneuma from
the Stoics to St. Augustine, writes that by and large
the hermetic concept of pneuma was that of "the aerial
envelop of the soul, which attached the soul to the
body". As such, he writes, the corporeal pneumatic
vehicle of the soul is an adaptation of the corporeal
medical concept of pneuma to platonic philosophy.
The material nature of spirit throughout this period,
therefore, was never doubted (Verbecke 1945:   321).
In fact it was not until the diaspora and the diffusion of Jewish thought into the Hellenistic world
that this conceptualization began to change. It was
only with St. Augustine, who stood on the threshold
between the classical period and the Middle Ages, that
a concept of purely incorporeal spirit, as sharply
contrasted with matter, was fully elaborated, but even
then, says Verbecke, the concept of spirit did not
totally lose its attachment to the physical realities
of air and vapor (1945:   387-388, 489).   In fact this
duality continued through the Middle Ages and the
Renaissance (Barach 1878; Walker 1958). Perhaps the
most sophisticated elaboration of this dual spirit is
seen in European Renaissance alchemy (Burkhardt 1974).

Seen in cross-cultural perspective the notion of
spirit, whether of a purely spiritual or a partially
corporeal nature, is an essential concept within any
mystical or magical cosmology since it functions to
link the world of direct empirical experience to the
occult forces and entities which operate beneath the
visible surface of things. C. G. Jung has expressed
this necessary relationship in the following way:
    The relative or partial identity of psyche and
    physical continum is of the greatest importance
    theoretically, because it brings with it a
    tremendous simplification by bridging over the
    seeming incommensurability between the physical
    world and the psyche (Jung 1972:231).
It is easy to see, therefore, why air, breath, wind,

291

smoke and vapors have been thought to form such
bridging vehicles in so many pneumatologies of the
world, since these aerial and gaseous phenomena
stand between the perceivable and the tangible on the
one hand, and the elusive and the unsubstantial on
the other. What better vehicle could one find, therefore, than smoke from a burning offering to carry the
invisible essences of concrete Andean resources to
the invisible spirits of the hills, spirits which
devour smoke-borne essences for their own nourishment
in a mysterious way perhaps not unlike that of human
digestive processes deep within the 'soul' or sonqo
of each man.

The Free Soul

     So far a picture of a corporeally based concept
of soul and spirit has emerged from the colonial
lexical and the contemporary ethnographic data.
Besides this, however, there also appears to have
existed some concept of free soul among the pre-
hispanic peoples of southern Peru. A free soul is
the extraphysical presence of a person which may
correspond with one or more of his soul aspects, and
which is that portion of an individual thought to
survive in some manner after the death of the body.

     We have no reliable lexical data on possible
pre-hispanic free soul beliefs as we do for those of
body and breath soul. However given the pattern of
such beliefs as it is observed today throughout
southern Peru, we may infer at least the outlines of
a free soul conceptualization as it may have existed
during the late Inca Period. This belief probably
centered on two or perhaps three free souls believed
to survive the death of the individual. At least one
of these souls was probably thought to have an autonomous existence apart from the body, and to travel
about during the individual's life time. These beliefs also appear to have been subordinate to the body
and the breath souls, and to have existed in both
lexical and conceptual variations from place to place.

     The only lexical information available from the
late sixteenth century which suggests the existence
of a free soul concept in pre-conquest Peru is the
Quechua term nuna. This word is listed by Gonçalez
Holguin in only five phrases, and all of these are

found within a single entry. Moreover each of these phrases reflect the Christian concept of incorporeal spiritual entities. The prominent term in each phrase however, is nuna which apparently had a meaning close enough to the Spanish concept of spirit to warrant its central place in these purely Christian phrases. Nuna spiritu, for example, is listed as a synonym of yuyak nuna, both of which are defined as el alma, 'the soul'. The Latin term spiritu may have been inserted to emphasize, or further refine, the Quechua concept along European lines. The term yuyak is an adjectival form of the Quechua term for 'mind, reason, intellect', and can be glossed here as 'thinking' thus the 'thinking' nuna, or the intellectual nuna. Since the Christian doctrine defined spiritus as 'pure intellect' (see St. Tomas Aquinas' treatises on 'Divine Government', and on 'Angels') it is highly likely that yuyak nuna was a Christian neologism used as a synonym for the hybrid (and to the missionaries) more precise expression nuna spiritu. Another possibility, however, is that in classical Inca the term nuna was indeed differentiated into 'mind spirit' and perhaps even 'breath spirit', 'heart spirit', etc. With no further data to go on, however, this remains pure conjecture. In fact, the former interpretation, that nuna is used here in a purely European sense, is perhaps the more realistic one.

Nuna is found in three other contexts which further indicate a non-Spanish sense of free spirit. Two of these are mana alli nuna, and alli nuna, literally 'bad spirit' and 'good spirit'. These terms are glossed 'demon' and 'angel' respectively. The third phrase is antay quiru nuna, glossed 'innocent angels like a new born child, or pure one' (antay quiru means literally 'new born'). Since angels and demons in European pneumatology were said to be purely spiritual creatures totally divorced from any material body, the use of nuna in these contexts further suggests a spiritual and incorporeal sense of the Quechua term. It is doubtful whether Gonçalez Holguin would have used this word in the way he did if its meaning had been too widely divergent from the European idea he was trying to convey. The fact, however, that this term appears nowhere else, and that Spanish loan words for angel and soul were brought into Quechua indicates that the term was not sufficiently close to the Spanish idea to warrant its general use. For example, Gonçalez Holguin does not use nuna in glossing the Spanish term espiritu, 'spirit'. Instead he gives <u>angel hina ucunnac</u>, literally 'like an angel, lacking a body'.

Once we have established proof that some notion of free soul did indeed exist in pre-conquest times, it is necessary to look at the contemporary ethnographic data to find out what general form it might have had. Caution should be taken, however, in the use of contemporary concepts in reconstructing prehispanic free soul beliefs. There are two reasons for this. First, a religious conceptual system may remain stable (or at least relatively constant in its essential elements) as long as it maintains a functional relationship with its ritual context, since the concept explains and supports the performance and the application of the ritual. In the case of contemporary free soul belief there are few associated rituals now practised, and none of those which are actually celebrated today exhibit the continuity of form and meaning seen in the ritual offerings made to the nature spirits, rituals which are so closely associated with <u>sonqo</u> and <u>samay</u>.

The second reason why contemporary free soul beliefs should be treated with caution, is the great deal of attention given this subject by the evangelizing Spaniards and by the generations of parish priests who followed them. This emphasis lead not only to lexical borrowing, but undoubtedly to conceptual syncretism as well. Despite all this, contemporary free soul concepts differ enough from the often repeated Christian doctrine to provide us with a clue for our reconstruction of pre-hispanic forms.

In the contemporary Quechua-speaking community of Kauri in the department of Cuzco, Bernard Mishkin reports that the prevailing concept of body and soul is as follows. Man consists of three parts: the <u>charan cuerpo</u> which is the flesh, literally the 'wet body', the <u>alma</u> which is located in the head, and the <u>animo</u>. Both these souls survive the death of the body. The <u>animo</u> goes to 'heaven' after death, but may return each year to earth on All Souls Day, November 2. The <u>alma</u> is thought to be a kind of guardian spirit, protecting men against attacks by malevolent spirits, and assuring successful harvests. Many people, says Mishkin, keep skulls in their houses. At night the souls (<u>alma</u>) which live in them converse with one another and with the souls of the living. They also arrange feasts, dances, etc.

among themselves.

The soul of an individual may also leave the body
to wander around. If a man wakes up with a headache
he says his soul has been on a trip and is tired. At
the feast of San Andreas held at the nearby district
capital, two men are selected each year to arrange
that part of the celebration which honors the souls.
Their title is alma alferez, and their ritual costume
consists of skull masks. Their responsibilities are
the pouring of libations and the organization of a
mock bull fight for the entertainment of the souls
(Mishkin 1963:467).

Informants in the peasant community of Punacancha
in the hills above the city of Cuzco have a similar
free soul belief, but without the ritual. The anima
is believed to go to the interior of a hill after
death where it is kept by the hill spirit. The alma,
however, "like moths", may flutter around the fields
and villages of the living. In the remote province
of Chumbivilcas, also in the department of Cuzco,
there seems to be very little emphasis on the notion
of free soul, however a duality of alma and anima
does appear.

From the above data it is clear that despite the
use of Spanish labels, the concept of free soul is a
dual one, much like other soul concepts throughout
South America. These data also reveal a general confusion of belief in free souls by contemporary
Quechua-speaking peasants, and a general lack of
interest by them in both free soul concepts and the
after life. Goblins and evil spirits, for example,
are not associated with the ghosts of the dead as they
are in so many other parts of the world, but rather
with malevolent place spirits and, in some regions,
with nak'aq, literally 'killers'. These are living
men who supposedly stalk the night trails killing
Indians and selling their 'fat' in apothecaries in
towns and cities.

Perhaps the most feared spectre is the condenado.
This monster is a person returned from the grave to
wander the hills at night physically devouring any
human being it meets. Condenados are also believed
to eat anything, even the very stones of the ground.
The only way they can be destroyed is by fire. One
becomes such a monster by committing particularly
grave antisocial acts in life. The point to note

here is that the condenado (a creation of the early
colonial period) has nothing to do with the ghost,
or the returning free soul, which is feared in so
many societies of the world, but rather with the
physical presence of the monster, and the direct
physical damage it can do.

This lack of interest in the after life appears
to have been a characteristic of pre-hispanic as well
as of contemporary belief in southern Peru. This does
not mean, however, that there was no belief in an
afterlife, but rather that it was of relatively small
importance in Inca religion, and thus less developed
than elsewhere. This lack of elaboration contrasts
with the elaborate ideas of free souls and of the
afterlife among the pre-hispanic Mexicans (Soustelle
1940). Gonçalez Holguin, for example, writes in the
introduction to his dictionary that the Indians did
not have words "for all spiritual matters, nor for...
the other life and states within it" (1952/1608/:10).
Also the various accounts of the chroniclers indicate,
as John Rowe puts it, that "Inca religion emphasized
ritual and organization rather than mysticism and
spirituality" (Rowe 1963:293). Within such a context
it is natural to expect that those soul aspects most
closely related to the behavioral features and the
physical processes of individuals would take prece-
dence over the more abstract notions of free soul,
thereby leaving the latter relatively undeveloped and
of secondary importance.

This seems to be reflected in the colonial lexical data as well where sonqo and samay suggest
basically the same senses throughout the meager literature, while there exists almost no lexical evidence
at all to show that some concept of free soul even
existed. A possible reason is that free soul concepts, because they were of only secondary significance, may have varied both lexically and conceptually
from place to place, while belief in body and breath
soul formed a common southern Peruvian theme. This
is suggested by the highly restricted use of nuna
(Gonçalez Holguin), and by the use of camaquenc as
'soul' by Santo Tomas, but its rejection by the 1586
lexicographer who was dealing with a slightly different dialect of Quechua language.

The Relationship of Body and Soul

The soul of a person is his essence, that is the constellation of attributes which account for the life and the character of individual human beings. Different cultural traditions weigh the behavioral, the emotional, the intellectual and the physical attributes of Man in different ways in the formation of their divergent soul concepts, thus revealing to the ethnologist a wide range of variation. These variations in turn appear to be based on two broad conceptual themes. One is seen in the Christian doctrine where the spiritual and the Material are conceptionally opposed to one another to form two distinct spheres of reality, with the spiritual always presideing over the material. The second theme is expressed in the Andean concept where matter and spirit are two rarely separable aspects of the same thing. The latter theme is by far the most pervasive, even characterizing the pneumatologies of the archaic period of Western culture as seen in the ancient Hebrew and the Homeric Greek languages.

Since matter and spirit are dichotomous realities in the Christian tradition, the Latin and the Spanish terms for 'body' and 'soul' stand in a semantic relationship of opposition to one another, thus reflecting in lexical usage the conceptual opposition which underlies it. This is seen in a number of contexts such as 'they slew him, and the soul flew from his body', or 'his soul was finally freed from its earthly fetters'.

In pre-hispanic Quechua, however, such a semantic relationship could not have existed since the central concept of soul was thought to be the potencies of corporeal organs, not some totally opposed spiritual force, and since the free soul seems to have been of a dual nature, each soul expressing perhaps two distinct sets of human or individual personality characteristics which were split up after death. Furthermore, there is evidence to suggest that there did not even exist a single word for body in the Spanish sense of the term.

The word used by the Spanish clerics in the colonial literature for body is ucu (uccu, uku). Gonçalez Holguin defines this term as 'body of Humans or animals', as do the other lexicographers. He also uses it in the typical European fashion, as

297

is also the case in all other colonial Quechua texts.
For example, _anima ppitin ucumanta_ means 'the soul is
separated from the body' (-_manta_ 'from'), and
ucuyquicta yayaytac checcallanpi kana animayquictaca
means 'take care of your body, but more so of your
soul'. In each of these sentences the Spanish term
for soul is applied and opposed to 'body' (_ucu_) in a
typical Spanish manner. Moreover _ucu_ is used in constructions expressing such Christian virtues as
'virginity' as seen in the phrase _huaccay chak_
llunpac uccucayninta 'he who preserves the purity of
his body, or virginity'.

Ucu, however, also meant 'body parts'. Gonçalez
Holguin defines _uccuycuna_ (-_cuna_ 'plural marker') as
'my body parts' (_mis miembros_), and the Spanish phrase
miembros del cuerpo (body parts) is glossed as
uccuycuna. The term _runaycuna_ is listed in both
entries as synonyms of _ucuycuna_. _Runa_ also means
'person' or 'human being'. Moreover the verb
ucunchani is glossed as 'to beat my body in each one
of its parts', and the phrase _huañunmi runay o_
ucuycuna cucuncayaspa means 'my limbs are without
sensation because of paralysis'.

If _ucu_ did indeed mean 'body' in the European
sense, then it would be reasonable to expect it to
continue in usage to the present day as does the
term _runa_. The word for body in modern Quechua,
however, is not _ucu_, nor in fact any other Quechua
term, but rather the Spanish loan word _cuerpo_. Presumably the Spanish form _cuerpo_ fit the Spanish concept better than did any native word available,
despite the attempt at extending the meaning of _ucu_
by the linguistic missionaries. In Inca times, therefore, _ucu_ probably meant not the body as an integrated
whole, but rather body as a set of parts.

If this were the case, the semantic domain of
body and soul, as realized in Inca terminology, was
appreciably different from the one which now exists
in modern Quechua. First of all, there was no generic
term for body then as there is today, but rather only
a cover term for the various parts which make it up.
(A similar case can be made for the lack of generic
terms in other domains of the classical Inca language
as well, for example the domains of color, plants and
animals). Secondly the concept of soul was inseparable from that of body and bodily functions (except
perhaps in the subordinate free soul notions), and as

298

such apparently played a more prominent role in Inca
times than it does today.

Conclusions

It was suggested at the outset that the body of
beliefs related to soul and spirit operating within
a given culture be labeled the pneumatology of that
culture. It was also stated that pneumatology, as
a phenomenon in its own right, is of special interest
to humanistic anthropologists since it provides insights into man's universal attempts at comprehending
his own, often puzzling nature, as well as man's
attempts at accounting for both the patterned and the
unpredictable in the world around him. In this
sense concepts of spirit and soul represent one of
the most primitive, and at the same time one of the
most durable means of explanation which the human
mind has devised.

Interest in soul and spirit beliefs played an
important role in the earliest theories of ethnology
as seen in the writings of Tyler, Frazer, Levy-Bruhl,
and Durkheim and Mauss. In recent times, however,
theoretical interest in this domain has wanned despite a vast increase in ethnographic and historical
data, and despite the development of models and
perspectives which offer far more explanatory power
than did the simple unilinear and functionalist
theories of the earlier ethnologists. It is therefore time that concepts of soul and spirit be re-
examined in their widest range of diversity among both
simple, non-literate cultures, and the sophisticated
literatures of the civilizations of the world. Such
an enterprise might be called ethnopneumatology, and
would have as its goals the determination of the
limits of variation in the realm of soul and spirit
beliefs as they are encountered cross-culturally,
and the definition of the commonalities which underlie this broad diversity. Another goal of this
enterprise would be to account for these variations,
as far as possible, in terms of the social, cultural
and environmental contexts in which they are found.
Ethnopneumatology would be of value to humanistic
scholarship by presenting an organized body of data
on this subject to related disciplines, as well as
by providing perhaps some explanatory insights into
this corner of the history of ideas.

The present essay might be seen as a contribution to ethnopneumatology since it has attempted to reconstruct the essential elements of Andean soul beliefs as they existed in southern Peru at the height of autochthonous Andean civilization. However with such a paucity of information available to us from this period it is impossible to draw any precise conclusions on the conceptualizations which underlay the lexical pattern we have been able to reassemble. It is clear though from what information we do have that the Inca conceptualization depicted the physical aspect of man as inseperable from that of his spiritual nature. This is consonant with Andean pneumatology in other domains as well, and illustrative of that pervasive second pneumatological theme mentioned in the last section, namely that "spirit", as the essence and the potencies of matter, is contained within corporeal objects and events, not opposed to them, and that these spiritual properties can only be made real through the physical world which embodies them. It is, in fact, this principle which not only accounts for the souls of man and animals, but also for the vital essences of Andean resources, and the animation of the Andean environment, all of which form the conceptual basis of native Andean religion in its various forms both past and present.

NOTES

1. The original sixteenth and seventeenth century orthographies, as used in the historical texts, will be preserved here when dealing with the colonial language. A phonemic orthography based on contemporary Cuzco Quechua will be employed elsewhere.

REFERENCES CITED

Anonymous 1951/1586/Vocabulario y phrasis en la lengua general de los indios del Peru, llamada Quichua. Printed in Lima 1586 by Antonio Ricardo. Edicion del Instituto de Historia de la Facultad de Letras. Universidad Nacional Mayor de San Marcos, Lima.

Avila, Francisco 1648 Tratado de los evangelios que nuestra Madre la iglesia nos propone en todo el año ... Lima.

Barach, Carl S. 1878 Biblioteca Philosophorum Mediae Aetatis. Containing the texts of Alfredus Angleus, de motu cordis, and of Costa Ben Luca, de differentia animae et spiritus descrimine. Innsbruck.

Burckhardt, Titus 1974 Alchemy: Science of the Cosmos, Science of the Soul. Penguin Books.

Custred, Glynn 1973 Symbols and Control in a High Altitude Andean Community. Unpublished Ph.D. thesis. Indiana University, Bloomington, Indiana.

Gonçalez Holguin, Diego 1952/1608/Vocabulario de la lengua general de todo del Peru llamada lengua Qquichua o del Inca. Edicion del Instituto de Historia. Universidad Nacional Mayor de San Marcos. Lima.

Hultkrantz, Åke 1953 Conceptions of the Soul Among North American Indians: A Study in Religious Ethnology. The Ethnographical Museum of Sweden, Stockholm (Statens Ethnografiska Museum) Monograph Series. Publication No. 1. Stockholm.

Jung, Carl G. 1972 On the Nature of the Psyche. In Collected Works. Vol. 6:231.

Mishkin, Bernard 1963 The Contemporary Quechua. In The Handbook of South American Indians. J.H. Stewart, editor. 2:411-470.

Onians, Richard B. 1973 The Origin of European Thought About the Body, the Mind, the Soul, the World, Time and Fate. Arno Press. New York.

Rowe, John H. 1963 Inca Culture at the Time of the Spanish Conquest. In J.H. Steward, editor, Handbook of South American Indians, vol. 2. The Andean Civilization Smithsonian Institution. Bureau of American Ethnology. Bulletin 143. Cooper Square Publishers, Inc. New York.

Santo Tomas, Domingo de 1891/1560/Arte de la lengua
Quichua. Julio Platzmann, editor. Leipzig.

Santo Tomas, Domingo de 1951/1560/Lexicon o vocabu-
lario de la lengua general del Peru. Ediciones
del Instituto de Historia de la Facultad de
Letras de la Universidad Nacional Mayor de San
Marcos. Lima.

Soustelle, Jacques 1940 La Pensée cosmologique des
anciens Mexicains. Paris.

Snell, Bruno 1953 The Discovery of the Mind: The
Greek Origins of European Thought. Harvard
University Press.

Van Peursen, C.A. 1966 Body, Soul, Spirit: A Survey
of the Body-Mind Problem. Oxford University
Press. London.

Verbecke, Robert 1945 L'Evolution de la doctrine du
pneuma du Stoicisme à S. Augustin. Paris.

Walker, D.P. 1958 Spiritual and Demonic Magic from
Ficino to Campenello. Warburg Institute.
London.

Zerries, Otto 1961 Die Religion der Naturvölker
Sudamerikas und Westindiens In Walter Kricke-
berg, editor, Die Religionen des alten Amerika.
Stuttgart.

AURALITY AND CONSCIOUSNESS: BASOTHO PRODUCTION OF SIGNIFICANCE

Charles R. Adams

It is not uncommon to encounter terms from diverse languages and cultures which have been incorporated into the metalanguages of anthropological
discourse--such terms as atlatl, couvade, lebollo,
kula, nommo, raga, shaman, tabu, karma, and piblokto.
The use of these terms indicates an anthropological
concern with intellectual incorporation, whereby
human knowledge, generated through multiple cultural
reflections on self and circumstance, is integrated
and utilized in the pursuit of understanding human
nature. These terms are 'signatures' recognizing the
authorship and creativity of their sources. But while
acquisition and maintenance of a polyglot discourse
language is not a primary anthropological concern,
that activity has implications extending far beyond
pragmatic and neologistic convenience. First, 'sig-
nature terms' acknowledge 'gaps' in anthropological
thinking that can be filled by the products of reflection in cultures other than the anthropologist's,
and secondly, their presence in anthropological discourse indicates that the knowledge and understanding
keyed by these terms have some broader applicability
than to the cultural experiences from which they derive, that is to the human condition in general.

The anthropologist, as R. R. Marett once noted,
"presides over a bazaar of experiments," collective
and individual cultural strategies which select for,
focus on, and elaborate understanding of different
aspects of human experience. Whether these 'experiments' are ludic, scientific, artistic, or ritualistic
in character, they are governed by hypotheses and
cultural presuppositions which define meaning and
value and the means of their production. These hypotheses, especially those concerning human nature and
its functioning, are primary targets of intellectual
incorporation, ethnographically through description

and cross-cultural translation and ethnologically
through the processes of status-elevation, comparison,
and application. It is in the context of these concerns that I wish to discuss a tenet of Basotho culture central to the domain of special experiential
activities called 'games' (lipapali): that aurality,
the experience of sounding and hearing, is a necessary
condition of human consciousness and the principle
mode for the production of significant interpretations
of the circumstances of living.[1] It is suggested that
this hypothesis addresses itself to certain lacunae in
the anthropological understanding of human perception
and that it has a potentially broad contribution to
make as a heuristic concept in the study of human
behavior.

The Basotho 'games,' in general, are discovery
procedures, processes for determining human significance, assigning value and meaning to human action and
circumstance. They consist of a variety of ways and
styles of constructing experiences systematically so
that conditions, evidence, and consequences can be
examined in controlled 'experiments'--events which
are as much inquiries into objective realities as
they are into the nature and qualities of human experience itself. Every individual is, in a sense,
a scientist, an "intelligence capable of learning by
experience" (Peirce (1940:98), and the Basotho 'games'
provide the kinds of experiences which they feel are
the optimal activities through which people conform,
inform, and reform themselves in their circumstances
of living. Most specifically, the 'games' are vehicles of understanding and consciousness.

The notion of 'games' and 'playing' encompasses
activities which range through ritual prayer and singing, competitive dancing, work songs, praise and
ridicule poetry, divination, jive songs, showing respect to inlaws, joking, and playing musical instruments, soccer, and hopscotch. Each particular type
and style of 'game' has its characteristic uses,
conditions, contexts, and social meanings, too numerous and varied to discuss here (cf. Adams 1974, 1978).[2]
It is sufficient to note that the 'games' are what we
call the temporal, dynamic, and performative arts:
singing, dancing, acting, poetic speaking, and playing
musical instruments, while the graphic and plastic
arts are excluded from the domain of 'games.'

The concept of 'game' (papali) or 'playing'
(bapala) is defined, in part, through its linguistic
roots and related terms: bapa, to make parallel or
commensurate; bapisa, to make parallel, conform, compare; papiso, comparison, similitude, metaphor. The
essential meaning of the concept is that of cohesions
and continuities, both those of individual life experiences and the social order, as the opposite of
'playing' is considered to be not work but 'war' (ntoa,
disruption, dispute, conflict, divisiveness, discontinuity). 'Games' are performed in situations marked
by conflict, crisis, and indeterminacy, whether
occurring socially or ecologically, in, for example,
rituals of social transition and political succession,
in coping with crop failure or cattle disease. As
devices of cohesion and continuity 'games' are invoked
to maintain what Csikszentmihalyi (1975) calls experiential 'flow' in reaction to the stasis of boredom or
the confusion of anxiety. But 'playing' is more than
a simple response to critical situations; it is also
performed in anticipation of crisis and in celebration
of cohesion and continuity in social and personal
life; it makes living coherent.

The Basotho 'games' are intentionally composed
and performed with specific ideational and pragmatic
objectives, and while they can be considered forms of
human adaptive reflex, theirs is an informed and consciously controlled reflexivity. Further, as artistic
forms the 'games' are creative and potent transform-
ative forces in their own right, capable of expressing
and actualizing "man's rage for chaos" (Peckham 1965),
the needs for surprise, arousal, and mystery, as well
as bringing order to disorder. The central import of
the Basotho 'games' in performance is to make evident
the qualities peculiar to their nature as expressive
and interpretive instruments in situations in which
those qualities are not apparent or perceivable. And
they can properly be regarded as sensuous vehicles of
understanding and consciousness, ordered perceptual
experiences, experiments.

Basotho 'games' are classified not so much according to their objective properties, their stylistic
features and attributes, but by the channels through
which they are performed and the perceptable qualities
inherent in those modes of production. Within two
acknowledged general ways of 'playing' ('sounding' and
'doing/acting'), four specific modes are recognized:
resounding on musical instruments (letsa), speaking

(bua), singing (bina), and playing (bapala) or acting. With the possible exception of the last category these types of 'games' have in common the exploitation and elaboration of auditory perception and the acoustical channel of communication.[3] Thus the hypothesis governing the Basotho human experiments called 'games' argues aurality, the experience of sounding and hearing, as the proper productive mode of perception on which consciousness, awareness, understanding, and interpretation of life's critical events are based. Our own cultural tradition, by way of contrast, has generated a similar, though contradictory, hypothesis about the perceptual basis of the human discovery process.

There is a long-standing bias of the Western cultural tradition which favors vision as the principal mode of human perception and the expressive and interpretive channel through which the more significant human abilities (e.g., reasoning, understanding, conscious reflection, self-awareness) are exercised. Little empirical evidence supports this bias, evidence of the kind for example that would clearly and specifically illustrate the effects perception through different sensory channels has on human adaptive and communicative capacities, or demonstrate particular relationships between a given mode of perception and its content. Nevertheless it is generally agreed that the sense perceptions in different channels vary considerably in both psychobiological and sociocultural ways. The 'vision bias' has had subtle and ubiquitous effects on our own thought and activity patterns; indeed, visual perception is thought to play a unique and major role in human experience:

> For nearly all animals, vision is an instrument of survival, but for most of them, those who stalk the jungle to those who flee, it is little more than that. For man on the other hand, vision is not only an aid to survival, but also an instrument of thought and a means to the enrichment of life. Even in prehistoric times men dwelling in caves painted pictures that must have been related to a compelling need to create visual images. The modern artist turns to his palette to express what cannot be said adequately in words. Because man is able to see in a certain way, he has been able to invent a written language that carries his message to large audiences and survives after the spoken word has vanished. The

scientist, confronted with concepts too difficult
to communicate verbally, constructs visual models
of mathematical or chemical formulations . . . .
Because of his eye and his brain, man is able to
ask certain questions and devise ways of answering them. He can speculate about his place in
the universe and build telescopes to extend his
vision into space. He can wonder about the
nature of life, and design microscopes that probe
deep into living cells (Mueller and Rudolph
- 1966:9).

The 'vision bias' links man's effort after meaning
with visual perception, making our history of scientific development seem primarily a 'vision quest,'
while Native American vision quests are perhaps mis-
named insofar as they involve auditory hallucination
and other sensational experiences no less essential to
spiritual understanding than visual sensation. The
enduring cultural themes whereby 'light and dark'
represent 'good and evil,' 'truth and falsity,' and
closely drawn analogies between emotional dispositions
and colors (e.g., blue moods, the red of anger, green
envy), reinforce our impression that vision is somehow a more important sensory mode than the others.
Far more cross-cultural research has been undertaken
on the topics of visual illusion and color classification than on the perception of timbre or tactile
qualities (see Lloyd 1972). And development of significant bodies of literature in, for example, the
field of audition in the works of Moles (1968), Tobias
(1970), Ostwald (1973), Ihde (1976), and Sebeok (1978),
is more recent than that in the fields of visual perception and optics. While other sensory abilities
seem neglected, the 'vision bias' pervades our concerns with safety, health and medicine, mysticism,
social classifications, religion, environmental psychology, and the fads of fashion and decoration (see
Birren 1961).

The contemporary American pattern of the 'vision
bias,' what Dundes (1972) calls a "seeing is believing"
syndrome, is reflected in numerous common language
expressions: 'evidence,' from Latin evidere, to see,
is the requisite basis of all true knowledge in
science as well as the courtroom; rather than 'smell
out' answers to our inquiries, we look for them in the
evidence. Legal hearings and artistic auditions are
at best preliminaries to more substantial interactions.
And it is believed that if someone can 'look you in

the eye' you can be assured of their honesty and sin-
cerity. A light bulb over the head of a cartoon
character signifies discovery, comprehension, an idea.
To say, 'you light up my life' has a feeling quite unlike 'you ring my chimes.' We look to people with
imagination and insight, visionaries, for leadership
and enlightenment, and, of course, leaders are expected to be shining examples. In face to face interactions we say, 'it's good to see you,' or 'hope to
see you again' and not 'it's good to smell you' or
'hope to feel you again.' And we say, that 'children
should be seen and not heard,' while things that are
heard but not seen, invisible 'things that go bump
in the night,' are feared.

While it involves a cultural hypothesis of some
strength, the 'vision bias' is not within its exceptions and paradoxes. For example, while 'hearsay' is
not an acceptable basis for judgement in legal procedure, courtroom activities consist of much 'saying'
and 'hearing,' 'talking' and 'listening.' And important social interactions and cultural communications are conducted in channels other than the
visual, especially in the arenas of political, educational, and religious activity where the acoustical
channel is exploited more than the others. Our
various paradigms of human behavior have not escaped
some of the paradoxes of the 'vision bias.' Psycho-
analytic theory, as one case, was strongly influenced
by Freud's personal aversion to musical experiences
and his preference for analyzing the content imagery of
literature and painting; this helped create "the very
curious phenomenon that psychoanalysis which contributed so much to our understanding of the dynamic
processes effective in works of art [and myth and
ritual], has done so little for our understanding of
the artistic activity which plays a greater role in
our lives than any other, namely music" (Sterba 1965:
96). Nor has the study of the musical experience been
particularly translatable to, or supportive of, the
models of human psychodynamics. Whatever the reasons
for Freud's personal bias, it seems to us somehow
justified by the wider cultural context of the 'vision
bias.' But the paradox persists: a field much concerned with the interpretation of emotional dynamics
has largely neglected a major medium of emotional
expression.

A certain challenge to the 'vision bias' is raised
by the Basotho hypothesis linking 'aurality,' the
experience of sounding and hearing, to consciousness
and understanding. Theirs is an 'aural bias,' encom--
passing not only the essentials of 'oral' traditions,
but sounds and hearing in general, and is a notion as
pervasive and deep-seated in Basotho cultural life as
the 'vision bias' is in our own. People make sounds
in singing, playing instruments, and poetic speaking,
not only for others to hear and understand but for the
cultivation of self-awareness and consciousness.
While more broadly conceptualized, the Basotho
'aurality' hypothesis approximates Blacking's observation about music, which "is not so much an immediately understood language which can be expected to
produce specific responses as it is a metaphorical
expression of feeling. It is primarily sensuous and
nonreferential and offers 'a representation of knowable facts, characteristic not of objective experience
itself, but of our consciousness of objective experience' [Donald Ferguson, Music as Metaphor, 1960:88]"
(Blacking 1969:38-39).

The Basotho concept of 'consciousness' (kutlo) is
translatable as sensation, apprehension, apperception,
consciousness, the feeling of being alive, conscien-
tious. Related linguistic forms are ikutloa, to feel
fit, strong, to be aware, to know what one means, to
think; boikutlo, sense, feeling, reaction, obedience;
maikutlo, thought, opinion, comprehension. 'Consciousness' or 'understanding' is directly linked, coordinate, with the specific sensory experience of 'hearing'
(utloa), indeed 'consciousness' and 'hearing' are
respectively in Sesotho the nominal and verbal forms
of the same linguistic root. In a manner quite analogous to our substitution of the activity of visual
perception for the nature or content of that sensory
experience, of 'I see' for 'I understand,' the
Basotho emphasize the equivalence of 'I hear' and 'I
understand.'

'Consciousness' and 'hearing' are psychobiological
phenomena of individual experience, but do not exist
in isolation; they are complementary to objective
and collectively expressible and interpretable phenomena, that is 'sounds.' In the same way that 'consciousness' and 'hearing' are linguistically based
coordinate concepts, 'sounding' (luma, to sound, make
a noise, resound, thunder) is coordinate with the
concept of social 'agreements' and their affective

309

bases: <u>lumela</u>, to have faith, be joyful, to consent; <u>tumellano</u>, accord, alliance, agreement, consensus--almost literally 'mutual soundings.' Highly organized patterns of sounds, in the 'game' forms of song and poetry, are the substantive means for the creation and expression of social 'agreement,' cohesion and continuity, in no small part because they constitute esthetically 'agreeable' experiences. But 'sounds' as 'heard' are also the vehicles of conscious interpretation, 'understanding,' and the assignment of cultural meanings to the particular patterns of cohesion and continuity desired in given circumstances of crisis.[4] The consciousness engendering experiences of Basotho 'playing,' essential components of rational adaptive and adjustive behavior, are well defined by another characterization of music, "the middle way between esthetic perception and the exercise of logical thought" (Levi-Strauss 1969:4).

The 'aurality' hypothesis is a complex of relationships between 'sounding,' agreement,' 'hearing,' and 'consciousness.' The pattern of these relationships constitutes a cultural <u>code</u>, socially motivated and psychologically motivating relationships between a domain of specific sensory vehicles of expression and interpretation and a domain of specific meanings, responses, and interpretations, between what Saussure (1966) called respectively 'signifiers' and 'signifieds' (cf. Bateson 1966, Eco 1976, Leach 1976). Said more simply, the 'aurality' hypothesis concerns culturally appropriate relationships between defined <u>means</u> ('sounding' and 'hearing') and purported <u>ends</u> ('agreement,' 'consciousness' and 'understanding').

It is indicative of both the depth and nature of emotional commitment to the 'aurality' <u>code</u> that its key relationships are linguistically marked. Sapir (1944) referred to such psycho-emotional patterns as 'illusions,' the feelings of relatedness or entailment engendered by the perception of similar sounding word pairs, <u>luma</u>: <u>lumellano</u>, and <u>utloa</u>: <u>kutlo</u> in the Basotho case. Additionally, these feelings, senses of the terms and their relationships, are cathected with the conceptual meanings of the terms and extended to the objects to which the terms refer. For clarification, consider one of the better examples of a linguistically marked and culturally pervasive code in English-speaking industrial societies, one some of the implications of which have recently been explored by Sahlins (1976), that governing the

310

relationship between goods and the good life.   That
these terms are partially homophonic, sounded and
heard alike, leads us to, and reflects, the 'illusion'
that the phenomena the terms refer to are alike, intimately and necessarily linked, bound with one
another, so that through the means of production, distribution, acquisition, and consumption of material
goods,the end, the attainment of a qualitatively good
life, is achieved.   Individuals are motivated by this
equation, they 'expect' certain satisfying consequences of their labor and interactions with material
things, and are frustrated, 'dis-illusioned,' if those
satisfactions fail to come about.   We cultivate the
'illusion' in our children when we say, 'if you are
good you can have a piece of candy (one of the goodies)
after dinner;' and in advertising goods are called
values (of which the good is one).   The 'illusion' is
socially reinforced by such constructs as a 'work
ethic,' and the sanctioning of those who would contradict the equation, threaten its continuance, by arguing that a 'bad life' is the principle consequence of
excessive materialism, or that a good life is to be
had only through means other than those concerned with
material goods.   It is by examining cultural codes of
conduct of this order that we can appreciate the dynamic articulations between symbolically expressed
ideational norms and values and empirically normal
behavior patterns and activities.   The Basotho
'aurality' complex, as a code of conduct in crisis,
has just this kind of dual normative pattern.   But in
its case, 'sounds as heard' are the 'goods' produced
and consumed in the attainment of a better life than
that offered up by the anxieties or boredoms of
critical situations.

    'Aurality and consciousness,' like 'seeing is be-
lieving' and 'goods and the good life,' is a cultural
hypothesis, a testable, confirmable or contradictable
proposition about human nature and a particular domain
of human experience.   It differs from the 'vision
bias' insofar as each different medium of expression
and interpretation "enjoys certain properties which
are subject to variability and which are, therefore,
the ultimate building blocks of the affecting work"
(Armstrong 1971:9) performed in that medium.   The
experienced qualities peculiar to 'aurality,' sounding
and hearing, differ from those of other sensory modes
and, the Basotho hypothesis assumes, are uniquely
suited to producing the kinds of affective responses

and interpretations which are the objectives of
Basotho 'games' and 'playing.' That is, it is through
'played aurality,' and not some other means, that
the feelings of psychosocial cohesion and continuity
are engendered, made perceptable and acceptable, enhance consciousness and understanding, and are discovered in critical situations where they were not
evident.

Implied by the foregoing is a puzzle, the relationship of sense and meaning, which has perplexed scholarship ranging across humanistically oriented and
scientifically focused concerns with art, the esthetic
experience, and human communication. Here, no attempt
is made at any substantive summary of the issues, nor
is any unique insight claimed, but they must be outlined in order to further consider the implications
the 'aurality' hypothesis has for the Basotho
'playing' strategy of producing significance, for
making life sensible and meaningful in critical situations. Basotho 'game' performances are as multidimensional, in sensory terms, as any human experience.
But the hypothesis argues that qualities peculiar to
'aurality' uniquely arouse 'conscious awareness' and
precipitate 'agreements,' that there is a necessary,
determinate relationship between 'aurality' and 'conscious agreement,' believing, accepting, understanding. In other words, the sensory experiences of other
channels are somehow inadequate means to achieve the
objectives of Basotho 'playing' because the 'messages'
of other media are different.

The assumption of uniqueness in expressive and im-
pressive channels enjoys support from different areas
of inquiry into human nature. Philosophical and
phenomenological perspectives on art and the esthetic
experience have long asserted the qualitative uniqueness and rich sensory particularity inherent in
different art objects. The arguments emphasize that
painting, poetry, music, sculpture, and so on, have
intrinsically different characteristics, which, as
perceived and experienced, create different and
unique patterns of feeling and interpretation, cultivate the 'esthetic sense' in different ways. Thus
artistic activity as a whole is multidimensional; it
contains many 'messages' and requires many different
'languages' for their expression and interpretation.
Psychobiological investigations additionally provide
some support for the notion of qualitative perceptual
uniqueness, based on substantive biological

differences between sensory channels. Visual and
auditory sensations differ since they are related to
different forms of energy, different neuro-physiolog-
ical perceptor mechanisms, and involve different
biochemical processes in the central nervous system.
While similar and cross-correlated, the various
sensory modes operate differently as neurophysiological
information extraction systems (Uttal 1973). But, how
then do the special arts express and impress upon us
universal and general understanding; why is music said
to be a 'universal language?'

An alternative viewpoint, evident in much recent
anthropological inquiry (similarly supported by
philosophical and biological arguments), particularly
the fields of symbolic, cognitive, psychological,
and structuralist persuasion, has emphasized the
trans-channel nature of cultural meanings--patterns or
forms, conscious and unconscious, which consist of
the highly distilled organization of multiple sensory
impressions into mental sets, cognitive categories,
codifications and interpretations of the world as
sensed--what in a wider context, has been referred
to as "the reason imposed from within on the relations
to an external order" (Sahlins 1976: 206). Consider,
for example, Leach's description of a ritual event,
one kind of the special experiential events in which
the Basotho 'aurality' code of conduct operates, where
he extends Levi-Strauss' (1969, 1973) 'orchestral
performance' metaphor of special human experience:

> But what actually happens is that the participants
> in a ritual are sharing communicative experiences
> through many different sensory channels simulta-
> neously; they are acting out an ordered sequence
> of metaphoric events within a territorial space
> which has itself been ordered to provide a meta-
> phoric context for the play acting. Verbal,
> musical, choreographic, and visual-aesthetic
> 'dimensions' are all likely to form components of
> the total message. When we take part in such a
> ritual we pick up all these messages at the same
> time and condense them into a single experience...
> But now I want to stress the added complication
> that, although the receiver of a ritual message
> is picking up information through a variety of
> different sensory channels simultaneously, all
> these different sensations add up to just one
> 'message' (Leach 1976:41).

313

This description additionally supports the 'aurality' hypothesis, but more in reference to the intentionally organized, composed, aspect of 'game' performances, the patterns and forms 'evidenced' in the various works of art, e.g., instrumental songs, praise poetry, telling riddles, and so on. Recall that the Basotho idea of 'playing' is quite literally 'making things parallel, commensurate, homologous,' and is linguistically related to the concept of 'metaphor.' Acoustical patterns in poetry, songs, jokes, riddles, and dances (e.g., hissing, stamping, clapping, ululating) are 'made parallel' with patterns perceivable through other channels, with social, ecological, economic, political patterns as they are presented to and in human actions.[5]

Metaphoric extension expands 'consciousness' by expanding the range of varied things that can be interpreted in a single, 'one message' meaning frame-- things that thus come into 'agreement.' There is only 'one message,' a trans-channel meaning or structure that is discernable in all channels of multisensory experience; one channel or idiom will do as well as any other as a basis of metaphor, and any channel can be arbitrarily and indeterminately selected--a tactile metaphor of 'smooth and rough' social interactions 'means' the same as an 'acoustical' metaphor of 'consonant and dissonant' social interactions. But is the meaning 'picked up' in such multi-sensory events, the same as that which ordered the performance of the events in the first place? If so, then what is the significance of engaging in multi-sensory experience? The basic question which confronts us in the 'aurality' hypothesis is how to account for the preference or value the Basotho place on the unique qualitative experiences of 'sounding' and 'hearing' (or our own preferences for visual sensations)--what determinate, necessary aspects of 'played aurality' motivate people to 'consciousness' and 'agreement,' to discover a 'quality of meaning,' a 'valued meaning' in coping with critical situations? In other words, what is the 'consciousness' of and the 'awareness' about. The question is not what happens in special experiential events, but how certain things happen.

The issue at present is not so much the advantages of single- as opposed to multi-channel communication or sensory experience, or their relation to 'conscious awareness,' value formation and affect, but the nature of the sense/meaning duality inherent in the 'aurality

code of conduct.' This duality is a widely recognized
characteristic of the audio-acoustic channel (though
by no means unique to it), the artistic works composed
in the medium, and the meaningful and feelingful concomitants of those work as experienced--the channel's
capacity for the simultaneous transmission and organization of semantic (meaningful) information (messages
and interpretations which are generally translatable
to other channels and media) and esthetic (sensual)
information (messages and feelings which are specifically not translatable) (Moles 1968:128-30). 'Aurality' is thus only a partially substitutable frame for
expressions and impressions in other channels, media
and idioms, only in its organizational aspect, as
musical and poetic works. But in its sensed, experienced aspect, 'aurality' imparts specific psycho-
biologically determined qualities which are valued as
those most necessary to meet and motivate human per-
severance through crisis. The 'aurality' hypothesis
asserts a partially necessary relationship between
what is required to meet crisis, 'consciousness' and
'agreement,' and how those are generated, motivated,
and created. More generally, the hypothesis points
to an articulation of the biological and cultural aspect of human behavior, artistically mediated and
coordinated (see Peckham 1965, Alland 1977).

There are numerous kinds, levels, special qualities of organized sounds and the hearing experience
which are valued by the Basotho in various circumstances of crisis. These situations are extremely
varied, ranging from the use of musical instruments in
herding cattle, singing lullabies, dancing in large
inter-village competitions, ridiculing and joking with
neighbors, playing soccer and singing hymns in church.
And the associated esthetic qualities and stylistic
canons of audio-acoustic performances vary accordingly,
as their variants are considered proper and potentially productive in each situation. But since the
'aurality code of conduct' is common to all these
special experiences, it is possible to mention some
general qualities of the 'sounding/hearing' complex
which especially stand out as interrelated foci of
the Basotho 'played aurality' strategies. Abstractly
these are energy (the relationships between motives,
meanings and the emotive forces of esthetic experience), time, (the feelings of growing, changing,
persevering, continuing, flowing, and cohesion (the
feelings of trust, belonging, not being isolated or

alienated, and coordinating the individual experience
with itself in relation to the collective experiences).

Taking his cues from the work of Kagame (1956)
Jahn has made the following observation about African
attitudes toward perception:

> 'Hearing' in the wider sense is a concept that
> includes hearing, smell and taste, so that per-
> ception is thought of in two main groups: vision
> and contact; . . . All forms of perception are
> passive and excite in the animal his memory or his
> 'innate instinct,' his drive, his greed, his
> lust. In man, however, they assist in knowledge.
> The animal hears and reacts, but man hears and
> understands (Jahn 1961:122).

Biologically, of course, human beings react to sounds,
they hear them, and are stimulated, aroused, driven,
and moved by the experience. And in the Basotho case
of 'aurality' (if not generally) some exception to the
notion of 'passive' perception must be made. The
Basotho make a distinction between simple affective
response (araba) and self-reflexive response (boikara-
bello), interpreted reaction, the exercise of responsibility. Neither are considered passive phenomena,
but differ as to whether one is acting or acted upon,
the mover or the moved, in the role of actor or re-
actor, playing or being played.

Insofar as 'sounding' and 'hearing' are dynamic
and energizing phenomena, they are closely related to
individual and collective senses of time and process.
Turner has recently observed that "anthropology is
shifting from a stress on concepts such as structure,
equilibrium, function, system, to process, inde-
terminancy, reflexivity--from a 'being' to a 'becoming' vocabulary" (Turner 1977:61). This shift is not
only helping reformulate an evolutionary perspective
in anthropology but through that interest revitalizing
its holistic scope, integrating, among other things,
biological and cultural concerns as well as humanistic
and scientific ones.

This change of focus in anthropological concern
is additionally having some effect on, or has been
influenced, by, a developing awareness of the importance of sensory channels other than the visual.
Hopefully this may help counterbalance the inordinate
emphasis placed on visual perception, which, while

316

widely recognized as a critical mode of structural and
spatial orientation, is unlike 'aurality' in that
"audition is the temporal sense par excellence" (Sebeok
and Ramsay 1969:127). And further "one's concepts of
time, duration, or speed . . . appear to be intimately
connected with auditory patterns. The main point
here is, of course, not so much this apparent separa-
tion of visual and auditory function with respect to
space and time, but rather that even such basic
notions as space and time in the observing individual
are built out of different kinds of perceptual experience" (Julesz and Hirsh 1972:294). And already
mentioned is the objective of 'played aurality' to
create the sense of continuity, personal and collective, of personal and social becoming, of movement and
growth.

Another pattern of the 'aurality' complex combines
'hearing' and 'consciousness' on the one hand, as a
phenomena of individual experience, with 'soundings'
and 'agreements' as 'representations, signs, evidence'
of those experiences in collectivity. Thus the code
articulates the change and developmental processes
of individuals in community. The Basotho define time
(nako) as the nexus of individual and collective experience, and of the perceived durable patterns of
social life and individual awareness of change and
variability (or between perceived social change
measured against individual sense of constancy): nako
ke litumellano lipakeng tsa batho, "time is the agreements between people."

The question of how human beings discover and
produce meaning and sense, how they engage in the
production of significance, is most important to our
understanding of the dynamic and developmental methods
through which people inform, conform, and reform themselves in their circumstances of living, of how a meaningful quality of living is or is not achieved.

Culture has to be seen as processual, because it
emerges in interaction and imposes meaning on the
biotic and ecological systems (also dynamic) with
which it interacts. I should not say 'it' for
this is to reify what is, regarded processually,
an endless series of negotiations among actors
about the assignment of meaning to the acts in
which they jointly participate. Meaning is
assigned verbally through speech and nonverbally
through ritual and ceremonial action and is often

317

stored in symbols which become indexical counters
in subsequent social contexts. But the assignment and reassignment of meaning must be investigated as process in the domain of resilience
possessed by each population recognizing itself
to be culturally perduring. For human populations are periodically subjected to shocks and
crises, in addition to the strains and tensions
of adjustment to quotidian challenges from the
biotic and social environments. These involve
problems of maintenance of determinate institutional structures as well as of creative adaptation to sudden or persisting environmental
changes, making for indeterminacy. (Turner 1977:
63).

The Basotho 'aurality' code of conduct in crisis
is a specific case of the emergent cultural process
of assigning meaning and sense, a generative model
for the production of significance, an attempt in defined situations to mediate the interpretation of
living and the sensed qualities of living. In other
jargon the process is called semiosis, "the process
by which empirical subjects communicate, communication
being made possible by the organization of signifi-
cation systems" (Eco 1976:316). Signs both represent
the world to our senses and the sense of ourselves to
the world, and the dynamics of the process inherent in
the dual nature of signs, as sensed and as interpreted,
that which links meaning and value (Morris 1964).

The tenet of Basotho culture exhibited in their
domain of activities called 'games,' and stated here
as an 'hypothesis' is that 'aurality,' sounding and
hearing, is a necessary condition of becoming conscious and the principle mode for the production of
significant interpretation of the circumstances of
living. As I understand it, the principle operates
as a code of conduct in crisis. As a code it is a
complex of motivated and motivating relations between
feelings and their interpretations which define the
proper Basotho conduct, 'playing' or performing, when
confronted with crisis. When faced with the discontinuity, conflict, anxieties, or boredoms of critical
situations, they create for themselves valued feel-
ings--feelings of energy, ability, being alive, having
faith, responding, flow, and coherence--experiences
somehow related to psychobiological response, and the
'code' links these feelings directly to the audio-
acoustic channel. The objective of 'playing' is to

318

engender these feelings and to create a consciousness
of them and agreement with them, to arouse some psychobiological potential and to shape that potential in
culturally meaningful ways, to create composure when
confronted with crisis. "Thus the forces in nature
and culture would be expressed in humanly organized
sound, because the chief function of music in society
is to promote soundly organized humanity be enhancing
human consciousness" (Blacking 1973:101).

This attempted exegesis of some of the implications of the Basotho 'aurality' hypothesis has been
undertaken without the advantages of dense description
and ethnographic analysis of the performance patterns
and situational contexts to which it is related.
While it is a premise or tenet informed by and operating in Basotho cultural life, an aspect of their
'experiments,' controlled experiences with living, it
is also a Basotho hypothesis about human nature and
its functioning. As a cultural hypothesis it challenges us not only to understand how it relates to the
articulation of sense and meaning in Basotho life, but
as well to consider the consequences some of our own
deep "biases" ("seeing is believing" and "goods and
the good life") have on the quality of our own experiences. It postulates definite relationships between
psychobiological dynamics and sociocultural processes,
between artistic activity and the contexts and conditions of its occurrence. Finally, as an anthropological hypothesis it directly challenges anthropological theory, methodology and understanding to explain,
evaluate, experiment with, and appreciate the human
phenomena to which it is addressed. In regard to such
a challenge the contemporary anthropological enterprise is somehwat wanting, not perhaps in the potentials of its diffuse collectivity, but through its
failure to create metalanguages appropriate to the
discussion of the dynamic cohesions of the cultural
and the biological, the scientific and the humanistic.
Ours is a melange of particularistic perceptions denying the historical mandate of a broadly evolutionary
and holistic discipline.

319

[1]Field research, upon which this paper is based, on Basotho __games__ and __playing__ was conducted in the Pitseng area of Leribe District, Lesotho (southern Africa), 1969-1970, and was supported by a Field Research Training Grant and Research Fellowship from NIMH whose assistance is gratefully acknowledged.

[2]Translating Sesotho __papali__ as 'qame' or 'playing,' while conventional, is potentially quite misleading. The concept is defined by an array of features different than those of our own cultural and scientific models of games and play behavior (Adams 1978). Essentially, 'playing' in Sesotho refers to a particular way of doing things and the products of that activity, 'games,' considered to be common to ritualistic, ludic, artistic, and scientific contexts.

[3]The last category, 'playing' or 'acting,' refers to kinetic and gestural performances, such as playing soccer, poker, or dancing without music, but is not so exceptional that it contradicts this paper's assumptions about 'aurality.' Sound is based on kinetic energy, in both its production and perception, and the auditory mechanism is an instrument of body orientation, coordination, balance, and motion perception in dancing and acting, as well as of hearing in music and speech.

[4]Far too few investigations have been made into the nature of the dynamic perceptual coordination of sounding and hearing. For example, Count (1973) has explored the phylogenesis of the relation between speech function (phasia) and symbolizing capacity (mentation) as a condition of the humanization process, but by neglecting to also discuss auditory function gives the impression that 'everyone has been talking with no one listening.'

[5]There is a large and well-documented corpus of traditional literature in Sesotho (see Guma 1967, Kunene 1971, Gérard 1971, Damane and Sanders 1974),

rather extensively analyzed for poetic structure and cultural meaning in its transcribed and written form (another relfection of the 'vision bias'). But in consideration of the 'aurality' hypothesis, it would be ethnographically more appropriate, and no doubt very revealing, to attempt an analysis of the 'musical'dynamics of this literature as it is 'played,' 'sounded,' and 'heard' in its various performance contexts.

REFERENCES CITED

Adams, Charles R.
    1974   Ethnography of Basotho Evaluative Expression
            in the Cognitive Domain Lipapali (Games).
            Unpublished Ph.D. Dissertation, Indiana
            University.

    1978   Distinctive Features of Play and Games: A
            Folk Model from Southern Africa. Paper
            presented at the session 'The Player's
            Perspective: Language Centered Research,
            annual meeting of The Association for the
            Anthropological Study of Play, South Bend,
            Indiana, 23-25 March 1978.

Alland, Alexander, Jr.
    1977   The Artistic Animal: An Inquiry Into the
            Biological Roots of Art. Garden City, New
            York: Anchor Press/Doubleday.

Armstrong, Robert Plant
    1971   The Affecting Presence: An Essay in Human-
            istic Anthropology. Urbana: University of
            Illinois Press.

Bateson, Gregory
    1966   Information, Codification, and Metacommuni-
            cation. In Communication and Culture:
            Readings in the Codes of Human Interaction.
            Alfred G. Smith, ed. Pp. 412-426. New
            York: Holt, Rinehart and Winston.

Birren, Faber
    1961   Color Psychology and Color Therapy. Hyde
            Park, New York: University Books.

Blacking, John
    1969   The Value of Music in Human Experience. In
            Yearbook of the International Folk Music
            Council. Alexander L. Ringer, ed. Pp. 33-71.

Blacking, John
   1973   How Musical is Man?   Seattle and London:
          University of Washington Press.

Count, Earl W.
   1973   An Essay on Phasia.   In Being and Becoming
          Human: Essays on the Biogram.   Pp. 213-297.
          New York: D. Van Nostrand.

Csikszentmihalyi, Mihaly
   1975   Beyond Boredom and Anxiety: The Experience
          of Play in Work and Games.   San Francisco:
          Josey-Bass.

Damane, M., and P. B. Sanders
   1974   Lithoko: Sotho Praise Poems.   Oxford: Oxford
          University Press.

Dundes, Alan
   1972   Seeing is Believing.   Natural History 81:10-
          12, 86.

Eco, Umberto
   1976   A Theory of Semiotics.   Bloomington and
          London: Indiana University Press.

Gérard, Albert S.
   1971   Four African Literatures: Xhosa, Sotho,
          Zulu, Amharic.   Berkeley: University of
          California Press.

Guma, S. M.
   1967   The Form, Content and Technique of Tradi-
          ditional Literature in Southern Sotho.
          Pretoria: J. L. van Schaik.

Ihde, Don
   1976   Listening and Voice: A Phenomenology of
          Sound.   Athens, Ohio: Ohio University
          Press.

Jahn, Janheinz
   1961   Muntu: Outline of the New African Culture.
          New York: Grove Press.

Julesz, Bela, and Ira J. Hirsh
    1972   Visual and Auditory Perception--An Essay of
            Comparison. In Human Communication: A
            Unified View. Edward E. David and Peter B.
            Denes, eds., Pp. 283-340. New York:
            McGraw-Hill.

Kagame, Alexis
    1956   La Philosophie Bàntu-Rwandaise de l'Ětre.
            Brussels.

Kunene, Daniel P.
    1971   Heroic Poetry of the Basotho. Oxford:
            Oxford University Press.

Leach, Edmund
    1976   Culture and Communication: The Logic By Which
            Symbols are Connected. Cambridge: Cambridge
            University Press.

Lévi-Strauss, Claude
    1969   The Raw and the Cooked: Introduction to a
            Science of Mythology I. New York: Harper
            and Row.

    1973   From Honey to Ashes: Introduction to a
            Science of Mythology II. New York: Harper
            and Row.

Lloyd, Barbara B.
    1972   Perception and Cognition: A Cross-Cultural
            Perspective. Harmondsworth, England:
            Penguin.

Moles, Abraham
    1968   Information Theory and Esthetic Perception.
            Urbana: University of Illinois Press.

Morris, Charles
    1964   Signification and Significance: A Study of
            the Relations of Signs and Values.
            Cambridge: M.I.T. Press.

Mueller, Conrad G., and Mae Rudolph, et al.
    1966   Light and Vision. New York: Time Incor-
            porated.

324

Ostwald, Peter F.
1973   The Semiotics of Human Sound. Atlantic
        Highlands, New Jersey. Humanities Press.

Peckham, Morse
1965   Man's Rage for Chaos. Biology, Behavior,
        and the Arts. New York: Schocken.

Peirce, Charles Sanders
1940   Logic as Semiotic: The Theory of Signs.
        In The Philosophy of Peirce: Selected Writ-
        ings. Justus Buchler, ed. Pp. 98-119.
        London: Routledge and Kegan Paul.

Sahlins, Marshall
1976   Culture and Practical Reason. Chicago and
        London: University of Chicago Press.

Sapir, Edward
1944   Grading: A Study in Semantics. Philosophy
        of Science 11:93-116.

Saussure, Ferdinand de
1966   Course in General Linguistics. New York:
        McGraw-Hill.

Sebeok, Thomas A.
1978   Sight, Sound, and Sense. Bloomington,
        Indiana: Indiana University Press.

Sebeok, Thomas A., and Alexandra Ramsay, eds.
1969   Approaches to Animal Communication. The
        Hague: Mouton.

Sterba, Richard
1965   Psychoanalysis and Music. American Imago
        22:96-111.

Tobias, Jerry V., ed.
1970   Foundations of Modern Auditory Theory. New
        York and London: Academic Press.

Turner, Victor
1977   Process, System, and Symbol: A new Anthro-
        pological Synthesis. Daedalus 106:61-80.

Uttal, William R.
1973   The Psychobiology of Sensory Coding. New
        York, Harper and Row.

TOUGH LUCK ETHNOGRAPHY VERSUS GOD'S TRUTH ETHNOGRAPHY IN
ETHNOSCIENCE: SOME THOUGHTS ON THE NATURE OF CULTURE*

by

Oswald Werner
Northwestern University

and

Allen Manning
Rock Point Community School

Sometimes one does not know what the problems were till
after they have been solved.**
-Bateson-

0.   Introduction
0.1 Definitions
0.2 Culture
1.   GTE in Werner & Begishe (1970)
2.   TLE in Werner et al. (1973)***
3.   Typology of Variation
3.1 Variation in Labeling
3.2 Variation in Attachment
4.   Epilogue
5.   References Cited

*This work was supported by a grant from NIMH, NH-10940
which is gratefully acknowledged. Although he did not
directly collaborate on this particular project the contribution of Kenneth Y. Begishe looms large. We are
equally indebted to many Navajos who have acted as our
consultants and whose knowledge and disagreements we
describe in the sections of illustrations.

The first paper I wrote as a graduate student for Professor Bidney was on The Nature of Culture and Language.
This paper is appropriately a continuation of that effort.

The Navajo orthographic convention is as follows: lh

0. Introduction.

This paper follows a simple outline. We start with theory and exemplify it in later sections by Navajo taxonomies of animals and plants.

First, we give a definition of God's Truth Ethnography (GTE). The presentation of the definition of Tough Luck Ethnography (TLE) is next. After the definitions we present some brief thoughts about the nature of culture to which we are led by our focus on TLE and especially individual variations of cultural knowledge as reflected in the Navajo taxonomies of animals and plants. This section is summarized by a list of nine axioms.

We then illustrate the nature of variation in Navajo cultural knowledge. First, by the taxonomic tree structures of Werner and Begishe (1970), The Taxonomic Aspect of the Navajo Universe. We present only the parts dealing with the knowledge of animals and plants. Our approach in this paper was GTE. It contains no discussion of variation.

Second, we illustrate the TLE approach by the animal and plant taxonomies of Werner et al. (1973), A Taxonomic Aspect of the Traditional Navajo Universe. We show that the GTE of Werner and Begishe (1970) is one possible variant in the TLE of Werner et al. (1973).

Third, we present a typology of variation encountered in the study of the above taxonomic samples. The list of actually occurring types of variations appears to be theoretically (formally) exhaustive, though we have not investigated that aspect explicitly.

We close with an epilogue about indications for further work in the theory of culture and the ethnography of variation.

---

for the barred l, 7 for high tone, and 8 (preceding the vowel) for nasalization. All other symbols are according to the Navajo standard orthography.

**I am grateful to Kevin Keating for this quote.

***Werner et al. is a cover term for that particular paper, the 150 plus pages of the monograph underlying the aforementioned paper and new data collected since the summer of 1972.

0.1 Definitions.

A definition of the principles of God's Truth Ethnography (GTE) and Tough Luck Ethnography (TLE) can be stated as follows:

Definition of GTE: An ethnography (or a partial ethnography) is God's Truth Ethnography if at some time after the initial fieldwork the ethnographer (and/or his/her staff) decides that it is time to write up the project and he/she (they) proceed to do so. The write-up can be further characterized as an attempt of the author'(s) to reach closure and to present a coherent picture of the people called XYZ.

This way of writing ethnographies can be likened to the learning of a culture by immigrants. At some point the immigrant feels that the new place is 'home.' He has integrated his view and he assumes he has a basically correct picture of what is going on. At this stage he claims that he knows the host culture.

We illustrate the above principle in "The Taxonomic Aspect of the Navajo Universe" (Werner and Begishe, 1970). In 1970, faced with a deadline (closure), Kenneth Y. Begishe and Werner decided that it was time to write down our observations made intermittently over the last six years. The result was a master taxonomy showing the classification of all things Navajo that were created or niilya7ii. It was the result of an anthropologist and his chief native consultant agreeing on what the taxonomic aspect of the Navajo universe was. The master taxonomy was presented to the public as God's Truth about the Navajo.

Subsequently we resumed work on the taxonomies representing the Navajo Universe for the new handbook of North American Indians. Meanwhile (independent of this project) we have become sensitive to the problem of individual variation as a key problem in ethnoscience and therefore ethnography. However, we did not see the principle of Tough Luck Ethnography clearly until we started writing the monograph (Werner and Manning, in preparation) underlying the handbook article.

Definition of TLE: An ethnography (or a partial ethnography) is Tough Luck Ethnography, if the ethnographer (and/or his/her staff) decide(s) before the commencement of the fieldwork that a cultural domain is thoroughly explored if and only if the data is rich enough so that it contains controversies, or disagreements among

329

consultants* in relation to a particular cultural domain.

Put another way: The greater the thoroughness of the discussion of controversies in some cultural domains the better the ethnography of that particular cultural domain. Or, the better one knows the controversies in a particular domain the more thoroughly one knows the cultural domain in question from the natives' point of view.

In our case, unique classifications are generally the result of work with a few or in most cases just one consultant. This also implies that our work as it has been presented is "A Taxonomic Aspect of the Traditional Navajo Universe" (Werner et al., 1973) rather than "THE Taxonomic Aspect of the Navajo Universe" (as we called Werner and Begishe, 1970).

A corollary of this approach is that our current work is the latest stage in our approximations of the taxonomic aspects of the Navajo Universe and that there is no last stage as long as Navajo culture exists and continues as a distinct identifiable entity.

0.2 Culture.

In 1935 Shapera made the statement ". . ., Culture is made up of individual variation from a traditionally standardized pattern." We hope the examples we present (Sections 1, 2 and 3) amply illustrate individual variation of Navajo taxonomic knowledge of animals and plants. If this variation is from a standardized pattern, that is much harder to demonstrate. To us, 'standardized pattern' and the notion of 'sharing' coincide. It therefore may be worthwhile to look at taxonomic variations and see what it is that may be shared.

Navajo taxonomies given in Sections 2 and 3 share, to a large extent, the inventory of their labels. This includes, in addition to the simple fact that all consultants speak Navajo, the following:

(1) The unique 'beginner' niilya7ii Things that were put there (created), which is apparently universally (at least passively) shared.

(2) All intermediate level terms, or named genera, especially if they are mono-lexemic, are shared.

---

*We prefer 'consultant' to 'informant' because it describes better our relationship with native speakers.

Binomials and more complex polynomials (none above quadru-
nomials) are shared less well though we must admit that
our elicitation procedure was not designed to specifically
test for sharing and/or non-sharing. In general, all consultants (informants) agreed on all the nodes we presented
to them. Even if they considered some labels strange or
attached to the taxonomies in strange places, they agreed
that such labels or their placement was peculiar (Who told
you that?!!) but at least possible.

(3) There was little disagreement about terminal
labels, though some people could recall more of them than
others.

The major difference we discern is the taxonomic
structure of experts versus that of laymen. This has two
aspects (see also Perchonock and Werner, 1969):

(1) The expert has an increased number of intermediate nodes.

(2) He also tends to further sub-classify the laymen's terminal nodes.

Interestingly the most profound disagreements
between consultants concern the placement and labeling of
intermediate nodes. The least shared aspect of taxonomies
is the place of attachment of particular labels within the
tree structures.

Thus, while it may be possible to postulate a
shared set of labels for any two versions of a taxonomy,
it appears much less likely that exact taxonomic structures are shared. To make matters worse, the appearance
of every new consultant (informant) makes both the set of
shared labels and especially the set of shared tree structures subject to possible drastic revision and re-
evaluation.

We are thus ready to formulate the first axiom of
cultural knowledge:

AXIOM 1: Cultural knowledge varies from individual
to individual both in quantity -- number
of labels -- and structure -- the connections of labeled nodes.

At present we cannot pinpoint why this is so, though
the findings of Bernard and Killworth (1973) are suggestive
(see Axiom 5 and ff). Some variation is necessary within
every social boundary. Other variation is the result of

331

eliciting <u>across</u> some social boundary. We will therefore briefly look at social/cultural boundaries next.

We agree with Colby (1973) that 'culture' should be viewed as an unbound variable. As such, it obtains its meaning from being bound to some unit such as 'Neolithic culture,' 'Navajo culture,' or 'Sailboat racing culture' (following Colby, 1973: 366).

This is not unlike other sciences. For example, the study of biology concerns itself with the study of living things. The concept 'life' is at least as diffi-cult to define as our concept of 'culture.' A definition of life is the ultimate goal of biology. The ultimate goal of anthropology is, in turn, the definition of cul-ture in some non-trivial non-simple sense. That is, such a definition comprises the entire content of a science and is therefore by necessity never closed. The domain of the major phenomena studied by a science is characteristically unbound. However, actual applications of study are always bound. Examples of binding are 'micro-biology,' 'the physics of fluids,' or 'Navajo culture.'

Viewing culture as a variable to be bound to some domain has multiple advantages. The binding can be made on the basis of social boundaries perceived by the native (e.g., Frank Gidding's 'consciousness of kind' [1922]). This is the solution generally preferred by anthropologists working in ethnoscience (e.g., Moerman, 1964). It can also be <u>quasi</u> arbitrary as the 'cultunits' or Naroll (e.g., 1970). This is the preferred solution for statistical cross cultural comparison. Finally, it is possible to combine both approaches -- as has been done by the major-ity of anthropologists in the past.

AXIOM 2:   The concept 'culture' is an unbound variable which must be bound for any and all applications.

COROLLARY: An ethnography or a partial ethnography is an application.

We agree with Bohannan that "every social group. . . has its own body of culture" (1973: 360). We add, how-ever, that the social group an investigator chooses for his purview depends on what he intends to do. Put another way, all bindings of culture are metonymic in character, be they derived from a native label or from an analytic category.

Our own choice of 'traditional Navajo' as our

binding label (in Werner et al., 1973) is a mixed, even arbitrary label. In a Navajo classification (see 2-v) we find dine7 People, t'a7a7 dine7 The real people, and Naabeeho7 The Navajo. However, even the label 'Navajo' though derived from a native term is questionable and ultimately metonymic, we restrict it to Navajos who speak Navajo although there are Navajos today who do not. Neither do we take into account an admittedly small number of bilingual Hopis, Paiutes, Utes and Anglos who also speak Navajo. To illustrate the arbitrariness further, nationalistic Hungarians count everyone who speaks Magyar as a Hungarian. In other words, even native labels are open to interpretation of its boundaries. It, like any other label, may single out a few or very often just one attribute and draw a line around it. But the boundaries of all concepts leak.

AXIOM 3: Any binding of culture -- by native label or by analytical category or by a mixture of both -- has fuzzy boundaries.*

Bound units of culture vary in size. On the highest level are what we have called, in the past, cultural universals pertaining to all humans. The largest bound unit of culture that we can think of is, therefore, 'terrestrial human culture,' though Wallace's (1961: 134) criteria can easily be extended to non-terrestrial, intelligent forms of life.

AXIOM 4: (At present) the largest bound unit of culture is 'terrestrial human culture.'

Following Bohannan (1973), the smallest bound unit of culture is the diad. But there is no need to stop there. Vygotsky (1962) states, we think correctly, that thought is social. Only autistic thought is 'truly' individualistic. One could argue that Vygotsky's (1962) 'inner speech' is an 'inner dialogue' or that social speech ought to be defined by its structure rather than by the number of perceivable participants (Litowitz, 1973: 4). Facts such as the necessity for a compartmentalized memory (e.g., Werner, 1974) in order to account for various types of cognitive behavior, the nature of conversion experience (Werner, 1973) and the relatively precarious integration of personality (e.g., its decomposition in schizophrenia) reinforce the notion that we may have to

---

*Fuzzy boundaries is intended as a graphic but nevertheless a technical term analogous to technical terms like fuzzy sets or systems of fuzzy logic.

look for our smallest units of culture below the skin of individuals.

AXIOM 5: The smallest bound unit of culture is an individual's -- possibly even part of an individual's -- cultural knowledge.

The last axiom eliminates the boundary between personality and a level of some bound cultural unit; a boundary that has been suspect at least since Sapir (1932) (see also the unique classification of plants by their use: 2-xix to 2-xxi).

Variation within a bound unit of culture can be explained in part but not exhaustively by social subgroupings. Each sub-grouping in turn may serve as a new binding of culture.

Theoretical computations of Killworth and Bernard (1973) emphasize the cultural atomization of human beings due to formal constraints on group structure. "An average individual is involved in three to four pseudo-closed networks, each of which contains seven to eight intermediaries" (Killworth and Bernard, 1974: 27). "Any group of more than 140 elements must form its own sub-groups, and in doing so produces its own formalized hierarchy to deal with this" (Bernard and Killworth, 1973: 50). Any consultant knows the people he knows, but knows only 70% of the people who are the friends and acquaintances of his friends. This knowledge fades very rapidly as one moves further away from the original consultant (Bernard and Killworth, 1973: 33). All this implies that each human being participates in very few primary groups that develop primary cultures. Bindings of culture to larger social units are the result of increasingly more tenuous social linkages as one moves out from individuals in intimate contact, to larger, less densly interacting groupings.

Other types of variation are normal and to be expected within social groups. However, at present we do not know which clusterings of 'contradictory understandings' (Ross, 1968: 12) mark a social boundary and which do not. In our Navajo example, social boundaries are suggested by 'ceremonial labels' versus 'secular labels,' by labels of 'younger Navajos' versus those of 'older Navajos,' and perhaps a few others. But none of these potential binding labels suffice to account for all of the variation.

AXIOM 6: Bound cultural units exhibit external variation of cultural knowledge in relation to other bound cultural units.

AXIOM 7: Bound cultural units also exhibit internal variation, no matter how small the
unit.

The nature of internal variation is problematic.
For the lack of a better term we will call such variation
contextual variation. A full range of contextual solutions requires answers to all possible question words.
That is, who? -- questions regarding social groupings,
role, status and division of labor; when? -- questions
about time; where? -- questions about space; what? --
questions about content; and why? -- questions about
motivations, values embedded in memories of past analogous
events. In other words, memories are part of the present
context which is provided by past experiences.

AXIOM 8: Cultural knowledge within any bound unit
of culture will vary with the participants (their role, status and division of
labor) -- who? -- time -- when? --
space -- where? -- content -- what? --
and assumed values and motivations --
why? -- as well as memories of similar
past events.

Bound units of culture 'stand still' only for the
unsuspecting anthropologist. For the participants it is a
constant 'becoming' rather than a 'being.' No elicited
corpus of cultural knowledge of some bound unit of culture
can exhaust the potential of all combinatorial possibilities, nor can such a corpus contain more than a small
fraction of all logically possible inferences. But new
combinations of old elements and new logical deductions
are being made by the members all the time. Members
stimulate each other in the exploration of the possibilities of their minds.

AXIOM 9: Cultural knowledge within some bound unit
of culture varies because the members of
that unit are continuously making new
discoveries of possibilities contained in
their minds.

Among our examples such processes may account for
the unique assignment of naat'a'ii Flyers to ch'osh
Unusual animals or the assignment of lho707' Fish to the
na'ash8o'ii Reptiles by some consultants.

As cognitive anthropologists we work close to the

335

individual end of the continuum of bound units of culture. Consequently we are in a favorable position to pay greater attention to individual variation and to the dimensions of individual variation: between and within bound cultural units. Tough luck ethnography is difficult, arduous, and almost always exasperating. Our need as humans to integrate cultural knowledge is overwhelming.

As anthropologists we must resist the temptations toward a more apparent than real cultural coherence. We must concentrate on a better understanding of the nature of the continuum of cultural units from the level of an individual all the way to the level of terrestrial human culture.

In the remainder of this paper we will exemplify our definitions and axioms with the domain of things that are alive according to the Navajo.

1. GTE in Werner & Begishe (1970).

In our first article on the topic of the taxonomic aspects of the Navajo universe, the domain of all living things was presented under several general labels:

(1-i)

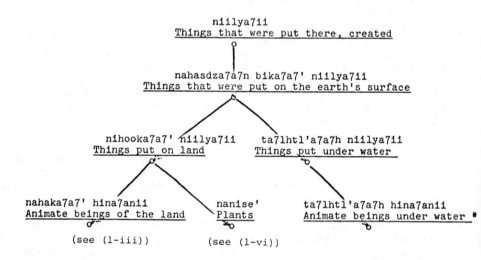

niilya7ii
Things that were put there, created

nahasdza7a7n bika7a7' niilya7ii
Things that were put on the earth's surface

nihooka7a7' niilya7ii
Things put on land

ta7lhtl'a7a7h niilya7ii
Things put under water

nahaka7a7' hina7anii
Animate beings of the land

nanise'
Plants

ta7lhtl'a7a7h hina7anii
Animate beings under water *

(see (1-iii))

(see (1-vi))

336

The things that were put there, created, were subdivided into four items ho7t'a7a7h niilya7ii things that
were placed above, nahasdza7a7nbighi' niilya7ii things
that were placed inside the earth, dine7 ba7niilya7ii
things that were put there for the benefit of the Navajo,
and nahasdza7a7nbika7a7' niilya7ii things that were put on
the earth's surface. In diagram (i) we show the last term
only. Although the sister nodes on this level and the
dominating node niilya7ii are by no means free of controversy for the sake of brevity and the aims of this paper
we have suppressed the discussion of these most general
Navajo concepts. They will be discussed in detail in our
forthcoming monograph.

The Navajo classification of living things in this
view does not have a 'unique beginner.' It is possible to
infer from the lexemic structure of the naming units the
following classification not explicitly stated in Werner
and Begishe (1970). Thus (ii) must be viewed as parallel-
ing (i):

(1-ii)

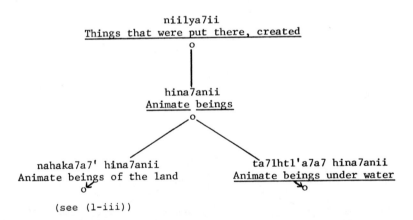

niilya7ii
Things that were put there, created

hina7anii
Animate beings

nahaka7a7' hina7anii
Animate beings of the land

ta7lhtl'a7a7 hina7anii
Animate beings under water

(see (1-iii))

In Werner & Begishe (1970) we did not expand the
item on the right further (ta7lhtl'a7a7 hina7anii Animate
beings under water). It contains all lho7o7' fish, the
underwater insects, and possibly others. The item on the
left was the label of the superordinate node of an
elaborate subtree, which is reproduced in the following
diagrams:

337

(1-iii)

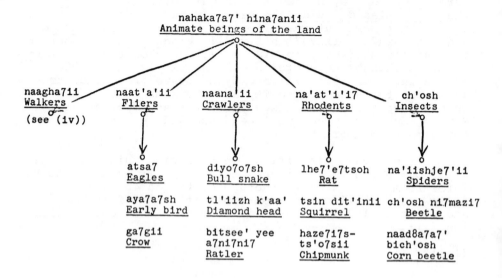

(1-iv-a)

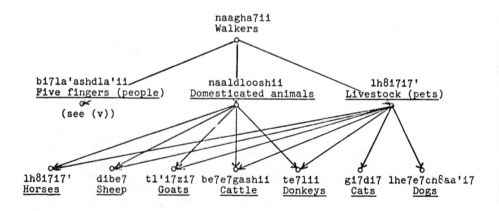

(1-iv-b)

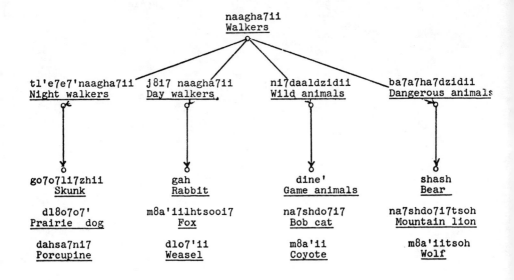

naagha7ii
Walkers

tl'e7e7'naagha7ii j817 naagha7ii ni7daaldzidii ba7a7ha7dzidii
Night walkers Day walkers Wild animals Dangerous animals

go7o7li7zhii gah   dine'   shash
Skunk   Rabbit Game animals Bear

dl8o7o7' m8a'iilhtsooi7 na7shdo7i7 na7shdo7i7tsoh
Prairie dog Fox   Bob cat Mountain lion

dahsa7ni7 dlo7'ii m8a'ii m8a'iitsoh
Porcupine Weasel Coyote Wolf

(1-v)

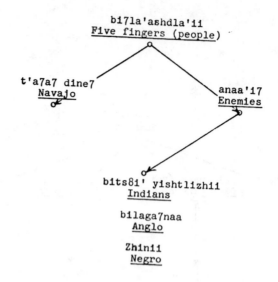

bi7la'ashdla'ii
<u>Five fingers (people)</u>

t'a7a7 dine7
<u>Navajo</u>

anaa'17
<u>Enemies</u>

bits8i' yishtlizhii
<u>Indians</u>

bilaga7naa
<u>Anglo</u>

Zhinii
<u>Negro</u>

(1-vi)

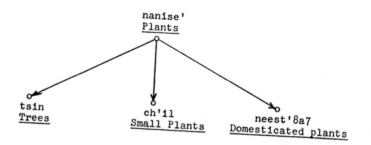

nanise'
<u>Plants</u>

tsin
<u>Trees</u>

ch'il
<u>Small Plants</u>

neest'8a7
<u>Domesticated plants</u>

Wherever several terminal nodes are given it can be inferred that more related terms are available. Thus the multiple terminal nodes and the small triangles signify further taxonomic structure.

This then is the taxonomic aspect of Navajo living things as presented in Werner & Begish (1970).

2. TLE in Werner et al. (1973).

Our discussion begins from the top down. We could not again elicit the term ta7lhtl'a7a7h niilya7ii Things put (created) under water. Therefore we did not consider it in the new presentation.

Our first surprise was the greater generalization of nanise' which we have glossed before as plants. Young and Morgan (1942) gloss nanise' as it grows about though they continue, that it usually refers to vegetation. Independently several consultants brought to our attention the fact that the following sentences are possible:

nanise' nooseelh Plants grow.

hina7anii nooseelh Animate things grow.

On the basis of this it was suggested that nanise' has in fact two positions in the Navajo taxonomy of living things: (1) as a most general concept referring to all living things whose major characteristic is that they do grow, and, (2) a less general usage referring to plants or vegetation. Consequently, we set up the taxonomic tree as follows (some detail omitted):

(2-i)

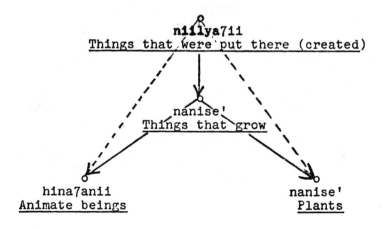

niilya7ii
Things that were put there (created)

nanise'
Things that grow

hina7anii
Animate beings

nanise'
Plants

341

This fact coincided with our previous insight that
if the same item referred to two different levels of a
taxonomy invariably the more specific application of the
term was more focal, or more closely to the focal awareness of Navajo speakers, or 'unmarked.'

However, by no means all consultants agreed with
the above picture. The first controversy that arose was a
relatively minor one. Several people refused to consider
nanise' as a possible superordinate node to the specific
nanise' Plants and hina7anii Animate beings. Their contention was that the two have no common node and both
should be suspended directly from niilya7ii Things that
were put there (created) (ultimately) or some of the
intermediate nodes graphed in the preceding section. This
latter view was largely the one we have presented in the
1970 paper. This aspect of the controversy is minor
simply because the view is contained in the one graphed in
(2-i) as shown by the broken lines. The two systems differ from each other only due to the removal of the generally interpreted nanise' Things that grow.

The third variant is much more serious. It was
presented to us by a group of very adamant young Navajo
male teachers. The group was mixed but while the women
teachers accepted the generalized nanise' Things that grow
as in (2-i) the men did not and proposed the following:

(2-ii)

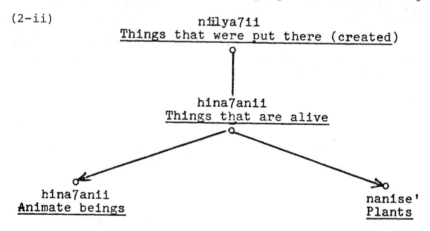

This arrangement again supports the generalization
that the more specific application (hina7nii Animate
beings) of two identical items is more focal than the more
general application (hina7nii Things that are alive).

Our first inclination was to dismiss this

342

arrangement as a case of interference from English. We argued that the verb hiina7 means It moves and therefore it is not applicable as a superordinate node for nanise' Plants. Furthermore, we assumed that the derived form iina' Life could be responsible for pressure via the English system used by educated Navajos on the use hiina7nii in its more general application. At present we do not know which influence to count more heavily. However, it has come to our attention that in traditional Navajo mythology statements like the following sentences are possible:

to7 hiina7 Water lives.

k807 hiina7 Fire lives.

or even

tse7 hiina7 Rock lives.

Considering that young men may be more intimately involved with the ceremonial religious tradition of the Navajo it is conceivable that the view shown in (2-ii) is the more traditional one. Alternately that nanise' Things that grow and hina7anii Things that are alive are possibly synonyms in their more general application. Furthermore, the synonymy may be context sensitive if hina7anii Things that are alive can be documented as a ceremonial term and nanise' Things that grow as a secular term. The secular ceremonial dichotomy in terminology seems to pervade many if not all Navajo systems of classification. The fact that women are generally less familiar with ceremonial terminology and the fact that they supported the version with nanise' Things that grow and objected to the generalized use of hina7anii supports our hypothesis.

We will present evidence in the classification of the birds that will argue for interference from English. Such interference, with the spreading of Anglo education among the Navajo, must be considered seriously wherever the evidence permits. In the foregoing case it seems that for the young Navajo teachers the influence of ceremonial knowledge and interference from English could converge.

We summarize our discussion in the next diagram. We have added the node labeled ch'osh Unusual animals simply because it does not seem to fit anywhere else. Note that this is again a more general use of the term than we have noted previously. The specific application is ch'osh insects which we will deal with below.

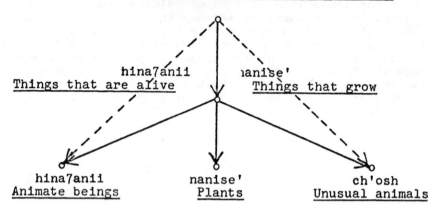

(2-iii)

niilya7ii
Things that were put there (created)

hina7anii
Things that are alive

nanise'
Things that grow

hina7anii
Animate beings

nanise'
Plants

ch'osh
Unusual animals

As before, for consultants who do not accept the general interpretation of either hina7anii Things that are alive or nanise' Things that grow the broken lines represent a special case of (2-iii) due to the transitivity of the relation of taxonomy.

The next discussion centers on the node labeled hina7nii Animate beings in (2-iii). So far we have listed only one label for the node. However, our consultants insisted that there are at least four equivalent labels that may fit at this (the more specific) level. The equivalent terms are: hina7anii Animate beings or perhaps more appropriately in this context Things that move; naagha7ii Things that walk; naaldeehii Things that walk plurally (more than two); and na7hididziihii Things that breathe. The interpretation of this type of synonymy is similar to such sets of synonyms in other languages: Each term contains the same full set of attributes of each other term (on the level to which it applies). At the same time each term also focuses or highlights a different one of the shared set of attributes. An English example is the synonymy of the following terms: 'being,' 'entity,' 'thing.' We claim their content is the same, but the first stresses existence, the second boundedness and the third its discreteness, or physical character. The above Navajo situation is even more complex.

Neither naagha7ii Things that walk, nor naaldeehii Things that walk plurally, nor na7hididziihii Things that breathe are possible superordinate nodes of ch'osh Unusual animals. However, hiina7anii Things that move is. On the basis of this information we assigned ch'osh to the more general application of hina7anii Things that are alive.

344

In the opinion of one very knowledgeable consultant ch'osh Unusual animals or Insects are hina7anii only in the summer. They are not alive and disappear in the winter. Thus, at least part time, in this man's opinion, ch'osh must be detached from hina7anii during the winter months with only its attachment to niilya7ii Things that were put there (created) remaining intact for the entire year.

The next level of our discussion may be summarized diagrammatically as follows:

(2-iv)

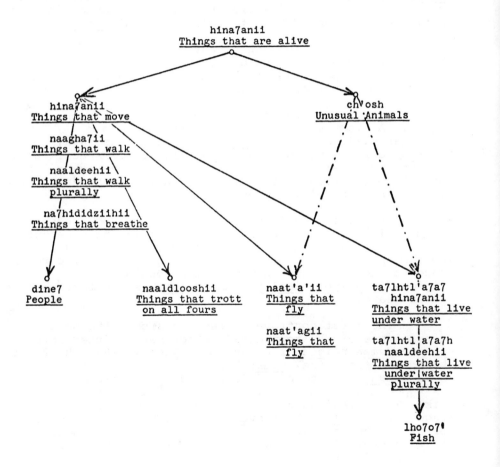

345

Here the term naat'agii Things that fly is notable.
In some parts of the reservation (e.g., around Rough Rock)
it seems to be the preferred term. However, almost everyone asserts that it is a ceremonial term. Some consultants even felt aya7a7sh should be included as a possible
third synonym for Flying things. However, we suspect
aya7a7sh seems most likely to be the ceremonial term only
for small birds with pretty feathers.

There is no question about the assignment of
lho7o7' Fish to ta7lhtl'a7a7 hina7anii Things that live
under the surface of the water. However, there is some
disagreement about the assignment of lho7o7 Fish to ch'osh
Unusual animals. Later on, with the classification of the
unusual animals, we will present further evidence for the
assignment of lho7o7 Fish to ch'osh Unusual animals.

In one case our consultant insisted that naat'a'ii
Flying things are also ch'osh Unusual animals. We show
these unusual features of the ch'osh subclassification
with broken lines of dots and dashes.

The classification of people starts with the term
dine7. A synonym, apparently a ceremonial term,
bi7la'ashdla'ii Their fingers are five is also available.
In the narrow sense naagha7ii Walkers refers specifically
to those who walk about on two legs. We have never heard
of any application of the term to other than humans or two
legged animals, e.g., birds.

The term naagha7 He walks about has a corresponding
form nijigha7 A human being walks about (among other possible interpretation of the so-called ji form, e.g.,
polite speech) which makes specific and/or emphatic reference to human beings. However, the possible form
nijigha7ii A specifically human walker is one that we have
never heard.

The first controversy centers around the most
general use of the term dine7, which may be interpreted as
either Human beings or as Any male human. Thus the first
branching from dine7 Human being is directly into dine7
Male humans and asdza7ni7 Female humans. This assumption
is supported by the possible interpretation of sentences
like Dine7 a7adi naagha7. A male (unspecified for color,
race, etc.) walks about over there. The basic dichotomy
of dine7 general term into specific males and females enters at every level on which dine7 may also be used in its
more specific senses.

Disregarding the division of dine7 Humans into

males and females at this level we find at least two, possibly three branches:

(2-v)

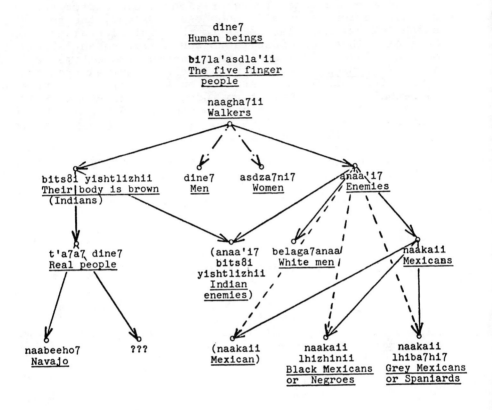

We do not know the precise range of the term bits8i yishtlizhii <u>Indians</u>. It is possibly a recent term. In the past (i.e., before contact) the terms ta7a7 dine7 <u>Real people</u> and anaa'i7 <u>Enemies</u> may have been sufficient.

Since that time Navajo life has undergone changes which are reflected in difficulties in the Navajo classification of people. The <u>Navajo proper</u> or t'a7a7 dine7 thus become a subordinate node under bits8i yishtlizhii <u>Indians</u>. At the same time t'a7a7 dine7 receives a wider interpretation which is difficult to gloss: It includes the Navajos proper for sure, but it also includes the

Northern Athapascans or dine7 nahadl8o7o7nii including the
hak'aaz dine'e7 Eskimo at least according to a few consultants who noted that the modified term dine'e7 usually
is reserved for Navajo clans. These clans also raise some
other interesting questions. The naasht'e7zhi7 for
example are the Zuni; therefore, one would expect their
classification as anaa'i7 enemies. However, the term
naasht'e7zhii may also refer to the Zuni clan among the
Navajos. Thus our consultants would list naasht'e7zhi7
once as t'a7a7 dine7 Real people and a second time as
anaa'i7 enemies. Obviously, all clans derived from the
names of former enemies are not only t'a7a7 dine7 but also
naabeeho7; if the later term indeed contrasts with t'a7a7
dine7. The situation is still complicated further by the
fact that naakaii may refer to Mexicans in general or to
the Mexican clan among the Navajos.

Both the classification of dine7, t'a7a7 dine7 or
naabeeho7 into clans does not exhaust the possibilities of
contextual ambiguities of the human terms. The following
subclassifications of dine7 People seem to be also appropriate:

(2-vi)

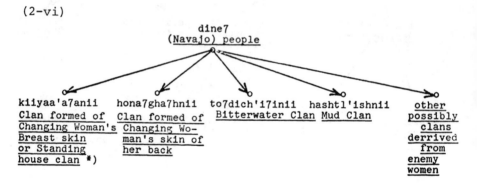

dine7
(Navajo) people

kiiyaa'a7anii — Clan formed of Changing Woman's Breast skin or Standing house clan *)

hona7gha7hnii — Clan formed of Changing Wo-man's skin of her back

to7dich'i7inii — Bitterwater Clan

hashtl'ishnii — Mud Clan

other possibly clans derrived from enemy women

(2-vii)

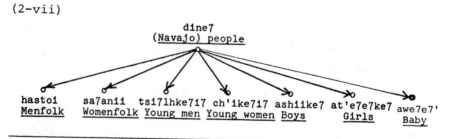

dine7
(Navajo) people

hastoi Menfolk

sa7anii Womenfolk

tsi7lhke717 Young men

ch'ike717 Young women

ashiike7 Boys

at'e7e7ke7 Girls

awe7e7' Baby

*The latter term is possibly a folk etymology of younger
Navajos.

348

(2-viii)

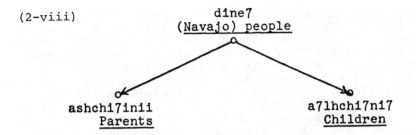

and finally based on the dichotomy indicated by dots and dashes in diagram (2-v)

(2-ix)

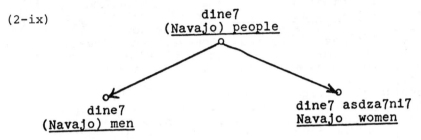

The classification of enemies is equally complex in its own way. There are the anaa'i7 bits8i yishtlizhii <u>Indian enemies</u>, though we have never heard this term. The term belaga7anaa <u>Anglos</u> usually refers to just the white men of the Southwest. In a wider sense this term may contain, but we cannot be sure at this point, the enemies that the Navajos acquired through their association with the United States and more specifically, through the last two World Wars.

These are among others the be7e7sh bich'ahi7 <u>Iron hatters</u> or the <u>Germans</u> and the bi'e7e7' lhichi7i7' <u>Red shirts</u> or <u>Russians</u>.

The final group of enemies are the naakaii <u>Mexicans</u>. We are not certain that the <u>Black Mexicans</u>, naakaii lhizhinii, and <u>Gray Mexicans</u>, naakaii lhiba7hi7, or <u>Blacks</u> and <u>Spanish</u> respectively are properly kinds of Mexicans. If they are, a third node of Mexicans proper is needed, as we have indicated in (2-v). We have graphed our uncertainty by placing the term between parentheses. The broken line of dashes is intended to imply the alternative classification.

The taxonomy continues with naaldlooshii <u>Trotters</u>. The most important category here seems to be lh8i7i7'

Domesticated animals. In the first paper (1970) we called naaldlooshii Domesticated animals. This is only partially true and rests on the fact that the trotters that come to mind first in everyday discourse are the large domesticated animals. But not all naaldlooshii are lh8i7i7' nor are all lh8i7i7' restricted to trotting animals. Among the lh8i7i7' Domesticated animals lhe7e7ch8aa'i7 dogs are probably also naaldlooshii, but this is uncertain for the mo7si7 Domesticated cats, Ta7zhii Turkeys and na'ahoohaii Chicken and all other potentially domesticable animals (mostly various small birds) are not naaldlooshii Trotters.

The dine' or dini' Game animals branch into b8iih Deer (or Deer like animals) and the aya7ni7 Buffalo or Buffalo like animals. All antelopes would fall into the first of these categories. However, the situation seems to be here similar to the one we will later encounter with leafy trees much more clearly. The antelopes, elks, moose, etc., may be referred to as b8iih deer like only if the precise classification is impossible either due to unfamiliarity with the animal (e.g., in a zoo) or inability to discern exact characteristics, perhaps at a distance. The situation seems analogous with aya7ni7 Buffalo. Some of our consultants reluctantly classified tl'i7zi7 alhchini7 Wild goats and dibe7 tse7tah Mountain sheep under aya7ni7 Buffalo while most of them preferred a direct attachment to dine' Game animals.

The dangerous animals, naaldlooshii ba7aha7dzidii are another category that cuts across classifications. Among the three branches only shash Bears are clearly and unequivocally dangerous, both physically and ceremonially. The Coyotes include, for example, m8a'ii dootl'izhii Blue-green coyote or Kit fox and ta7b8aah m8a'ii Water's edge coyote or Racoon which are definitely not considered dangerous in any sense. Both seem to be (as we shall see) questionably naaldlooshii Trotters. Thus even the classification of all coyote like animals as trotters is disputed by some consultants. Among the Cats na7shdo7i7 only na7shdo7i7tsoh Big cat or Mountain lion is unambiguously dangerous.

The na'at'i'ii Staggerers or Animals that move in a line overlap in interesting ways with naaldlooshii Trotters. It appears that large(r) four legged animals are always classified as naaldlooshii Trotters, the small(er) animals are always na'at'i'ii Staggerers. Some in between sized animals are both, while some smaller animals are questionable, so (broken lines):

350

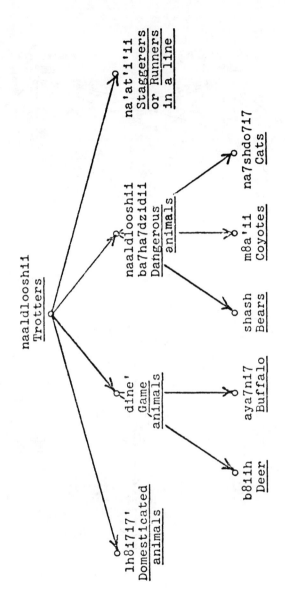

(2-xi)

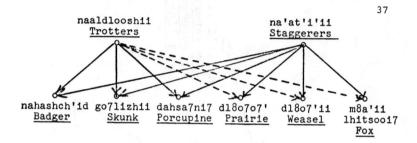

(2-xii)

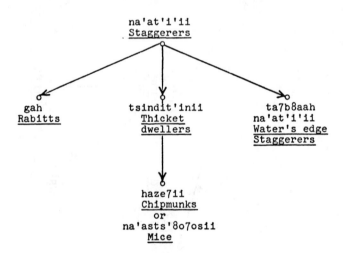

There are about 10 different species mentioned
under the label we have named either Chipmunks, haze7ii,
or alternately na'asts'8o7osii Mice. Consultants differ
as to which term is subordinate to the other. One of our
consultants classified d18o7o' Prairie dog in this category but that attachment was emphatically rejected by all
others. Similarly the classification of Prairie dog,
d18o7o7', under gah Rabbit was rejected by all but one
consultant.

The influence of education in English became clearly apparent in the classification of the Flyers,
naat'a'ii. We were assisted by two younger Navajo men in
the preparation of the preliminary diagrams which we sub-
mitted in various forms for comment to consultants who
were only casually or occasionally associated with our
project. The top levels of the tree were as follows:

(2-xiii)

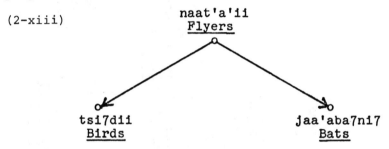

The right node for Bats, jaa'aba7ni7, was terminal
without any further subdivision. The left node was superordinate to all birds which includes the Eagles, atsa7,
the Owls, na'ashjaa', the Crow and Ravens, ga7agii, and
all other birds in the Navajo universe. Our 1970 classification was in accord with this view. It was largely
the view of Kenneth Y. Begishe, a young educated Navajo.

Our subsequent work with more traditional and older
Navajos quickly established the fact that the view represented in (2-xiii) did not coincide with theirs. There
was unusual agreement among these traditional people. The
alternate diagram is given below.

The use of aya7a7sh at the highest level is probably out of place. In most contexts it refers to birds
used in ceremonies or in ceremonial equipment because of
their pretty colored feathers. Most likely on further investigation it will constitute possibly a cross cutting
classification to the small birds proper, **tsi7dii (see
below for the explanation of the double asterisks). As we
have pointed out before, the term naat'agii seems to be

(2-xiv)

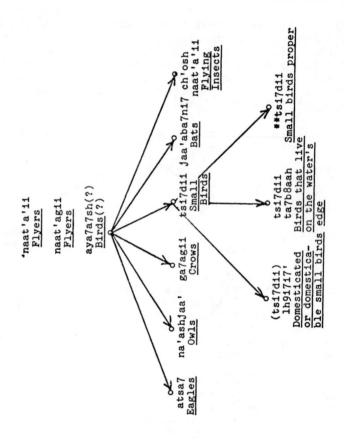

ceremonial though at least with some Rough Rock families
it appears to be the predominant secular term too. The
classification of naa't'a'ii can be interpreted traditionally where it would include only animate beings. With the
advent of airplanes, chidii naat'a'ii, or flying cars,
these may also be classified in this taxonomy. The possibility for this is implied by the cross cutting with the
classification of insects, i.e., with the ch'osh
naat'a'ii, Flying insects. By at least one informant the
jaa'aba7ni7 Bats should also be classified among the flying unusual animals, ch'osh naat'a'ii, one level above the
more specific flying insects, cho'sh naat'a'ii.

We could have included a node for dangerous birds.
However, this is frought with similar problems as the previously discussed node of dangerous animals, naaldlooshii
ba7ha7dzidii. Here only one group, the owls, na'ashjaa'
are clearly dangerous because they are harbingers of bad
omens, usually some close family member's impending death.
Smaller birds in the English owl classification are not
classified as na'ashjaa' owls. Only young Navajos classified consistently tsi7diihd8oohii, Screech owl, among the
owls probably on the basis of the English translation. As
its name implies it is a tsi7dii Small bird and is classified as such by all traditional consultants.

The Eagles, atsa7 are perhaps dangerous but min-
imally so. There was considerable disagreement since they
are trapped for their feathers, unlike the owls who are
dangerous descendents of the mythological Flying Monster.
It is further possible that the ceremonial use of atsa7
Eagles would place them into the ayaa7sh classification.
At this point we simply don't know. We know, however,
that all small birds of prey, e.g., biizhii Western night
hawk and others, fall into the small bird, tsi7dii, category, whereas the large hawks are clearly ats7a Eagles.

There is some controversy about the assignment of
ga7agii the Crows and ravens. One consultant felt they
should go with the Eagles atsa7, while others would rather
have them with the tsi7dii Small birds. Most seemed to
prefer a separate classification altogether.

The tsi7dii lh8i7i7' Domesticated or Domesticable
small birds are just that. They cross cut with lh8i7i7'
pets or domesticated animals. Tsi7dii ta7b8aah naaldeehii
Water's edge birds similarly cross cut with the ta7b8aah
naaldeehii Things that live (plurally) on the Water's
edge. It is not clear whether tsi7dii naa'eelhii Small
floating birds, usually ducks constitute an independent
node or whether they are part of the tsi7dii ta7b8aah

naaldeehii Water's edge birds.

The 'pseudo' node **tsi7dii Small birds proper implies that all other small birds are listed under this
node but it should not be construed as a dominating node
but as a single node standing for the large number of over
100 or more small birds in the Navajo universe.

Finally, in the case of the Flying insect Ch'osh
naat'a'ii we have about 50 species. These were further
subdivided by only one consultant as follows:

(2-xv)

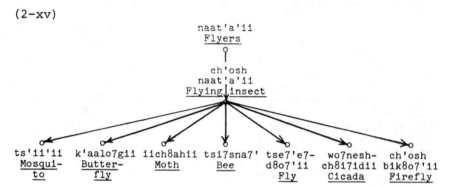

Where each node has several species under it. The flying
ants wo7lachi7i7' naat'a'ii were classified under ants,
wo7lachi7i7, though the cross classification with
naat'a'ii Flyers is unavoidable.

The next item is the classification of things that
live under water, ta7lhtl'a7a7h hina7anii.

The 'pseudonode' **ta7lhtl'a7a7h hina7anii Things
that live under water (proper) dominates all living things
that live under the surface of the water, mostly fish. We
are not certain if tsi7dii ta7lhtl'a7a7h hina7anii Small
birds living under the surface of the water are properly
split off at this point, or as a result of a pervading
cross cutting classification by locomotion versus habitat.
The Small birds living under the surface of the water contain the diving birds, that is, various ducks, geese and
loons. The Watersnake, to7tl'iish, is clearly an Under
water dweller, yet at the same time part of the snakes and
therefore of the Unusual animals, ch'osh. Conceivably all
ta7lhtl'a7a7h hina7anii Dwellers under the surface of the
water could be classified as kind of ch'osh, Unusual
animals. As the classification of the unusual animals

356

(2-xvi)

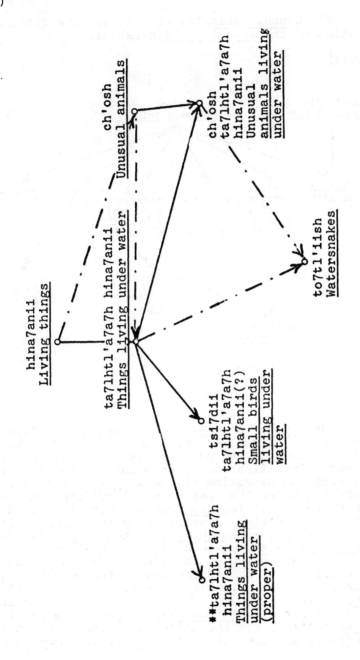

will show (following) this is likely in at least two possible ways.

The <u>Unusual animals</u>, ch'osh, are the final classification of the <u>animal world</u> hina7anii:

(2-xvii)

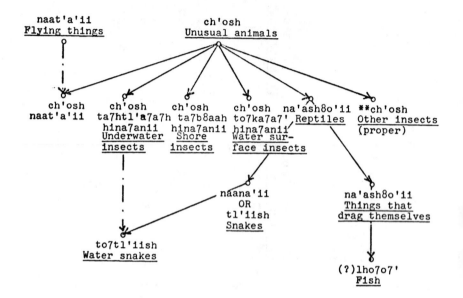

The <u>Flying insects</u>, ch'osh naat'a'ii (looking back at 2-xiv) are classified under both heading of the <u>Fliers</u>, naat'a'ii, and the <u>Unusual animals</u>, ch'osh. This pervasive cross classification is true for all the following nodes with the exception of the <u>Reptiles</u>, na'ash8o'ii, and the species under the 'pseudo node' *ch'osh, on the right which contains all <u>Insects</u> that are not classified by locomotion, i.e., <u>Flying</u>, naat'a, or by the three habitats, ta7htl'a7a7h <u>Under the surface of the water</u>, ta7b8aah, <u>At the shore of water</u>, or to7ka7a7', <u>On the surface of the water</u>. The ambiguity of the term ch'osh as <u>Insect</u> in the more usual and by far more common interpretation whereas ch'osh as the <u>Unusual animals</u> is less common. All <u>Reptiles</u>, na'ash8o'ii, are to be found here. These are subclassified into the <u>Things that slither</u>, naa'na'ii, or the <u>Snakes</u>, tl'iish, and the na'ash8o'ii <u>The things that drag themselves</u>, or generally the <u>Lizards</u>, <u>Gila monsters</u> and

Salamanders. One of our consultants insisted that the
fish, lho7o7', belong to this category also. Thus we have
here another possible cross classification with
ta7htl'a7a7h hina7anii the Dwellers under the surface of
the water. Another consultant insisted that all the
birds, that is the eagles, atsa7, through the small birds,
tsi7dii, are all to be classified under ch'osh Unusual
animals. The only unifying principle that we could find
for such assignment is the fact that almost all unusual
animals, ch'osh (with the exception of the bats,
jaa'aba7ni7), burst forth from eggs. To the best of our
knowledge only Gladys Reichard (1950) tried to relate the
term ch'osh insects to the verb stem for bursting forth --
ch'osh, for example in the Navajo term for soda pop,
to7dilhch'oshi7, used on the Western Reservation. Although it would make good sense to classify for example
caterpillars ch'osh ditl'ooi7 Hairy insect (and several
other designations) with the Slitherers or Snakes,
naana'ii or possibly with the na'ash8o'ii, The draggers,
or generally Lizards, we are unaware of such an assignment.

Although there is no paucity for specific names for
plants, easily and well over 300, the animal classification
seems to outstrip the classification of plants considerably. We are able to give only two competing classifications or plants: the first generally agreed upon by all
our consultants save one, the other given by the disagree-
ing consultant who also proclaimed the first classification wrong headed. The lack of richness in the plant
classification is the more striking to us since at least
two of our consultants are considered specialists on
plants. The person giving the classification by use (the
second version) is not so considered.

The term che7ch'il or tse7ch'il Rock weed or oak
was classified by all our consultants under tsin Tree,
while its lexemic structure would imply that it ought to
be under ch'il Weeds. At present we have no resolution
for this anomaly. In the category of tsin Trees there are
to be found the rudiments (?) of further subclassification. Apparently cha'olh Pinion pine, t'i7i7s Cottonwood,
and ts'ah Sage bush may be used as generic terms for con-
iferous, desiduous trees and bushes respectively. However, this use is permitted only under unusual conditions:
only in cases where the exact identity of the tree or bush
is not ascertainable.

In previous classifications of the Navajo plant
world we have included categories such as azee' Medicines,
neest'8a7, Edible plants, ba7ha7dzidii Dangerous ones and

(2-xviii)

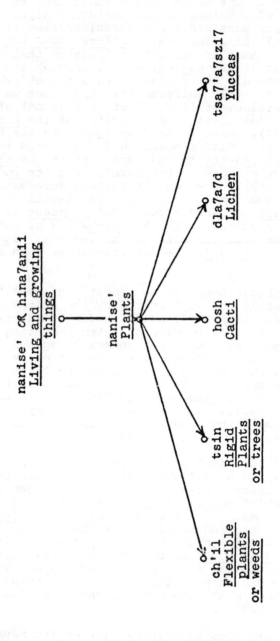

na7t'oh Tobaccos. Among these only the last is a term of
the classificatin of plants. The category of dangers cuts
across several domains. This is usually ritual danger
rather than just a physical one. The edible plants cross
cut the five categories of plants; there are edible
species in each category. Still on a much larger scale
the Medicine, azee', classification cuts across the entire
universe of animal, vegetable and minderal objects.

Finally the classification of the yuccas tsa'a7szi7
is controversial. Some consultants claim it is a kind of
Cactus, hosh, others that it is in the ch'il or Weed category. Still others prefer to place it separately. As
such it is the smallest subcategory of plants with only
four sub-members.

The only classification of plants by use that we
were able to elicit is as follows.

The classification we present is not the complete
tree as given to us by our consultant. A subtree should
be imagined under each one of the nodes ·of (2-xx) as implied by the subtree under nanise' dine7 bi'azee' Medic-
inal plants of the Navajo. We did present this classification to one other consultant who was somewhat over-
whelmed. However, he latched on immediately to the
classification of the Useless plants, nanise' dine7 doo
choyoolh'i7inii and especially the Grey cactus, hosh
Ẋiba7ha7, by asserting "We eat them all the time."
Whether it is possible that different species of cacti are
called by different names in different parts of the Reservation we do not know. That could explain such a disagreement, since the two men lived a considerable distance
from each other.

(2-xix)

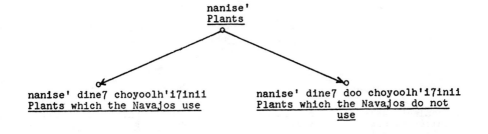

nanise'
Plants

nanise' dine7 choyoolh'i7inii
Plants which the Navajos use

nanise' dine7 doo choyoolh'i7inii
Plants which the Navajos do not
use

(2-xx)

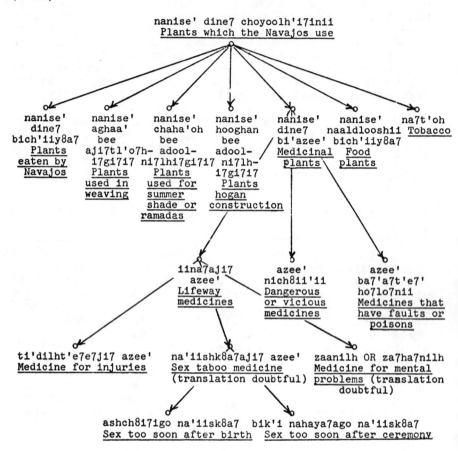

(2-xxi)

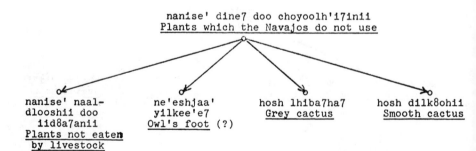

3. Typology of Variation.

In the preceding section we established the fact that there is considerable variation that an ethnographer uncovers if he sets his mind to looking for variation and controversy. In the first subsection we will attempt a typology of the kind of variation that can be posited for taxonomic structures. Subsequently in the following subsection we will illustrate the types of variation by examples found in our preceding Navajo sample.

3.1 Formal Types.

There are two types of possible variation in a taxonomy: (1) variations in labeling; (2) variation due to different attachment of nodes and edges (arrows) to other parts of a tree structure. Although the types we have discovered so far appear to be exhaustive we are not prepared to claim exhaustiveness at this point in our studies.

3.1.1 Variations in Labeling.

We distinguish five types that are not entirely independent of each other. Our examples will show variation whenever possible from a less rich system (on the left side of the page) to a richer system on the right side of the page. If such a view is not possible it will be specifically discussed.

(1) Multiples Labels with Synonymy (MLS) (S = semantic relation of synonymy). The same node has two synonymous labels (a) and (b), and possibly more.

(3-i)

(a) S (b) ...

There are several examples in the classifications presented. Perhaps the most notable is Graph (2-iv). Hina7anii living/moving things was the preferred term of most of our consultants. However, everyone understood naaldeehii Things that walk plurally from Haile (1942). Few consultants use it on the Western Reservation. Na7hididziihii Breathers was used by a few of our

consultants. Naagha7ii, <u>Walkers</u> (usually on two legs) as
can be seen from comparing (2-iv) with (2-v) appears on at
least two levels. The four terms are claimed to be
synonyms. Each highlights a different aspect of essentially the same bundle of attributes. On the other hand,
while our consultants seem to accept this synonymy, it
could be our ignorance and their ignorance. One of us
thought <u>mammal</u> and <u>placental</u> were synonyms in the same
sense until confronted with biological evidence.

(2) Multiple Labels Without Synonymy (-MLS). A
label in the same position in the taxonomies T(1) and T(2)
of two individual consultants (or in two taxonomies
elicited at different times) by the same consultant have
different labels that are not synonymous (not S):

(3-ii)

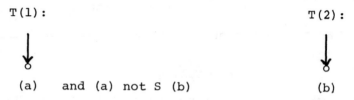

T(1):   T(2):

(a)   and (a) not S (b)   (b)

We don't have a unique example. The graph (2-xii)
combines -MLS with Label Reversal (see (3)).

(3) Label Reversal (LRL). Whereas in taxonomy
T(1), (a) dominates (b), in the other T(2), (b) dominates
(a):

(3-iii)

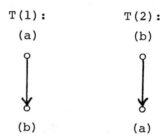

T(1):   T(2):
(a)   (b)

(b)   (a)

The two labels under tsindit'inii <u>Thicket dwellers</u>
or <u>squirrels</u> (2-xii) exhibit these characteristics. If
haze7ii <u>Chipmunk</u> is the superordinate node, as some consultants claim then there are under it, a node haze7ii
<u>Chipmunk</u> proper, and various species of <u>mice</u>,
na'asts'8o7sii. If na'asts'8o7sii <u>Mice</u> is the

superordinate term, as is the claim of others, the picture is reversed.

This example is, therefore, also an example of Duplication of Label and Label Reversal ((4) and (5) below). Clearly type (2) or (MLS) is related to type (3) or (LRL). In the former the leftover node is not part of the taxonomy, while in the (LRL) case both remain in the taxonomy but in a different hyerarchic relation to each other.

(4) Duplication of Label (DPL). The same label appears on two (or more) levels of a taxonomy:

(3-iv)

(a)

(a)

There are numerous examples of (DPL) in our (2-i), (2-ii), (2-iii), (2-iv), most notably (2-v) to (2-viii) in the classification of people and in others. Interestingly in 'context free' (in a most generalized context) questioning consultants' preference is the lower, more specific interpretation of the same label.

(5) Duplication of Label (DPL) with Label Reversal (LRL). Three nodes are labeled (a) (a) (b) in taxonomy T(1) and (a) (b) (b) in the other T(2):

(3-v)

Our best example of (LRL) is illustrated by (2-i) to (2-iii). First, in Navajo, the meaning of a term most close to focal awareness (or in the most generalized context) is the more specific use of the term. The

controversies always center around the more general use.
Most of our consultants agreed that among <u>living things</u>,
nanise' was the most general concept. This <u>was based</u> on
the fact that nanise' and the verb nooseelh <u>it</u> <u>grows</u> are
related.

A group of younger men insisted that the most general node was hina7anii <u>Living things</u> derived from motion
verbs. At first we thought this was the result of
acculturation. Subsequently, we felt that it was a
combination of more ceremonial and also more male knowledge and in addition possibly also acculturation.

3.1.2 Variations in Attachment.

We distinguish eight types. Again these are not
necessarily completely independent of each other. We follow the left/right side of the page convention as before.

(1) Topgrowth (TG): Taxonomy T(2) has one more
general node than taxonomy ((i) is new node label) T(1):

(3-vi)

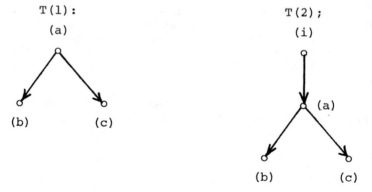

T(1):   T(2);
(a)   (i)

(b)   (c)   (a)

                               (b)   (c)

In our sample we have no examples of topgrowth.
This in part is an artifact of our eliciting. We concen-
trated on variations of attachment rather than variations
of labeling. Usually we presented all the labels we collected for assembly into taxonomies. It seems to be at
least part of general passive knowledge of many tradition-
al Navajos that niilya7ii <u>Things</u> <u>that</u> <u>were</u> <u>put</u> <u>there</u>
(<u>created</u>) is the recognized 'unique beginner.'

(2) Bottomgrowth (B): Taxonomy T(2) has one (or
more) more specific level(s) than taxonomy T(1) ((i) is
new node label):

366

(3-vii)

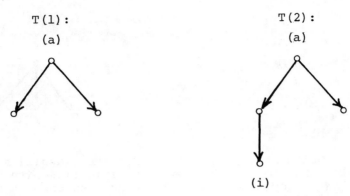

T(1):

(a)

T(2):

(a)

(i)

Our most extensive example is diagram (2-xix) and diagrams (2-xx) and (2-xxi). This classification, or (BG), of nanise' <u>Plants</u> is unique to one consultant. When it was presented to others they said something equivalent to "how interesting."

(3) Ingrowth (IG): A new taxonomic level is inserted in taxonomy T(2):

(3-viii)

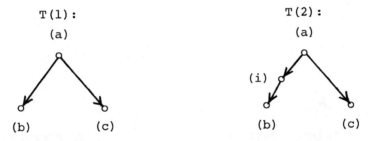

T(1):

(a)

(b)   (c)

T(2):

(a)

(i)

(b)   (c)

Our best example is (2-xiii) and (2-xiv) respectively. Younger consultants inserted by IG the node tsi7dii <u>Birds</u> between naat'a'ii <u>Flyers</u> and the rest of the birds (2-xiii). Older Navajo objected and claimed tsi7dii is the proper label for <u>Small birds</u> only (2-xiv). We are assuming that the equivalence of tsi7dii with <u>Birds</u> was forced under pressure by the English folk taxonomies which demand a label like <u>Birds</u>.

(4) Middlegrowth (MG): Taxonomy T(2) has more diversity on a level than taxonomy T(1):

367

(3-ix)

T(1):　　　　　　　　　　　T(2):
(a)　　　　　　　　　　　　(a)

(b)　　　　(c)　　　　　(b)　(c)　(i)

　　　　Our best example comes from the classification of
people. Due to the Navajos' identification with the
foreign policy of the United States, new enemies were
acquired, i.e., new nodes were attached to anaa'i7 <u>Enemies</u>
(2-v). These are neither belaga7anaa <u>Anglo</u> nor naa<u>kaii</u>
<u>Mexicans</u>, but include such peoples as be7e7sh bich'a7hi7
<u>Iron hats</u> or <u>Germans</u>, and be'e7e7' lhichi717' <u>Red shirts</u>
or <u>Russians</u>.

　　　　Middlegrowth (MG) has an inverse that could be
called Node Removal (NR). That is, a node which was present in taxonomy T(1) is absent in taxonomy T(2).

(3-x)

T(1):　　　　　　　　　　　T(2):
(a)　　　　　　　　　　　　(a)

Other inverses are conceivable by simply reversing T(1)
with T(2). Any instance of a consultant now knowing a
term that another does know constitutes a valid example.

　　　　(5) Laticization (LA)* (or paradigmatization):
The new node (i) in T(2) is dominated by two nodes. This
may be also interpreted as Bottomgrowth (BG) with convergence:

---

*We chose 'laticization' because the resulting formal
graph is called a 'semi-latice.'

368

(3-xi)

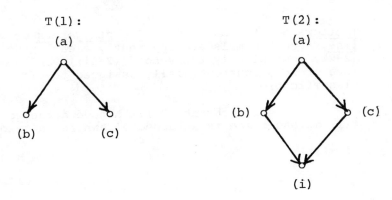

A possible alternate explanation of Laticization
may be as follows:

(3-xii)

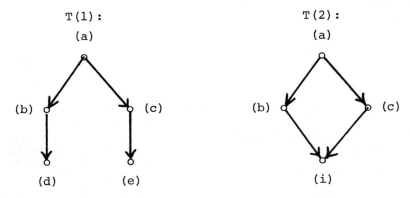

where (i) may be identical with either (d) or with (e).
If the two alternatives are empirically differentiable
then (3-xii) could be classified as a Variations in labeling.

Laticization is generally prevalent especially in
the animate kindgom nanise' or hina7anii Living growing
things. By including labels like ji7naagha7ii Daywalkers
and tl'e7e7'naagha7ii Nightwalkers as we did in (1-iv b)
even more legitimate cross classifications can be created.
The two labels are the classification from one or several
gambling myths and may or may not be unique to them.

The most interesting laticization (classification
and their cross cutting) is among the naaldlooshii

Trotters and the na'at'i'ii The staggerers or walkers in a line. Some animals are apparently clearly the first (2-x), some clearly the second (2-xii), and some can be more or less controversially assigned to either (2-xi) classification.

(6) Reattachment (RA): A node attached in taxonomy T(1) at one place is attached elsewhere in taxonomy T(2):

(3-xiii)

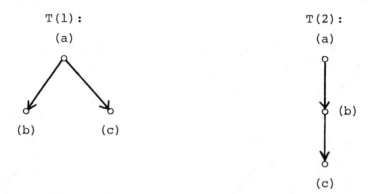

T(1):
(a)
(b)   (c)

T(2):
(a)
(b)
(c)

All consultants kept the fish, lho7o7' close to the high level node of ta7lhtl'a7ah hina7anii Dweller under the surface of the water (2-iv). Only one consultant insisted on placing lho7o7' Fish under na'ash8o'ii (2-xvii). We were unable to ascertain whether lho7o7' Fish was to be attached to the specific level of na'ash8oii The Lizards, or to the general na'ash8oii The Reptiles. Although we have drawn in (2-xvii) the former solutions we have indicated the alternative (which seems more likely) as well.

(7) Orthogonal Taxonomies (OT): Taxonomies T(1) and T(2) have identical ancestral (superordinate) nodes; however, at some point they branch into separate independent sub-taxonomies with a common ancestor.

In the Navajo sample such orthogonal taxonomies seem to occur only in the classification of People, dine7. In diagram (2-v) the dot and dash lines indicate this phenomenon. Whereas the taxonomy drawn with solid lines in one possible subtree to be drawn under dine7 People, the subtree of dine7 Men and asdza7ni7 Women is another tree with the same origin but independent of the first. Diagrams (2-vi), (2-vii) and (2-viii) show three additional possible interpretations of the subtrees dominated by the dine7 People node. All of these sub-taxonomies are

370

exclusive of each other and represent a different point of view. In other words, there is considerable complexity here that does not clearly appear in the simple diagrams. Such orthogonal taxonomies always seem to imply laticization, while the converse is not the case: Laticization does not imply orthogonal taxonomies.

(3-xiv)

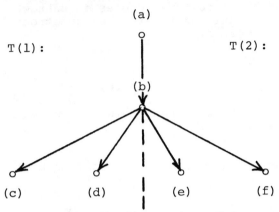

(a)

T(1):

(b)

(c)   (d)   (e)   (f)

T(2):

This completes the discussion of types of variation. Obviously many more examples for each type can be cited.

4. Epilogue.

We need a cultural theory that can explain how individuals, each with a different knowledge of his world, can communicate with each other and form viable social units that can then create a corpus of cultural knowledge of their own.

This paper is merely a continuation of work along these lines. We are especially indebted to the work of D'Andrade (1970) and the papers of Bernard and Killworth (1973 and 1974). D'Andrade measured and tried to explain the large percentages of unique cultural knowledge among members of homogeneous social groups. Bernard and Killworth have made inroads in discerning the formal theoretical constraints on social groupings that impose severe limits on the homogeniety of human cultures.

This paper tries to show that individual variation of Navajo taxonomic knowledge about animals and plants includes all possible formal structural types of variation. However, these types are not uniformly distributed

over all possible cultural sub-domains. There appear to
be at work constraints that limit the number and type of
variation that can be tolerated by the entire system. We
know very little about the operation of such constraints.
Our knowledge is rudimentary when it comes to formal
theoretical limitations. Unfortunately, reliable empirical investigations are lacking as well.

How individual minds, i.e., memories, each with a
cultural knowledge of its own, interact in order to form
social and hence cultural wholes is unknown. To us these
are key empirical and theoretical questions to be answered
by future research.

5. References Cited.

Bernard, H.R., & P.D. Killworth, 1973
    On the Social Structure of an Ocean-Going Vessel
    and Other Important Things. Social Science
    Research 2:145-184.

Bohannan, P.J., 1973
    Rethinking Culture. Current Anthropology 14:357-
    365.

Colby, B.N., 1973
    Comments on Bohannan 1973. Current Anthropology
    14:366.

D'Andrade, R.G., 1970
    Culture Shared and Unique. m.s.

Killworth, P.D., & H.R. Bernard, 1974
    Catij: A New Sociometric and its Application to a
    Prison Living Unit. Human Organization 33.

Giddings, F.H., 1922
    Studies in the Theory of Human Society. Macmillan.
    "Consciousness of Kind" p. 161-67 passim.

Hill, J.K., 1968
    The Culture of Retirement. Northwestern University
    Dissertation.

Litowitz, B., 1973
    Personal communication.

Moerman, M., 1964
    Farming in Ban Phaed. Yale University Ph.D. Dis-
    sertation.

Naroll, R., 1970
   The Culture-Bearing Unit in Cross-Cultural Surveys
   in Naroll & Cohen 1970: 721-765.

Perchonock, N., & O. Werner, 1968
   Navajo Systems of Classification: Some Implications of Ethnoscience.   Ethnology 8:229-242.

Sapir, E., 1932
   Cultural Anthropology and Psychiatry.   Journal of
   Abnormal and Social Psychology 27:229-242.   (Reprinted in D.G. Mandelbaum, 1963, Selected Writings
   of E. Sapir, University of California Press,
   pp. 509-521.)

Schapera, I., 1935
   Field Methods in the Study of Modern Culture Contacts.   Africa 8:315-328.

Vygotsky, L.S., 1962
   Thought and Language.   MIT Press.

Wallace, A.F.C., 1961
   Culture and Personality.   Random House.

Werner, O., with K.Y. Begishe, 1970
   The Taxonomic Aspect of the Navajo Universe, Proceedings 39th International Congress of American-
   ists, Lima, Peru, (August, 1970) pp. 27.   (To
   appear in Vol. 5 of Proceedings.)

Werner, O., A. Manning, & K.Y. Begishe, 1973
   A Taxonomic Aspect of the Traditional Navajo
   University.   (To appear in Handbook of North Amer-
   ican Indians, Smithsonian Institution.)

Werner, O., 1974
   The Synthetic Informant Model.   (Proceedings of the
   9th International Congress of Anthropological and
   Ethnological Sciences.)   In Monton.   W.C. McCormack
   & S.A. Wurm (eds.), Language and Thought.   Anthro-
   pological Issues, pp. 171-184.

Werner, O., 1974
   Intermediate Memory: A Central Concept in Ethnoscience.   Communication and Cognition 7:281-314.

SYMBOLS AND COGNITION[1]

V. A. Howard
Harvard University

1. Three Perspectives on Symbolism

It is customary amongst humanists and social scientists to label as "symbolic" virtually any object, action, or event that is not just being itself, which is to say, being literal or perhaps just literally being. Myths, for instance, are said to have literal, exoteric significance for those who take them at face value but only symbolic, esoteric significance, if that, for those who take them to be myths (Bidney, 1953, p. 302). And if symbolic status is supposed to mark a sophisticated understanding of myth, precisely the opposite flight from symbolism to literal formalism is thought to evidence an aesthetically enlightened attitude towards art. Between symbolic myths and nonsymbolic art lies a confusion, more exactly, an ambiguity in our common notion of symbolism that leads me to question the twin assumptions that art, myth, or anything else is less symbolic for being literal or exoteric and more symbolic when esoteric, allegorical, or metaphoric.

On the one hand, there is a broad usage of the term 'symbolic' roughly synonymous with anything that carries meaning in any of a variety of ways: literal or metaphoric descriptions, expressive or deadpan portraits and gestures, simple or complex codes, straightforward, ironic, or allegorical narratives, traffic signs, and silhouettes on lavatory doors. On the other hand, a much narrower usage of 'symbolic' tends to restrict the term to whatever wears its meaning up rather than on its sleeve, to the metaphorical and allegorical, the hidden, latent, deeper, more general and recondite. Thus Moby Dick read as a simple sea story is "symbolic" on the former usage but not on the latter, a difference that would hardly matter if it were not for the fact that on any view language, particularly complex, descriptive language, must be placed very near if not at the apex of human symbolic development. By the same token so must the number system, pictures, codes, music notations, diagrams, and maps, which amounts to a special plea for the broader usage for theoretical purposes with the proviso that something needs be done to distinguish among the various types of symbols in ordinary and extraordinary use. Little violence is done thereby and some clarity gained, since on the broader usage, things classed as "symbolic" on the narrower usage turn out to be

375

symbols of symbols: a whale description expressing Evil, a fish depiction representing Jesus, an odyssey narrative exemplifying heroism, endurance, or human frailty. The task is then to give an account of these various "simple" and compounded symbolic functions--of description, depiction, representation, expression, exemplification, and the like.

Some progress has been made in this direction in recent years which I hope to bring to bear on the topic of cognitive growth. Meanwhile, for what follows it is useful to distinguish three perspectives on the study of symbols, the first two of which reflect the aforementioned ambiguity in our common view of symbolism. First and more closely allied to the narrow usage is what might be called the interpretive perspective. The question here is what does a particular symbol or collection of symbols mean; their "levels" of meaning, specific and general, literal and metaphorical; their diachronic history and, where appropriate, ethnographic variations. The quest for the meaning of symbols may range from learning to use a particular form of symbolisation, say, language or music notation, to questions of style in art or of the nature of artistic, scientific, historical, or religious understanding. Included under this heading would be aspects of the work of lexicographers, art critics, cultural anthropologists, and historians but foremost and most obviously, the efforts of Everyman to understand and communicate about his world.

Corresponding to the broader colloquial view of symbolism is what I shall call the functional perspective. It concerns how particular items--gestures, utterances, inscriptions, objects-- acquire their symbolic functions to describe, name, depict, express, and so forth. Put another way, what are the relations that sustain a particular symbolic function and its contribution to meaning? To answer that question is the prime task of semiotics construed as propounding a general theory of symbols but also of interest to logicians, linguists, and philosophers.

Beyond these is the cognitive perspective concerned with the role of symbols in the growth of knowledge and perception in the individual; such questions as, How do symbols of various kinds mediate perception and thought? Do symbols emerge in regular sequences and through some sensory channels rather than others? In short, what are the psychological processes required or most frequently involved in the acquisition and mature use of different sorts of symbols? Such matters are fundamental to any theory of instruction and constitutive of theories of learning and thus occupy educators and psychologists alike.

Clearly, the aforenamed perspectives are complementary and, to a degree, intersecting rather than exclusive realms of inquiry. Which is to say, that it is as fruitful to distinguish what something means from how it means from how we learn what it means as

376

it is folly to separate them. Indeed, in what follows I shall be concerned with the role of symbols in cognitive theory from a functional point of view; that is with the general theory of symbols in the context of cognitive psychology. By examining aspects of Bruner's work on cognitive development, chiefly his three-stage theory of cognitive growth, I hope to show not only psychology's indebtedness to past philosophical theories of symbolism but what it has now to learn from more recent philosophical work on symbolism. Before getting on to that, however, a brief word needs saying on the contribution of a theory of symbols to a theory of cognition.

2. Meaning, Function, and Cognition

Talk of intellectual growth is talk about the growth of meaning in general, not just as it pertains to language, but to whatever enables us to understand and make our way in the world. Hence, talk of meaning inevitably involves a consideration of the mediating power of symbols primarily as instruments of cognition and secondarily of communication. This is not to underrate the importance of communication for cognitive growth but rather to underscore the logically prior purpose of symbolisation to facilitate understanding in the widest sense of the term. Without understanding communication would not only fail, but there would be no need of it.

I am suggesting to approach the concept of meaning in this context in terms of symbol functions. However, unlike the "meaning is use" formula, until recently so fashionable in philosophical circles, the notion of a symbol function assumes neither that all meaning is linguistic nor that it is initially clear what it is for something to be "used" or to function as a symbol of a certain kind. On the contrary, it is the aim of a general theory of symbols (or semiotics) to determine the conditions under which something, for instance, two contiguous circles, may function as a symbol of a certain sort—two letter O's, two zeros, or Little Orphan Annie's eyes. While linguistics has made brisk progress along these lines towards illuminating the structures and functions of language, our theoretical grasp of the non-languages remains most tentative and unsure. The weakness reaches into other fields.

Cognitive psychologists generally, and Bruner in particular, have been criticised for reinstating an out-moded "theory of ideas" in their reliance upon images, icons, maps, pictures, schemas, and other so-called "inner representations" to explain behaviour they would otherwise consider inscrutable (Schwartz, 1968). The charge is that to explain one inscrutable by another is not only to beg the question, but, even worse, to put it beyond experimental access. To that extent, a picture or image in the head is theoretically more troublesome than a pain in the neck. The latter at least has spatio-temporal locale, perceptible quality,

377

and measurable intensity.

The irony is that we are not much better off with a picture
in the hand. The situation is not unlike the philosopher's joke
which runs, "What is time? (Pause) That is time!" For a picture
is more than mere pigments on canvas just as language is more than
uttered vocables or numbers a set of numerals. What more is not
likely to be found by closer inspection of whatever things have
pictorial, linguistic, or numerical status, nor of their referents
(since there will often be none), nor in any special relations of
similarity, contiguity, causality, or conventionality supposed to
hold between certain kinds of symbols and their referents. Rather,
we are in the position of having to take all such symbol "vehicles,"
their referents, if any, and special relations to them as so many
phenomena to be explained. For that no mere taxonomy based on
these phenomena will do; for what is there to indicate when two
things that are similar, contiguous, or causally related are also
(or therefore) symbolically related? Does a hammer necessarily
symbolise every other hammer, or the hand that holds it, or the
nail it drives? One supposes that it could "by convention", but
that suggestion comes uncomfortably close to a <u>petitio principii</u>
when left to rest there.

A theory of symbols, to be adequate, must explain the aforementioned phenomena by explicating the relationships of reference,
of formation, and of structure that sustain the pictorial, linguistic, or numerical functions. On the analogy of logical, notational, and other sorts of <u>systems</u> of symbols, a theory of symbols
endeavours to bring all types of symbol systems within a common
comparative perspective. Further details of symbol systems will
come to light as the discussion proceeds. For the moment, it
suffices to say that if the aim is to facilitate a broad theory
of cognitive growth of, say, Brunerian or Piagetian proportions,
what is required is an equally broad, though rigorous, theory of
symbols encompassing the whole range of symbol systems in everyday
and specialised uses to serve as armamentary and desideratum for
further empirical theorising about their acquisition, development,
and influence on cognition.

A major advantage of the functional approach is that it
avoids the fallacy of "psychologism" which, ironically, afflicts
certain areas of psychology more than linguistics or philosophy.
That is the tendency to view meaning as a mental process or event
such that the meaning of a symbol is taken to exist temporally
"in the mind." As already mentioned, the reification in the mind
of various schemas, images, and the like has not gone unnoticed by
critics of cognitive psychology.

The tendency to psychologism is perhaps natural enough.
When we read, for example, we understand what we read, and the

process of understanding may well consist in a series of conscious states. But to leap from that observation to the conclusion that the meaning understood is a mental event is to confuse acts of understanding with the meaning understood. The same point can be made about knowledge in general which, no less than meaning, is irreducible to peculiar mental states dredged up by an effort of introspection. If meaning were a mental event, it would exist only so long as those events and vary with each different state of consciousness evoked by a symbol from one individual to another and from one occasion to another for the same individual. It would then be impossible to speak of words, sentences, or any symbol as having the same meaning for more than one individual on more than one occasion; and with that sacrifice of publicity of meaning would go all possibility of communication as well (Greenlee, 1973, pp. 30-31). The consequences are thus far worse than simple empirical inaccessibility.

Since on the functional approach meaning is not an event, still less a mental event, these consequences are avoided. To inquire how a symbol functions relative to other symbols of that kind in a system of symbols be it a word, image, map or graph, eliminates much, though not all, of the mystery and lack of access that accrues to so-called "inner representations," which difficulties accrue no less, though perhaps less obviously, to symbols outside the head as well.

3. Bruner's Theory of Representations

The sandy soil of semiotics has given rise to some amazing varieties of terminological growth slithering like Triffids across the landscapes of aesthetics, music theory, art history, linguistics, education, media studies, cultural anthropology, and, of course, cognitive psychology. Bruner's selection, partly home grown, of the foot loose flora divides "representations" into "enactions," "icons," and "symbols." The choice of terms little matters except to note for clarity's sake that while for Bruner symbolism is a subset of representation, current theoretical usage, following the broader colloquial usage aforementioned, is just the reverse: representation along with description, expression, et cetera, being one amongst many other forms of symbolisation. (Cf. Goodman, 1968, Intro. and Ch. 1) To avoid the greater confusion of forcing current usage on Bruner's texts, the context of discussion will usually suffice to indicate which usage is being observed. Failing that, the terms "representation" and "symbol" enclosed within quotes will indicate when the special Bruner usages are intended.

The pivotal role of "representations" in Bruner's theory of cognitive growth is iterated throughout his work in such statements as, "[W]e shall be concerned with intellectual growth as it is affected by the way human beings gradually learn to represent

the world in which they operate--through action, image, and symbol."
(Bruner, 1966, pp. 5-6) Or more elaborately,

It is fruitful, I think, to distinguish three systems of
processing information by which human beings construct
models of their world: through action, through imagery,
and through language. A second concern is with integration,
the means whereby acts are organised into higher-order en-
sembles, making possible the use of larger and larger units
of information for the solution of particular problems.
(Bruner, 1964, p. 1)

Bruner shows himself aware of the difference between the
functional and cognitive perspectives distinguished above when,
alluding to Braine's (1963) account of the emergence of the "P(x)"
syntactical structure in baby talk (pivot-plus-open-word phrases
like "Allgone Mommy," "Allgone candy," "Allgone bye-bye"), he
makes two methodological observations. First, "The linguistics must
be moderately clear before the relevant psychological question can
occur to us"; and second, "A formal linguistic description is not
a psychological explanation of the origin or nature of the speaker's
behaviour." (Bruner, 1966, p. 3) Unhappily, both points get lost
in the shuffle of "enactions," "icons," and "symbols."

On the issue of linguistic clarity, Robert Schwartz (1968)
exposes a desperate lack of it in the trichotomy of "representations" in a well known review of Studies in Cognitive Growth.
There he notes that "[S]uch a classification, even as a way of
distinguishing among purely external models of representation, is
difficult to maintain and most certainly requires argument for its
justification." (1968, p. 175) Well and good except for the slight
suggestion that it might somehow be easier or different for the
external modes. This is by no means to deny whatever psychological differences there may be, say, between adding a list of numbers
in one's head and doing it on paper, but rather, that those differences have anything to do with the arithmetical function of
addition. Schwartz never quite settles on the fundamental point
that the features distinguishing various kinds of symbols, being
logical and systemic, not psychological, are therefore quite independent of any differences between their "internal" and "external"
manifestations, however interesting in other respects those differences may turn out to be.[2]

Neither are those features likely to be captured by a jerry-
built taxonomy that fails to keep its basic kinds distinct, a
point that Schwartz does make and most tellingly.

What [he asks] is to constitute representation by action?
Are hand signals in a sign language, the conductor's
baton movements, silent films or cartoons, learned facial
expressions and gestures all to be lumped together as
enactive? Similarly, what is it that makes representational

380

systems iconic? To say that the 'iconic' label applies
to systems that are similar to representation by painting
or drawing does not tell us whether or not we are to con-
strue graphs, maps, diagrams, music, smoke signals, Chinese
ideographs, stop lights, etc. as iconic systems. When it
comes to the category of 'symbolic representation,' the
situation is even worse and the label less informative;
for each of the other types of system, when functioning
as a system of representation, likewise involves symbols
of one sort or another. What would then be crucial is
not that a particular system makes use of symbols but
whether there is something distinctive in the kinds of
symbols it uses or in the way it employs these symbols.
(Schwartz, 1968, pp. 175-176).

Schwartz further argues that it is difficult to understand
how "enactions" such as knot tying, tool using, or bicycle riding
"stand for, refer to, indicate, signal, connote, or denote anything," and therefore, "how it can be maintained that we represent
and come to know our world through them." (p. 176) This carries
the case a shade too far. On a more generous construal of knowledge as inclusive of procedural 'knowing how' as well as propositional 'knowing that' (Ryle, 1949, Ch. 2), it is perhaps not so
difficult to see how, on philosophical grounds alone, it might
be maintained that we come to know our world partly through direct
physical action. Such in any case would seem closer to Bruner's
intentions. Nonetheless, Schwartz is surely right to point out
that such actions do not in and of themselves represent or symbolise the world, though they may well involve symbols such as a
conductor's gestures, an instruction manual, or a Sergeant Major's
grimace.

Bruner's failure to achieve even his modest aim of being
"moderately clear" on the classification and analysis of symbols
merely puts him in company with the majority of humanists and
social scientists who, like him, fail to live up to his second
aforementioned methodological caution, namely, that "A formal
linguistic description [or any symbol description] is not a psychological explanation of the origin or nature of the speaker's
behavior." (p. 6 above) This time the wayward influence comes
from philosophical rather than psychological tradition, from exactly the opposite tendency from psychologism: physicalism, which
locates most of the essential features of symbolism in the physical and sensible properties of whatever things happen to be symbols.
Its influence on Bruner's views is considerable.

4. Symbols and Sensibility

Philosophical symbol theorists of whatever persuasion have
tended to assume that how a symbol functions, to depict, signal,

381

or describe, depends on certain relations between symbol and referent determined by the physical-sensory characteristics of the symbol itself: whether it is similar to its referent (icons); spatial-
ly or temporally contiguous (indexes); or conventionally associated to a referent (symbols) (Peirce, 1902).[3] Accordingly, some
kinds of symbols appear to be more "artificial," "conventional,"
or "abstract," at least in the sense of having fewer roots in
direct perception than others, for instance, mathematics and language versus natural signs (indexes) and pictures. From this perspective flow such familiar dichotomies as those between the verbal and the nonverbal, the verbal and the visual, the discursive
and the presentational, the literary and the plastic arts--each
as theoretically confusing as initially convenient ways of sorting
symbols into types.

Peirce himself humourously confessed to "triadomany,"[4] and
once in its thrall, it is difficult to see beyond the layer upon
layer of trichotomies superimposed, like so many conceptual epi-
cycles, one upon the other. However, stepping back for another
look, it is clear that even assuming the physical-sensory properties of the symbol vehicle to be constant, the ways of symbolising
are highly variable relative to a given symbol vehicle. "A picture
in one system may be a description in another." (Goodman, 1968,
p. 226) Or a word like 'love' is transformed into sculpture by
Robert Indiana. Conversely, there can be many physical-sensory
vehicles for a given mode of symbolisation. Language is usually
visual and verbal, less commonly gestural or tactile, and hence,
nonverbal, either way giving the lie to our most common categories for separating language from the nonlanguages. And since two-
and three-dimensional visual objects, gestures, and sounds may
equally represent (Howard, 1975, p. 207), any hasty identification
of the representational with the visual or pictorial is hasty indeed. It is evident, therefore, that types of symbolisation cut
across physical and sensory modalities in ways rendering any
classification of the former based upon the latter highly suspect.
What limitations might then be expected regarding the sorts of
things that can be symbolised in certain ways? The answer is virtually none. Though a Tabby-depiction, a Tabby-description, and
a Tabby-mime differ amongst themselves in many important ways,
they all refer to the same cat. And if, as we must, we allow for
expression, then sounds can be pictured, colours sounded, feelings
painted, thoughts felt, and the unspeakable rendered in words.
It is only some theory that tells us otherwise.

Bruner inherits most of the questionable trends of the older
semiotics compounding them by a few of his own--in particular, by
attempting to make his own trichotomous taxonomy conform to the
demands of a developmental theory of cognition. The result is a
set of quite literally disembodied "inner representations" supposed
to be the mental analogues of their physically defined originals.

But more serious difficulties than the ontic status of nonphysical
physically defined symbols in the head flow from the failure of
this entire approach to keep separate functional from cognitive
questions. And once again, these difficulties come back to plague
"outer" as much as "inner" representations.

Speaking of the genesis of "representations" in the individual, Bruner says, "Their appearance in the life of the child is
in that order [enactive, iconic, symbolic], each depending upon
the previous one for its development, yet all of them remaining
more or less intact throughout life--barring such early accidents
as blindness or deafness or cortical injury." (1964, p. 2) Schwartz
traces the likely course of Bruner's thought leading up to this
conclusion, starting from the observation that,
>...as children develop, changes occur in the kind of
>properties they take as essential and tend to key on when
>seeking to identify, recognise, or remember objects. He
>[Bruner] believes further that these properties fall
>into three neat and distinct categories: those related to
>(1) the object's function, (2) the object's colour, size,
>shape, and other 'surface' or 'pictorial' qualities, and
>(3) the abstract or relational properties of objects.
>This, however, Bruner somehow takes as an indication that
>there must be three modes of representation, each specific-
>ally suited for and essentially limited to its correspond-
>ing property kind. (Schwartz, 1968, p. 178)

This is fine as far as it goes, but it does not go far
enough; for it is not merely "somehow" (as if by accident) but by
the confusion of hypothesis and definition engendered by his taxonomy of symbols that Bruner is led to these, it must now appear,
self-prophetic conclusions. To illustrate: if one is initially
persuaded that a "symbol" as contrasted with an icon or enaction
"represents things by design features that include remoteness and
arbitrariness" (Bruner, 1964, p. 2)--that whatever is a symbol
has these properties--the tendency then is to make them defining
characteristics of "symbols." Eventually, as happens with Bruner,
nothing is apt to be labelled a "symbol" unless it has those properties; in which case, a statement that began its career as an
overt empirical intuition or hypothesis ends up as a closet taut-
ology.

To object that symbols usually do take some sensible form,
and, moreover, do seem to emerge in predictable sequences and sensory modalities is futile; for such sequences and modalities as
correlated with types of symbolisation is exactly what we should
like to learn in fact, not in definitional fiction. And that can
be accomplished only if one's taxonomy of symbols meets the condition of logical independence from the facts about sequences and
sensibility to be discovered. Otherwise, one's taxonomy forces
rather than fits the facts. In one sense, this is but to draw

383

out the message for Bruner's own work of Bruner's own dictum that a linguistic or symbolic description is not a psychological explanation.

Further evidence that Bruner's taxonomy of symbols constrains rather than explains the facts can be seen from the obvious fact that enactions and icons also may be "remote" and "arbitrary" from their referents; that is to say, could be "symbols" by Bruner's own criteria. The classic "Thumbs up!" gesture or the colour coded London Underground map are as remote and arbitrary from the things to which they refer as any words used to describe those very same things. As a hypothesis, the claim that "symbols" are remote and arbitrary whereas enactions and icons are not, being more the children of perception than of convention, would appear to be plainly false. On the other hand, if one accepts the two properties as part of a definition of "symbolic" as opposed to enactive and iconic systems, it is inevitable to underestimate the complexity and versatility of the latter and to encounter further problems in accounting for their mature forms. In other words, "symbols" are construed as inherently more complex with enactions and icons falling placidly into line as relatively easier to grasp, simpler forms of pre-symbolic representation. (Cf. Bruner, 1964, esp. p. 2 and 1968a, Ch. 2.) It takes but a moment's reflection to realise that the relative simplicity or complexity of a symbol accrues not to its type but to the uses to which it is put. This point will come up again later on in another connection.

One last caveat. It is no good trying to save the situation by insisting on the first in order of appearance of simple icons in children while acknowledging the complexity of adult icons (Bruner, 1966, p. 30). For as Schwartz argues, "...even if children's images are in fact limited in the ways he [Bruner] claims, it is hard to see how these features are a necessary result of or easily explainable in terms of the supposed pictorial nature of imagery." (1968, p. 177; italics mine) Beyond that it may also be noted that it is hard to see why such limitations as apply to children's actions and images should not strictly apply to their "symbols" too, particularly language, the evidence for which is old and ample (Brown, 1958). Bruner would, of course, be the last to deny such limitations on early "symbolism" (1968a, esp. Ch. 1), but it is perhaps most difficult of all to see how a theory that downgrades certain types of symbols for the sake of arranging a developmental sequence of them can comfortably accomodate those limitations.

5. Towards an Instruction of Theory

What can be recommended to make the relations between symbols and cognition easier for a psychologist of Brunerian ilk? No doubt it is time to cancel out the old debt to philosophical semiotics and take out a new loan. Fortunately, some fresh hard currency has come available in Nelson Goodman's Languages of Art, An Approach to a Theory of Symbols. (1968) Though ostensibly a book in aesthetics, it is first and foremost an attempt to delimit the outlines of a general theory of symbols inclusive of such topics as metaphor, expression, representation, realism, work identity, forgery, the uses of notations in art and science, and analogue and digital systems of measurement. Furthermore, in stressing the function of symbols primarily as instruments of cognition--of understanding and perception--and secondarily of communication, Goodman's approach is well suited to the purposes at hand.

The core of the book is Chapter 4 entitled, "The Theory of Notation" which, amongst other things, sets out a matrix-measure of symbol systems consisting of five, mutually independent logical requirements by which different symbol systems may be compared and contrasted in terms of their conformity or lack of it to any or none of the five requirements of a "strict notation." Two of the requirements are syntactic and three are semantic. A nontechnical description of them would run as follows:

Syntactic disjointness--the property of segregation amongst the characters of a symbol scheme,[5] such as the letters of the alphabet, numerals, Morse Code, or standard music and dance notations;

Syntactic finite differentiation--depending upon the feasibility of assigning marks or inscriptions to at most one character in a disjoint scheme, a feature distinguishing the "articulate" schemes of language, codes, and logical and mathematical notations from the "dense" schemes of representational systems like paintings and sketches the essential elements of which are not, unlike handwriting, for instance, assignable to a disjoint scheme;

Semantic disjointness--the property of segregation amongst the reference classes compliant with a symbol scheme, a feature which, when combined with syntactic disjointness, is characteristic of notations though not of language which is syntactically but not semantically disjoint; that is to say, class intersection and inclusion, prohibited by this requirement, are ubiquitous properties of all natural languages;

Semantic finite differentiation--depending upon the ordering of reference classes such that the members of those classes can be correlated with the inscriptions of one character at most in the symbol scheme, a feature distinguishing digital from analogue systems of measurement, graduated from ungraduated scales, say, of temperature or hardness, or unit from interpolated reading of a clock face;

Nonambiguity--requiring that no two reference classes be correlated with inscriptions of the same character, again, a feature of notations like the Dewey Decimal book retri val system though not of words like 'cape,' 'pipe,' or 'man' (meaning male human or mankind).

To avoid any possible misunderstanding of the proposal to use these logical properties of a strict notation to measure other symbol systems, it is not being claimed that all other types of symbols must somehow be reduced to notational systems; nor that notational systems are any better or worse, except for certain purposes, than other systems; nor that notations are inherently easier or more difficult to "read" or to learn than other symbols; nor that any realm, domain, mark, inscription, object, or event is in itself notational or nonnotational; nor even that notationality is the only suitable measure of symbol systems for the purposes at hand.

Rather, the logical features of a strict notation are merely listed here without technical explanation or supporting arguments primarily to suggest how they may be used in combination with other properties of symbol systems to characterise the differences amongst them in ways independent (1) of any physical-sensory properties of whatever things are used as symbols of a certain kind; (2) of any physical-sensory properties of whatever things are symbolised; and (3) of any psychological facts pertaining to the acquisition, development, and mature use of symbols of whatever kind.

Assuming the minimum, that Goodman's theory of notation achieves at least the moderate clarity Bruner desires at the level of "formal description," it should be clear also that the theory meets the latter's second methodological requirement of being independent of a psychological explanation of the nature and origins of symbol using behaviour in the individual. A brief illustration making use of the aforementioned categories to show the principle differences between notational and linguistic systems may help to make some of these points a bit more concrete.

As an example in common use of a mostly notational system, a musical score is recoverable from the sounded pitches and durations it uniquely determines, barring some redundancy in the scheme (e.g., C#, D♭) and nonnotational instructions (e.g., dynamic marks, figured bass, expression words). This mutual recoverability of score and performance, possible only in unambiguous and disjoint systems, serves the double purpose (as do most art notations) of guiding performances as well as identifying a work through good and bad performances by many performers. By contrast, in the notational system of language, in this instance English, a given man may conform simultaneously to 'featherless biped' and 'English gentleman' and numerous other descriptions, none of which is uniquely the description which denotes him. It is perhaps not too misleading to say that predication--the capacity to assert that something is the case--is gained at the expense of the mutual recoverability of symbol and referent in notational systems. Hence, whereas the written and sounded characters belonging to the symbol scheme of language are segregated (disjoint and differentiated), its field of reference is not, resulting in a semantically dense, nonnotational <u>system</u>.[6] A major advantage of this approach is that it does not matter where one begins, with language, pictures, or notations, with simple, complex, multiple, or compounded systems; it is always possible to give a run down of the essential functional features of a symbol in near or distant comparison with others.

6. The Processes of Symbolisation

What changes might one expect in the cognitive perspective to result from such alterations in the functional perspective on symbolism as just proposed? Basically these: a more rigorous, elaborate, and versatile analysis of symbol systems; one that keeps the logical clear of the psychological aspects of symbolism; but in such manner as to promote a more fecund working relation between them. These changes are perhaps most apparent on reconsidering questions of the relative complexity, sensible forms, and sequencial emergence of symbols left off at the end of Section 4. I hasten to add that it is not my aim so much to suggest answers to these questions as to clarify them and to suggest a possible reconstrual of Bruner's own answer to at least one of them.

Earlier it was argued that many so-called enactions and icons turn out to be "symbolic" by Bruner's criteria of the latter (p. 10 above). It also happens that many symbols in common use do not fit any of his criteria being neither "simple," "static," or "concrete" enough to fit the first two categories nor restricted enough in ways demanded by his criteria for "symbolic" status-- musical scores, blueprints, and telegraphic codes, to mention only three. Besides "remoteness" or "displacement", Bruner (1966, pp. 32-41) lists three other defining features of "symbols" in his special sense of the term: "categoriality," "semanticity," and "discreteness"; or roughly, class membership, conventional or "arbitrary" reference, and character segregation or alphabetisation. All four belong paradigmatically to language. Possibly Bruner intends them to be necessary <u>and</u> sufficient for language though merely necessary for anything else "symbolic," but nowhere is this made clear, and the details need not detain us. It suffices to say such criteria are far too narrow to define the "symbolic" and that Bruner is guilty of an incipient "linguophilia" by virtually identifying the category of the "symbolic" with language.

On the other hand, he allows that "images...can be <u>infused</u> with the properties of symbolic functioning, as can tool-using involving action." (1966, p. 30; italics mine) Infused? Does this mean that acts and images may themselves become "symbolic"? Or that they are sometimes combined with language, or both? And how, finally, are these "infused" systems to be analysed ranging as they do from strict notations at one extreme to dense, representational systems at the other? Bruner is left with no recourse but to label them first 'enactive' or 'iconic', lacking a matrix fine enough to capture their differences, and then later endow them with 'symbolic' status by verbal fiat; for, held strictly to accounts, there is nothing in his taxonomy of "representations" that would allow for this transformation. And, after all, it is not a real transformation anyway, but an artificial promotion of symbolic types, as it were, required by the original arrangement of enactions, icons, and symbols in order of increasing complexity and difficulty.

Aside from the philosophical sources already mentioned, whence comes the psychological support for such a view of symbolism? Even Schwartz's suggestion (p. 9 above) of a correlation between symbol types and property kinds, doubtless a legacy of the older semiotics, is compatible with a high degree of complexity within each type. A more direct route, seemingly based on fact, would proceed from the observation that children are somehow better at interpreting pictures than language, and, by (invalid) implication, that notational symbol systems are more difficult to assimilate than dense, representational ones. The distinction between functional and cognitive perspectives on symbolism alone would show the inference to be invalid. Beyond that, two specific considerations weigh heavily against it.

First is the fact that some "enactive" notations, like a wagging finger of warning, can be so simple as to consist of but one character, while some pictorial "icons" exhibit complexities of composition and expression accessible only to the mature, well educated eye. Other, yet undisclosed, evidence is required to show something inherent to either the representational (in this instance, depictive) or notational (in this instance, gestural) modes rendering the former easier to learn than the latter.

A second consideration is Bruner's own observation (1968b) that children pass though an initial "ostensive" phase of symbolic development. Once the logical kinships between simple, one or two character notational schemes and more complex ones are grasped, then it emerges as a distinct possibility that the child's first symbolic activity is of a basically <u>notational</u> kind; and that notationality is the original inroad to both pictorial and linguistic systems.

Clearly, the mere fact of looking at a picture is no evidence that is is being "read" as a pictorial symbol. Further, it is plausible to conjecture that the child's first encounters with pictures will draw upon earlier experiences of deictic gestures or "ostensiveness" in such manner as to treat certain classes of pictures as syntactically equivalent characters in a simple notation denoting a cat, dog, or other familiar object while ignoring its representational properties. In other words, the adult's cat-picture could well be the child's primitive cat-notation with coextensivity of reference preserved on either interpretation. Thus, and this is the point of these speculations, it is hasty to assume either that the child's interpretation is pictorial or that the ostensiveness of his interpretation accrues to pictorial status. By the same token, the likelihood of a notational reading would seem greater where no alternative to ostensiveness yet exists. Interestingly, a "post-pictorial" reading is not unusual for cognitive adults when, for instance, we treat pictorial road signs or the male and female silhouettes on lavatory doors as different sets of equivalent characters indicating their respective hazards to avoid. But here I must quit, at the end of a logical criticism, at the threshold of a revised empirical theory.

7. Summary and Prospect

I began by distinguishing the functional question of what features of symbol systems set off one from another while sustaining the varieties of reference possible within each from complementary questions of interpretation or the psychology of symbolism. After delimiting the role of a theory of symbols in a theory of cognition, and turning to a case analysis of Bruner's theory of "representations," it was discovered that he intuits the general demands of that role but lacks a suitable player to fill it.

By tracing its philosophical roots and psychological uses, Bruner's theory of "representations" was shown to suffer from the twin afflictions of psychologism and physicalism rendering it self prophetic and inadequate for a developmental cognitive theory. Goodman's approach to a theory of symbols was suggested as being more suitable to the demands of cognitive theory than any remnant of the older semiotics in providing an articulate matrix-measure (the theory of notation) of the varieties of symbolic functions besides being logically independent of any psychological findings. Certain changes in empirical theory were seen to flow from this more complex view of symbolism as consisting of so many _systems_ of symbols, including my tentative suggestion of an initial notational phase as the entree to a much wider variety of early symbol activity in children than allowed by the trichotomy of "representations" currently in vogue amongst psychologists and educators.

In taking care to distinguish the functional from the cognitive perspective on the topic of symbolism, it has been my ultimate objective to set them in proper mutual perspective. As the logician Quine (1973, pp. 1-3) recently observed, "Given only the evidence of our senses, how do we arrive at our theory of the world?" is a question of empirical psychology of evident philosophical dimensions and interest involving the quest for the "roots of reference." This provokes a host of similarly bi-focal questions of far reaching significance. Such as: Is initial symbol acquisition restricted to one or other sensory modality, symbol system,

or combination of both? Is some other type of symbol, for example,
the deictic gesture, first in order of appearance? If so, how
are other forms of symbolisation built up from this simple beginning? Or is there perhaps a wider range of symbolic activity from
the not so simple beginning? How does information, on some proper
analysis of that puzzling notation, admit of multiple symbolic
manifestation; and which amongst them are more economical for certain educational purposes or levels of learning? Do not some individuals exhibit definite symbolic or sensory "preferences":
language versus mathematics, the visual versus the auditory? Are
such preferences due entirely to nature or partly to nature? And
how ought they to be taken account of in various instructional
contexts? Finally, where an aversion amounts to a dysfunction,
what use have alternate symbol schemes and systems to compensate
for learned dysfunctions as well as those due to brain damage?[7]

Contiguous, interdisciplinary investigations such as these
questions exemplify span the range of Bruner's theories of cognition, of learning and development, and of instruction. Less con-
spicuous, but threading through them all, is his theory of "representations" which, if not the centre piece, is nonetheless of
central importance to the pursuit of the rest. I have been arguing
for nothing short of a major revision at the core.

FOOTNOTES

[1]An earlier version of this paper was delivered to the British Philosophy of Education Society in London, 6 January 1976.

[2]But see his footnote number 2 on pp. 173-174.

[3]Though not an unfair statement of the common coin of Peircean semiotics, the complete texts reveal an overall position closer to the one advanced herein than does the tradition growing out of his works. For an excellent critical assessment of Peirce's views of the theory of "signs" in the larger context of his philosophy, see Greenlee (1973).

[4]Cited in Greenlee (1973, p. 34).

[5]On the important difference between a symbol scheme and a symbol system, see Goodman (1968, p. 143ff). Roughly, a symbol system consists of a symbol scheme correlated with a field of reference.

[6]For a detailed discussion of these matters, see Goodman (1968, p. 120; 151; and 181-185).

[7]For a survey of recent work in the neuropsychology of brain damage and its effects on symbolic capacities, see Gardner (1975).

Bidney, D. Theoretical Anthropology. New York: Columbia University Press, 1953.

Braine, M. D. S. "The Ontogeny of English Phrase Structure: The First Phase," Language, 1963, 39, 1-13.

Brown, R. "How Shall a Thing be Called?", Psychological Review, 1953, 65 (1), 14-21.

Bruner, J. S. "The Course of Cognitive Growth," American Psychologist, 1964, 19, 1-15.

Bruner, J. S. Toward a Theory of Instruction. New York: W. W. Norton, 1968a.

Bruner, J. S. Processes of Cognitive Growth. Clark University Press, 1968b.

Bruner, J. S. Beyond the Information Given, edited by J. M. Anglin. New York: W. W. Norton, 1973.

Bruner, J. S. and Olson, D. R. "Symbols and Texts as the Tools of the Intellect," in D. R. Olson (Ed.), Media and Symbols: The Forms of Expression, Communication, and Education. 73rd Yearbook of the NSSE. Chicago: University of Chicago Press, 1974.

Gardner, H., Howard, V. and Perkins, D. "Symbol Systems: A Philosophical, Psychological, and Educational Investigation," in D. Olson (Ed.), Media and Symbols: The Forms of Expression, Communication, and Education. 73rd Yearbook of the NSSE. Chicago: University of Chicago Press, 1974.

Gardner, H. The Shattered Mind, The Person After Brain Damage. New York: Alfred A. Knopf, 1975.

Goodman, N. Languages of Art, An Approach to a Theory of Symbols. Indianapolis: Hackett, 1976.

Greenlee, D. Peirce's Theory of Signs. The Hague: Mouton, 1973.

Howard, V. "The Convertibility of Symbols: A Reply to Goodman's Critics," The British Journal of Aesthetics, 1975, 15 (3), 207-216.

Peirce, C. S. "The Icon, Index, and Symbol," (1902) Collected Papers, vol. 11, 2.274-2.308. Cambridge: Harvard University Press, 1960.

Quine, W. V. O. The Roots of Reference. LaSalle, Ill.: Open
    Court, 1973.

Ryle, G. The Concept of Mind. London: Hutchinson, 1949.

Schwartz, R. Review of Studies in Cognitive Growth. The Journal
    of Philosophy, 1968, 65 (6), 172-179.

ABOUT THE AUTHORS

Dennis Michael Warren, associate professor of anthropology at Iowa State University, received his B.A. in biology from Indiana University (1974). He has taught high school science in a secondary school in Ghana, and has conducted research on indigenous knowledge systems among the Bono of Ghana and the Yoruba of Nigeria. He is currently serving as a rual development specialist for the Agency for International Development in Ghana.

Bruce T. Grindel, associate professor of anthropology, received his B.A. in anthropology from Northwestern University (1963) and his Ph.D. in anthropology from Indiana University (1969). He has conducted research on education and social change among the Sisala of Ghana and on the religious life of the southern United States. Currently, he is editor of the Anthropology and Humanism Quarterly.